More Praise f
The Quran: Epic and Ap_____y__

'Infuses the field of Quranic Studies with a breath of fresh air... The avenues of interpretation that the work opens up have the potential to occupy generations. Not only does Lawson's contribution show how both Muslims and non-Muslims can participate meaningfully in reading the Quran, the work is a vivid reminder of a prophetic saying on the virtues of the Quran: its wonders will never cease, and scholars will never be satiated by its study.'

Mahan Mirza, Professor of the Practice, Contending Modernities, Kroc Institute for International Peace Studies, Keough School of Global Affairs

'In this rich and erudite study of the epic and apocalyptic aspects of the text, Lawson adopts and elucidates many of the habits of ancient readers, and the result is a greater appreciation for the Quran's sweeping aesthetic, literary and spiritual grandeur. *The Quran: Epic and Apocalypse* is also invaluable for its deep engagement with recent...scholarship, and its venturesome analyses of minoritarian Muslim exegetical works. Like a thoughtful and generous conversation partner, Lawson asks interesting questions, avoids dogmatic scholarly or religious statements, and leaves us with a lot to think about.'

Kristin Zahra Sands, Professor of Islamic Studies, Sarah Lawrence College

'...offers numerous fresh and important insights regarding Islam's most sacred text. Grounded in meticulous analysis of the Quran's religious and literary dimensions, this volume takes an entirely new direction in identifying and studying its epic and apocalyptic qualities. It is a must read for anyone interested in comparative religious studies, or indeed in cultural and literary history.'

Sebastian Günther, Professor and Chair of Arabic and Islamic Studies, University of Göttingen

'By attending to the Quran's epic as well as its apocalyptic voice, Todd Lawson proposes to liberate Western readings of Muslim scripture from their current obsessions. It is difficult to imagine a timelier or more necessary scholarly intervention. And when the Quran finally acquires the audience it deserves, i.e., one capable of bracketing theological pre-commitments (pro or con) and appreciating it for the re-visionary work of...literature that it is, Professor Lawson's book will be recognized as a major contribution towards that long overdue cognitive shift.'

Peter Matthews Wright, Associate Professor and Chair, Colorado College Department of Religion

About the Author

Todd Lawson is Emeritus Professor of Islamic Thought at the University of Toronto. He has taught in the field of Islamic Studies for over forty years and published numerous books and articles in Quranic Studies and related topics. He lives in Montreal.

THE QURAN

Epic and Apocalypse

TODD LAWSON

ONEWORLD
ACADEMIC

Oneworld Academic

An Imprint of Oneworld Publications

First published by Oneworld Academic 2017

ISBN 978-1-78607-227-6
eISBN 978-1-78607-228-3

Typeset by Silicon Chips Ltd
Printed and bound by Clays Ltd, St Ives plc

Oneworld Publications
10 Bloomsbury Street
London WC1B 3SR
England

For Bahiyyih, Ludovic & Shelby

Contents

INTRODUCTION   XI

1. THE QURAN AS EPIC   1

2. THE QURAN AS APOCALYPSE   27

3. AN APOCALYPSE OF REUNION: *THE EPIC OF JOSEPH*   57

4. DUALITY AND OPPOSITION: *THE APOCALYPTIC SUBSTRATE*   76

5. WATER AND THE POETICS OF APOCALYPSE   94

6. CHAOTIC COSMOS AND THE SYMMETRY OF TRUTH   116

7. JOYCEAN MODERNISM IN QURAN AND TAFSIR   132

CONCLUSION: *EPIC AND THE DOMESTICATION OF APOCALYPSE*   169

ABBREVIATIONS   175

GLOSSARY   177

ACKNOWLEDGEMENTS   184

NOTES   187

APPENDIX   216

BIBLIOGRAPHY   218

INDEX   237

We shall show them Our signs in every realm of the natural world and in their own souls until it becomes clear to them that this is the Truth.

Is it not enough that your Lord witnesses everything?

(Q41:53)

سَنُرِيهِمْ آيَاتِنَا فِي الْآفَاقِ وَفِي أَنْفُسِهِمْ حَتَّى يَتَبَيَّنَ لَهُمْ أَنَّهُ الْحَقُّ أَوَلَمْ يَكْفِ بِرَبِّكَ أَنَّهُ عَلَى كُلِّ شَيْءٍ شَهِيدٌ

Introduction

Divine grace comes to the help of a man menaced by earthly confusion and ruin – this is the framework of the vision.

Erich Auerbach, *Figura*

T he Quran belongs to humanity and to the reading experience of humanity. This is part of its self-definition. We attempt to look at some of the religio-aesthetic workings of meaning generation in the book to help understand why it is so loved and to help us navigate what is frequently a very challenging text. By isolating the epic and apocalyptic dimensions of the Quran it is hoped that such familiar concepts and categories will aid the interested reader, especially the one who wishes to understand Islam and Muslims and sees in this understanding a way to neutralise the poisonous spew about Islam to which we are all steadily subjected through broadcast news, newspapers and government communiqués. Muslims are nearly one quarter of the population of the planet, after all. It makes sense that their central sacred text should be read and understood by their fellow earthlings. It is also hoped that the approach offered here will be of interest to Muslims themselves who may also see its potential as a bridge between literary and religious cultures and perhaps even a stimulating perspective from which to encounter this sacred text.

In the process of describing the overall coherence of the Quran's message as epic and apocalypse we do not wish to suggest that such exhausts the meaning of this extraordinary book. However, it may open otherwise unrecognised doors to the richness of the Quran. Some of the sub-topics that will recur from time to time are: covenant, divine glory, divine presence, divine signs, an apocalypse of reunion and recognition, typological figuration and, of course, revelation. These are, it is hoped, discussed below in a way that opens the text to a wider readership among people of all religious persuasions and none. No book has had a greater impact on the history of humanity and the development of world culture. I think it is not an exaggeration to say that to make it part of the educated global citizen's reading – what used to be thought of as "soul formation" – is a desideratum of some urgency.

THE QURAN AS EPIC

Whatever else an epic does for a culture or a community, it provides a dictionary for the language of self-identity, of 'mythography', and the broader cultural code. The epics we are familiar with: *The Iliad*, *The Odyssey*, 'Gilgamesh', *The Aeneid*, *The Shahnameh*, *The Divine Comedy*, *Paradise Lost*, *The Marriage of Heaven and Hell*, *Ulysses* and *Finnegans Wake* are all distinguished by an explicit and self-consciously contiguous (if sometimes difficult-to-follow) narrative theme. Much the way the combined Old and New Testaments have come to be seen as the great code of Christian/Western culture, the Quran has for long been seen as such for Islamic/Islamicate culture, even if this understanding has not been made explicit.[1] In the Quran, narrative coherence is frequently stimulated to life in the mind of the audience/reader, as a function of what has been aptly called its 'referential nature'.[2] In this instance, the Quran may be compared to a musical improvisation upon a familiar melody, which is sometimes present, sometimes alluded to or echoed, and sometimes present by being completely absent – aniconic.

The much remarked atomistic, discontinuous, fragmentary approach to the Quran which seems to be celebrated in the standard *tafsir* corpus notwithstanding, it is clear that Islam and Muslims nonetheless acquired and developed a coherent notion of who they were and are, and that the title of Hodgson's famous trilogy *The Venture of Islam* does indeed say something important and accurate about the history of Islam and the culture it produced: it could just as easily have been called *The Epic of Islam*. It is possibly from the vista supported by the unassailability of this epic certitude, triumph and attendant cultural confidence that the atomisation of the Quran in *tafsir* was seen as utterly harmless – 'nonthreatening', and perhaps simply expressed a pure, vertical, 'scientific' desire to come to terms with and explore the sacred epic ethos at what might be thought a narratologically molecular level.

As scripture the Quran fulfils many roles and functions, as text it is possible to think of it as a distinctive cornucopian text, containing within it many different genres, all somehow united and made to cohere through two opposing literary 'energies': 1) that of apocalypse and 2) that of epic.[3] By opposition is meant the idea that apocalypse occurs in the context of social and cultural disturbance and change, while epics are symbolic of stability and bespeak or valorize a status quo. Obviously, the Quran is quite dissimilar to those epic poems mentioned above from the point of view of form, performance setting, narrative flow, notions of morality and cultural identity. However, it will be seen that there is more than enough resonance between the form and contents of the Quran and the epic genre (whether Homeric or other), as this has come to be understood and problematized in contemporary scholarship, to warrant such an exploratory investigation.[4] Among other very intriguing, and in this context somewhat paradoxical, developments in this recent scholarship is the recognition of the influence of older Near Eastern epics on the formation of Homer's two great books.[5] In what follows, some of this recent scholarship will be highlighted in order to help demonstrate that there are important, perhaps even decisive, similarities between the Quran and what we now understand by the word 'epic', from the point of view of function and form. A brief quotation from one of the most recent reference works on the ancient epic will make what might otherwise be thought a rather far-fetched comparative exercise more immediately promising:[6]

> In potential size, epic is hugely ambitious, undertaking to articulate the most essential aspects of a culture, from its origin stories to its ideals of social behaviour, social structure, relationship to the natural world and to the supernatural. The scope of epic is matched by its attitude: as Aristotle noted, it dwells on the serious. (Even its meter, says Aristotle, is 'most stately and weightiest' . . . *Poetics* 1459 b34–5.) Epic, the ultimate metonymic art form from the per-spective of its *pars pro toto* performance, is on the level of ideology a metonymy for culture itself.

In order to clear up any possible misunderstanding of my purpose, I would like to state in no uncertain terms that I do not wish to demonstrate in this book that the Quran is 'mere' literature. Nor do I wish for a moment to suggest that an explication of the epic qualities of the Quran somehow explains away its status as the Word of God. Rather, this exploration may be easily seen as an attempt to come to more precise terms with its form and function. One way of conceptualising this attempt is, in fact, to consider the Quran in its dignity as divine revelation. Sacred scripture is – in line with the Quran's own theory of revelation – revealed in the language of the people to whom it is directed (Q14:4). That is to say, the Quran contains much that corresponds to what might be considered the 'epic expectations' of its audience, its *qawm*. This audience, the 'Nile to Oxus' or Mesopotamian 'sectarian milieu' – it is perhaps unnecessary to emphasize – was one for whom the epic in various forms had helped to supply, define and refine values, history and identity since time immemorial. We are concerned with drawing attention to what may be designated the 'epic voice' of the Quran. The model for such an exploration is taken from Northrop Frye's study of the Bible in which he wishes to emphasize that while the Bible is literature, it is more than literature.[7] Frye self-consciously avoided theology in these works to concentrate on literary features to demonstrate how these had been instrumental in articulating a religious or spiritual vision, while at the same time lending unity to the Bible.[8] In the case of the Quran, what might otherwise be mistaken for 'mere literature' should be considered the medium through which the divine message is relayed. As with Frye and the Bible, we are not primarily interested here in the Quran's theological content although it frequently happens that religious ideas are deeply implicated and even explicated in the course of the discussion. Rather, we are interested in the medium by which that theological content was communicated. This medium is, for lack of a better word, literature. Thus, the title of Issa Boullata's landmark book is quite germane: *Literary Structures of Religious Meaning*.[9] We are concerned with the epic aspect of or dimension of literature. Put another way, I would like to test the idea that the Quran may be partly seen and read as a skeletal or even refracted epic. Clearly, viewed from this perspective the main thrust of the narrative is the unfolding of history, beginning in the pre-creational timeless, mythic setting of the Day of the Covenant and stretching to the 'end of the world' with the Day of Judgment. In the course of this unfolding, various divinely appointed heroes experience numerous tests, challenges and persecutions – *peripeteias* – in order to protect and promote the master and, as it unfolds, epic notion of the oneness of God. It is epic in terms of scale because it applies to the universal humanity present at the Day of the Covenant (the Day of Alast Q7:172), where this humanity is defined not as Arab or Muslim, but simply as 'the tribe/ sons of Adam' (*bani Adam*) – 'humanity'. This epic journey, and various subsidiary ones, unfolds in the course of the Quranic performance and kerygma. The unfolding is not always smooth or 'entertaining'. Rather, it is frequently broken, implicit, and sometimes apparently abandoned altogether. Yet, it is the core narrative of the Quran.

The main point is that the Quran may be read – especially in the context of its own time and place – as a harbinger of a specific modernity in its reworking and critique of epic as it had been transmitted to an audience of the Nile to Oxus region since pre-antiquity through the poems of Homer, Gilgamesh, or the Alexandrian Romance, among others. The Quran tacitly critiques such epics because they are, in the first place, not centred on the oneness of God, and God's plan for humanity. Earlier epics are, by comparison, ethnocentric, limited in vision. With the Quran, we have a combined literary and religious theophany that may be thought to have begun with the Hebrew Bible and its precursors. The Quran does not have a 'chosen people' as such, but rather affirms that all people, all humanity, are 'chosen'. It is the universality of the Quranic epic that allows us to compare it, and observe it in conversation with other epic traditions. This does not mean it is not sacred scripture. Indeed, the very assertion of the oneness of God as a guarantor of the oneness of humanity keeps its religious and scriptural/revelational character always foremost. This is nowhere more dramatic than in the precreational scenario mentioned above, the Day of the Covenant. Here, according to the Quran, the history of humanity and consciousness were born at the same time. It is an epic birth.

Simply put, if the Quran is read in the chronological order of revelation (Arabic tanzil), the subject matter and form of the verses strongly suggests a version or rendition of apocalypse, especially with the affirmation of revelation from an unseen realm through the agency of a supernatural being, the nearness of the Hour, natural dislocations, and catastrophes of a miraculous nature entwined with the theme of Judgment, and the breathtaking absence of any hint of narrative movement, apart from the simultaneous movement and stillness of apocalypse. However, when read in the current Quranic or 'Uthmanic' order, the order of what is referred to in Arabic as the mushaf, the situation is quite otherwise. After a few brief introductory verses of invocation, prayer and petition, we are fully involved in the historical beginnings of humankind on earth with the story of Adam, followed by the story of Moses and so on. *Surat al-Baqara,* it has

recently been argued, is really a tightly structured book of education, telling the community who they are and where they came from[10] – precisely
one of the purposes and preoccupations of the epic genre.

It is important to recall that the mushaf order almost perfectly reverses
the tanzil order of the revelation so that the newer suras of the Quran are
those that open the book, while the book closes with those suras that
were the first to be revealed. An examination of the epic dimension of the
Quran will help not only the 'Western reader' but also any reader of the
text, who, if the daunting mountain of textual commentary composed in
every century since the codification of the Quran is any indication, also
had difficulty from time to time in understanding perfectly the structure
of the text. In other words, such an exploration may also help solve the
perennial question recently voiced anew in Carl Ernst's fine book *How to
Read the Quran:* why does the so-called Uthmanic codex assume the form
it has today, beginning with the longest suras and ending with the shortest,
an arrangement which almost perfectly reverses the chronological order
of revelation. Here, it is simply and fairly stated: '[No] one really knows
how or why the fixed arrangement of suras took shape in this way.'[11]

In elucidating the epic elements of the Quran, its epic substrate, we may
achieve some insight into this problem. The insight may be stated rather mne-
monically: If read in the tanzil order of revelation, the Quran sounds like an
apocalypse; if read in the order of the mushaf, the Quran sounds like an epic.
It is not that if read in mushaf order the Quran somehow becomes another
book, that it is now not holy scripture and it has become 'secular literature'.
It is that when read in mushaf order its narratological landscape is different
than if read in tanzil order. The narratological landscape does, of course,
influence theology. The historical record of Adam and Eve, the children of
Israel and Moses and Pharaoh with which the mushaf begins is not accidental
or neutral vis-à-vis Islamic theology and sacred history. Recent work on the
biblical canon has, for example, demonstrated that the biblical order, when
compared with other versions of the psalter and the Psalms, raises a number
of questions largely to do with a messianic or Christological structure of the
canon.[12] If we then compare and contrast the various roles common to each
genre we are left with a working – and therefore provisional – conclusion
that those who performed the widely attested (Arabic *mutawatir*) duty of
casting the Quranic text in its final form wished to convey and emphasise the
narrative, sacred history message over and above the more abstract, poetic,
imagistic and ahistorical mood of the apocalyptic passages of the Quran. And
because of the vastness of the scope of this *Heilsgeschichte* and the struggles

of its heroes, the narrative is heard and read with the tonalities of the epic. Ultimately, the arrangement of the Quran stands as an authorial gesture of the first importance. The mushaf emphasises the epic voice and dimension of the Quran. As sacred epic, then, the Quran is concerned not with a particular ethnic group (unlike previous epics), rather it is concerned with forging a new group for which it is providing a universal narrative. The new group is humanity. This is not a mere literary achievement; it is an epoch-making shift in religious consciousness.

The epic structure of the Quran is more fully explicated in Chapter 1, 'The Quran as Epic'. The subject is taken up again in Chapter 3, where it is combined with a discussion of certain apocalyptic aspects of the story of Joseph as told in the Quran's sura 12. In Chapter 6 the epic challenge so characteristic of Islam, namely the transformation of savagery into civilisation, is discussed in terms of the extra Quranic notions of chaos and cosmos, together with the Quranic ideas of ignorance and knowledge. Here, education itself may be thought the path of the epic journey with the Prophet in the role of master educator. Finally, in Chapter 7, the epic substrate of the Quran is again the basis of a comparison of two other instances of dramatic and profound literary innovation and their relation-ship to a more recent modernity and the cultural creativity arising from the dynamics in play between change and tradition.

THE QURAN AS APOCALYPSE[13]

> An apocalypse is a supernatural revelation, which reveals secrets of the heavenly world, on the one hand, and of eschatological judg-ment on the other.
>
> John J. Collins, *The Dead Sea Scrolls*

Deriving from the New Testament's Apocalypse or book of Revelation, the first work to bear such a generic designation, the term 'apocalypse' from the Greek word for disclosure or revelation, ἀποκάλυψις, here refers to dire and violent happenings that will presage the end of the world, a world in which Christians are persecuted by evil worldly powers. Such an end represents the consummation of the divine plan, as well as the end of that unjust world. Scholarship in religious studies, especially since the middle of the twentieth century, has established that the genre of apocalypse is a complex literary and social historical phenomenon that comprises three separate categories intimately related in historical and individual religious experience: eschatology, social movement and literary genre. The Islamic instance provides an instructive example of how these three modes or manifestations of apocalypse influence one another and then separate into self-contained categories once again.[14]

The word 'apocalypse' is also dangerous because it can be understood in so many different ways, some of them accurate and some of them inaccurate. It is not, for example, possible to extract the notions of 'disaster' or 'catastrophe' or even 'end of the world' from this originally Greek word. The word may have acquired these connotations and secondary meanings in the course of its eventful life in scripture, commentary, literature high and low, and culture in general, including television news programmes and films. But it means 'revelation'. When thinking about the Quran as an apocalypse we are primarily concerned with its literary qualities. Since apocalypse means 'revelation' and since it is as revelation that the Quran defines itself with regard to both its form and its contents it is of particular interest to look at the Quran according to the standard scholarly understanding of the word and the genre of literature to which it applies. John Collins, the dean of contemporary apocalyptic studies, has written:

Apocalypse, as the name of a literary genre, is derived from the Apocalypse of John, or Book of Revelation, in the New Testament. The word itself means 'revelation,' but it is reserved for revelations of a particular kind: mysterious revelations that are mediated or explained by a supernatural figure, usually an angel. They disclose a transcendent world of supernatural powers and an eschatological scenario, or view of the last things, that includes the judgment of the dead. Apocalyptic revelations are not exclusively concerned with the future. They may also be concerned with cosmology, including the geography of the heavens and the nether regions, as well as history, primordial times, and the end times. The judgment of the dead, however, is a constant and pivotal feature, since all the revelations have human destiny as their ultimate focus.[15]

Collins has elsewhere emphasized that apocalypse has a narrative framework and that its purpose is 'to interpret present, earthly circumstances in light of the supernatural world and of the future, and to influence both the understanding and the behaviour of the audience by means of divine authority'.[16] Divine authority is nowhere better petitioned than through the mode of revelation, the lexical meaning of apocalypse.

Revelation is in fact so much a part of what the Quran is that one could say that it is the main topic of the book and, for that matter, the main character. It is in the service of the idea and event of revelation, or apocalypse, that the dramatis personae of the Quran are presented, are described, act and summon the audience to the highest standards of human behaviour and ethics. This Quranic call (*da'wa*) or kerygma is primarily raised through a four-part process of revelation: God>Angel>Prophet>Humanity. As God is utterly unknowable and inaccessible (*munazzah*, transcendent) direct communication does not occur. Rather the divine message is entrusted to an angel identified eventually as Gabriel who discloses it to the chosen prophet, in this case Muhammad. Muhammad, in turn, completes the process of revelation by communicating this message to his audience, which according to the Quran, is humanity (*al-nas*). Thus, the requirement of Collins' definition, that the revelation be 'mediated by an otherworldly being to a human recipient, disclosing a transcendent reality' is perfectly met. That this reality has a spatial and temporal dimension is also a Quranic presupposition, especially with regard to the characteristic theme of paradise (*al-janna*, the garden) as a feature of the hereafter (*al-akhira*). This otherworldly region is described frequently and in great detail throughout the Quran together with the mention of the eschatological 'Hour'.[17] The content and structure of the message, when compared with the characteristics of apocalypse as defined by Collins and his colleagues, would appear to conform so perfectly as to present us with a textbook example. The sad irony is that none of the exciting work on apocalypse carried out over the last century addresses the interesting examples found in the Quran.[18] As a subject of modern apocalyptic studies, the Quran is virtually unknown.

The suitability of considering the Quran as an apocalypse is immediately apparent when comparing its form and contents with those distinguishing features of apocalypse isolated in the literature. Of course, it is important to note that the Quran may fulfil such criteria in its own distinct manner. We have already drawn attention to the first major characteristic, revelation. Here the Quran is quite straightforward. Its own self-image is given repeatedly throughout its verses (*ayat*, 'signs, portents', sing. *aya*) where the Arabic word translated as 'verse' actually denotes a process of miraculous revelation and where other Quranic words are understood as synonyms for this process (see Glossary: Revelation/Apocalypse) even if their semantic structure is different. For example, nazala/tanzil actually means 'to come down' rather than to 'remove a covering', which is the basic meaning of the Greek apocalypse. There, what was removed was the lack of understanding about why the early Christian community should suffer so much persecution, and also the 'covering' or mystery about the future was removed so that this same community would be reassured that indeed a great apocalyptic reversal of fortune would shortly ensue, and the current wretched state of the followers of Jesus would be traded for prosperity and worldly power while the current persecutors would fall from power. In this connection, in several passages of the Quran a near perfect Arabic cognate of the Greek ἀποκάλυψις (apocalypsis) is also found. The word *bayan* and its derivatives occurs over five hundred times in the Quran and frequently indicates that true understanding of the divine purpose is being revealed or explained, *and* that the explanation also happens to be beautiful and compelling. A less frequent Quranic word, *kashf*, actually does mean 'uncover'. More on the Quranic 'terms of art' vis-à-vis apocalypsis is presented in Chapter 2.

The self-avowed purpose of the Quran is to teach humankind what it did not already know (Q96:5), to reveal new knowledge. The question of narrative, the next feature of apocalypse according to our definition, arises when we study the Quran not so much for what is said or taught, but how the message is presented. Narrative emerges as one of the chief means whereby the divine message is communicated to its audience. The Quranic narrative timeframe has a beginning, middle and end, even if the overall structure of the Quran (which may be thought of as endless or perhaps circular) does not reflect this narrative convention. The beginning of the 'story' is indicated at Q7:172 on what is called the Day of the Covenant. The Quran explains, in the supra-logical language of myth, that here God, at a sacred and mysterious time before creation, drew forth all the future generations of humanity from the loins of the first prophet Adam. He then addressed them with the supreme existential question: 'Am I not your Lord?' The immediate, unanimous response was 'Yes indeed!' (*bala*). In this same verse, the narrative end is also indicated. God explains that this question was posed so that on the Day of Judgment none could say that they had been unaware of the covenant – their obligation to obey the laws of God – and would thus have no excuse for having been unfaithful to it. Between the Day of the Covenant and the Day of Judgment the apocalyptic narrative develops according to a set pattern whereby God periodically sends prophets and messengers to humanity to remind them of and renew this original covenant, and to provide guidance in the form of instructions and examples of how to apply these laws and to conduct life. The chief examples are the prophets and messengers themselves, whose holy lives furnish the believers with the best example or pattern (*sunna*) on which to model their behaviour. This aspect of the narrative has been repeated many times and has been presented, according to the Quran text, to every community on earth (Q10:47). Even though the Quran itself only mentions twenty-five such prophets and messengers, the Islamic tradition, taking its cue from the basic cosmopolitan vision of humanity taught by the Quran, posits no less than 124,000 such figures as having been sent by God to every human community that has ever existed. All humanity has, whether they remember it or not, received revelation from God and is implicated in the primordial divine covenant described at Q7:172.

During the earliest period of Muhammad's preaching, from approximately CE 610, the End or Hour was thought to be very near. It is in fact not completely obvious that this feeling about the nearness of the Day of Judgment or the Hour grew any less in the latter part of his message when he had become the leader of a powerful community. The various markers of the expectation of the Day of Judgment are found throughout the Quran in both its earliest and its later pronouncements. This feature was first thoroughly studied by Paul Casanova in his groundbreaking *Mohammed et la fin du monde: étude critique sur l'Islam primitif* (Paris, 1911). Unfortunately, Casanova's views were harshly criticized by leading contemporary Islamicists and this book and its highly suggestive thesis was more or less ignored for over half a century. The Quranic words for a great historical, eschatological anagnorisis, whether this be understood to pertain to the broad historical plane or restricted to the arena of individual experience (as it eventually came to feature in the writings and lives of those we like to refer to as 'mystics') are many and varied. The most common is 'the Hour' (*al-saʿa*) occurring some forty-eight times. This may be related to the multiple mentions of 'the Day', 346 times, many of which refer explicitly to the Day of Judgment, or the day in which all good will be distinguished from all evil. Similarly, the idea of God's 'command' or 'cause' (*al-amr*), frequently synonymous with the Hour, occurs some 150 times in various combinations and contexts. But the earlier revelations are distinguished by their powerful description of such apocalyptic events as the cleaving of the moon (Q54:1), the crumbling of mountains into 'tufts of wool' (Q101:5), or the day on which none shall find any helper but God (Q86:10).

Another characteristic feature of the Quran explored at length in Chapter 3 is the role that duality, opposition and symmetry play in expressing its apocalyptic message and spirit. This is shown to be an integral part of the 'text grammar' of the Quran, providing continuity in what might otherwise be susceptible to becoming a disjointed and disconnected reading experience. The proliferation and concatenation of oppositions and dualities, far from communicating any kind of dualism – a concept foreign to the Quranic conception of God, powerfully expresses and reinforces the transcendent oneness so essential to Islam's version of ethical monotheism.

The Quran, whether it is speaking of a future time or not, is profoundly concerned with the judgment of humanity and so may be said to be primarily occupied with the transformation of human behaviour. In the early days of the revelation, Muhammad and his followers were severely persecuted and harassed because of the threat they posed to the status quo. Thus it may be that much of the Quran is meant to console the believers as they suffer for accepting or even merely understanding the revolutionary message of the prophet Muhammad. That message was: there is only one God. Such a theological emphasis had grave implications for the existing society, an oligarchy of tribal aristocracy whose fortune and existence would appear to have depended and flourished precisely on the traditional polytheism of the Arabs. Therefore, the monotheism preached by Muhammad was not mere theology, but a 'modernity' that challenged the entrenched social and cultural mores of his time and place. He and his followers suffered accordingly and the Quran 'came down' to console them and assure them of ultimate victory. This quotation from another leading scholar of biblical apocalyptic, is quite germane even though it is not speaking about the Quran:

> In the pressing need to define spiritual identity in the face of challenge, and to sustain hope, a basic perspective is nevertheless identifiable around which apocalyptic systems grow: it is the perspective of apocalyptic eschatology which furnishes a way of viewing reality which denies the apparent superior position of opposing groups of any validity vis-à-vis divine purpose.[19]

Among other apocalyptic themes and motives isolated by research in Jewish, Christian, Zoroastrian and other cultural spheres, a few are worth signalling here due to their irresistible application to the form and contents of the Quran and the history and development of the Muslim community, from its beginning as a harassed remnant to its status as a world power. Thus, the grid of features first isolated in a landmark issue of *Semeia*,[20] is reproduced, with some modification, in Chapter 2. It offers a schematic guide for reading the Quran as an apocalypse, or at the very least a text eminently susceptible of the interpretive readings of an apocalyptic imagination: visions, otherworldly journeys, otherworldly mediator, reaction of recipient, primordial events, salvation, resurrection, forms of afterlife, otherworldly regions and beings, paraenesis by revealers (in this case God through the angel and Muhammad), instructions to recipient (Muhammad and his audience) and narrative conclusion.

Islamic eschatology is clearly apocalyptic in form and content, focusing as it does on ultimate judgment of the wicked and the good, another world, and an end to time. The end time of the world and the end time of the Muslim community or individual are somehow conflated. Individual salvation or damnation replaces concern with the actual end of the world. The apocalyptic vision frames Quranic eschatology and conditions the entire text, regardless of specific topic or subject otherwise at hand. Key Quranic terms such as the hereafter, paradise and hell are pertinent markers of apocalypse as eschatology. Even more important is 'the [approaching] Hour', or 'the Appointed Time'. The Hour is inevitable (Q40:59) and cannot be delayed or hastened (Q35:12). Its time is known only to God (Q43:85). Nonetheless, the heavens and the earth are even now 'heavy' with the Hour (Q7:187). The approaching event, however designated, is a prominent topic in both Meccan and Medinan suras, where, together with descriptions of paradise and hell, it ranks as one of major themes of the Quran. Among the most dramatic events associated with the Hour, synonymous with impending occurrences referred to as the divine cause (*al-amr*), the happening (*al-waqi'a*), the resurrection (*al-qiyama*), and the calamity (*al-qari'a*), are the following: the splitting of the moon (Q54:1), a massive earthquake accompanied by mass terror (Q22:1–2), disbelievers surrounded by clouds of fire (Q39:16), mountains crushed and scattered 'like carded wool' (Q20:105; 27:88; 52:10; 56:5; 70:9; 101:5), the earth illuminated by divine light (Q39:69), the presence of all previous prophets (Q39:69), the broadcasting of the deeds of all humankind (Q39:69), universal judgment and dispensing of justice (Q39:69), believers' entrance into paradise, and polytheists' abandonment by their gods (Q30:12–16). Through such tropes of intensity, the apocalyptic, messianic and visionary-cum-experiential élan of the Quran and the hadith is preserved in scripture where its rhetorical power has remained undiminished and perhaps even enhanced with the passage of time.[21]

The early Islamic community has a suggestive affinity with the type of religious community classified in the literature as apocalyptic, for example Qumran. The factions that emerged after the Prophet's death also employed and exploited the rhetoric of apocalypse: proto-Shiʿis, with their multiple fissiparous developments, and their opponents. Muhammad's preaching was interpreted as involving the establishment of a saved community in an Islamic iteration of the Abrahamic theme of a divine remnant (*baqiyyat allah*; Q11:86). Quite apart from the portents of the end found frequently in the short 'hymnic' suras of the Quran, the hadith literature also portrays an urgent expectation of an end to history that must be faced by the community. Many hadith reports attributed to the Prophet speak of the nearness of the Hour in greater detail, sometimes including specific dates. A dramatic example of this is the 'booth like the booth of Moses' hadith, which features the Prophet instructing two of the faithful not to bother making overly sturdy mosques of brick and wood but rather counselling them to use more convenient thatch structures because the 'the divine decree' (*al-amr*) was due to happen at any moment. Such a focus in Islam's scripture is naturally and inevitably linked to those numerous messianic or apocalyptic movements that have been a feature of Islamic history from the very beginning, eventually emerging also from Sunni, Shiʿi and Sufi traditions.

A significant motif of post-Quranic apocalyptic literature focuses on events in the five holy cities of Jerusalem, Alexandria, Antioch, Constantinople and even Rome; something that may indicate a vision among early Muslim groups of the conquest of all Christendom in one triumphant gesture. Much apocalyptic and messianic lore is used as validation, sometimes post-eventum, for the major political dynasties of Islam, including the Umayyads, the Abbasids, the Fatimids, the Ottomans, the Safavids and others. Likewise, groups and movements who disputed the authority of such triumphant religio-political powers all relied to one degree or another on a specific interpretation of Quranic *apocalyptica*, especially with regard to eschatology and the centrepiece of Islamicate religious authority: the institution known as *walaya*, a complex term that suggests numinous presence, devotion and guardianship as well as political, moral and spiritual authority, simultaneously with allegiance to this same authority. Such apocalyptic historical movements include the Kharijis, the Uthmanis, the Kaysanis, the Qarmatians, the Khurramis, some of the activities of Hallaj (922) and his followers, the Abbasid revolution (749–50), the Hurufis, the Nuqtawis, the Sarbadarids, the Ni'matullahis, the Shaykhis, the Babis, the Baha'is, the Mahdi of Sudan, the Ahmadis, the Iranian Revolution (1978–9), al-Qaeda, and others. So pronounced and pervasive is this feature of Islam that it stimulated various apocalyptic and messianic movements among Jews and Christians within the abode of Islam. It was not only the marginalised of Islamicate society who sought to calculate the precise time of the end of the world and to offer descriptions, based on the Quran and the hadith, of the events that will accompany it, but also such prominent figures, among others, as Kindi, Ghazali, Suhrawardi, Ibn Arabi, Ibn Taymiyya, Ahmad Sirhindi, Sayyid Qutb, Mawdudi and Ayatollah Khomeini. Of course, contemplation of such themes and imagery need not result in a political or historical vision, and many of the mystics of Islam offered a more purely existential and personal interpretation of such material.

Islam sees itself as having arisen in the midst of a transformative crisis in a society that had strayed much too far from a monotheistic ideal and which, as a result, was beset by numerous social and spiritual ills: economic injustice, rampant crimes of betrayal, absence of compassion, widespread violence and savagery. The Hour that the Quran preaches is simultaneously an hour of self-awareness and of social responsibility. The message is cast in a venerable language of images and symbols well known to its immediate audience. That Muhammad was the last prophet is a doctrine that perfectly conforms to the apocalyptic vision of his revelation as this has been preserved by the faithful. The question remained for generations of followers, who thus form a true apocalyptic community: when and how does this divinely ordained Hour occur? In a sense, the riches and achievements of Islamic civilization that are now the heritage of a global humanity, are also the result of the various answers to this question offered by its most talented and most creative minds over the last fourteen centuries.

In the following chapters a few key ideas will be repeated. Some of these require little elucidation but some are less familiar. In the discussion of epic we frequently refer to the 'alphabet of prophets' construed by Islam through the Quran. By this is meant the way in which the highly cosmopolitan and plural humanity addressed by the Quran is supplied a scriptural warrant. The details of the warrant will be found mentioned from time to time in Chapters 1, 3 and 6. Another technical formula, mentioned above and used in the following pages is 'trope of intensity'. This refers to those highly charged Quranic statements such as the cleaving of the moon, the reducing of mountains to wool and even such compelling images as those found throughout the Quran in the Light verse (Q24:35), the Throne verse (Q2:255) and elsewhere. The point is that whatever else these images portend, in the first place they are rhetorically and poetically striking and as such this literary intensity conditions everything else in the Quran, even those more prosaic passages that may carry comparatively little poetic or apocalyptic 'music' by themselves. The coinage is meant to try to capture some of the pre-exegetical or pre-canonical, pre-critical vitality of the text. The studies collected here rely heavily on the insights of a few scholars, beginning with Northrop Frye whose literary approach to the Bible has been influential. Michael Zwettler's work on typological figuration brought this inestimably important literary device to my attention in the first place. The covenant features repeatedly in the following pages and is discussed from – one hopes – a sufficiently varied diversity of perspectives that its repeated mention does not become tedious. It is only relatively recently that Islamic scholarship has begun to give the role of the covenant and its renewal in Islam its proper due as it has been for generations a bona fide topic in biblical studies. Here covenantal studies are in a similar predicament with epic and apocalypse. John J. Collins' work on apocalypse has been enormously influential to the point of revelatory, as will be seen. His name appears frequently. In addition, the ideas of Erich Auerbach, Angelika Neuwirth, Muhammad A. S., Abd al-Haleem, Wadad al-Qadi, Norman O. Brown and Henry Corbin have also been very important.

Finally, the literary energies of both epic and apocalypse seem to converge and focus on the problem of identity, perhaps the single most central theme of world literature. Through the Quran's epic and apocalypse, the longitude and latitude of humanity are plotted and some idea of the road travelled and the road ahead illuminated. This illumination may be seen as the chief unifying feature of the Quran.

Chapter 1

The Quran as Epic

C ontrary to the apparent meaning of many of the earliest more explicitly apocalyptic suras and verses of the Quran, the world did not end, time did not end, the mountains had not been turned into tufts of wool: the Hour had not come. Rather, the followers of Muhammad had become triumphant in the 'sectarian milieu' and life had gone on. A new religious community had acquired more or less permanent features. The epic voice of the Quran explains these features, gives them content and a rationale in the context of an otherwise chaotic welter of religious identities. This is the power and function of the epic. The epic voice of the Quran is sometimes more fully expressed and sometimes less. And though this is not the only voice heard or read in the Quran, it may be one of the more significant. Where the epic feature appears vestigial and undeveloped, it is always the case that it has been taken up in extra-Quranic literature to be fleshed out and made more fully epic, say, in the *Sira* of Ibn Hisham.[1] Of course, both the apocalyptical and epical personalities of the Quran also intertwine, creating something of a literary fugue. In some cases, the Quranic apocalypse is rendered more epic than other apocalypses, and in some instances the Quranic epic is rendered more apocalyptical than other epics. This is a unique and characteristic feature of the Quran and its recognition will help scholars and readers come to terms with its otherwise *sui generis* character.

The epic form and mode has come to us from before antiquity – it is a distinct cultural bestowal, crystallising, for example, with Gilgamesh in the Ancient Near East and Homer in the Ancient 'West' (to name only two of the most influential for Western literature). That it has contributed to the formation and composition of the Bible is well accepted. Indeed, ancient Hebrew epics may have simultaneously contributed to and been influenced by the evolution and development of the form.[2] The history and development of the Persian epic tradition has long been a topic of great interest.[3] Indian culture also esteems an ancient epic tradition.[4] Then, there is of course the Arabic oral 'folk' epic itself, much-studied from a number of angles.[5] It is therefore quite understandable that elements and vestiges of the epic are traceable in the Quran, some more prominent than others. This has not been brought out into the open sufficiently, the question possibly getting 'confused' or conflated with some understanding of 'religion' as distinct from or even opposed to 'literature' as such. But, if the epic is a metonymy of culture and that culture is also deeply imprinted with what we are fond of calling religion, then it seems sensible to try to account for some of that religiosity through its metonym.[6]

Pursuing the Quranic epic voice is in the service of saying something quintessentially true about both the Quran itself and Islamicate culture in general, something that seems to have especially eluded scholarship on the Quran. If we can rely on electronic searches, there are, for example, only eighteen occurrences of the word 'epic' in the six volumes of the magisterial *Encyclopaedia of the Quran*. And these fleeting instances pertain not to the Quran itself, but frequently to various literatures that are perceived to be in conversation with the Quran – indigenous, cultural epics with which the Quran entered into conversation as a result of the expansion of the *dar al-Islam*.[7] The recent penetrating analysis of the vernacular Quran in the Balkans represents the kind of brilliant and illuminating work on the relationship between orality, textuality, folk epic and 'Quranic epic' that can be done.[8] The earlier study of the role of epic in conversion in Central Asia is equally suggestive.[9] More explicit concern with epic in an Islamic setting, especially Central Asia, has reasonably enough centred on poetry and performance, and frequently the relationship between orality and narrative. The great Persian national epic of Firdawsi has generated its own library of excellent scholarship.[10] However, in all of this scholarship there is virtually no recognition of the epic Quran.

In the most recent scholarship on epic, there is sometimes a reference to the 'standard handbook definition' of the genre. This, of course, implies that current scholarship on the epic has gradually moved away from the traditional definition. And, in fact, this is the case. Such divergence or, if you like, progress, in epic scholarship is guided by the insight that epic had for too long been the emblem of successful, triumphant societies and civilizations. The erroneous assumption was that it is these cultures that produce and own epics, while the ones that were defeated do not. Such a fallacy has been exploded in, for example, the brilliant Introduction to *Epic Traditions in the Contemporary World,* which clearly dissolves this and several other 'clouds of glory' clinging to the notion of epic.[11] Here, we wish to make a first step by reading the Quran, studying it, with reference to precisely the standard or traditional definition, especially since the culture for which the Quran was and is an emblem and metonym was also remarkably triumphant. This is by way of opening up the question.

It is the article by Revard and Newman in *The New Princeton Encyclopaedia of Poetry and Poetics*[12] that is frequently referred to as the standard definition of the genre. The opening paragraph of that article succinctly encapsulates the breadth, depth and scope of the genre as it had generally come to be understood by the time of writing this classic description:

> An epic is a long narrative poem that treats a single heroic figure or a group of such figures and concerns an historical event, such as a war or conquest, or [a] heroic quest or some other significant mythic or legendary achievement that is central to the traditions and belief of its culture. Epic usually develops in the oral culture of a society at a period when the nation is taking stock of its historical, cultural, and religious heritage. Epic often focuses on a hero, sometimes semi-divine, who performs difficult and virtuous deeds; it frequently involves the interaction between human beings and gods. The events of the poem, however, affect the lives of ordinary human beings and often change the course of the nation. Typically long and elaborate in its narrative design, episodic in sequence, and elevated in language, the epic usually begins 'in the midst of things' (*in medias res*) and employs a range of poetic techniques, often opening with a formal invocation to a muse or some other divine figure, and frequently employing elaborate formulaic figures, extended similes (usually termed epic or Homeric similes), and other stylized descriptive devices such as catalogues of warriors, detailed descriptions of arms and armor and descriptions of sacrifices and other rituals. Recurrent narrative features include formal combat between warriors, prefaced by an exchange of boasts; accounts of epic games or tournaments; and fabulous adventures,

sometimes with supernatural overtones and often involving display of superior strength or cunning. Epic incorporates within it not only the methods of narrative poetry but also of lyric and dramatic poetry. It includes and expands upon panegyric and lament. With its extended speeches and its well-crafted scenic structure, it is often dramatic and is perhaps with the choral ode the true ancestor of ancient drama.

The epic is thus understood as containing or displaying a number of predictable features or conventions. They may be listed as follows:

1. Epic is frequently the first or oldest literary work (whether oral or textual) in the culture, and is usually very long
2. Opens *in medias res*
3. The setting is vast, covering many nations, the world, or cosmos
4. Begins with an invocation to a muse
5. Starts with a statement of theme: *praepositio*
6. Makes use of epithet
7. Makes use of epic similes and figures
8. Contains long lists: *enumeratio*
9. Features long and formal speeches
10. Shows divine intervention in human affairs
11. Features 'star' heroes who embody the values of the civilisation
12. Is performed before an audience.

The above list will serve as a point form guide for the preliminary and necessarily brief discussion that follows. Though it is not mentioned in Revard and Newman, one might add a thirteenth factor, namely that the epic frequently generates numerous commentaries and/or types of performance. As such, it may also be considered an 'open' work, as per Eco's widely influential discussion.[13] Doubtless, one of the reasons for a disinclination to see the Quran in its epic dimension is because of the notoriously daunting narrative discontinuity of the text. Recently, however, there have appeared numerous studies elucidating the mechanics, rhetoric and poetics of Quranic coherence, especially with regard to ring composition/chiasmus.[14] The role of ring composition and chiasmus in oral composition was first brought to scholarly attention in studies of *The Odyssey*. So, we come full circle: to the degree that the mysterious narrative structure of the Quran has been unappreciated, so has its epic dimension. We can now appreciate more acutely why, though the narrative flow and continuity 'on the page' of the Quran may be problematic at the 'molecular' level, the overall coherence and identity – its 'centre of narrative gravity' – is never really in question. It is argued below in Chapter 3 that it is precisely the recurring figure of duality that helps to establish the Quran's continuity in the face of such apparent discontinuity.[15] Here, we observe that another guarantor of this same continuity is the epic vision of the Quran: the relentless and compelling epic energy suffusing the text exemplifies a concern with the journey, spiritual heroism, the affirmation of a distinct code of moral values, the assertion of community identity, and other traditional epic problems and topics. The Quran's epic role and function is also unmistakable in its status as the first book in Arabic and, furthermore, in its being a long composition that rhymes from beginning to end – something the uninitiated may be forgiven for mistaking as poetry.[16] This fulfils the requirement that the epic be in elevated, not to say 'liturgical' or artistic language. As such, it offers a cognate to other seminal, culturally foundational texts such as the poems of Homer, 'Gilgamesh', and *The Aeneid*, to name only three. One should not fail to mention here the culturally foundational role of this elevated, 'exalted' Quranic Arabic excerpted, as it were, from the Quranic text/context. The *Fatiha* – the first sura of the Quran – as the opening (perhaps better, 'overture') for the mushaf does triple duty as the (first) invocation to 'the muse', in demonstrating the distinctively Quranic instance of an epic beginning *in medias res*, and in stating the introductory theme. We will look at each of these three Quranic versions of standard epic conventions in turn.

Before embarking on this, it might first be useful to reacquaint ourselves briefly with the meaning of the term 'muse'. Today the word stands for an agent of inspiration and is frequently used figuratively in a variety of contexts, often having nothing to do with classical Greek mythology, in which the muses were nine goddesses, daughters of Zeus, who were the sources of knowledge of all the arts and sciences, and whose aid was traditionally petitioned before beginning a given work, in this case epic poetry, whose muse was Calliope.[17] The typical petitioning of a muse in the traditional epic is thus more directly concerned with the poet asking for inspiration. It is obvious that the Quran's *the Merciful, the Compassionate* (*al-rahman al-rahim*) or *Lord of the worlds* (*rabb al-alamin*), is much more than a mere muse, and that the anthropomorphism and polytheism of the

Greek tradition could not be more repellent to Islamic religiosity, piety and spirit. However, the two traditions do agree on one extremely important factor: the role of inspiration. In both cases the 'literary phenomenon' is identical, but the actual source of the inspiration is also decisive, as was shown conclusively by Zwettler.[18]

Here in the Quran we have the distinctive and familiar invocation, the *basmala*. If this is not an explicit request, such may be thought implied: *In the name of God the Merciful the Compassionate* is thus a comparatively indeterminate prayer that can mean 'with the help of God', 'on the authority of God', or 'By God', as in an oath. The mood is continued with the opening words of the next verse, known as the *hamdala*: *Praise be to God* (*al-hamdu'li-lláh*). The prayer and petition here seem obvious. Since God is the author of the Quran, why would there be any more explicit request for 'poetic' help? Such a point is made most explicit at Q17:16 when the prophet is instructed to *not move your tongue*. The *basmala*'s ubiquity throughout the Quran tends to argue for its role as an invocation, naturally not to a muse but to the one and only 'God of Islam'. Its doubling with the *hamdala* at the opening of the mushaf emphasises the specifically monotheistic and epic character of the Quran: the Quran is using the epic convention of the invocation, but it doubles as an invocation to God. As such, it is a rewriting or recasting – a critique – of the traditional epic. In musical terms, it may be thought a transposition into the 'key of monotheism'. Part of the point of this critique is, again, to universalise the epic and simultaneously personalise it. This will become clearer below where the subject of the epic hero and the Quran is addressed.

With the *Fatiha* as the beginning, the mushaf also begins *in medias res*. The persistent and variously evoked imagery of the road or the path in the Quran is first introduced here with the mention of the *sirat al-mustaqim* (*the right path*). The exact wording is: *ihdina al-sirat al-mustaqim* (*Guide us to* (or *on*) *the straight path*). Regardless of which preposition one chooses, the idea of a path suggests being in the middle of the action, the process or progress – from a beginning to an end. Such a structure also depends upon the frequent use of flashbacks so common in the epic form, such as the kind we find immediately following the *Fatiha* in Q2:30ff and *passim* throughout the Quran. The path, no matter how it is construed, is between two poles: the Day of the Covenant mentioned later, and the Day of Doom or Judgment, mentioned here. So, the Quran begins with *Surat al-Fatiha* in an invocation of the straight path that, it is assumed, we are already on (*in medias res*) after invoking God, the Most Merciful, and alluding to the end of the epic journey, the Day of Doom, Judgment Day. It is not, however, until we get to Q7:172 that we discover – or are reminded – in detail of the 'egg' from which this long, dramatic, formative history emerged.[19] The Day of the Covenant is, for the Quran, the beginning of time, being, and history in the same way that Genesis is the beginning for the Hebrew Bible. It is also the beginning of consciousness.[20] Having been born on the Day of the Covenant, every time consciousness is deployed, it represents – in a sense – a remembrance (*dhikr*) and imitation, re-enactment or performance (*hikaya*) of that primordial event. Thus, the Quran, the mushaf, begins in the middle of things. Ultimately, of course, the Quran is not fully at ease with these traditional categories: beginning, middle and end. It unfurls its particular character in serene disdain for such relative banalities. The *totum simul* identified by Brown[21] is also perhaps a useful way of thinking of Quranic textual flow/narrative. But, narrative in the standard understanding of the term is also extremely important for the Quran's epic function. Whether we take as our historical beginning the story of Adam and Eve, first encountered in the Quran at Q2:30, or the Day of Alast, the opening of the book assumes we are on the path from that event headed for the last event. All of us, the prophet-hero, humanity and the individual, are precisely and firmly *in medias res*. So, after an invocation, namely the *basmala,* of the Quranic muse, God (an invocation that is repeated so often that it has become one of the epic formulae of the book), and after beholding ourselves on a path (whether the straight one or the wrong one), we discover we are in the midst of the action. It is normally the hero who is thus situated, but the Quran in some sense wants to implicate everyone in the heroic quest. It is important to repeat that the road, by whatever Arabic word it may be designated, is one of the more frequent themes and metaphors in the Quran and that as such it also assumes the role and function of the epic simile, mentioned above as number 7 in the list of epic conventions.[22]

But it is not only the Quranic vocabulary that points to the epic orientation of Islam and the venture of Islam. Corbin, many years ago, described in some detail the way in which the heroic epic evolved, under the impress of Islamic culture and civilisation, into something he called the mystical epic.[23] Though he did not explicitly deal with the Quran's epic dimension in this elegant study, it may be assumed that he was not unaware of the Quranic 'seeds' of epic heroism that also fed the evolution of the Islamic mystical epic. One of the stages in between might be thought of as the common-or-garden religious epic. The path of righteousness is indicated not only in the famous *sirat al-mustaqim,* but also in countless key Quranic and extra-Quranic words and titles, such as *sabil, nahj, muwatta', sira, madhhab* and so on. And while it would take a few centuries for such travel to be reconfigured and revalorised as 'progress' in the contemporary sense, it nonetheless captures the meaning of 'Pilgrim's Progress'. Without the preoccupation with the metaphor of movement from one place to another, journeying and travelling – whether such preoccupation be Quranic or extra-Quranic – a great deal of what is distinctive about Islam and Islamic culture would be lost or simply absent. Thus, the statement of theme is clear: praise and petition to be on the right path and to be pleasing to God. The rest of the book demonstrates in detail how this is to be achieved and how the opposite is to be avoided. The *Fatiha*, in presenting the theme of the Quran, has long been said by the exegetical tradition to encapsulate the entire book through a celebrated, oft-quoted hadith ascribed to Ali that may be paraphrased thus: everything that is in the previous scriptures is in the Quran, everything that is in the Quran is in the *Fatiha*.[24]

Traditional genre-definitions of the epic mention the importance and function of lists. A prime example of such a list can be found in the catalogue of ships that sailed from Greece to Troy (Book 2, pp. 484–759 of *The Iliad*), and the 'Catalogue of Women' by Hesiod. Catalogues bespeak cultural wealth and plenitude and may also provide something of a 'reality effect' in addition to universalising the message and, in some cases, such as biblical genealogies, paying homage to various members of the audience. In the Quran, we find catalogues of both material and spiritual 'items'. This is not surprising since the concerns of the Quran may be thought equal parts 'spiritual' and 'material' (without, however, being dualist). One of the most populous lists in the Quran is spread from the beginning to the end (and may also thus be considered another marker of continuity). The divine attributes and names number well over several dozen, beginning with the most frequent, *al-rahman* and *al-rahim*.[25] The next major list would be the fifty-five various names for the Quran the Quran itself uses, mentioned by al-Suyuti in the *Itqan*.[26] The list of suras may also qualify as well as numerated lists of verses, both of which together actually constitute the Quran. A long list of the twenty-five prophets and messengers mentioned in the Quran is certainly relevant. In addition there are much shorter lists of the false gods of the *jahili* period: al-Lat, al-'Uzza, and Manat (Q53:19–20); Wadd, Suwa', Yaghuth, Ya'uq and Nasr – the gods of the people of Noah (Q71:23); *al-taghut* – 'false gods' (Q16:36 and Q39:17).

There are, in addition, the more restricted lists of the various religions and their holy books: Yahud, Nasara, Sabi'un, Majus, *al-Tawrat, al-Zabur* and *al-Injil.* But the fewness of actual names of religions and scriptures here can be misleading. After all, the Quran affirms that a revelation has been given to every human community through a prophet or messenger (Q35:24); that the Quran does not mention all of them (Q40:78); and, that such revelation has been in the language of the particular community (Q14:4). The 'alphabet of prophets' that emerges from the Quran goes quite beyond the function of the normal epic list to provide a key to the unlocking of the various mysteries entailed in the chaos of religions greeting observers and denizens of the 'sectarian milieu'. Furthermore, this cultural feature – prophets – is identified as being distinct from mere 'poets', a group with which it might otherwise become confused.[27] Thus a theoretical list of communities takes shape in the Quran. Such a theoretical list is the basis for the vast literature of so-called heresiographical works and tales of the prophets, more properly considered works of comparative religion in the cosmopolitan context in which they were composed. Such a list of nations, languages and races is again evoked in Q49:13:[28]

> People, We created you all from a single man and a single woman, and made you into races and tribes so that you should recognise one another. In God's eyes, the most honoured of you are the ones most mindful of Him: God is all knowing, all aware.

A list of types of human response to the divine message also emerges, for example, *Muslim, mu'min, ahl al-kitab, kafir, mushrik, fasiq, munafiq, shahid,* and *radd.* There is a list of levels of paradise and levels of hell, more or less symmetrical, and a list of various nations such as al-Rum. There are potential 'lists' of communities that have passed away as suggested by the frequent locution, or some variation of, *that is a community that has passed away* (Q2:134), *how many a community have We destroyed?* (Q7:4) and so on.[29] Such references may be considered placeholders for later elaboration by the tradition; just as the twenty-five Quranic prophets open a catalogue section for the eventual 124,000 prophets and messengers acknowledged by the Islamic tradition. Angels, though mostly unnamed and mentioned eighty-eight times, provide the basis for a list. The pillars of religion (*passim*) and the pillars of faith (Q2:177) represent two more lists.

Other kinds of books and literary – whether oral or textual – 'sources' suggest another list: *asatar al-awwalin, shi'r/sha'ir, kitab/kutub, suhuf* and all of the technics, tools and media of literacy mentioned in the Quran from the mysterious and transcendent *al-lawh al-mahfuz* to the *signs of God* (*ayat*) that are to be read by all believers. Günther's suggestion that even various verbal formulae, such as *allama al-insan*,[30] indicate a culture of literacy is quite to the point: there is a list of literary sources, again whether actual or theoretical, oral or textual, embodied in the Quran. The mysterious letters also form another list, as do the verses/signs and suras themselves, as mentioned above.

A major 'list' for consideration is the one indicated in the frequent Quranic concern with 'all [created] things' (*kullu shay'*, *passim*), which function also as 'signs of God' (for example, at Q41:53). Such a list is obviously not fully elaborated or itemised, but there are several eloquent and moving passages which list features of the creation and its subservience to God, such as Q4:190. Thus, the entire 'contents' of the cosmos and the soul – in addition to the signs/verses of the Quran itself – are brought within the purview and literary sovereignty of the epic vision of the Quran. Just as the various genealogical chains in the Bible may be seen to constitute a variation on the epic list, so we might consider the laws in the Quran a similar variation on the conventional epic list. Modern and classical scholars tend to agree that there are five hundred verses of legal import in the Quran; this constitutes a rather long list in itself:

> Among the multitude of exhortations and prescriptions found in the Quran, there are a good number of legal and quasi-legal stipulations. Thus legislation was introduced in select matters of ritual, alms tax, property, and treatment of orphans, inheritance, usury, consumption of alcohol, marriage, separation, divorce, sexual intercourse, adultery, theft and homicide.[31]

Thus, while the nomothetic function of the Quranic legal pronouncements need not be questioned, by looking at the same material as literature, specifically epic, we are given a new understanding of the text. *Surat al-Ma'ida* (Q5) is a fine example, listing many commands and prohibitions, from the status of the individual, to concerns of the community, to rules for interreligious relations. Such laws have been seen as naturally separable (and therefore 'listable') from the more universal principles contained in the Quran and particularly in this sura:

> Sūra 5, revealed at Medina, marshals a list of commands, admonitions and explicit prohibitions concerning a great variety of issues, from eating swine meat to theft. References to the Jews and Christians and their respective scriptures recur throughout. In Q5:43 God asks, with a sense of astonishment, why the Jews resort to Muhammad in his capacity as a judge 'when they have the Torah which contains the judgment of God'. The Quran continues: 'We have revealed the Torah in which there is guidance and light, by which the prophets who surrendered [to God] judged the Jews, and the rabbis and priests judged by such of God's scriptures as they were bidden to observe' (Q5:44). In Q5:46, the Quran addresses the Christians, saying in effect that God sent Jesus to confirm the prophethood of Moses, and the Gospel to reassert the 'guidance and advice' revealed in the Torah. 'So let the people of the Gospel judge by that which God had revealed therein, for whomever judged not by that which God revealed: such are sinners' (Q5:47).[32]

Lists are thus an important feature of the Quran. As such, their presence represents an epic convention in distinctive Quranic form.[33]

Related to lists in the case of the Quran, the epic convention of the epithet looms rather significantly. The traditional notion of the epic epithet is, for example, the famous Homeric 'rosy fingers of dawn', or references to Agamemnon and Menelaus as 'the two eagles', or the evocative 'wine-dark sea'. These epithets are conventions and mannerisms (verging on what the ungenerous might call cliché), frequently repeated stock phrases in Homer's poems, and serve to move the action along with a minimum of verbiage. They are also touchstones of familiarity, adding to the continuity of the poems. They have helped define the epic genre. In the Quran there are numerous locutions that serve the same purpose.[34] To begin with, we might consider the divine attributes again. Doing double duty as an example of an epic catalogue or list, they also function as epic epithets. In the Quran their identity is almost never questioned, and they add variety and information about the otherwise utterly unknowable God. In this way, these epithets orient the reader/listener and provide familiarity. Apart from the divine names and attributes, such familiar Quranic formulae as 'the life of the world' (*hayat al-dunya*), and verbal formulae such as 'for those who have minds to know' (*ulu'l-albab*), also function as epithetical 'shortcuts' and embellishment. Also to be mentioned are the various names of the Quran itself: *al-dhikr, al-tanzil, al-kitab*, in addition to all of those other figurative self-references that populate the text.[35] There is certainly no space here to examine everything that might be considered epic epithets in the Quran but, in addition to those mentioned, we could briefly add also the epithet 'all [created] things', and the frequent phrase mentioned in the previous section: the community that has passed away, and the numerous Quranic warnings to 'not trade' for a paltry price the signs of God, the next world, or belief.

Closely related to the epic convention of the epithet is the epic or Homeric simile.[36] An epic simile is one through which the entire scope or concern of a given epic may be stimulated to life. Sometimes referred to as an extended simile, it is seen in such phrases as 'Apollo came like the night'. We see in the Quran various characteristic tropes or similes, such as 'to purchase this world with the next with a paltry price' or the repeated use of 'so which of your Lord's bounties will you deny' in Q55. A more abstract but nonetheless instructive Quranic simile occurs with the glorious Light verse (Q24:35), whose other, darker, half (Q24:36) is frequently forgotten in the dazzling light and beauty of its language. Another similar example is the Throne verse (Q2:255), which resonates with all those other Quranic uses that employ throne imagery.[37] These key Quranic moments would seem to function very much like the epic similes in Homer and other poems. The *Fatiha* itself may be seen to fulfil a fourth function as an epic simile, particularly with reference to the extended imagery of the straight path and those who have been led to it. The parables of the two gardens and their owners also fall under this category; other possible epic similes or metaphors are humanity, revelation and unity. These are extended comparisons in some way key to the extended argument of the Quranic epic. Throughout the Quran numerous 'simile moments' occur which are important both for the general, if refracted, epic narrative (important, that is, for keeping the 'action' moving), and for supplying essential information pertinent to how and why the narrative moves. Here it is interesting to emphasise again that the divine attributes, mentioned above, may also function as epic similes in which God, ever remote – as per the epic simile in *Surat al-Iklhas* (Q112) – is nonetheless connected to the world and the epic action of the prophets and humanity through such divine 'emotions' as wrath and mercy.[38]

But there is also a sense in which the entire Quran, in its recounting of the history of humanity as call and response to the divine message, is one long grand or operatic epic simile. And here we approach the sense in which revelation (the Quran) is its own hero. Typological figuration, so key to the Quran's method, dictates that Muhammad is Moses and Jesus in the poetic or spiritual sense and it dictates that his community is also their community: what happened to the earlier group will happen to them.[39]

When read in terms of its epic voice, the Quran *is* a long speech, the speech of God through an angel to Muhammad. In addition, other brief speeches populate the text. It is perhaps even less necessary to dwell at great length on this particular epic convention. As revelation, the Quran is by virtue of its very 'self', concerned with and emblematic or illustrative of divine intervention in human affairs. It is God, after all, who is speaking, and it is God who is addressing and challenging humanity precisely on the grounds of His having intervened in the past: communities who obeyed Him prospered, those who did not were destroyed. It is God who will ultimately judge all humanity on the Day of Judgment. But here we are introduced to a meta-dimension of the problem in observing that not only does the Quran speak about divine intervention, it *is* divine intervention. Thus do the contours of the Quranic epic become more and more discernible. Though the story adumbrated in the Quranic epic could not be told in a single sitting, or even a single day, the story is so important that the shorthand version – the mushaf (that is the Quran) – available on the best possible authority, may be told and or recited (performed) in the course of a single day. As indicated above, the timeframe is from before creation to the Day of Judgment, and the spatial canvas is equally grand. The Quranic chronotope is epic indeed.[40] Within this time-space continuum numerous, if not near-infinite, features are noticed, valorised, sacralised or condemned.

All of the cosmos, creation, humanity, time and history are the subject of the Quran. The scale of action could not be more vast. Although there is no need to 'prove' this, a few features of this vast scale are offered here: the action of the Quran starts, as was mentioned above, on the Day of the Covenant. Actually, the 'action', or at least the scene, has to begin even before the Day of Alast, because even here we are introduced to already fullyformed (if not yet created) characters, such as Adam, to say nothing of the pre-existent God Himself. This pre-existent beginning is characteristic of the Quran, setting it apart from other creation myths. Certainly, many creation myths begin in some kind of chaos before creation. However, the Quran distinctively posits something else as the substrate upon which creation proceeds, suggesting that chaos is really a human 'creation' and has nothing to do with God or His plan.[41] The end, or the 'final cause', is the aforementioned Judgment Day towards which all creation is wending. The vastness of the temporal scale is matched by an equally enormous spatial canvas, a spectrum of place and space reaching from the atom and the sperm, and the space(s) they occupy, to the expanse of the seven heavens and beyond. This spatial continuum is further divided into planets, nations, villages, seas, lakes, rivers, stars and so on. Into this vastness enter, of course, 'all [created] things', animal, vegetable, mineral, human, angel and jinn. With the entry of humans also comes an attendant moral spectrum, or spatiality, through which the drama of choice and faith are acted out in a wide variety of human relationships from the familial to the tribal, the national, the mercantile, the military, the prophetic and so on. As has been remarked many times, the paucity of detail in many of these instances is also a characteristic feature of the Quran's expressive style, but not one that has diminished its kerygmatic appeal or epic call (*da'wa*). Here, it may be thought to have worked an opposite magic, by relying upon the reader or listener to fill in the blanks, the epic becomes personalised perhaps to a degree not quite encountered in other scriptures and epics. The lack of historical detail is here just as productive as a wealth of historical detail might be. The *tafsir* tradition is, of course, a permanent record of just how well the audience is able to fill in the blanks, or to put flesh on the skeletal epic of the Quran.[42]

THE HERO OF THE QURAN

If we are to be thorough in our exploration of the Quran as a special kind of epic, we had better start looking for a hero before too much more time passes, not least because the hero appears to be the single most important element of a given epic. The word 'hero' of course comes from a Greek word meaning 'protector' and we may discuss at our leisure precisely what the hero thus protects in the case of the Greek epics, but it is likely to emerge that it is identity and ethos, which are among the most prized treasures. In the case of the Quran and Islam, our epic hero protects the truth of divine oneness, which of course paradoxically protects the audience, reader and believer who then also become protectors of the same truth. In this final section of our brief exploration of the epic substrate of the Quran, we return to the place we started, with the standard definition of the genre. Here we are concerned only with this fragment of the definition:[43]

> [Epic] treats a single heroic figure or a group of such figures and concerns an historical event, such as a war or conquest, or [a] heroic quest or some other significant mythic or legendary achievement that is central to the traditions and belief of its culture.

The hero is an essential element of the epic. Even though Aristotle himself argued that this aspect can be overemphasised, the hero has emerged as the central point in that not only are the exploits of a single individual retold for edification and entertainment (not necessarily separated), but the hero as single agonistic player embodies the virtues and ethics esteemed by the audience of a given epic. But the above definition also points to something beyond the usual notion of the hero as single actor in a story, namely the idea that the heroic role may be assumed by numerous individuals. In the Quran, Muhammad emerges as an epic hero in the context of all the other heroes who have been sent by God to reform humanity, namely the twenty-five prophets and messengers explicitly mentioned and the vast number (eventually fixed at 124,000) accounted for in theory by the developing tradition. Muhammad's role is in fact defined and elucidated by identifying his office with those earlier named prophets, most of whose roles and lives are defined in much greater detail than his, at least in the Quran itself.[44] The epic struggle here is largely the one that seeks to replace savagery with civilisation.[45] In the course of this quest, this Herculean labour, the hero has been typified as going through a series of more or less standard stages in the service of the epic struggle. It was Carlyle who first detected the epic nature of Islam's self-image in his famous, though today little read, analysis of Muhammad as hero of the prophetic type.[46] Joseph Campbell, in his widely influential *Hero with a Thousand Faces*, also refers, sparingly, to Muhammad and Islam in the course of delineating his own, somewhat idiosyncratic and controversial, heroic code or profile. The scheme may be briefly summarised as entailing for the hero an unusual, difficult, miraculous, or otherwise remarkable birth into a sacred or noble lineage; summons to a challenge; a helper, otherworldly or not, and protective, sometimes magical or supernatural objects; crossing-over: the hero leaves the natural world and begins his journey or quest; the hero is tested to prove his worth; the hero usually leaves his home to find safety from the opponents; the hero frequently returns home after the epic journey, victorious and powerful and especially with the ability and wealth to bestow largesse on his helpers and community.

To take Campbell's theory much further than he himself did in the case of Muhammad, we will offer a brief sketch of the way in which the Prophet's life story as alluded to in the Quran and more fully detailed in the *sira* (or 'life' as in biography) may be thought to conform to that scheme.[47] To speak of the life of Muhammad as an epic is not the same as speaking of the Quran as an epic. Given, however, the inseparable-ness of the two sources and the incessant cross-fertilisation between them reflecting identity, ethos and praxis, it is certainly not irrelevant to focus briefly on the figure of the prophet, after which we will address certain other manifestations of the heroic, more directly and arguably 'Quranic'.[48]

Muhammad's birth, boyhood and adolescence up to his marriage to Khadija is of course not told in the Quran, but it is told in all its compel-ling detail in the *sira*.[49] The *sira* is umbilically wedded to the Quran as that which makes the adamantly referential and allusive nature of that text understandable to its audience. His conception and eventual birth is signalled by a light emanating from his father Abd Allah's forehead. His father, a descendant of Meccan 'royalty', the son of Abd al-Muttalib, dies before the birth of his son. (It should be remembered that much of the first part of Ibn Hisham's edition of the Ibn Ishaq biography is in the manner of establishing precisely this royal or aristocratic lineage.) The predestined birth had also been foreshadowed by the vow of Abd al-Muttalib to sacrifice his son, the Prophet Muhammad's father – a plan that was abandoned for the ransom of a number of camels. And his mother dies while he is still very young. Thus, we have the familiar theme of the disadvantaged and yet highborn beginning of the hero. Muhammad's receipt of revelation and the concomitant (re-)establishment of monotheism in the place of exist-ing polytheism, a restoration of true religion, is certainly in line with the Campbellian theory. A challenge emerges in Muhammad's status as *ummi*, meaning either 'illiterate' or 'unlearned' in religious texts; the rampant polytheism, materialism and brutality of his society; and his relatively lowly social status as a result of his orphanhood. It is in the early period of his orphaned life that the signs of prophecy are recognised by the Syrian monk Bahira, adumbrating the helper motif that emerges more fully after the first experience of revelation on Mount Hira in the mythically-charged cave.[50] Quite apart from the long list of sacred relics that Muhammad is said by tradition to have become heir to, the Quran first casts the angel of revelation in the role of helper and the experience of revelation and the contents of revelation as the supernatural protection the (now) prophet will need to accomplish his task. Shortly after, of course, other helpers emerge: Khadija, Waraqa, Abu Bakr, and eventually all of the Companions and by extension the *umma* itself. Muhammad's *miʿraj* qualifies perfectly as an instance of 'crossing-over', and though the details are not in the Quran, the Quran is almost universally read to refer to it (Q81:19–25; Q53:1–21). But, prior to the *miʿraj*, the actual experience in the cave on Mount Hira may be thought a textbook example of this mythic crossing over into an enchanted realm. The description of Muhammad's experience is decisive: first an encounter with a supernatural, nearly monstrous, being followed by a profound fear and refusal of the communication or charge.[51] Here, the helpers become instrumental in reassuring the Prophet who fears that he has somehow become a despised poet. His other name, Mustafa – 'Chosen' – indicates the divine choice of Muhammad, and his pre-prophetic life is generally regarded as the proving ground for this choice, during which he exemplified all of the noble and heroic qualities that he would continue to manifest throughout his life. Chief among these tests are his confronting the entire weight of Arab custom – *sunna* – with the changeless *sunna* of God (see for example Q17:77 and 33:38, 62).[52] This battle for civilisation would play out over his lifetime. Of course, the Hijra perfectly qualifies as exile, flight from persecution.[53] In the biography of the prophet, the typical return to the 'real' world after the crossing-over is conflated with the establishment of the Medinan *umma* after the return from the night journey, the *miʿraj*. Later, the Prophet's victorious return to his beloved Mecca will add another layer of drama to this standard heroic motif. With his triumph and conquest and the support and allegiance he attracted from the various tribes, he is now the very personification of 'protector' and able to dispense the bounty (spoils) of his success upon all whom he esteems as members of his nation, the *umma*. The relevance of each of these stages to the heroic life of Muhammad may be more fully elaborated and illustrated with regard to the Quran and the *Sira*. For the time being, we simply wish to register the compelling nature of this schema for a study of the epic substrate of the Quran and Muhammad's heroic role in the founding of Islam.

There are other ways in which the hero has come to be understood and which may also help illumine the epic dimensions of the Quran, though not necessarily in traditional terms. Other candidates for heroic status in the case of the Quran are God, the community, humanity as such and the reader/listener. After all, the divine attributes may also be seen as human attributes of an otherwise transcendent God whose heroic quest is to lead humanity to some kind of enlightenment, whether by hook or by crook.[54] That the audience of the Quran is challenged to the same heroic standard as the Prophet (and prophets) is axiomatic of monotheistic kerygma and is an example of the call to what has appositely been called 'moral athleticism'.[55]

So, while warfare, battle, spying, scheming and deceit may not hold the same prominent place in the Quran as they do in other more conventional epics, they certainly have a prominent role, part of which is to function as a metonym for the journey of the soul from the Day of Alast to the Day of Judgment, *the* heroic journey from ignorance to enlightenment. Here enlightenment seems to function in tandem with the more traditional epic quest for immortality, as in Gilgamesh.[56] The Quranic *jihad* of such multifarious renown, and to which every believer is summoned, is really a call to this same heroism, whether it be on the battlefield of military combat or the battlefield of spiritual struggle, the epic (compare *batal*) dimension is unmistakable. Subsidiary heroic features, such as the bestowal of boons in the form of wealth or comfort, are also traceable in the Islamicate veneration of hospitality, an invocation of the ultimate hospitality of paradise, which, in the last analysis, is causally linked with the heroic triumph of the Prophet Muhammad.[57] The ultimate boon is of course true civilisation in place of the pre-existing savagery (*jahl*).

While obviously not an epic in the traditional sense, there is enough 'epic energy' prominently in operation in the Quran to do the work required: the nation of Islam is born, its credentials presented, the identity of the new community encoded, the purpose of life made clear, and the chaos of religions transformed into the understandable product of the history of the relation between God and humanity. While the foundational literary epics are seen, from the point of view of traditional – especially Abrahamic – monotheism, to spring from a 'pagan' (that is, unacceptable to Islam) tradition, it should be remembered that even in Homer there is veneration of *the* god, *Theos*. If the sacred olive tree of Greek religion resonates typologically with the olive tree that is now 'neither of the east nor of the west' (Q24:35) we are not arguing for cultural and/or 'conscious' borrowing. We only wish to point out structural and 'grammatical' homologies representing distinct and freestanding separate cultural complexes. However, the splendorous role of the olive in the Quran may be thought a simultaneous climax of both epic and apocalyptic energies in the mode of 'glory' (Greek *kleos)* – a motif quite characteristic, whether in dramatic or theological garb, of both the epic and the apocalyptic tradition. The hero achieves, or perhaps better, participates in, glory. But this glory, in the case of Muhammad (and in counterpoint with the pre-Islamic cognate of pride/*fakhr*), is in some ways a reflection of the everlasting and sublime glory of the one and only God whose name in Arabic is Allah.[58]

The epic repertoire calls for the hero-leader to overcome the rebellion of his people,[59] a theme that may be considered one of the major preoccupations of the Quran. In the case of the Quran, the hero preserves and protects the correct means of worship (namely tawhid) against which such rebellion is cast as operating. And the movement from Mecca to Medina may be seen as an example of the kind of protection Aeneas accomplished when he rescued his gods and brought them to a place where he might be free to worship them. In one sense, Muhammad's success in establishing an *umma* in Medina may be thought the climax of a minor or subsidiary epic in which the primordial covenant is re-enacted and the moment thus preserved in perpetuity. But in the Quran the larger 'framing' epic seems to present us with another hero, namely humanity itself. *Al-nas, al-insan, banu Adam, al-khalq* and *al-bashar* are all words that acquire something of a heroic tonality in the unfolding of the Quranic message and which acquire a distinct role in the Quran. Part of this heroism must surely be involved in the epic task of 'understanding' through reading/audition of the Quran's account of everything. It is, after all, with humanity as hero fallen on difficult times that the Quran begins, the specific humanity of Mecca whose prayer is reflected in the *Fatiha*. While the prophets and messengers are charged with their heroic tasks to promote the message of divine unity, their audiences are also charged with, in the nature of things, a perhaps equally heroic duty. Here the antagonists are civilisation and savagery, and it is in Islam and the Quran that civilisation acquires special status as a religious value. *Jahl* is its opposite, so that the *hizb al-shaytan* (Q58:19) are those who reject knowledge and succumb to the expedient of savagery. The image of the Prophet Muhammad as hero is in reality death-less. This has most recently been demonstrated in works of anthropology, but is enshrined in the Islamic tradition itself.[60]

The serpentine and broken, allusive, or refracted manner in which the whole story unfolds – perhaps similar in some ways to the vagaries of the *qasida* – is never told *seriatim* from beginning to end, except in *Surat Yusuf* (Q12) which begins at the end of the first third of the mushaf. Indeed, in light of what we now know of the importance of chiasmus and ring structure for the composition of the Quran, it may not be wrong to consider the twelfth sura as the chiasmic 'centre' of the epic Quran. Parts of the narrative stream are most frequently glimpsed from time to time in the context of other tell-ings and it is left to the audience to stitch the various segments together and/or to supply missing information. Such a technique of storytelling is tried and true, guaranteeing audience interest through audience participation – a kind of secondary authorship. From this point of view, it could be argued that it is not so much the fact that the Quran is an epic, but that the other-wise disparate elements explicitly told or alluded to have been 'epicised' by the audience.[61] *Surat al-Baqara* sets the tone and general structure of the Quranic epic through the basic story of revelation and instruction in which God's prophets are heroes set against odds, and their communities are similarly tried. Success is assured both in this world and in the next. What follows from *Surat al-Baqara* may be thought a number of tellings of the same epically-charged *da'wa* or kerygma: revelation, acceptance/rejection, success and prosperity/failure and destruction. And, all of this is still firmly on the straight path of epic literary expectations that culminates on the Day of Judgment. More symmetry.

The heroics of the prophets are, of course, of special interest because they emulate and reflect most closely the heroics of the standard epic hero. Miraculous or auspicious birth; lowborn status; removal from home or exile and return; encounter with supernatural spirits, angels, guides; given a message or task; rejected in the prosecution of the task; brought low only to rise again triumphant.

That the Quran inherits an epic voice and theme is no surprise. What the Quran does with this inheritance is interesting in the extreme, as if it improvises on a set form to provide a new iteration, a 'modern' and commensurately challenging rendition of the familiar genre. With the Quran one senses a now stronger, now weaker, presence of the epic genre. As mentioned above, if one begins reading from the beginning of the mushaf the epic form is suggested. If one begins with the earliest revelations, reading chronologically, one feels oneself in the presence of apocalypse. But because of the effect of the peculiar scriptural feature, dubbed by Brown *totum simul*, it matters not where we begin to read, once we understand the epic scope. This can come only from immersion in the text:[62]

> Once a verbal structure is read, and reread often enough to be possessed, it 'freezes'. It turns into a unity in which all parts exist at once, which we can then examine like a picture, without regard to the specific movement of the narrative. We may compare it to the study of a music score, where we can turn to any part without regard to sequential performance.

While it is problematic to use the technical term 'canon' with regard to the Quran, it is nonetheless true that the arrangement of the final text of the Quran stimulates the same kinds of questions that may be found discussed in scholarship on the biblical canon.[63] Canon is as much about the relationship between form and content as it is about what has been deemed worthy to preserve. Arrangement of canon is just as much an authorial gesture as the composition of verses or suras. Depending upon the order in which the various parts of a discourse are read, the meaning may be utterly changed. Though it has been hinted at in the past, we still do not have a fully fledged study of how, for example, the arrangement of the exegetical hadith in, say, al-Tabari, represents an original authorial gesture despite the protestations to the contrary of al-Tabari himself.[64] The study of the way in which the Psalms are arranged in the canon likewise has produced a large library of scholarship in which the intention of the arrangement of the canon is energetically debated.[65] It is not necessary to list here an exhaustive catalogue of how form becomes content in the case of the arrangement of books, we only need imagine rearranging the Bible, putting the book of Revelation first and the book of Genesis last, to gain some insight into the centrality of arrangement to the purpose of this or that text/discourse. With the Quran, it is as if the 'conservative' epic form domesticates and tames the sometimes opposing and even antagonistic or socially disruptive literary energies of apocalypse. Such energies have recently been the subject of suggestive analysis in a comparison of Homer and the Bible.[66]

To the degree that the Quran may be performed, heard and read as an epic, its continued and unparalleled appeal and sanctity may be more clearly understood. Far from disappearing, the epic in all its forms, including the Quranic, continues to exercise a strong hold on the psyche and the imagination; in religious language, the soul. That the Quran is perhaps the most read book in the world is not a function only of the laws and ordinances it articulates but derives from the compelling story it tells about the venture of humanity – and this on the highest possible authority. This story accounts for the great variety among humans and their societies and also accounts for the underlying unity which is, in any case felt to be there, but with the Quran's eloquent gospel of cosmopolitanism, stemming from the originary unity portrayed in the Day of the Covenant verses, is now taken as a non-negotiable divine teaching.

This brings us finally to the very important aspect of performance,[67] especially as it may pertain to a study of the Quran. While the bibliography on this is meagre, it is nonetheless an open secret that the Quran in fact is coterminous with, and unthinkable without, performance. The original revelations were performed, first by the Prophet Muhammad himself, then the readers and reciters who have, in imitation of the Prophet's *sunna*, performed the Quran from the very beginning. Believers also perform the Quran, at least to God and themselves, in the course of their private devotions. Public performances of the Quran have always existed and always entailed competition. Thus, as for the view that epic lives mainly as an oral performance the Quran can easily be implicated in the genre. In the discussions of epic between orality and textuality,[68] the Quran also is seen to have an important if unexplored interest. But if we stay with the idea that an epic is most epic when it is performed (and not merely read as a written text) we can easily accommodate the Quran once more, whose stories and heroes, whose sense of history and justice, are a permanent and important element of the worldview of a quarter of the world's people, regardless of their relationship with the actual printed book. It is wired into the culture; the culture is thus something of a performance or embodiment of the Quran and the Quran a metonym for its culture.

CONCLUSION

Whether we wish to use the word epic or not, the 'clear light of history' shines on the unprecedented spread of Islam from the backwater of the Hijaz to the Hindu Kush mountains in the East and the western coasts of Africa and southern Europe in less than a hundred years. A key element in this was the spread of the Quran over such a vastly variegated cultural, geographic and linguistic territory, a territory that would come to be known as the abode of Islam (*dar al-Islam*), the place where true worship is cultivated and protected. Here, Islam sets the moral and ethical tone, supplies the language of social intercourse, provides a universal narrative of beginnings in the form of Quranic cosmogony for the various populations, supplies and adjusts the names and identities of otherworldly spiritual beings, teaches a universal narrative of endings in the form of Quranic eschatology, teaches also a universal natural history, and claims for this teaching the highest possible authority. The result is that a 'citizen' of the *dar al-Islam* can journey from one end of the Islamic world to the other and, while much of what is encountered will be strange and new, a very impressive amount of the cultural *imaginaire* will be familiar and even 'feel like home'. This is, by any measure, a truly epic achievement, and one that likely could not have been predicted a hundred years earlier. One of the ways this was achieved, it seems possible to speculate, was the way in which the Quran acknowledges and validates the histories of all these various ethnicities and linguistic groups, by virtue of such verses as Q10:47, *li-kulli ummatin rasul:* 'Every nation has a divine messenger' who, presumably, also teaches that there is no human community that has not had the benefit of divine teaching from a messenger of God, even if we have lost the record of this. Furthermore, each nation has been taught the divine message in its native language so that the message be as clear as possible, as in Q14:4, *wa-ma arsalna min rasulin illa bi-lisan qawmihi li-yubayyina lahum:* 'We have sent no divine messenger except in the language of his people *so that the message be clear.*' Thus, each nation's history, according to the Quran, is dignified by a pre-existing relationship with the one God. It may be that those pre-existing epics with which the Quran frequently meshed, and which the Quran frequently validated, may have easily been understood as a remaining record of a long-ago and otherwise perhaps half-forgotten divine revelation. The epic voice of the Quran emerges as a great universaliser validating the quest and struggle of all of humanity in whatever place it may be found. The nature of this epic voice is, of course, uncompromisingly monotheistic and God-centred. The heroes of the Quran are the virtuoso servants of God whose main task is to eradicate the opposite of monotheism and to teach the godly virtues of ethical monotheism. We are aware of how the early histories of the Muslim community came to see a simultaneous acknowledgement of, and break with, the so-called *jahili* past. The record of this transformation is to be found in the new vocabulary of the Quran, especially when compared with the oral literature of the pre-Islamic period. It is designated in the sources as a move from savagery to civilisation. The same general pattern may be discerned in all those places where Islam established itself, and part of this transformation has to do with reorienting the universally encountered epic struggle in its various forms and within the various cultures of the *dar al-Islam* so that it becomes a truly universal – in Islamic terms – epic struggle with God at the centre and the various pre-Islamic cultural heroes, either through typological figuration or other so-called 'literary devices', brought into the fold of the Islamic worldview.

The epic voice or mode of the Quran is that which is privileged and made obvious in the mushaf to such a degree that it may help explain the final arrangement of the Quran. Would such an epic élan be as easily discerned if the revelation were read only in the chronological order of revelation? Rather the mood of the 'performance' would be entirely different, conditioned by a much more direct concern with the nearness of the Hour and all of the accompanying powerful apocalyptic forecasts, symbols and imagery, promises and threats. Even so, this apocalyptic 'music' is never absent from the experience of the Quran. It is a distinctive and characteristically incessant leitmotif and may be thought to provide the 'soundtrack' for the master epic we have been discussing here. The mix – or fugue – is heady indeed. To recognise the Quran's apocalyptic and epic voices and their contrapuntal relationship is to observe something quite essential about the way in which the Quran commands and grips an audience, the way it teaches, and the way in which its readership, its audience, develops its attachment to the book. Through its own verbal artistry, it somehow brings together in one place epos, mythos and logos (each of which depends upon words and language) to nourish the individual soul and the community through validating the historical identity of each reader/believer and pointing the way to a fulfilment of the destiny implied in this historical identity as disclosed to all humanity on that long ago yet ever-present Day of Alast.

The hero is a protector, and a suggestive translation for this word is the Arabic *wali* (guardian, friend), a word still frequently, if inadequately, translated as 'saint' in much of the relevant literature. However, it is nonetheless instructive that for the article 'Heroes and Hero Gods' in Hastings' monumental and venerable encyclopaedia, the reader interested in the Islamic instance is referred to another article, namely 'Saints (Muslim)'.[69] The distinctive and ubiquitous Islamic 'institution' and technical term for spiritual and religious authority, *walaya,* may indeed offer some clues about the nature of the Quranic epic and heroism. Quite apart from its very rich and malleable semantic charge, through which it denotes a powerful cluster of mutually enhancing, generative meanings (friendship, protection, guardianship, loyalty and even love) it also bespeaks a mutual activity (or verbality) by which both the subject and object are somehow united in participation in this friendship, guardianship, loyalty and love. While the word is frequently used to refer to highly accomplished spiritual heroes, whether in Shiʿism or Sufism, it is important to note that it is actually God Himself who is designated (nearly fifty times) the *wali*, par excellence, in the Quran (for example Q2:102, 120 and 257; Q5:68; Q6:51 and 70; and Q9:74 and 116, to list only a few). By virtue of their relationship to God, prophets and messengers and their communities are also understood as bearers of *walaya* (see for example the explicit designation Q5:55). Our Quranic heroes are thus indicated. Heroism is no longer, according to the Quran, the prerogative or fate of one outstanding person from the past. It becomes the desideratum of the entire community who see the Prophet and Messenger as a perfect example (*uswatun hasanatun,* Q33:21 and Q60:4).

With the Quran at the centre of Islamic religious experience, the epic value of all believers is affirmed. All of creation reiterates the absolute value of life and its meaningfulness (as for example in Q43:51). Through participation via the act of reading or recitation, the individual rehearses and re-performs the story in uncountable ways and through uncountable circumstances. Here we return to Corbin's important observations about the act of reading and imitation (*hikaya*) through which the reader or reciter actually becomes identified with the spiritual heroes of the tradition, and through which the epic quest and struggle of an Esfandyar, the *al-mahki anhu*, becomes the epic quest and spiritual challenge of the reader/reciter *al-haki*.[70] There is no reason to assume that the process would be any different in the case of the heroes of the Quran whose lives and stories are constantly recited by the believer/reader. This bespeaks a natural development within the rich spiritual heritage of Islam, its valorising in equal parts both the role of society and the role of the individual, its emphasis on the meaningfulness of life. The vast cultural and religious achievement and transformation that is associated with the name 'Islam' certainly suggests the category and adjective 'epic'. It is therefore little wonder that it is possible to trace this epic spirit to the Quran itself.

Chapter 2

The Quran as Apocalypse

These people have no grasp of God's true measure. On the Day of Resurrection, the whole earth will be in His grip. The heavens will be rolled up in His right hand – Glory be to Him! He is far above the partners they ascribe to Him! The Trumpet will be sounded, and everyone in the heavens and earth will fall down senseless except those God spares. It will be sounded once again and they will be on their feet, looking on. The earth will shine with the light of its Lord; the Record of Deeds will be laid open; the prophets and witnesses will be brought in. Fair judgment will be given between them: they will not be wronged and every soul will be repaid in full for what it has done. He knows best what they do. (Quran 39:67–70)

The Quran may be distinguished from other scriptures of Abrahamic or ethical monotheistic faith traditions by a number of features. The first of these is the degree to which the subject of revelation (as it happens, the best English translation of the Greek word ἀποκάλυψις /apocalypsis) is central to its form and contents. In this the Quran is unusually self-reflective, a common feature, incidentally, of modern and postmodern works of art and literature. It is not only a revelation, but repeatedly identifies itself as revelation and this identification is also revelation. It is acutely and uniquely self-referential as far as content, form and function are concerned.[1] In short, the Quran may be thought of as the 'main character' of the Quran. In studies of the Quran, the word 'revelation' is usually a translation of tanzil, 'sending down' a word with a very different semantic shape than apocalypse, which means 'to uncover' (and is thus akin to ἀλήθεια / aletheia). However, there are other Quranic words that also denote or connote revelation; some of these have a closer semantic correspondence to apocalypse. Such etymological problems notwithstanding, it is beyond discussion that revelation is the form, function and self-image of the Quran, and that finally these lexical questions emerge as moot or tangential.

So heavy with expectation, the Quran also distinguishes itself from other scriptures of the Abrahamic faiths in the degree and intensity with which it dwells on the question of afterlife *and* the vividness of that afterlife. In this context, the afterlife may be understood as a theatre for the dramatic performance and operation of the glory of God at a most intense level. Revelation is intimately linked with what is called in biblical and apocalyptic studies, a 'glory motif'.[2] There are, besides revelation and paradise, many other moments of glory in the Quran, but in the following exploration of paradise we will restrict reference to two: covenant and divine presence (*al-sakina*). Paradise, covenant and divine presence are discussed and explicated through reference to the Quranic literary features of enantiodromia (the interplay of duality, opposition and symmetry) and typological figuration. The hope is to demonstrate that these topics and literary functions are among those parts of the Quran that carry the apocalyptic theme most vividly and dramatically. Naturally, the more standard ideas of eschatological judgment and the afterlife are also touched upon. This chapter is organised as follows: first, a brief outline of the history of apocalyptic scholarship in biblical and related studies; second, a brief outline of the study of apocalypse in Islamic and Quranic scholarship; third, paradise as an apocalyptic motif in the Quran: covenant, glory and divine presence (*sakina*); and fourth, a brief conclusion setting forth the main results.[3]

APOCALYPSE AS LITERARY GENRE

In this context, it is important to first point out that the word apocalypse denotes only 'unveiling' or 'revelation'.[4] It does not denote 'destruction' or 'catastrophe' or even necessarily eschatology.[5] It only connotes these things by what might be thought literary accident. From this point of view, what came to be a very important book entitled The Apocalypse of St John (known also as The Apocalypse of Jesus Christ) was profoundly and powerfully concerned with eschatology and the 'end of the world' as that world was perceived to be a wicked impediment to the plan of God. So, the otherwise unremarkable or at best, possibly unusual word acquired considerable heft and presence when it was chosen as the title for the last book of the New Testament as we know it today. Indeed, there seems to have been a considerable early inner-Christian debate as to whether or not the Apocalypse of St John should be considered part of the canon. (For example, it is not in the original Syriac Peshitta.[6]) It is this 'literary accident' that has led to the eventual prominence and notoriety of the term as a designation for a category of literature and a designation for the attendant cosmic events and prophecies in what we solipsistically refer to as Western culture. Prior to this 'accident' it had no history as a marker of genre, as a type of eschatology or social/religious movement, though certainly there had existed books and writings concerned with these topics.[7] Because of its somewhat accidental use as the title of the last book of the New Testament[8] (for which it also happens to be the first word of that text) and because of the arresting, dire, dramatic, entertaining, exotic, frightening and comforting contents of that book, 'apocalypse' has also come strongly to connote (and incidentally denote) all of those things – that is, the content of the book – as well. Thus, apocalypse is a technical, generic designation and applies first to form and second to content.

The book of Revelation shares a suggestive concept, if not titular word, with one of the more frequent names by which the Quran itself is known and referred to, namely *The* Revelation – *al-tanzil*. Like the Quran, its contents are determined by the distinctive historical, psychological and social conditions of the audience to whom it was first addressed.[9] This audience was, of course, the early Christians suffering not only Roman and Jewish oppression and persecution but also the disarray and insecurity attendant upon the lack of clearly demarcated and universally acknowledged strong and effective leadership. Thus, the purpose of this particular revelation (Greek Ἀποκάλυψις Ἰωάννου, The Apocalypse of John): to comfort and reassure the community through a narrative of more or less constant rhetorical intensity that, ultimately, they would triumph against the forces of evil (what is referred to in the literature as an 'apocalyptic reversal', that is, of fortune),[10] as Hanson pointed out.[11]

Far from being a narrative of despair and destruction it is a narrative of hope. (It is only a narrative of despair for those who may be identified as the holders of power and authority condemned by the revelation/

apocalypse.) The mode of the message, divine revelation, is in the service, among other things, of establishing the highest possible authority for this comforting and encouraging information. But the mood of the discourse is along the lines of sharing a divine secret with the audience.[12] The wealth of frequently strange and 'supernatural' detail is in the service of creating a special 'reality effect' and lending credence to the proposition that all of this irrefutable information – including the details of judgment (who will be rewarded and who will be punished) – comes from an unseen, mysterious, all-knowing, and divine source. It is, of course, also entertaining in the etymological sense of 'gripping'.[13]

But the content of the book of Revelation, it has been argued, is not responsible for its place of prominence in the Bible. Rather, it is the ascription of that book, its revelation and composition, to 'John' – now generally further specified as John of Patmos – who until fairly recently was usually identified as the author of the Gospel of John, that is the disciple John and the author of the various epistles bearing his name. It is possible that this identification, more than the actual contents of the book, has made it such an object of veneration, meditation and exegesis, and that has assured its continued and important place in the canon. It should be remembered, however, that there are many other texts that never made it into the canon although they were attributed to important biblical figures, such as the Gospel of Peter, the Gospel of Thomas, the Acts of Thomas, Paul's Third Epistle to the Corinthians (which is, actually, accepted as canonical by the Armenian Church) or the Apocalypse of Peter. Thus, there seems to have been something about the Apocalypse of John beyond the mere attribution to the disciple that made members of the early church accept it as part of their scripture, while they were not willing to accept similar claims brought forward with regard to other similar texts. This 'something' is doubtless the contents of the book. Another argument claims that such content would otherwise have cast the document beyond the pale of acceptability, and it would have languished with other similarly fantastic and/or dubious texts on the margins of the theological library had it not been for the attribution.[14] Over the last century, the study of apocalypse has burgeoned, producing a more or less distinct and self-contained area of scientific study broadly termed 'apocalyptic' or 'studies in apocalypticism'.[15] Whereas formerly, while the book of Revelation was certainly considered just that, and was to be fully and gratefully received as the divine word in Christianity, there was at the same time a disinclination to encourage its study or in fact to pay too much attention to it. It meant *something*, but we must not meddle in things beyond our abilities, and clearly the strangeness of Revelation indicated in no uncertain terms that it was largely 'over our heads' – a mystery.[16] As Collins points out, 'Theologians of a more rational bent are often reluctant to admit that such material played a formative role in early Christianity. There is consequently a prejudice against the apocalyptic literature which is deeply ingrained in biblical scholarship.'[17] The last few generations of biblical and related scholarship, however, have attempted to grapple earnestly, and with minds freed from such prejudice, with what it has simultaneously sought to define as a genre. This highly variegated and productive process bore impressive fruit in the three-volume *Encyclopedia of Apocalypticism* (1999). There, a broad and concise definition of apocalypse is offered: 'the belief that God has revealed the imminent end of the ongoing struggle between good and evil in history'.[18] This definition is reduced from one formulated previously by the same author, and quoted earlier in the Introduction.

Reading this definition, the question immediately arises as to why the Quran and Islam have not been of more interest to scholars of apocalyptic. We forbear from responding to such a question until the conclusion. For now, suffice it to say that even in this recent encyclopaedia, which sees as its primary purpose the exploration of the apocalyptic element in the 'three Western monotheistic faiths of Judaism, Christianity, and Islam', Islam, in fact, occupies comparatively little space and the Quran itself even less.[19] In the meantime, it is widely acknowledged that there are 'apocalyptic' aspects to the Quran (for example the so-called 'hymnic' suras), just as there is near universal resistance to considering the entire text – as we do here – a bona fide apocalypse.[20] To be clear, it is also assumed that a text can be more than one thing at the same time and to say that the entire text is an apocalypse does not exhaust the possibilities or circumscribe the field of enquiry. Rather, we hope for the opposite: to widen the approach. The Quran today remains virtually unknown as a subject of apocalyptic scholarship as this has come to be largely and quite variously configured. It has not really been invited to (or if invited has not attended) the rather sumptuous banquet of contemporary apocalyptic scholarship.[21]

Current scholarly consensus is adamant that a great disservice to at least the genre of apocalypse is done if the term is taken to mean destruction *tout court*. Rather, the term is now understood to stand for a composition

whose nature may be very briefly summarsized as: 'a supernatural revelation, which reveals secrets of the heavenly world, on the one hand, and
of eschatological judgment on the other'.[22] In order that the reader may
be assured that the identification of the Quran as apocalypse does not
depend solely upon the lexicological and terminological coincidence of
the equivalence 'revelation/apocalypse', we provide in the Table below,
a brief list of key constitutive elements of the genre as now recognised in
apocalyptic studies, studies no longer restricted to biblical and apocry-
phal texts but which take into their purview the study of world literature,
whether ancient, modern or contemporary and in a variety of languages
representative of a variety of cultures.[23]

Over-reliance on such lists has been criticised because they tend to
be much too abstract, schematic and imprecise.[24] It has been argued that
apocalypse is best thought of as entailing three levels of analysis and study:
genre, eschatology and social movement. The study of apocalypse as 'literary genre' would bracket off all considerations of history and theology
to focus on the literary form and contents of the particular apocalypse
being studied. The study of apocalypse as 'eschatology' concentrates on
the religious and theological ideas about only the 'end things'. Thus, it goes
beyond the more purely literary investigation to isolate the way in which
a particular text, or indeed social movement, teaches about and considers
the last things. These last things can pertain to the more purely historical
events in 'time' or they may refer to the last things as they pertain to a
more existential or spiritual realm, the realm of the soul. Most commonly,
eschatology refers to a combination of both of these 'fields of action'.
Finally, the study of apocalypse as 'social movement' is an investigation
into the history and culture of groups or religions whose primary identity
is derived from and constructed on a view of the immediate future and
rescue from tyranny, wickedness and persecution.[25] Their actions and
teachings are all connected to a great cosmic or catastrophic event about
which they alone have accurate (secret) knowledge. A table, such as that
below, may be thought, therefore, to 'indiscriminately mix the three levels'
of analysis and 'include features which are randomly distributed among
the writings in question' (namely Jewish, Greco/Roman, Christian and
Zoroastrian apocalypses). In Hanson's words, they are 'too abstract to
define such a living entity'.[26] Yet, such a list, as the table indicates, seems
to speak with startling pertinence to the literary form and contents of
the Quran.

Apocalyptic themes and motifs with Quranic cognates

APOCALYPSE	QURAN
cosmogony	Quranic creation narrative
primordial events	Day of the Covenant, Q7:172
recollection of past	stories of the prophets and their communities
ex eventu prophecy	moot
persecution	persecution and rejection of prophets and followers; year of the elephant, Ma'rib dam
other eschatological upheavals, the end	*al-sa'a, al-amr, al-waqi'a, al-akhira*
judgment/destruction of wicked	punishment/leading astray
judgment/destruction of the world	*al-sa'a, al-amr, al-waqi'a*
judgment/destruction of otherworldly beings	*jinn*
cosmic transformation	*khalq jadid*
resurrection	*passim*
other forms of afterlife: angels and demons	heaven, hell, *barzakh*
pseudonymity/anonymity	authorship of the Quran
ambiguity and multivocality	*passim* (cf. *tafsir*)
glory motif	divine presence, *tajalli, sakina, al-haqq*, divine names, signs, the word, the book
illocution	e.g. numerous *qul* passages
aurality	oral composition and aural reception, *tajwid*/performance tradition
cultural hybridism	numerous loanwords, hybrid eschatology (perso-semitic)
orchestration of authorial voices	various grammatical persons as actor, actant, narrator in Quran
literary forms and devices	*saj'*
time and history periodised and determined	time fully controlled and transformed, periodised
enantiodromia	*passim*
otherworldly revelator/angel	Gabriel
closure	*yuwm al din*
truth	*al-haqq*
revelation	*tanzil, ba'th, kashf, bayan, haqq, ayat*

With such considerations in mind, it is of immediate interest to observe that, in fact, all of the items in the above list occur with greater or lesser frequency and intensity in the Quran and that the Quran, studied as apocalypse, may offer the student of the genre new aspects to consider, or the opportunity to consider a familiar problem in its Quranic manifestation: the topic of the Quran as divine and serious 'entertainment' (viz., in the sense of 'that which holds' not in the sense of mere amusement). The dramatic aspects of apocalypse, in which the Quran itself is the main character of the revelation, is surely also of some interest in the attempt to elucidate the charismatic hold it has on the reader.

APOCALYPSE IN THE STUDY OF ISLAM AND THE QURAN

In general, studies of the Quran avoid the word apocalypse and its derivatives, even though it certainly embodies enough apocalyptic subject matter to at least raise the question of whether or not it is an apocalypse. One of the reasons this may be so relates to an early twentieth-century dispute in Islamic studies among French, German and Dutch scholars. The effects of this dispute may be thought to haunt contemporary Quran scholarship. In 1911, Paul Casanova published his famous – soon to be considered infamous – *Mohammed et la fin du monde*, in which he sought to put forth a completely new view of the eschatology of the Quran and Muhammad's views on the 'end times'. According to this theory, the Quran contains the same eschatological ideas as the New Testament. Casanova read the history of Islam, the life and career of the Prophet Muhammad, and the travails of the early community in the context of apocalyptic eschatological tension. Casanova differentiates three stages:

1. In the first period, Muhammad expects the imminent end of the world;
2. In the second, he hesitates and explains that he does not know any longer whether the hour is near or far;
3. In the third period, he is completely preoccupied with his duties as military leader and legislator for the community now formed; he lets the question finally fall and dedicates himself to the necessities of the present hour completely.[27]

The Casanova thesis was quickly discredited, first by Becker[28] and then by Snouk Hurgronje,[29] and his ideas remained marginalised for several decades by dint of the apparently more appealing interpretations of Islamic history and the life of Muhammad put forth by such eminent scholars as Richard Bell, Montgomery Watt, Harris Birkeland, and the robust and influential ensuing tradition.[30] Today, as has been recently pointed out, many of these arguments against Casanova would be judged quaint and/ or biased. How contemporary Islamic studies, whether by Muslim scholars or 'Westerners', has come to avoid privileging the eschatological and apocalyptic content so much in evidence in the Quran itself is a fascinating story which Shoemaker sees beginning in the nineteenth-century methodological debates between two important German scholars, Ewald and Baur, about the study of early Christianity and the ministry of Jesus. The effects of the debate have continued to make themselves felt until today. Shoemaker's final word on the subject is germane:

> Indeed, when the eschatological traditions of the Quran and early Islam are evaluated according to the same standards used in reconstructing the historical Jesus, the results suggest a need to move beyond modern scholarship's prophet of social justice in order to recover, as once was similarly necessary in the study of the historical Jesus, the eschatological warner who stands at the origin of this global religious tradition.[31]

PARADISE AS APOCALYPTIC MOTIF

Paradise is a distinctive, defining theme of the Quran due to the frequency with which it is encountered, either as, *janna* (= "garden") which, together with its plural form *jannat* occurs over 120 times in the Quran, or by one of the several other synonyms or near synonyms denoting it. Some of these auxiliary terms are: *adn* (Eden) (6),[32] *al-na'im* (bliss) (7), *firdaws* (paradise) (2), *al-ma'wa* (refuge) (2). Kinberg has noted other Quranic words that through exegesis eventually came to be understood as synonyms for paradise:[33] *dar al-salam* (abode of peace) (2), *dar/jannat al-khuld* (eternal abode/garden) (1 each), *dar al-muqama* (eternal abode) (1), *maqam amin* (secure place) (1), *maq'ad al-sidq* (seat of honour) (1), *dar al-muttaqin* (abode of the pious) (1), *dhat al-qarar* (high ground) (1,

Q23:50), *tuba* (blessed) (1), *illiyyun/illiyyin* (exalted realms or creatures) (1 each), *rawda* (meadow) (1), *rawdat al-jannat* (heavenly meadow) (1), *husna* (best, most beautiful, bliss) (17), *al-akhira* (the hereafter) (71), this includes usages in which *dar* (abode, dwelling place) also occurs. Unlike the others, the term *dar* may refer to either paradise or hell, depending upon context.[34] A number of Quranic words or concepts not mentioned by Kinberg may also evoke paradise: *ridwan* (divine good pleasure, approval and acceptance) (8), *salsabil* (fountain in paradise) (1), *kawthar* (frequently understood as a river in paradise) (1), *sakina* (divine presence) (6, see above), and even the root *s-l-m* (divine peace) (140). In the same way, words such as *kufr* (ingratitude, unbelief) or *al-ghayb* (the unseen) (48) suggest hell (and therefore paradise through enantiodromia) or the invisible spiritual realm which is, of course, the final destination of souls (*al-ma'ad*). In addition, such important passages as Q7:172 (see below), and its mythic presentation of a time and place beyond time and place in the divine presence, may also be considered a direct reference to the presence of God – in other words, paradise. With these various usages – and many more yet to be marshalled but for which there is no space here to do so – paradise is implicated in most (if not all) of the Quran, either through direct reference or through the rhetorical gesture of referring to something by mentioning its absence (apophasis, aniconism) or its opposite (enantiodromia, paralipsis, irony).

Paradise, a myth and symbol of such amplitude, is not only multiple and variegated with regard to its comfort, ease and pleasures, landscape, vegetation, inhabitants and weather, it is also multiple and variegated with regard to the numerous terms and adjectives with which the Quran refers to it.[35] (In the Bible it is only in Revelation that we find anything approaching the *sustained*, sumptuous descriptions found here.[36]) The promise and description of paradise certainly continues, bolsters and elaborates strong ethical and moral thematic elements[37] and the general élan of the Quran we are so accustomed to identifying as the *raison d'être* of the afterlife: an inducement for acceptable behaviour and an argument against bad behaviour: *al-amr bi-l-ma'ruf wa-nahy an al-munkar.* However, paradise is also a message of mercy and forgiveness and is thus concerned with or speaks to an additional dimension of a personal existential awakening. In the eschatological logic of the Quran, paradise (*al-janna, al-jannat, al-firdaws*) is a subset of the broader category of the afterlife or hereafter, *al-akhira.* In keeping with this (largely binary) eschatological and apocalyptic logic,[38] its mention immediately brings into view several related categories and topics. The primary topic is hell-fire (*al-nar, jahannam, al-jahim*). Following this come the specific and characteristic geography, material culture and inhabitants associated with these 'places': the camphor fountain (*al-kafur*), the river of abundance (*al-kawthar*), pure spouses (*huris*), abundant rivers (*anhar*). The mention of such pleasures – comfort, ease, water, wine, milk – also stimulates the Quranically educated imagination to register opposing, related categories and topics in addition to hell and those things associated with these 'places': the bitter accursed tree (*al-zaqqum*), pus as beverage (*al-ghislin*), fruit as repulsive as the heads of devils (*kaannahu ruʿusu l-shayatini*).[39] As an example of eschatological symbolism, both scenarios are of course poised in 'fearful' or apocalyptic symmetry with life on earth, pre-mortem. They reflect both each other and the existential verisimilitude of being in the world. This dynamic of duality also pervades the rest of the Quranic text so that whenever oppositions are encountered, and they are encountered very frequently, paradise and hell are also part of the subtext. Paradise is a space where divine mercy is made effective and real. Such associations are simply unavoidable for the 'Quranised' consciousness,[40] and a prime example of the symphonic manner in which the Quran generates both meaning and aesthetic experience.[41]

THE GLORY MOTIF

Of the several literary and religious textual features isolated and characterised by recent scholarship as elements of apocalypticism or criteria by which apocalypticism may be identified, the so-called 'glory motif' figures prominently.[42] Glory is a word that combines power, authority, presence and light.[43] The original Hebrew word *kvod* connotes 'heaviness' and solidity (perhaps along the lines of the Arabic *samad*), but in its usage throughout the Bible it acquired other features. From being protected and hidden in the ark of the covenant after the exile it became portable beyond the holy of holies as when it visited the prophet Ezekiel in the form of the throne-chariot (*merkabah*) of God (Ezekiel 10) where the glory of God is especially visible in the fiery wheels 'within wheels'.[44] Ultimately, the meaning of glory is 'that which makes it possible to perceive or sense the presence (Hebrew *shekhina*) of God or the Lord'. Thus, light and

Quranic Arabic roots related to the glory motif

ASPECT OF THE MOTIF	ROOT
glory as power and authority	*'-z-m* (128); *'-z-z* (119); *j-b-r* (10); *k-b-r* (161); *m-j-d* (4)
light, fire and appearance	*d-w-'* (6); *j-l-l* (2); *j-l-w* (5); *n-w-r* (194); *s-f-r* (12); *s-n-w* (3); *sh-r-q* (17); *t-l-'* (19); *w-h-j* (1); *w-q-d* (11); *z-h-r* (1); *z-h-r* (59)
communication (including understanding, learning) and revelation	*'-y-w* (382); *'-r-f* (70); *b-sh-r* (123); *b-y-n* (523); *d-b-r* (44); *dh-k-r* (292); *f-h-m* (1); *f-q-h* (20); *k-l-m* (75); *k-sh-f* (20); *l-b-b* (16); *n-dh-r* (130); *n-t-q* (12); *n-z-l* (293); *q-l-b* (168); *sh-'-r* (38)
presence, propinquity, immediacy and relation	*'-n-d* (201); *h-w-l* (25); *l-d-n* (18); *q-b-l* (294); *q-r-b* (96); *s-k-n* (69); *w-j-d* (107); *w-l-y* (231); *w-s-l* (13)
praise and glorification	*h-m-d* (68); *s-b-h* (60); *s-l-m* (140)

splendour are frequently associated with the idea, as is the more abstract notion indicated by the word 'presence'. (We will return below to the Arabic cognate for *shekhina, sakina*.) For the purposes of this very brief and preliminary examination of the glory motif in the Quran we must be content simply with listing some relevant Arabic roots.

This Table does not take into consideration all of those key prepositions which in the proper context communicate proximity to or contact with divine glory (for example *bayna* (with or without *yaday*), *bi-*, *'inda*, *lada*, *li-*, *ma'a*, *min*, *qurb*). Nor does it take into full consideration the ubiquitous theme and feature of the divine names and attributes, all of which – whether singly or collectively, are instances or moments of the manifestation of divine glory. But there can be no doubt about the presence and prominence of a glory motif in the Quran. Indeed, it may be said that the glory of God is made manifest whenever revelation occurs or is rehearsed. And, as with most topics in the Quran, a positive and a negative perspective are also traceable. A negative aspect of glory (*fakhr*) as vainglory, is highlighted and condemned in numerous passages: 'And turn not thy cheek away from people in [false] pride, and walk not haughtily on earth: for, behold, God does not love anyone who, out of self-conceit, acts in a boastful manner' (Asad's translation, Q31:18; compare also Q57:20 and

Q20:131). Such condemnation, in obvious conversation with pre-Islamic usages, serves here to offer a foil against which the status of the divine is drawn more finely. This is in perfect harmony with the binary mode of discourse so prominent throughout the Quran.

Pursuing the motif or theme of glory in the Quran, then, quickly becomes an exercise in looking at both the forest and the trees at the same time, and brings into sharper focus the oft-quoted words of Constance Padwick that the Quran is of a special order: 'these are not mere letters or mere words. They are the twigs of the burning bush, aflame with God'.[45] On the one hand, the entire 'recital' is a theophany: a manifestation of God, appearance of the divine; and on the other, the theophanic text is replete with words and ideas and verbal gestures each of which may be thought to indicate an occurrence of the divine presence or to be understood as doing so. However, it is also clear, even before a thorough survey of the vocabulary of glory is available, that glory as power, presence and mode of communication is a major theme of the Quran. Hundreds of verses are indicated in the roots and topics mentioned above. Certainly, such glory is indicated in the opening epigraph of this chapter, quoting Q39:67–70. Glory in the Quran is an example of the coalescence of form and function: the glory and greatness of God is the main message of the revelation that is an action of this same glorious God. Nowhere in the Quran (or for that matter any place else, except perhaps the beatific vision in Dante),[46] is this idea of divine form and function as glory and revelation made more explicit than in the sublime and ravishing Light verse (Q24:35, here in the Arberry translation).

> God is the Light of the heavens and the earth;
> the likeness of His Light is as a niche wherein is a lamp
> (the lamp in a glass,
> the glass as it were a glittering star)
> kindled from a Blessed Tree,
> an olive that is neither of the East nor of the West
> whose oil wellnigh would shine, even if no fire touched it;
> Light upon Light;
> (God guides to His Light whom He will.)
> (And God strikes similitudes for men,
> and God has knowledge of everything.)[47]

This expresses the luminous aspect of glory; however, the equally celebrated and beloved Throne verse (Q2:255, here Arberry) expresses the
power, authority and (omni-) presence of glory:

God
there is no god but He, the
Living, the Everlasting.
Slumber seizes Him not, neither sleep;
to Him belongs
all that is in the heavens and the earth.
Who is there that shall intercede with Him
save by His leave?
He knows what lies before them
and what is after them,
and they comprehend not anything of His knowledge
save such as He wills.
His Throne comprises the heavens and earth;
the preserving of them oppresses Him not;
He is the All-high, the All-glorious.[48]

Q7:143 became a *locus classicus* for later medieval exegetes such as Ibn Arabi
(1240) in their attempts to explicate the workings of the self-manifestation
of divine glory, *tajalli*. It is the Quranic version of Moses' encounter with
God which is, in a sense, a replay of the original covenant, to be mentioned
shortly in the same sura at verse 172:

When Moses came for the appointment, and his Lord spoke to
him, he said, 'My Lord, show Yourself to me: let me see You!' He
said, 'You will never see Me, but look at that mountain: if it remains
standing firm, you will see Me,' and when his Lord revealed Himself
to the mountain, He made it crumble: Moses fell down unconscious.
When he recovered, he said, 'Glory be to You! To You I turn in
repentance! I am the first to believe!'[49]

The final key verse is Q41:53, the famous 'signs' passage in which the function and distribution of the signs of God's glory and presence are made
clear: they are everywhere, in the cosmos and in the souls of individuals. It
is understood, of course, that they are also in the Quran since it is a Quranic

verse that communicates this knowledge. 'We shall show them Our signs in every region of the earth and in themselves (*fi l-afaq wa-fi anfusihim*), until it becomes clear to them that this is the Truth (*hatta yatabayyana lahum annahu al-haqq*). Is it not enough that your Lord witnesses everything?'[50] This last verse, more than any other, summarises the Quranic theory of signs which, in the present context, is also a theory of glory and its transmission by and from its glorious source. It explains why the so-called natural world is a reflection of divine glory: the sun, moon, stars, water, the change of seasons and everything else. This natural realm is perceived as a theatre for the meaningful symphony of divine glory as is the human spiritual or psychic realm.[51] And all of this is explained in detail through the divine verses, literally 'miraculous signs' (*ayat*) of the glorious Quran.

TYPOLOGICAL FIGURATION

In the context of the present discussion, glory is of course remarkable in itself and as a marker of apocalypse. The apocalyptic symmetry, which may be thought to generate the light of glory, is at work not only in the trope of duality but also in typological figuration. The connection among the three central nodes of glory mentioned above, paradise, covenant and divine presence (*sakina*), is expressed through this powerful literary device of extraordinary imaginative vigour. Though typological figuration has been a key to understanding the composition and audience of the New Testament,[52] it has not really attracted the wide attention of Quran scholars. However, whatever attention it has attracted has been sufficient to demonstrate its intimate connection to the Quranic production of meaning.[53] The figure is so pervasive in literature that we sometimes forget it is functioning and it becomes transparent. So, in the Bible Egypt frequently stands for evil, darkness and oppression.[54] Babylon and Rome in the Bible function as antitypes and also represent the original Egyptian evil. Jonah delivered from the fish is seen by Christian readers as a prefiguration of Christ's resurrection. In Roman mythopoeic history, Augustus is simultaneously Romulus, Aeneas and Caesar.[55] Mary may be, as in the Quran, identified through typological figuration with Maryam of the Hebrew Bible,[56] and the ark of the covenant in Christian thought.[57] Jesus, through the Christian reading of the Hebrew Bible and prophetic history is seen as the second Adam, or a figuration of the prophet Joseph,[58] Moses (based on

Deuteronomy 18:15), Elijah or John the Baptist (Luke 9:7–9) or the Lamb of God. This literary device also serves to identify the Prophet Muhammad with every other prophet sent by God in an exclusive brotherhood of specially chosen emissaries of truth (*al-haqq*) and bearers of revelation, just as his community represents all earlier prophetic communities intent on vanquishing and combating evil to worship the one true God.[59] Even if the functioning of the device is so pervasive as to be transparent or undetected, like water for a fish, it nonetheless remains a very powerful component of the imaginative habitat of Quranic consciousness.

From its own point of view, Islam is the third in a series of three stages of what might be called a succession of typological readings or exegeses of scripture: 1) Hebrew Bible; 2) New Testament; 3) Quran.[60] These three scriptures are united in their concern with divine glory, presence and, of course, covenant. And, we see from the Islamic perspective that this same typological hermeneutic simultaneously unites and distinguishes each of these scriptures and communities. The workings of typological figuration and interpretation, especially in the instance of Abrahamic religion, has perhaps been best characterised by Northrop Frye.

> Typology points to future events that are often thought of as transcending time, so that they contain a vertical lift as well as a horizontal move forward. The metaphorical kernel of this is the experience of waking up from a dream, as when Joyce's Stephen Dedalus speaks of history as a nightmare from which he is trying to awake. When we wake up from sleep, one world is simply abolished and replaced by another. This suggests a clue to the origin of typology: it is essentially a revolutionary form of thought and rhetoric. We have revolutionary thought whenever the feeling 'life is a dream' becomes geared to an impulse to awaken from it.[61]

The aptness of this insight for the Islamic instance and the literary workings of the Quran would appear to be borne out by the very fact and reality of what might be called the 'mood of protest' of the formative years of Islam. Thus, a 'mere literary device' is both imbued with and expresses the imaginative energy of apocalypse, other terms for which might include 'spiritual revolution', 'paradigm shift' or 'enlightenment'. The apocalyptic revolution, as Collins says, is first and foremost 'a revolution in the imagination'.[62]

COVENANT

Glory and divine presence permeate the Quran and are encountered when it is encountered. In the Quranic historiography of revelation, the very first instance of their appearance is at the Day of the Covenant (*'ahd, mithaq*), recounted at Q7:172:

> When your Lord took out the offspring from the loins of the Children of Adam and made them bear witness about themselves, He said, 'Am I not your Lord?' and they replied, 'Yes, we bear witness.' So you cannot say on the Day of Resurrection, 'We were not aware of this.'

This is the day on which all three communities were part of a greater unity, that of humanity, *banu Adam*.[63] Such primordial unity had been a secret, but now it is disclosed and in the process of disclosure solves numerous problems facing the young community, not least of which is the problem presented by the 'chaos of religions' (sometimes referred to as the 'sectarian milieu') out of which Islam may be seen to have arisen.[64] With the doctrine of the covenant, the unity of humanity under one God is not a mere 'political' expediency but an eternal, inviolable, sacred truth. The luminous spirit of that day of intimacy and unity in the covenant, an occasion for the manifestation of divine glory, circulates through every word and letter of the Quran. And through typological figuration the reality of the primordial covenant is enhanced, elaborated, given substance; it is repeated through the line of prophets and in the recitation of the Quran.

Apocalypse is characterised by urgency and intensity. Paradise and hellfire are two mutually exclusive and, paradoxically, mutually enhancing tropes of intensity.[65] They are also spatial. From a literary point of view, they balance each other. As for time, the counterpart of space, there are two similarly balancing tropes of intensity. The epic scope of the Quran proceeds from or begins with the first of these intensity tropes, namely the Day of the Covenant described at Q7:172. When God posed the key Quranic question: Am I not your Lord? All humanity, there assembled for the occasion, responded with an enthusiastic (in the literal sense) and immediate: Yes indeed! (Arabic *bala*).[66] The presence of God on the Day of the Covenant is repeated and fulfilled on the Day of Judgment that in its symmetry with the great gathering on the Day of Alast[67] provides literary and apocalyptic balance. The Quranic covenant is the place where everything began. The return may be thought to be to that same place of the covenant, though now embellished with the effects and contents of the process or 'adventure' of consciousness: paradise or hell. Its lavish description may be seen as a way in which this intensity – an intensity of nearness, presence, expectation and encounter (*ittisal*, 'attaining connection with', or *ma'iyya*, 'propinquity, nearness' as distinct from *ittihad*, 'unification with') – may be repeated, replayed, re-experienced through precisely remembrance (another name for the Quran – *al-Dhikr*). The primordial Quranic paradise of human unity and harmony is made 'present' through a literary, imitative recital (*hikaya*) and an unbroken reiteration, prolongation and continuance of this first moment. And it is a moment which, in the characteristic supra-logical presuppositions of myth, is beyond space and time 'before creation'. That it is beyond time and place, however, does nothing to vitiate or weaken the spiritual and existential intensity of the drama of the covenant. Quite the reverse, its mythic nature produces the opposite effect.

Apocalypse induces the intuition that time is that which keeps everything from happening at once, and language is that which articulates meaning out of the undifferentiated transcendent – from our pre-enlightened point of view – *massa confusa,* to keep everything from being said at once and to thus be understandable and meaningful here in the sublunar realm.[68] Put another way, it reminds us of the true nature of reality and history.[69]

Between the beginning and the end, however, divine presence recurs in various forms. This presence is, of course, an apocalypse, whether from the point of view of the revelations themselves, the 'miraculous signs' which have been placed in the souls, in the cosmos and in the book (Q41:53) or the more dramatic descent from time to time of the apocalyptic 'divine presence' (*sakina*, see below).[70]

The Day of the Covenant remains solidly and firmly established in the mind of the Quran, the mind of Islam and Muslims, as the beginning of everything; most importantly, as the beginning of consciousness and the beginning of history. Such is a major component of what might be termed Islamic 'soul formation' or religious and spiritual imagination: the education of the soul. From a literary point of view, such intensity may only be balanced by its opposite, namely the end of everything or the destruction of the world, time and consciousness of these 'things'. A word from the Islamicate mystical vocabulary for this event is annihilation (primarily of 'self'), *fana*. The Quranic word for it is the Hour, *al-sa'a*. Paradise functions in this context as a promise of intensified or 'abundant' (compare John 10:10) life and the continuance of the primordial intensity of love and intimacy indicated at Q7:172. Indeed, the entire Quran and its contents may be thought of as a (perhaps operatically) prolonged instance of textual melisma – to borrow a technical term from the tradition of religious chant in the Christian tradition – in which the controlling 'syllable' is precisely the covenant mytheme of Q7:172.[71] Such revelatory music provides both a causal and typological argument for the unity of the Quranic prophets and their communities.[72] In this, all contents also simultaneously refer to and depend upon the promised denouement of *al-akhira* – the next world.[73] The light surrounding all Quranic statements is generated by the glorious and awesome relationship between the Day of the Covenant and the Day of Judgment.[74]

One of the chief accomplishments of typological figuration is the manipulation or control of time; in the same way music may be thought to control and exploit time and its illusions of movement and sequence. Thus, the reading act may become a 'technique of ecstasy' in the sense that the ephemeral self – as a construction or function of space/time – is escaped and the true identity of the reader/believer is instantly 'found' at the primordial moment of the covenant 'beyond time and space', the Day of Alast (compare *wajd*, 'ecstasy' derived from *wajada*, 'to find' from which is derived *wujud*, 'existence, being').[75] Time, after all, has the habit of making us think that only the present is real.[76] Quite apart from this collapse or erasure of historical time which Quranic typological figuration accomplishes,[77] existential and 'normal' historical time is also quite malleable in the hands of the apocalypticist. Through historical periodisation – another marker of apocalypse[78] – (*jahiliyya ≠ islamiyya*, or the 'times' of the various pre-Islamic prophets and their communities) and similar narratological embellishments, 'dumb' and 'amorphous' time is transformed into eloquent, teleological and monumental or epic history.[79] Muhammad's virtuoso performance is no exception. With the replacement of mindless time (*dahr*) and formless space with Quranic history and place, and then the erasure of this same construction, to return to 'the presence of God' at the 'moment of covenant', a formidable, imaginative power is deployed and enacted. To be in Quranic time and space is to be at the beating heart of apocalypse where past, present and future all meet and whose worldly/*dunyawi* distinctions somehow disappear altogether. Instrument and music merge. Performer, audience and performance – as in a dream, become one. After all, it is a relatively recent development in Western culture, at least, which saw the severe separation of two previously rather imperfectly delineated groups: performers and audience. And 'literal reading' of scripture is also a relatively recent preoccupation. Ancient readers tended to read typologically and poetically.[80] To chant the Quran, *the* reminder (though the word seems pallid in the present context) of the covenant, is to cause the divine presence (*sakina*) to descend and literally to enchant the now sacred space. The architecture and structure of such enchantment is sturdier than a cathedral.[81] The divine presence, so conjured, communicates and anticipates something of the essential reality of paradise.

A suggestive example for comparison with the experience of Quranic space/time is found through the medium of the magnificent fresco in the crypt of the Cathedral of Anagni. Surrounded by the images and events disclosed in the Apocalypse, the biblical book of Revelation, which adorn the contours of the ceiling of the crypt and were conceived by an unknown artist from the twelfth century, one may be moved to ponder how this virtuosic, essentially artistic, performance struck the medieval beholder.[82] The natural questions arising to our beholder are: Did all of these events already happen? Are they destined to occur in the future? Or, are they actually happening now? The crypt itself answers 'Yes' to all three questions and in recognition, the observer silently nods in understanding. This understanding or reading derives partly from the skill of the painter and partly from the observer's own experience of being in this particular apocalyptically charged, enchanted 'divine' space.

Obviously, in the case of the Quran the reader/auditor is surrounded, absorbed in and engulfed not by graphic images, but by the sonorities and meanings of the Quranic theophany, which include frequent, sumptuous depictions of paradise. The noetic and experiential effect (compare *hal*) may be thought similar: awareness, enlightenment, recognition.[83] Prophetic utterance is somehow timeless, and constitutes a tense of its own – the 'prophetic perfect'.[84] Now the world is experienced as singular and undifferentiated – a reflection of the transcendent unity of God, ontologically prior to what might be considered a continuous process of creation. It is as if the past the present and the future are all 'in the same room'. In this case, the room is the enchanted room 'sung into being' and defined and built by the recitation. The room is the Quran or rather, the space that vibrates with its sound, intoning the revelation. So, even though the original covenant 'has occurred' somewhere in the remote and mysterious placeless and timeless (*la makan* and *la zaman*), it is potentially revivified and relived at every moment of passing time with the same message: we are all now united as we were 'then'. The process, the content and the form the message takes is apocalyptic, revelatory: *al-haqq*. On the Day of the Covenant, glory was experienced fully and completely. In the world (*dunya*), glory is experienced intermittently. While it may be that some spiritual athletes (ἄσκησις / *askesis* < asceticism) and virtuosi experience it more steadily, it remains for most a fleeting and interrupted experience. Paradise, however, is the promise of a return to the primordial presence of glory and intimacy indicated at Q7:172. Thus, glory connects what has been characterised as the three cardinal periods of Islamic time: the primordial covenant, the life in or of the world, and the hereafter.[85] One dramatic symbol of this intermittency (and simultaneous eternity), during the ephemeral vagaries of being in the world, is found in the Quranic word *sakina* and its various descents into time.

DIVINE PRESENCE: *AL-SAKINA*

The function of this distinctive Quranic 'character', scholars agree, relates to the experience of the divine presence and glory pre-mortem, as it were.[86] The *sakina*, undoubtedly an emblematic evidence of Islam's Abrahamic genealogy, occurs in the Quran when important 'sacramental' requirements are felt: first, under the tree of oath-taking at al-Hudaybiya (628/6), we have a typical figuration of the cosmogonic Day of the Covenant (highlighted above) and simultaneous celebration of an Abrahamic genealogy for which it is also an instance of typological invocation. Al-Hudaybiya was of course inestimably important for the future of Islam, establishing as it did a detente between the Prophet Muhammad and the Quraysh of Mecca. Second, the divine presence 'descends' at the Battle of Badr (624/2), when help and encouragement were sorely needed. Third, it appears during the *hijra* (began 13 June 622), when the Prophet and Abu Bakr were seeking refuge in the cave and the *sakina* descended and inspired confidence and faith so that the Prophet could also encourage his companion. The circumstances of the three remaining instances are akin to the above: the establishing of authority, the reassuring of both Muhammad and the believers, and an experience of the presence and glory of God.

As a sign of the divine presence, the *sakina* is also an example of the many ways in which the glory motif functions in the Quran. Again, it may be said that the glory of God is made manifest when revelation occurs. What distinguishes the other world from this world, in the logic of the Quran, are the added degrees and intensities of propinquity, either to divine reward (nearness) or divine punishment (remoteness). *Al-sakina* is a timeless (though periodic) emblem (and personification) of this intensity, mentioned six times in this form of the verbal root *s-k-n*. To give a clearer idea of the way in which the Quran privileges this spiritual reality, we list here the six verses in the order in which they appear in the mushaf. Note how the topic of covenant or agreement is invoked in the last two:[87]

1. Their prophet said to them, 'The sign of his authority will be that the ark [of the covenant] will come to you. In it there will be [the gift of] tranquillity *(fihi sakinatun)* from your Lord and relics of the followers of Moses and Aaron, carried by the angels. There is a sign in this for you if you believe.' (Q2:248)

2. Then God sent His calm down to His Messenger *(thumma anzala Allahu sakinatahu 'ala rasulihi)* and the believers, and He sent down invisible forces. He punished the disbelievers – this is what the disbelievers deserve. (Q9:26)

3. Even if you do not help the Prophet, God helped him when the disbelievers drove him out: when the two of them were in the cave, he said to his companion, 'Do not worry, God is with us', and God sent His calm down to him *(fa-anzala Allahu sakinatahu 'alayhi)*, aided him with forces invisible to you, and brought down the disbelievers' plan. God's plan is higher: God is almighty and wise. (Q9:40)

4. It was He who made His tranquillity descend into the hearts of the believers *(huwa l-ladhi anzala l-sakina fi qulubi l-mu'minina)* to add faith to their faith – the forces of the heavens and earth belong to God; He is all knowing and all wise. (Q48:4)

5. God was pleased with the believers when they swore allegiance to you under the tree: He knew what was in their hearts and so

He sent tranquillity down to them (*fa-anzala l-sakina 'alayhim*) and rewarded them with a speedy triumph. (Q48:18)

6. While the disbelievers had fury in their hearts – the fury of ignorance – God sent His tranquillity down on to His Messenger (*fa-anzala Allahu sakinatahu 'ala rasulihi*) and the believers and made binding on them [their] promise to obey God, for that was more appropriate and fitting for them. God has full knowledge of all things. (Q48:26)

In all but one case (Q2:248) the *sakina* is sent down directly by God and is thus, in line with the Quranic technical lexicon, a revelation or apocalyptic event – an obvious event (and trope) of intensity and encounter with the divine presence echoing the primordial encounter described at Q7:172.[88] In the hadith literature, as is well known, this virtue or 'sacramental value' is extended to apply to the 'normal' recitation of the Quran by the believer. Thus, the idea, belief and perceived reality that whenever the Quran is chanted this same glorious, reassuring, peace-inducing presence descends with the recitation and literally enchants the space in which it is chanted – *and the covenant becomes renewed*. Such enchantment is of course exponentially enhanced and intensified through the verbal artistry of the Quran which we are not discussing.[89]

CONCLUSION

In addition to all of the above tabulated and listed elements of apocalypse present in the Quran, several of them may be thought to converge and indeed be harmonised in the controlling topos (or perhaps better *temenos* / τέμενος) of paradise, which then emerges as the harmonic centre of apocalyptic synergy in the Quran. Paradise accounts, directly, for a significant portion of the contents of the Quran, significantly more than the five hundred or so verses of content dedicated to legal and prescriptive matter.[90] However, if we consider indirect references to paradise, the situation is even more impressive. From this perspective, even the 'unapocalyptic', 'rational', 'unpoetic', 'unhymnic' laws and regulations of the Quranic legal code may also be thought to pertain to and evoke paradise inasmuch as their obedience or disobedience has direct bearing on whether the individual will be admitted to paradise or its counterpart, hell, in the post-mortem drama of salvation and damnation of the Quran. It has been shown, in biblical and apocalyptic scholarship (including studies of the Dead Sea Scrolls and the Qumran community) that calendars and other legal prescriptions, rather than being the opposite of apocalyptic, actually harmonise with the apocalyptic vision of a text or series of texts, depending upon context.[91] This, in fact, is one of the more persuasive elements in judging the Quran an apocalypse, as opposed to simply noticing this or that apocalyptic verse or sura. The mood and mode of apocalypse actually takes over the entire text, similar to the way in which the book of Revelation is present throughout the entire Christian Bible, even though it is the last book.

It is superfluous to attempt a differentiation between chronologically later revealed so-called Medinan and the chronologically earlier revealed so-called Meccan suras on the subject of paradise, even though the actual topic of the last day is less explicit in the Medinan suras.[92] The idea unites both periods in that there is a direct correspondence between an individual's deeds and their 'eschatology'. The subject or 'target' of apocalypse – of revelation – is precisely humanity, whether as individual or community. Paradise, as noted, is the key to understanding the spirit of Islam.[93] It certainly continues and reinforces the strong ethical and moral elan we are so accustomed to identifying as the *raison dêtre* of the afterlife. But it also adds an overlay, an additional dimension of a personal existential awakening and experience by repeating or replaying the experience of presence indicated at Q7:172. Here the much-loved and much-quoted hadith of the Prophet is germane: 'Men are asleep and when they die they awake.'[94] The moments of descent, when the event of the covenant is recalled (as in *dhikr*), are in this connection so many preludes or foretastes of the great awakening referred to in the hadith. Such foretastes of paradise, through evocation of the glory and intimacy indicated in the verse of the covenant, abound. With these prefigurations of awakening (enlightenment/apocalypse), the subject may indeed 'ascend' through various stages until the presence or vision of God is experienced. A defining and controlling model for this experience is the prophet's journey and ascension that came to figure prominently early on, both as an exegesis of otherwise mute and mysterious Quranic statements and as an example to be emulated or aspired to.[95] (Compare for example here the traditional hundred 'abodes' of *al-janna*, in which *firdaws* – paradise – is frequently, though certainly not always, the highest.) It may be added that the traditional interpretation of this powerful, living, spiritual *Bildungsmythos* as a somewhat comedic explanation of the institution of the ritual prayer service (*al-salat*) is an obvious ploy for taming the otherwise potentially destabilising and perhaps 'dangerous' energies of a profound personal and authoritative spiritual or mystical experience. The story is, in some ways, an attempt at domesticating the apocalypse.[96] Doubtless, this was sincerely felt to be for the best.

Paradise as an otherworldly supra-rational location is, as in the table on p. 33, a recognised marker of apocalyptic literature. But, paradise is especially interesting because of the number of other apocalyptic themes that are directly connected to it: triumph of good over evil; judgment; strange and fantastic beings; typological figuration; enantiodromia; glory motif; true home; the foil and consummation for time/history and periodisation; synaesthesia; and divine presence. In this, paradise may be thought the conceptual chiasmic centre of the entire Quran, where the other contents of the book meet as spokes of a wheel.[97] It was an earlier wheel, after all, that represented the 'escape' of *kvod*, divine glory, from the now 'occupied' temple to join and comfort the Jews in their painful exile. *Kvod* is at the very foundation for the study of the glory motif in the Hebrew Bible. Glory in the Quran is known by a number of names and situations. As has been repeatedly demonstrated here, it is frequently brought to light through duality, opposition and symmetry in the Quran, and their narrative and doctrinal issue of typological figuration and oneness.

The consideration of the Quran as an apocalypse invites questions about the nature of apocalypse, what it has meant, what it means in current scholarly discussions, and why the category is or is not useful in the study of religion and literature generally, and in the study of the Quran and Islam specifically. It is hoped that this discussion demonstrates the unique usefulness of such methodological tools as a generic notion of apocalypse for the study of the Quran. We have seen that when paradise is described in the Quran it is certainly not mere literary allusion. Rather, due to the complexity, interconnectedness, harmony and mutual resonances of the images – that is to say the literary nature of the discourse – along with their eternal/final implications, one might refer to the cultivation of an 'apocalyptic sensorium'. It is such a sensorium that is now in operation and deployed and employed by the audience, believer and reader. The eyes and ears that register the descriptions of paradise are organs of the imagination – an apocalyptic or revelatory imagination. The secret of paradise is revealed in the Quran through this sensorium. The apocalyptic sensorium is the one that leads beyond the earthly diurnal world to a new (but not completely different)[98] realm.

A more intense trope than the end or destruction of the world can hardly be imagined and, in literary and perhaps psychological terms, this 'negative intensity' is balanced by the positive intensity of paradise and its Quranic description-cum-celebration. Intensity is a 'venue' or 'occasion' for truth-telling, as in natural catastrophes, wars, famines, funerals, weddings and births. During such occasions one delivers oneself of the truth. Thus, the mere notion of 'the Truth' (*al-haqq*), carries apocalyptic resonances of certainty and finality. Such truth and honesty are demanded by virtue of the Hour and end of days imagery. Intensity is also encountered, read and experienced in numerous other Quranic passages, or – perhaps better, at various Quranic 'moments' (sing. *waqt,* compare *al-sa'a*). Some of these more conspicuous instances are the 'moment' and very idea of revelation (apocalypse), *bayan, kashf, tanzil, haqq,* which is of course everywhere in the Quran, and may be thought particularly 'thickened' at such celebrated passages as the Light verse, the Throne verse, the Night of Power or the descent of the heavenly table, *al-ma'ida.*[99] All descents/revelations are moments of disclosure, encounter, recognition and intensity. The language used to describe them is therefore perforce experienced as a trope of intensity and understood also as a lexicon of intensity since such communication is the main event of the Quranic apocalypse: meaning and form are perfectly fused. The Quran is more concerned with revelation than with anything else, including God/Allah, prophets and community. From this perspective, each of these separate subjects function as occasions or modes of revelation (literally *asbab al-nuzul*). However important they are for Islamic religious thought and practice, they are second in importance to the event (compare *al-waqi'a*) of revelation, without which there would be no knowledge of any kind. It is useful here to think of such 'major themes of the Quran' as first order or 'master' occasions of revelation/apocalypse, and the traditional *asbab* as secondary or subsidiary or contingent occasions of revelation.

It is not being argued here that the Quran be somehow squeezed into a category determined by etic, non-native, invasive or 'neo-colonialist' considerations and 'outsider' practitioners in a gesture of neo-Orientalism. Rather the opposite idea is key: the Quran, because it embodies so much in common with current scholarly notions and definitions of apocalypse (while simultaneously displaying obvious departures), may offer insight

about such a genre and its structures, limitations and dynamics. To the
extent that the New Testament acquires meaning in the context of a
Holy Bible having a beginning, middle and end (Genesis, Life of Christ,
Revelation), it is also the case that it is an apocalyptic text read and imagined by an apocalyptic community.[100] To the extent that the Quran focuses
on revelation, the Day of Judgment, paradise and hell it is also the book
of an apocalyptic community, a book in which every letter and every
word, every verse and every sura is imbued with the same intensity and
'presence' (*sakina*). One might suggest that paradise in the Quran, while
certainly an eschatological theme, is also more. A provisional taxonomy
may go like this: eschatology in the key of speculative or dialectical theological, philosophical and mystical 'religious' discourse is a subject and
result of logocentric scholarly pursuit. Eschatology in the key of prophecy
is something else. To articulate an only somewhat circular argument,
the distinctive nature of Islamicate apocalypsis may be understood more
perfectly by focusing on the Quran, in contradistinction to extra-Quranic
material and historical events. And, it brings us closer to understanding
the nature of a sacramental dimension in reading the Quran. As Hodgson
said so eloquently:

> For the Quran continued, as in Mecca and Medina, to be a monu-
> mental challenge. In its form, it continued, even after the ending
> of active revelation with Muhammad's life, to be an event, an act,
> rather than merely a statement of facts or of norms. It was never
> designed to be read for information or even for inspiration, but to
> be recited as an act of commitment in worship; nor did it become
> a mere sacred source of authority as the founding of Islam receded
> into time. It continued its active role among all who accepted Islam
> and took it seriously. What one did with the Quran was not to
> peruse it but to worship by means of it; not to passively receive it
> but, in reciting it, to reaffirm it for oneself: the event of revelation
> was renewed every time one of the faithful, in the act of worship,
> relived the Quranic affirmations.[101]

Suppose our knowledge of the Quran began only recently with a discovery of mysterious scrolls in a desert cave. Suppose we had no Muslim
community, no Islamic history, no Islamic science or civilisation to help
us read these scrolls. Is it conceivable that we might mistake these Quran

scrolls for the central text of a long vanished apocalyptic community whose ideas about the next world, colourful and fantastic as they might appear, nonetheless are understood to make perfect sense in the context of one of the more prevalent genres of late antiquity? There seems to be little reason for us to continue to avoid referring to this powerful and glorious imagery of a transcendent realm and its role in the reward and punishment – the judgment – of good and evil, as apocalyptic.

The prejudice of Church scholasticism towards the book of Revelation mentioned earlier may have been inherited and elaborated by modern and some contemporary Quranic scholarship, through a long and complicated process, resulting in a strange political correctness. Note this strong statement transcribed from a medieval and dismissive critique of the Quran's paradise discourse: 'All these descriptions of paradise suit only stupid ignorant people who are inexperienced and unfamiliar with reading texts and understanding old traditions, and who are just a rabble of rough Bedouins accustomed to eating lizards and chameleons.'[102] Surely, the descriptions of paradise in the Quran are no more outlandish or fantastic than the contents of the book of Revelation. Perhaps it is the tendency to think of 'apocalyptica' as simultaneously irrational, marginal and peripheral to a conceptualised necessary mainstream that has given rise to a tendency – out of well-meaning respect – not to consider the Quran an apocalypse (whatever else it may *also* be).[103] Of course, not all judgments have been so negative, as we have seen.

Another reason for the neglect of such a potentially fruitful and stimulating method for the study of the Quran centres on the undesirable (and accidental) associations with the mere word 'apocalypse' and its untutored and colloquial acceptance as destruction and violence. A third possible reason for such neglect relates to the role of narrative in most definitions (and instances) of the apocalypse genre. The perceived absence of a continuous narrative, or the perceived presence of a deeply flawed and defective narrative layer of the Quran, has long been a bulwark of Western studies of the Quran. Recent scholarship, however, has drawn attention to an unmistakable (but heretofore elusive, if not totally unrecognized) chiasmic narrative structure in the Quran, a structure that derives from oral composition and is found throughout human history in orally composed poems and narratives of numerous cultures and societies. The discovery of the ring or chiasmic structure of the Quran's longer suras and sequences of shorter suras has shone floods of light on the study of Quranic narrative.[104]

Sometimes referred to as 'Semitic rhetoric', this structure entails the deployment of a series of symmetries which direct attention towards the centre of the composition which thus emerges as the main point of the text both physically and conceptually, in contrast to the main point of a text being located at the conclusion, as is the case in other types of compositions. In addition, various distinctive features of the text, such as duality and typological figuration, have been shown here to provide a coherent and powerful narrative core for the entire book. It emerges that the Quran may be simultaneously an apocalypse and whatever else it so obviously is: prophetic scripture of ethical monotheism. The two modes need not be mutually exclusive. Furthermore, parallel suggestions about the epic dimension of the Quran is likely to shed more light on the fascinating topic of the narratological complexity and coherence of the Quran.[105]

The purpose here has been to highlight the Quranic mode and mood of apocalypse as expressed through the theme of paradise and precisely as that which constitutes the pre-canonical[106] or pre-exegetical setting of the text. Thus do we understand or hear the voice of the Quran – before it became an object of study by the learned Muslim and non-Muslim traditions – in its apocalyptic or revelatory musicality. By musicality is meant that the grammar of the performance and the grammar of a text merge – audience and performance merge so that the audience is part of the performance or revelation. There is circularity and closure, a sense of 'home' very much akin to the effect of music.[107]

Paradise in the Quran is a comprehensive and symmetrical depiction of the world we know; yet it somehow takes us out of that world through a gnostic or noetic apocalypse in the imagination. These striking artistic qualities somehow suffuse the entire text of the Quran and lend it its specific identity and unmistakable character. Certainly, such qualities are also found in other scriptures (for example the Song of Songs, the book of Nahum), but their pervasiveness throughout the entirety of the Quran (a book of approximately the same length as the New Testament) is quite definitive. Thus, these features and their profusion are simultaneously what seem to set the Quran apart from other scriptures while paradoxically providing a link to them. But, most importantly, they may provide evidence for the ebbing of an originary apocalyptic imagination as it gave way to a more domesticated Islam. In terms quite foreign to the present instance, it helps us understand how in Islam heresy became orthodoxy. Obviously, the apocalyptic imagination did not disappear completely.

Recent scholarship has discovered and analysed the apocalyptic centre of such various historical Islamic (and therefore religio-political) movements as the Abbasid rise to power,[108] the various claims to religious authority among Muslims in general,[109] the rise of the Ottomans,[110] the Safavids,[111] the Hurufis,[112] the Babis and the Baha'is,[113] the Ahmadiyya,[114] as well as even more recent and contemporary phenomena.[115] However, the source of such apocalyptic imaginative and spiritual energy in the Quran – whether as text or document, scripture or prophecy – remains to be fully understood, described and appreciated.

Chapter 3

An Apocalypse of Reunion
The Epic of Joseph

INTRODUCTION

The Quran is not without a centre of narrative gravity despite its notoriously challenging narrative flow. This becomes especially apparent when we are being told about the experience of particular prophets or messengers with their proper community. History and the rise and fall of civilisations and cultures are punctuated by the appearance of these special envoys, according to the Quran – thus their epic struggles in the divinely inspired effort to guide humans from ignorance to enlightenment and from savagery to civilisation in whatever community they have existed (prophets have been sent to all of them, according to Q16:36). However, such narrative continuity is frequently difficult to detect on the page. In these instances, certain characteristic Quranic literary features maintain the integrity and coherence of the whole in the absence of explicit and continuous, unbroken narrative dramatic movement. The following is an attempt to discuss, in sequence, 1) typological figuration as it pertains to 2) the story of Joseph, concluding with a focus on one of the main 'characters' in the story, namely, the famous shirt (*qamis*), which functions as a touchstone of narrative continuity and as a symbol of Joseph's spiritual journey and travails. This exploration starts from a premise that the Quran and *tafsir* are both literature. Typological figuration, a venerable and powerful literary device, is in both instances one of the central keys to an otherwise sometimes opaque Quranic narrative continuity. In this chapter it will be seen that typological figuration functions beyond the confines of 'mere' literature to inform Islamic piety and religious thought.

TYPOLOGICAL FIGURATION

While typological figuration has long been recognised as an important and persuasive literary feature of the Bible and even its exegesis, the Quran and the vast literary web that it generated have not yet been subject to the same kind of thorough examination we find, for example, in Leonhard Goppelt's classic study. There it was demonstrated beyond any possible doubt that the authors of the New Testament saw in the life and teachings of Jesus a typological fulfilment (*cum* repetition) of a variety of distinctive themes and motifs and 'promises' of the so-called Old Testament. The New Testament is, through typological exegesis, a *tafsir* of the Hebrew Bible and the mission of Jesus is perfectly and seamlessly identified (at least for the authors and their readers) with what has come before. As a result, there is no doubt about the identity of such Old Testament types as 'the Lamb of God' or 'the Suffering Servant'. Even the experience of Jonah in the belly of the whale is seen as prefiguring the mission and role of Jesus, especially his period in the tomb before the resurrection.[1]

Typological figuration is, of course, found frequently in many other contexts outside the strictly religious. Since Goppelt's foundational work on the power and prevalence of typological figuration at work in the New Testament, we have grown accustomed to recognising this literary figure and its persuasive rhetorical and poetic efficacy in various settings. It represents history in a series of conceptual, as distinct from verbal, rhymes. Often we see it at work in studies of history and historiography, ancient, modern and contemporary. In the 'logic' (which transcends logic) of typology, Augustus can be both Aeneas and Romulus redivivus at the same time. It has been suggested that our own confidence in the process of, and one might add the structure we give to, history is probably derived, whether wittingly or unwittingly, from the compelling symmetry and meaning that typological figuration delivers.[2]

Typology says that the old world has ended, a new one is about to be born. Those who perceive this shift and are sympathetic to it, such as the early followers of the Prophet Muhammad, will be persecuted and ostracised for merely 'understanding'. The understanding is that Muhammad represents the new return of the life-giving, divine, ancient and eternal, prophetic spirit. Therefore, this new and numerically insignificant community depends upon the revelation for encouragement, solace, and promise that 'it will all work out' despite the serious hardships and obstacles it will undoubtedly be its fate to encounter and suffer. (Paradise, for example, is typically described in the Quran when the Hour or the Last Day is mentioned.[3]) Typology is a figure that unites time, harmonises it and gathers it together: 'the type exists in the past and the antitype in the present, or the type exists in the present and the antitype in the future'.[4] This reflects a basic attitude towards the world and one's place in it with regard to the passing of time. What was formerly mere time past is now, as a result of the prophetic imagination, history. So it assumes heretofore unimagined importance and, at the same time, the mystery of this great secret/importance is revealed.[5] The past is now seen as part of a process through which 'meaning' may be identified with human experience. Interpreting Shi'i theological philosophy on the problem of time and history, Henry Corbin's well-known observation is impossible to ignore: 'Our thinkers perceive the world not as "evolving" in a horizontal and rectilinear direction, but as ascending: the past is not behind us but "beneath our feet".'[6] Such a statement actually may go to the heart of a general Islamic view of time and history, and thus has implications far beyond an understanding of Corbin's basic sources, as in this statement from the *Encyclopaedia of the Quran*:

> The entire world in all its variety was created by the one creator at one particular moment. It follows that oneness was the ideal state for it at all times and that to which it should always aspire. As the beginning was one, so the expected end of the world is one for everyone and everything. Whatever is and takes place in between these two definite points of created time, no matter how varied in detail, follows a set overall pattern. Thus the history of the past and of the future, including that of the present, is fundamentally uniform. No distinction between the three modes of time need be made by the observer of human history.[7]

This may be akin to what al-Qurtubi (1273) was referring to when he characterised the Night of Power as the point where all time meets, *jami' al-dahr*. Michael Sells has spoken eloquently in this same connection about what one might call a 'sacrament of time and history' or, perhaps better, an 'icon of time and history' and its centrality for Islamic religion in his classic article on the Night of Power:[8]

> The Christian mystics, John the Scot Erigena and Meister Eckhart, both emphasized the combination of perfect and imperfect tenses as essential to an intimation of the 'eternal moment', the moment that for Eckhart always has occurred and always is occurring, and which in his Christian interpretation corresponds to the eternal birth of the son of God in the soul. (p. 249 n. 27)
>
> Through such aural, syntactic, and thematic inter-twining among the *ruh* passages involving creation, revelation, and *yawm ad-din*, of which the above example is only one of many that could be cited, the spirit takes on a temporal multivalence. The occurrence of the term *ruh* within these three distinct moments engenders an inter-textual acoustical-semantic dynamic that plays against the separation of the three moments and transforms normal understandings of time. (p. 254)
>
> The connection between *ruh* and *qadr* in *surat al-qadr* suggests that this transformation of time into a primordial unity is an aspect of *qadr* ... Translators of the Quran have tended to choose terms like 'power' for *qadr*, terms that express only one side of the semantic field. It is my view that 'destiny' might come closer to expressing the mutivalence of the term, though no single English term would seem sufficient. (p. 255)
>
> The classical interpreters emphasize the storing up of future events in the *laylat al-qadr*, a phenomenon that represents the containment of a span of time (whether one year or all time) within a single moment. (p. 256)

Even if all the details of this new meaning are not completely clear now, they will be made clear in due course. When this happens, the present magically becomes the antitype or repetition of previous history but with the added luminosity of truth revealed, and fulfilled: the code cracked.[9] We now understand, and a mystery we may not even have recognised as existing previously is now solved. Such understanding may also acquire the features of revolution, as when the past is simply obliterated and rendered no longer pertinent. As we saw earlier, Northrop Frye uses the image of waking from sleep to describe the workings of typological figuration.[10]

The prominence of typology in the Quran and *tafsir* as a hermeneutic presupposition or strategy suggests an association of this literary conceit with what has so aptly been described as the 'apocalyptic imagination'.[11] It is important to observe that not only does typology move through time and transcend time (Frye's words) but, in fact, typology frequently erases or collapses time. It does this by insisting that in the presence of God all things are somehow happening at once.[12] Time is that which 'sorts them out' for human consumption. It is the obliteration of time, perhaps somehow analogous with the splitting of the atom, that would seem to summon up the powerful literary energies and concerns of bona fide revelation and focus them into an apocalypse.

The constant recurrence of the pervasive figure of typology throughout the Quran provides one bank, if you like, for the narrative stream flowing through the Quran from 'beginning' to 'end'.[13] The overall structure is much the same as that described in the sura of Joseph some years ago: circular[14] and chiasmic.[15] The Quran has no beginning and no end, although it contains within its sphere numerous discrete narratives, each with their own beginnings, middles and ends, whether explicit or implicit.

Note that typological figuration applies to both the prophets and their communities. The first Muslims compared, and in some sense identified, themselves with the ordeals experienced by the children of Israel and the followers or *qawm* of all other prophets. And, in the nature of things, this was as it should be. Hanson's observation, quoted earlier, that apocalypse is used to take power away from evil forces and to comfort the apocalyptic community is germane here.[16]

The typological iteration or rendering of Muhammad's prophethood points to the erasure of time and history in a persuasive and compelling gesture of the prophetic imagination. All time is dissolved or redissolved into the original moment characterised by the Quran as the Day of the Covenant (Q7:172), a time outside time in a place beyond place that may indeed be seen as a symbol or metaphor for what has recently come to be discussed in other, more scientistic settings as the birth of consciousness.[17] The apocalyptic secret is revealed: the chaos of mutually exclusive, historical religions is now transformed into a harmony of periodic divine revelation, the reading of which is made possible by the newly proclaimed (yet simultaneously ancient, viz., *badi*')[18] alphabet of prophets and divine messengers who are shown to be profoundly related and of one purpose. This new alphabet forms the language for the proper reading of the past.

The nightmare of history is dealt with by demonstrating exactly how illusory and ephemeral 'time as history' is. It is awareness, consciousness, understanding and their like that are, by comparison, substantial and permanent (though atemporal and supraspatial) and therefore superior to vulgar and mere history. This is one reason why it may be possible to translate *islam* as 'enlightenment'. Obviously, this is not a literal translation. However, based on the philology of Ignaz Goldziher and Toshihiko Izutsu, it is arguable that the true opposite of *jahl* 'ignorance, savagery' is not *ilm* 'knowledge' but rather *hilm* 'moderation, patience, civility' for which Islam, especially in its adjectival form *islami* and used in diametrical opposition to *jahili* and its permutations, may be seen as a near synonym.[19] The *halim* is the 'civilized man', as opposed to the *jahil*, the 'barbarian'.[20]

Based on comparison and contrast between two principles, typological figuration (ultimately dependent upon the symmetry and duality so clearly and unambiguously at work in the Quran) may be thought to articulate in a special and distinct way the characteristic apocalyptic èlan of the Quran by standing for that great secret that the Prophet Muhammad and the Quran unveiled to the chaos of religions that confronted him and that he himself confronted on behalf of God. The secret is none other than the interconnectedness and kinship of all prophetic messages, their prophets and their followers.[21] This is part of what is called in the Islamic tradition 'spiritual truth' or 'reality'. The shirt of Joseph, about which more below, is a perfect emblem or symbol of this spiritual truth.

Another key characteristic of typological figuration is that it is generative. Once the basic pattern is introduced, it becomes a matter of the natural, fluent and unstoppable 'logic of the imagination'[22] to apply it to a number of different contexts and subjects. Thus we see typological iterations of the Prophet Muhammad in the characterisations of such subsequent figures of religious authority (viz. *walaya, khilafa, imama*) as the first four caliphs (and, in a sense, all subsequent caliphs), the imams of the Shi'a, the great imams of the legal tradition and religious culture (compare, for example, al-Shafi'i's *Risala* for the distinctive image of the Prophet Muhammad that inhabits that work), and last but certainly not least, the sufi sheikh, who may be considered a holographic or 'virtual' reiteration (viz. *mazhar*) of prophetic authority. Thus typological figuration, together with other similarly ubiquitous and characteristic literary structures of the text, is clearly communicated, both in meaning and form, to a vast readership and audience far beyond Arabic linguistic boundaries.[23]

THE STORY OF JOSEPH IN THE QURAN AND EXEGESIS

With such a clear, consistent and paradigmatic basic message, it is perhaps in the nature of what might be termed 'anti-narratological relief' that the Quran itself is far from presenting a unitary discrete narrative, from its 'beginning' to its 'end'.[24] The only sura of the Quran universally recognised to have a 'proper' beginning, middle and end is the sura of Joseph (Q12).[25] Thus it is possible that the main protagonist of the sura, as a paragon of beauty, is also a paragon of order and meaning and typological figuration, which has its own inherent beauty or aesthetic.[26] The conclusion of this sura emphasises the happy reunion of Joseph with his people and most significantly with his father, Jacob. In the course of telling the story of Joseph and the relationship implied for the current audience, Muhammad himself is seen, by virtue of his spiritual/typological kinship with all of the prophets and messengers, as being reunited with his true family, who in the very act of reunion/recognition (compare *'irfan, ma'rifa*) are given a new measure of divine guidance, another revelation.[27] Such a reading is in line with the distinctively Quranic formal and stylistic identity between history's movement (type/antitype) and the pervasive Quranic motif of 'pairing' (*zawj/tazawwuj*).[28] Typological figuration expresses a longed-for consolidation of scattered, exiled, dissipated forces, in the life both of the individual and of society.[29]

On the model of the New Testament (the New Covenant) as a commentary on the Hebrew Bible (the Old Covenant), the Quran is a commentary on earlier scriptures, their traditions and their faith communities. Through the typological identification of the Prophet Muhammad with all previous prophets (both known and unknown), the Quran may be thought to decode the great baffling and terrifying 'nightmare of history' and its chaos of religions, and point a way out.[30] It reveals or perhaps more accurately, lifts the veil (Arabic *kashf* = Greek *apokalypsis*) covering the true nature of the relationship between historical reality, spiritual reality and social reality. Most importantly, of course, it makes clear and non-negotiable the relationship between God and the world through prophethood and messengership, without which there would be no understanding or meaning. And inasmuch as the heart of this revelation or apocalypse is articulated in the 'return' of the prophetic reality to his people (as, for example, the type of the reunion of Joseph with his tribe), then it may be thought an apocalypse of union or reunion and recognition, what Aristotle called anagnorisis.[31]

The story of Joseph in the Quran is among the favourites of Muslims in general. It is considered the 'best of stories' (Q12:3), because it is a more or less extended and consistent narrative, unlike other suras of the Quran.[32] According to al-Tha'labi (1036), author of *The Tales of the Prophets* (*qisas al-anbiya*), the story of Joseph is the most beautiful 'because of the lesson concealed in it, on account of Joseph's generosity and its wealth of matter, in which prophets, angels, devils, jinn, men, animals, birds, rulers, and subjects play a part'.[33] Joseph's generosity is especially portrayed in his dealings with his treacherous brothers whom he supplies with grain and forgives.

The contents of the sura present something of an integrated expression of the fundamental thrust of Islam, whether from the point of view of personal religiosity and spirituality, or from the broader perspective of humanity's communal religious life. As with many suras of the Quran, this one also emphasises the connection of Islam with previous religions. The number of verses in sura 12 approximates the number of suras in the Quran itself.[34] And the sura of Joseph has been singled out[35] by various exegetes throughout *tafsir* history as one that lends itself to discussion because, unlike many other suras of the Quran, it presents a comparatively sustained narrative. At the same time, like other suras, it is replete with many topics considered to be key to the Islamic religion in general and the authority, role and vocation of prophethood in particular. Thus, this sura brings together all of the various concerns, themes and otherwise perhaps disparate aspects of the Quranic vision under one roof, in one place. (Or, in line with the central metaphor informing the word 'text', it may be seen as weaving together in one 'tapestry' those elements so distinctive of the Quran.) The same is said of *Surat al-Baqara*,[36] but the difference between the two is clear. With regard to uniting the message of the Quran in one compelling and entertaining narrative, the frankly operatic sura of Joseph 'outstrips' *Surat al-Baqara* by many leagues.

The figure of Joseph as a spiritual hero and prophet has also been the subject of several Islamicate works. For example, Ibn Arabi took up the Quranic Joseph in his *Fusus al-hikam* as a basis for his discussion of the spiritual imagination and the role of interpretation or 'proper understanding' (*ta'wil*) of the signs of God, because this topic is also central to the unfolding of the Quranic story.[37] The sura has also been the subject of commentaries and elaborations. To Abu Hamid Ghazali (1111) is ascribed a mystical *tafsir* on this sura.[38] The same work has been ascribed to Abu Hamid's younger brother Ahmad (1126) and is published as *Ahsan al-qasas*.[39] Other titles for this work are *al-Durra al-bayda* and *Bahr al-mahabba wa-asrar al-mawadda fi tafsir surat Yusuf*. The latter title was apparently published in Bombay in 1894. Verifying the precise authorship of this 'Ghazalian' work remains to be done. Another example of the interest in the sura is the eighteenth-century *Natijat al-tafasir fi surat Yusuf* by one Shaykh Ya'qub b. Shaykh Mustafa al-Khalwati, completed in the year 1720. This work collects excerpts from commentaries by a variety of authors including al-Maturidi, al-Nasafi, Fakhr al-Din al-Razi, al-Qurtubi, al-Qushayri, al-Tusi, al-Zamakhshari, and the 'books of preachers'.[40] In addition to these commentaries, *GAL* lists several others with some duplication.[41] A *Tafsir surat Yusuf* is ascribed to the Safavid-era philosopher Mulla Sadra (ca. 1640), although the catalogue cited lists only a *Tafsir surat Ya Sin* for this author.[42] There is mention of another work with the title *Ahsan al-qasas*, this time by *Taj al-ulama* al-Naqavi, grandson of the famous Dildar Nasirabadi (1820), who studied in Mashhad and Karbala,[43] and who was apparently 'the first Indian to return to India as a recognised mujtahid, having studied under Bihbahani in Karbala. He was instrumental in establishing the Usuli school in Oudh and also for a campaign against Sufism.'[44] This work was published in Azimabad, presumably sometime before 1894, the year of the author's death. Another *Tafsir surat Yusuf* is ascribed to one Ahmad b. Asad b. Ishaq, about whom no other details are given.[45]

In addition to studies in Arabic and other Islamic languages, the sura of Joseph has also attracted attention from 'Western scholarship'; as of this writing there are a few monographs available on the Quranic Joseph story.[46] Those who have studied the sura have approached it from a variety of angles. Biblical and Quranic comparison is probably the best represented.[47] However, there are discussions of its exegesis,[48] dramaturgical 'subtext',[49] its general literary features,[50] the symbolism (of the cloak, for example),[51] the portrayal of love,[52] ambiguity, betrayal, reunion, filial piety and cosmology;[53] in short, 'all things (*kullu-shay*')'.[54]

An indication of the importance that the story of Joseph has had for the Shi'a is the many titles of *tafasir* devoted solely to it in *Dhari'a*, a multi-volume bibliographic survey of Twelver Shi'ism. Volume 1 lists three separate works, two of which were written in the nineteenth century.[55] Volume 4 lists ten separate entries, one of which is the previously mentioned work of *Taj al-ulama*'.[56] The first entry (no. 1512) is the above-mentioned work by Mulla Sadra. The first line of the work, which al-Tihrani quotes, is the same as that said to begin the *Tafsir surat Ya Siin* (Q36) in the Sipahsalar catalogue quoted by *GAL*. The ninth entry is ascribed to yet another descendant of Dildar, one Muhammad b. al-Sayyid Dildar Ali Naqavi al-Nasirabadi al-Lakhnavi (1908). Given the well-attested antipathy of the Usuliyya towards the Shaykhis, and by extension the Babis, it is most interesting that the descendants of the great Indian Usuli scholar felt called upon to compose commentaries on the sura of Joseph, perhaps as a corrective to the by then well-known, or at least infamous, imitation of the Quran by the Bab, which was also based on the sura of Joseph.[57] The Babi enormity may have also been behind the decision to publish (in 1849) the above-mentioned *Natija*.

The sura of Joseph has particular meaning for Shiʿism. In addition to the distinct relevance of the motif of hiddenness, the sura may be thought especially relevant to and reflective of the syntax and morphology of the grammar of Shiʿi piety in a number of other instances.[58] Not least among such resonances is the role played by the perfect transformation of time into history, a history in which betrayal and injustice are changed for faithfulness and justice. The symmetry of the narrative is the first signal of this. As already mentioned, this sura is prized by the greater Muslim tradition as the shining example of Quranic narrative perfection. Unlike all of the other 113 Quranic suras, this one is structured by the three *sine qua non* elements of both myth and story as such: a beginning, a middle and an end. Thus, on the one hand, it may be thought most artificial (as in literary artifice) and, on the other, a most accurate reflection of the Islamic religious ethos, which includes the proper ending of the story of humanity with the Day of Judgment. Its special attraction for Shiʿism comes into play in the drama of the envy, jealousy, betrayal and lies of Joseph's brothers.[59] In addition, the theme of patience (*sabr, sabr jamil*) is personified in Jacob and is especially pertinent to the religious idea of 'waiting [viz. for the hidden imam]', *intizar*. The characteristically Shiʿi institution of *walaya* is signalled at Q12:101 and alluded to rather obliquely at Q12:84. God and His representative are the proper rulers of society (no other prophet except Solomon is cast as a ruler). Thus, Joseph assumes the features of the *verus propheta* so frequently discussed by Corbin in his studies of Ismailism and Shiʿism. This is not to minimise the idea of interpretation (*taʾwil*), mentioned more times in this sura than in any other. Another distinctive feature of sura 12 relevant to Shiʿism is that the word *bab* or its plural *abwab* occurs in it more than in other suras. For this reason, it might have been thought to represent more fully than others the, again, characteristically Shi'i mystery of *babiyya,* that is, the way in which divine authority is made present and operative in the world: identifying the 'door' through which the divine enters the world and through which the world accesses the divine. There is exegetically productive ambiguity in the term centred on the problem of whether the 'door' is to God Himself or to the hidden imam.[60] Finally, *surat Yusuf* is an appropriate subject in Shi'ism because of a long tradition that reveres the story of Joseph as representing the spiritual mystery of *taqiyya,* or pious concealment, which is so important to Shi'i religiosity in general. Here the absence or hiddeness of the imam may be regarded as a species of *taqiyya.*[61]

In the Shi'i hadith literature, it is said that the 'master of this divine cause' (*sahib hadha l-amr*) (that is, the Qa'im) bears a certain resemblance to Joseph, one example being that this expected 'proof' (*hujja*) is to attain eventual sovereignty over the world at some particular time (*waqt min al-awqat*), just as Joseph gained sovereignty over Egypt.[62] In another report the story is told of how Joseph discovered the signs of *nubuwwa* in himself,[63] and an explanation of how Joseph became a *hujja* is given.[64] In the *Ikmal al-din* of Ibn Babawayh, it is mentioned that God has named Joseph 'Unseen' (which is also one of the names of the Qa'im) in Q12:102 when He said, 'That is of the tidings of the Unseen';[65] and the proper greeting for the Qa'im is 'Peace be with you, O remnant of God.'[66] The word *baqiyya,* which denotes the divine remnant and also perhaps indicates, through a related 'cloth association', the shirt (*qamis*) of Joseph, is a major topic in messianic Shi'i discourse, where the term *baqiyyat allah* is always a reference to the imams' authority, *walaya,* in addition to being an honorific for the hidden imam, based partly on the exegesis of Q11:86: 'That which God leaves is best for you if you are believers/*baqiyyatu llah khayrun lakum in kuntum mu'minin.*'[67]

Muhammad Baqir Majlisi (1699 or 1700) is quoted as saying that the *sahib* of 'this cause' bears resemblance to four prophets, Moses, Jesus, Joseph and Muhammad, and that the prison of Joseph symbolises the occultation of the imam.[68] The Mahdi will have a basket in which he carries relics of all the prophets, including the 'cup' of Joseph.[69] When the Qa'im comes, there will be great disagreement about the Quran[70] and he will know all of the Quranic sciences, including *tafsir, ta'wil,* and *nasikh wa-mansukh.*[71] It is mentioned that the Qa'im will appear between the *rukn* and the *maqam* (reference to the sanctuary in Mecca), and the people will take an oath on a new book.[72] In a very long commentary on a verse in his major work, *Ziyarat al-jami'a*, in which reference is made to the 'return' (*raj'a*) of the imams, Shaykh Ahmad Ahsa'i (1826), founder of the above-mentioned Shaykhi school, mentions several, sometimes conflicting, hadiths on the subject. The return of the Qa'im will take place during the month of Jumada I, and before his advent (*khuruj*) there will be seven years of famine and little rain, 'like the years of Joseph'.[73] This obviously refers to Joseph's interpretation of the dream of the 'king' (Q12:46–9). Here Ahsa'i also mentions the tradition from Majlisi, which says that the Qa'im will say what none other has said, and will promulgate a new book that will be difficult for the Arabs (to accept) (*kitaban jadidan wa-huwa 'ala l-'arab shadid*).

THE SHIRT OF JOSEPH AND THE FIGURATIVE GENERATION OF SPIRITUAL TRUTH

If Joseph is an emblem of order and meaning, then his most famous possession, his shirt, may be thought a metonym for the same. It is therefore of the most serious interest that this shirt, whose origins according to Islamic tradition are to be sought in the furthest remote past, represents the origins of prophethood itself and the clothing of Adam.[74] The shirt or mantle (*kisa*), in some form, becomes the credential of all subsequent prophets, playing a number of discrete roles within the sura and Islamicate cultural life. That is, every subsequent prophet is both himself and the actual 'shirt of Joseph' that carries his scent ('*arf* a word related to *ma'rifa*, knowledge, recognition); a complex bouquet redolent of many connotations, themes and motifs.[75]

Scent is a frequent metaphor for 'spiritual' reality.[76] Despite its requiring a caveat here, one of the reasons the term 'spiritual' continues to be useful, especially in the context of Islamic (-ate) material, is that it captures in religious language the energy and vitality of what in other contexts may be considered from a literary angle: it is precisely the powerful literary device of typological figuration that is captured by the term.[77] The ultimate symbol of this literary/spiritual process or dynamic, this metaphorical and metonymical creative and revelatory energy, is Joseph's garment, which the Quran calls a shirt (*qamis*) and the Hebrew Bible calls a coat of many colours (*kethoneth passim*).

Like a number of other important terms in the singular sura of Joseph, the shirt appears in several key contexts that may be thought to mark important narrative transitions in the story. In the first mention, the idea of the garment, if not the actual garment itself, is used by the perfidious brothers to demonstrate that they had done nothing wrong (Q12:18). The false garment's appearance with false blood marks the departure of Joseph from Canaan and his journey to Egypt. The second appearance is when Joseph's actual garment exonerates him from the crime and sin of lust (Q12:25–7), and by extension ingratitude (*kufr*). It marks the beginning of his imprisonment, when his true gifts as a man of God and divine knowledge are destined to be revealed, and as a result of which his status in Egypt is elevated beyond what anyone might have reasonably predicted. The third appearance is after the truth has been revealed, the denouement, as it were. For all intents and purposes the story has ended, needing only the quick succession of the events that follow to burn the truth of the story into the minds of the audience. Joseph tells his astonished brothers, who could never have imagined that their despised brother might have achieved such success, notoriety and power in Egypt, to take his shirt with them back to Canaan where Jacob languishes blind, in grief and separation from his beloved son, Joseph and, by association and dramatic action, Benjamin (Q12:93). They are commanded to lay the shirt on Jacob's face so that the 'supernatural' divine healing power of the shirt, its smell, fragrance, perfume, will restore Jacob's eyesight, eyesight that was 'washed away' in weeping for his beloved son (Q12:84). In a subsequent complex scene, the power of the shirt and its perfume is dramatised in a most compelling manner.

The instant the Canaan-bound caravan of Joseph's brothers crosses the border from Egypt we have what would be called in cinema a cutaway to Jacob's bedside. There is probably no more moving or powerful vignette in the Quran. The grieving, languishing, aged prophet and patriarch of Israel, despairing of the continuance of his prophetic line and the loss of his two favourite sons, is suddenly stimulated, practically resurrected, to new life and joyous hope. His beloved Joseph lives:

And as soon as the caravan [with which Jacob's sons were travelling] was on its way [and out of Egypt], their father said [to the people around him]: 'Behold, were it not that you might consider me a dotard, [I would say that] I truly feel the breath of Joseph [in the air]!'(Q12:93–4 Asad translation adapted.)

Both Sunni and Shiʻi exegetes agree that the reason Jacob knew his son was alive was because of the special scent the shirt bore, the shirt that the brothers had with them in the returning caravan. The final scenes of the sura represent a circular closure[78] of a narrative exemplified in what may be called an apocalypse of reunion.[79] Here the love of Jacob for Joseph, also originally (if tacitly in the Quranic text) symbolised by Jacob's gift of the shirt, is consummated in the migration of the entire family from Canaan to Egypt, to live in exalted status more or less undisturbed (at least for a while) as a vindication and dramatic proof of the efficacy of the God of Jacob, His power and, of course, superiority.[80] The story of Joseph, whether in the Hebrew Bible and tradition or in the Quran, represents also what may be thought a true model of the epic drama of the Hebrew people and, as in the case of the Quran, the Muslims. Such an epic may be on the grand historical scale, or on the scale of the interior spiritual life of the soul.[81] In the Quran, the story of Joseph has an added function in that it represents the thickening or intensification and perfection of heretofore imperfectly completed narrative gestures in its partial and somewhat aborted telling of the stories of other prophets. The sura of Joseph is the apex of the Quranic narrative art and, coming as it does 'protected' near the centre of the mushaf, it functions as a reminder, an unambiguous statement of the Quranic 'theory of prophethood and salvation' that may be only incompletely or partially detected elsewhere in the book.[82] It thus functions in the same way as the clear statement of a melodic theme does in the context of what might otherwise be challenging or opaque improvisation and variation.[83] It is here that the reader is given the whole truth about the prophetic office. It delineates in dramatic form and much detail the basic curve of the life and career of one chosen by God to carry and relate a special message, a revelation. In reading 'the best of stories' one can readily contemplate and understand the life of the Prophet Muhammad: his birth, his destined greatness from an early age, his rejection by his relatives, his love of women, his piety and steadfastness, his ability to reveal the true meaning of events, his position as wielder of political and social authority, his wisdom, beauty, fairness, patience, betrayals, the hiddenness of his true greatness until the appointed time, his concern with the unknown Hour, with law, with forgiveness and, of course, with civilisation.[84]

The shirt of Joseph is an especially apt emblem of typological figuration. The typological weaving, generation and embellishment of this unique textile (< text, credential, revelation, information) narreme (a word not yet admitted to the *OED*) is a distinctively Islamic process, fascinating to trace throughout the exegetic literature.[85] In a sense, all fabrics are related, either positively or negatively, to the shirt of Joseph. That is, it may be seen to represent 'fabric' itself, a metonym for culture, civilisation, the cross-connected lines of the various fates of humans and human fate as such.[86] As a fabric it is related to all clothing, including veils, and as such is capable of concealing and revealing, frequently at the same time. This suggests the mystical process of *iltibas* or amphiboly that Corbin analysed in the writings of Ruzbihan Baqli (1209).[87] The shirt is also a symbol or emblem of the passage of time and narrative development, and, by association, all narrative continuity. It is a bearer of the heavenly scent of Joseph and all prophets, because of its intimate relationship (viz. *walaya*) to both the prophets and its point of origin, God. Like *walaya* itself, a category explicitly mentioned in Q2:101 and obliquely alluded to in Q12:84, it protects, distinguishes, comforts and identifies its bearers and those who participate in (affirm) their *walaya*.[88] That the shirt is one symbol for all salvation history (*Heilsgeschichte*)[89] is also suggested by the fact that it only occurs in the sura of Joseph and that this sura, based on features of its form and content discussed above, may be seen as a kind of Quran 'in miniature'.[90] That is to say, if the shirt is the centrepiece of the sura, and the sura itself is the centrepiece of the Quran with regard to narrative art and coherence, then its primacy is compelling. This would appear to be one of the points of traditional exegesis, whether Sunni or Shi'i. In this vast body of literature, there is a clear consensus that Joseph's shirt is one of those 'divine artifacts' or 'evidences' that come from the unseen realm (*al-ghayb*) in which it is mandatory for believers to believe.[91] This is in addition to the striking way in which its own specific narrative structure, brilliantly explicated by Mustansir Mir in his 1986 article 'The Quranic Story of Joseph, Plots, Themes, and Characters', offers numerous clues for the way in which the Quran itself may be read, thus cracking another code.

The symbol of the cloak may be seen to have developed out of the ancient practice of holy men and diviners, who kept the 'exterior world at a distance' by wearing a special robe.[92] In Shi'i works reference is often made to 'the people of the cloak' (*ahl al-kisa'*), who are specified as Muhammad, Ali, Fatima, Hasan and Husayn.[93] Shi'i writers use this designation to express the idea that Muhammad's special qualities were transmitted to his progeny through contact with his mantle. Corbin called attention to the powerful role of exegetical typological figuration in the early consolidation and identity building of Imami Shi'ism. He pointed out that it represents a major moment when the famous scene of the *mubahala* is typologically identified in the *Tafsir* ascribed to al-Hasan al-'Askari (874) with the annunciation of Jesus:

> The vastness of theological meaning found in this scene by Shiite meditation may be measured by the fact that the *tafsir* attributed to Imām Ḥasan 'Askarī, the eleventh Imām of the Duodeciman Shiites, expressly establishes a typological relation between the Koranic verses [especially Q33:33, see also Q53:3–4 and Q81:19–29] evoking the Annunciation and the conjunction of the Holy Spirit with Jesus, and this scene in which Gabriel the Holy Spirit joins the five hypostases of the original Imāmate. It is precisely here that Shi'ism inaugurates the transition from Angel Christology to Imāmology.[94]

The word *qamis* appears in the Quran only in sura 12, where it is mentioned six times. First at Q12:18, where Joseph's brothers are described as having put false blood on his shirt in an attempt to deceive Jacob, claiming that a wolf had eaten their brother. At Q12:25–8 the *qamis* figures prominently in the well-known episode with Zulaykha, Potiphar's wife, where the guilt or innocence of Joseph is determined by whether the shirt is torn at the front or the back.[95] An interesting comment on this scene occurs in the *tafsir* of the Sufi Sahl al-Tustari (896). The entire ordeal has as its purpose a demonstration of the efficacy of divine 'proof' (*burhan*) without which Joseph would have been abandoned to his 'defeated' (*maghlub*) condition because 'he had permitted the desire for Potiphar's wife to rise in his lower self'.[96] In the context of the entire narrative, such 'defeat' is dramatically contrasted with Joseph's eventual role as powerful minister, which he wins as a result of properly interpreting the Pharaoh's dream. Indeed, so important is this ultimate rise to power and victory, which in the event must also include victory over the self as well as over the perfidious brothers, that the key phrase is repeated in this sura: 'Thus did we empower Joseph over the land', *wa-kadhalika makkanna li-Yusuf fi l-ard* (Q12:21, 56).[97]

Finally, for the present discussion the most important mention comes at Q12:93. Joseph's brothers have finally recognised him as a highly placed official in Egypt, whereupon Joseph instructs them: 'Go, take this my shirt, and cast it on my father's face, and he shall recover his sight; then bring me your family altogether.' When Ja'far al-Sadiq (765) was asked about the shirt of Joseph, he responded that when Abraham was burning in the fire (Q21:68–9), Gabriel came down with the shirt and clothed him with it so that he would not be harmed. Abraham gave this shirt to Isaac, who gave it to Jacob. When Joseph was born, Jacob gave the shirt to him. It was this shirt, originally sent from heaven, by which Jacob detected the scent of Joseph (Q12:94).[98] Al-Sadiq was then asked what became of this shirt, to which he responded that the shirt stayed with the descendants of Joseph and is now in the possession of 'our Qa'im' because all the prophets inherit knowledge and other things from one another.[99]

The author of the encyclopaedic Akhbari Shi'i lexicon *Mir' at al-anwar* says of *qamis* that its exoteric meaning is well known, but that its *ta'wil* is connected with the words *thiyab* and *libas*.[100] The first word is defined as representing the knowledge with which the imams have been endowed, and by extension refers to *walaya* proper.[101] The second word carries a complex of meanings that include, together with the idea of garment, 'deception'.[102] For the former, al-'Amili-Isfahani refers to several verses in the Quran, among which is Q2:187, where it is stated that spouses are as a garment to each other. For the latter, he cites Q2:42, in which those who disguise the truth with falsehood are condemned. Ultimately, however, the word *libas* is seen as a symbol of the *walaya* of the imams.[103]

In his commentary on *al-Qasida al-lamiyya*, Sayyid Kazim Rashti (1843) takes the opportunity to dilate on the implications of the word *qamis*, which occurs in one of its verses.[104] The poet has compared the curtain (*satr*) of the tomb of the Prophet with the *qamis* of Joseph, stressing that the spiritual 'fragrance' of the former is far greater than that of the latter.[105] Rashti says that however powerful the fragrance of the shirt of Joseph might have been, it cannot compare with the much stronger power of the curtain of the Prophet's mausoleum. Interestingly, the power of the shirt comes from Joseph's having worn it, rather than from the heavenly origin of the shirt. Jacob could detect its perfume from a great distance, because both he and Joseph were a 'single aspect' of the 'seal of the prophets' (*lama kana Ya'qub*

wa-Yusuf ʿalayhuma al-salam wajhan min wujuh khatam al-anbiya ʾ).
Presumably this means that Jacob could detect his son's presence precisely
because he also was a bearer of *walaya* and therefore in reality they were
one and the same. Since Joseph's shirt acquired its 'fragrance' (spiritual
power) from physical contact, the fragrance acquired from physical close-
ness to the Prophet's tomb must be even stronger. Therefore, while it was
the power of the fragrance of the shirt of Joseph that caused Jacob's physical
sight to be restored, the perfume of his Muhammadan 'shirt' (that is, the
satr of the tomb) is incomparably stronger and will give spiritual sight to
those who regard it with the 'eye of reality'.[106]

In an interesting, if marginalised, literary gesture in *Tafsir surat Yusuf*
by Ali Muhammad Shirazi (1850), known to history as the Bab, it is argued
that the *qamis* of Joseph represents a power equivalent to the *satr* of the
tomb of the Prophet. The symbol of the shirt of Joseph is immediately
associated with the bees mentioned in Q16 (*surat al-nahl*), which reflects
an early Shiʿi identification of these bees with the imams, for just as the
bees produce honey 'in which there is a healing for mankind' so the
imams dispense healing knowledge.[107] Such an apparently incongruous
and abrupt association of the bees with Joseph's shirt is quite typical of
the Bab's method throughout this commentary. The Bab seems to take the
bees out of thin air. This air is actually the exceedingly rich atmosphere of
the Shiʿi exegetical tradition.

CONCLUSION

The story of Joseph has a special place in Islam and in the Quran. It may
be offered that while Abraham and/or Moses have frequently been considered the ideal exemplar for Muhammadan prophecy,[108] a study of the
shirt of Joseph suggests that this *qamis* may have also served as a veil for
another possibility. It is actually Joseph who represents a truer type, or
at least a more complete type, for the Prophet, whether among Sunni
exegetes or Shiʿi. In this amplitude of Quranic detail and narrative there
is rhetorical power.

There is a special attraction in Shiʿism for the story of Joseph, but it is
central to Islamic religion for a number of reasons. The *qamis* of Joseph is
an efficient emblem of the Islamicate notions of prophethood, revelation
and *walaya* because it bears their scent, a scent that is at once complex

and unmistakably borne upon the shirt, or cloak, that both reveals and conceals. In poetry, the shirt of Joseph is equated with the 'Muhammad (*centifolia*) rose', recognised as having the most complex perfume of any of the roses. The *Tafsir surat Yusuf* ascribed to al-Ghazali lists seven different types of scent borne upon the *qamis* of Joseph.[109] Furthermore, because of its function as a marker of narrative progression in the sura of Joseph, it is also a symbol of historical continuity-within-change, eschatological hope and order in the face of chaos. This scent carries all of the information we have been given in the sura and in the Tales of the Prophets, in addition to summoning up the remembrance of the primordial covenant, a reunion of all of those 'children of Adam' (humanity) who, before time, joined in their assent to the sovereignty of God. Perfume is the perfect conveyor of this powerful coincidence of opposites and one that distinguishes itself among all other sensory experiences because of the way it conjures the past, making it one with the present and giving the experience of an obliteration of distance between the subject and the object.[110]

Chapter 4

Duality and Opposition
The Apocalyptic Substrate

Since the Quran and indeed Islam are both largely defined by their deeply engaged and prolonged celebration of revelation, it is perhaps somewhat mysterious that the study of Islam and the Quran has only recently taken seriously (again) the concepts and categories of apocalypse/apocalypsis, apocalyptic and apocalypticism as a factor in its early history, social formation and doctrinal élan.[1] Of these three modes, only the historical aspect has really captured the imagination of scholars of Islam over the last few years. Thus, a recent detailed study of the question focuses on early Arabic literature in which various battles and skirmishes are related in apocalyptic terms.[2] Such a study sheds much valuable light on the nature and development of early Islamic history and captures, no doubt, the frustrations and aspirations of the people in whose midst such chronicles were composed. Here, however, we will examine the problem of Islam and apocalypse from a purely literary perspective, concentrating on a theoretical or virtual entity known as a 'pre-canonical'[3] or perhaps more to the purposes of this exploration, a 'pre-exegetical' Quran. Under this rubric, it is possible to read the Quranic text as being formed by and containing several of the standard features of a genre of literature widely recognised as apocalyptic. These include various categories of themes, motifs and other features that biblical scholarship and studies of the Ancient Near East especially (but certainly not exclusively), Iranian studies and indeed anthropology have identified.

Despite the two very suggestive, if not revelatory, and influential definitions of apocalypse from John Collins quoted in the Introduction, there is a curious and persistent disinclination to read the Quran as an apocalypse. Recent consideration of this problem by Collins himself elicited this cautious and judicious, if categorical, statement: 'the Quran is not an apocalypse, even though it contains many apocalyptic elements'.[4] It is hoped that the following discussion will help to nuance such conclusions as they may be applied to a distinctive Islamic social, historical and religious context. It may be that part of the problem resides in the assumption that if we consider the Quran an apocalypse, then we cannot consider it anything else. There is some sense in which it is felt that an apocalypse represents the vestiges or literary tidal residue of a vanished community or sociological movement. Clearly, Islam is here. Thus, we may be in the presence of an interesting and distinctive instance of literary apocalypsis: an enduring apocalyptic community whose structure, nomothetic and religious horizons are determined and fixed by reference to a true apocalypse. This should surely be of some interest to scholars of religion.

The recent excellent and thorough study of extra-Quranic Islamic texts by David Cook, referred to above, has shed much light on apocalypticism as a social movement and even a genre of Arabic literature within the early period of Islam. Here there is a clear realisation of the importance of the genre for a discussion of the Quran, but there is also a clearly stated certitude that the Quran is 'probably not an apocalypse' even though it contains many features of standard apocalyptic discourse, indicated by several 'key words'.[5] There is scant acknowledgement that Islamic studies may have something very important to gain from biblical studies on the problem. Rather a single quotation, of a similar verdict by a fellow Islamicist is all the evidence we are given: 'the apocalyptic sense . . . is not strong in the Quran'.[6] Thus there is no engagement with the rather sophisticated and well-developed methodologies within precisely the very scholarly tradition that identified, defined and nuanced the problematic of 'apocalypse' to begin with. The matter is rendered even more interesting and perhaps compelling in the context of Cook's negative assessment. To be fair, Cook's chosen subject was not the Quran. But his comments, along with other more positive ones from other scholars, encourage a further critical examination of the question.[7]

The reasons for an allergy to biblical scholarship are perhaps not hard to find, but we will forbear here from further discussion or speculation except to say that the absence of an 'apocalyptic approach' to the Quran may also be the result of a much too narrow understanding of apocalypse. Apocalyptic revelations are not exclusively concerned with the future, though this is frequently a component. As such, apocalypse is not defined only by its interest in and description of the end of the world or great and violent cataclysms of the immediate future. What has emerged from the scholarship is an appreciation of the fact that the apocalyptic imagination expresses itself in a number of ways. By broadening the definition of apocalypse, recent work has made it possible to focus on the way in which the genre communicates intensity of experience through revelation. Indeed, within the context of such an evolved understanding of the category, references to the end of time or the end of the world may be seen as a means whereby the apocalyptic mood of the original revelatory experience is communicated through something we might provisionally term a 'trope of intensity'.[8] The purpose here is to explore how the Quran may be seen as a unique example of literary apocalypsis through using these same sources.

In studying the Quran as an example of the genre of apocalypse we must also be prepared to accept that not all aspects of apocalypse (as currently understood) will necessarily be found in it, or at least, not all features will be present in exactly the same way they are in the apocalypses that have thus far merited the attention of those who study the genre. According to traditional studies, apocalypse is a subgenre of revelation, and there is a close relationship between the words of the prophets of the Hebrew Bible/Old Testament and the imaginative landscape of the apocalypses. In this connection, and to state the obvious, it may be that in a Quranic apocalypse we should not be surprised if the emphasis on the Hebrew Bible is much less than in other apocalypses. What may be expected to take its place is precisely the pre-Quranic Arabic religious culture as this is preserved and retailed in the Quran itself (see below the example of Thamud). Thus, we are interested in discussing what may eventually be seen as a unique example of apocalypsis in the Quran. The value of this is that it helps us to refine our expectations of the text. That there can be no understanding without genre, a view formulated most famously by the literary critic E. D. Hirsch Jr, would seem a fairly sensible observation.[9] Heretofore it has been common to think of the problem of genre with regard to the Quran in the light (or shadow) of the tautology 'the Quran is an example of a genre of literature that has only one example', which, at the very least, may be thought unhelpful with regard to the literary study of the Quran. Another more optimistic approach has been to define the Quran as a repository of a number of genres and literary forms.[10] The pursuit of the Quranic apocalypse undertaken here is in the spirit of attempting to articulate something meaningful and helpful that may be thought to connect these subgenres in a satisfactory and illuminating way and show how the Quran may be viewed as an example of a more widely recognised genre of religious literature that reflects the religio-literary expectations and culture of the Nile-to-Oxus region of Late Antiquity.

If the genre 'apocalypse' is useful for looking at the Quran as a whole (and is not restricted to the so-called early apocalyptic/'hymnic' verses), then it may help address some of the more imposing complexities of the text, whether from within or without the Islamic tradition. Among other general developments in the world of scholarship on the apocalyptic since Casanova's ill-starred venture,[11] and doubtless the most important one, is the advance in the study of apocalyptic as a genre associated with the names of biblical scholars such as Gunkel, Koch, Smith, Hanson, von Rad, Collins, J. Z. Smith and many others. As a result of their collective endeavours, the genre has been 'defined' to a highly evolved degree by the employment of a grid that indicates numerous topoi, figures and motifs thought to be constitutive of apocalypse.[12] There is not space here to discuss all of these elements, but I will attempt to demonstrate how a selected cluster of them is present in the Quran: duality (distinct from – but not excluding – 'dualism'), opposition, symmetry and its evocation and, perhaps most interestingly, typological figuration. These are seen as providing the foundational thematic and formal substrate for much of what is characteristic of the Quranic theophanic discourse and provide the conceptual and figurative basis for such other important elements and markers of apocalypsis present throughout the Quran as: history and its periodisation, judgment of the living and the dead, glory and its articulation, description and evocation, the detailed description of other worlds and realms (for example paradise and hell), to name only the most prominent. Obviously, anyone familiar with the Quran, and especially professional Islamic scholars, will not be impressed by the 'news' that paradise and history are major Quranic preoccupations. Nor will they be surprised to hear about the pervasive presence of duality and the glory motif. However, it is hoped that this exploration succeeds in demonstrating that in fact these apparently old and familiar subjects or problems are stimulated to new life by considering them as defining, interlocking structural elements of the Islamic apocalypse, the revelation of the Quran.

DUALITY AND OPPOSITION

Symmetry, rhyme and meaning are all expressions of duality, or perhaps more accurately 'syzygy'. That is to say, for a notion of 'meaning' to exist, we must have two elements: 1) the thing and 2) its meaning.[13] In the case of rhyme, it is meaningless to think of rhyme with only one element. The rhyme obviously depends at least upon the existence of two words that sound the same. And, what is especially important for this discussion, duality automatically elicits or evokes its aniconic 'other half', tawhid (> *wahda* – 'oneness'), which in the case of the Quran and Islam is always a transcendent (*munazzah*) oneness.[14] Tawhid actually means 'making one'; it is a divine commandment which believers must strive to obey. The interplay of conceptual and substantive oppositions and dualities is a prominent feature of both the form and content of the Quran which the reader/believer must experience as a unified message that speaks of the overarching divine unity suffusing creation.

Opposition here may not always indicate antagonism; rather its first meaning is 'two things facing each other, or being compared with each other'. Obviously, one form of such 'spatial' positioning may include and involve enmity and antagonism. Taken together, or in 'apocalyptic harmony' with a number of other salient and distinctive features, it represents one of the more prominent apocalyptic leitmotivs of the Quran. Taken by itself, a thorough study of the interplay and prominence of duality and opposition, something far beyond the scope of the present chapter, would shed much light on the distinctiveness of the form and contents of Islam's holy book. One conclusion offered here is that the Quran may be distinguished from other scriptures and holy books by the degree to which the text is suffused with and informed by a preoccupation with duality (not dualism). This follows on from the profound observation, made nearly thirty-five years ago in a landmark study of the Quran focusing on *Surat al-Rahman* (Q55), that the duality at play in such crescendo moments gives us immediate access to and experience of the literary power of the Quran.[15] In a more recent context, it has been pointed out that:[16]

> A central feature of the Quran is contrast: between this world and
> the next . . . between believers and disbelievers, between Paradise
> and Hell . . . scholars have found truly remarkable patterns of con-
> trasts: angels and devils, life and death, secrecy and openness, and
> so on, occurring exactly the same number of times.

The presence in the Quran of some other literary attributes and features
of apocalyptic establishes a context for the study of Quranic enantiodromia.[17] Whether or not this means that the Quran represents a 'genuine'
instance of apocalypticism, it nonetheless remains that the prominence
of this device, in the context of others, renders the Quran susceptible of
a reading expressive of something called an apocalyptic imagination.[18]

The play and ultimate eradication (or at least taming) of opposition
may in fact represent, as Eliade suggested, the 'eschatalogical syndrome,
par excellence'.[19] Exemplified dramatically in other literatures by the
child playing with the snake or the lamb lying down with the lion, such a
coincidentia oppositorum 'is the sign that Time and History have ended'.
The explicit coincidence of opposites is really only one of the modes of
duality and opposition among many others expressed throughout the
Quran. But it should be pointed out that wherever they are found in the
Quran they are susceptible of coalescing in the kind of union spoken of by
Eliade. Diametric oppositions and dualities may also stand for emblems
of totality, even prior to the 'event' of union or eradication:[20] here they
would represent poles of a spectrum separated by all the various related
permutations and graded instances of their intervening elements and
intensities. The prime example is the frequent Quranic 'what is in the
heavens and what is in the earth and whatever lies between the two (for
example Q18:15; Q25:59; Q30:8; Q32:4; Q44:38; Q46:3; Q50:38). Here
'heavens' and 'earth' are simultaneous opposites and defining points on a
grand scale of totality. The opposition ceases when time and history cease,
when earth becomes heaven, a kind of apocalyptic inversion.[21] On this
pattern one could, presumably, 'think with' any of the other numerous
pairs of Quranic oppositions.

Another key expression of the motif or figure of duality is less structural
or formal and more concerned with actual meaning: ambiguity and/or
vagueness, both in the actual text itself and in the reception of the text and
its various symbols, tropes and types, which add up to another feature of
apocalyptic, namely indeterminacy. From the tension and apprehension

produced by indeterminacy comes certitude, its opposite. But it should not be lost sight of that such indeterminacy is a key feature of any true apocalypse and that attempts to emasculate the apocalypse by considering it 'mistaken' or 'deceitful' or 'inconsistent' betray a lack of appreciation for the symbolic dimension of narrative.[22] Collins, relying on Ricoeur for ballast, offers the following very useful critique of some current apocalypse scholarship:[23]

> The tendency of much historical scholarship has been to specify the referents of apocalyptic imagery in as unambiguous a manner as possible. This enterprise has indeed contributed much to our understanding of passages like Daniel 11. Yet Paul Ricoeur has rightly protested against the tendency to identify apocalyptic symbols in too univocal a way. This tendency misses the element of mystery and indeterminacy which constitutes much of the 'atmosphere' of apocalyptic literature. In short, Ricoeur suggests that we should sometimes 'allow several concurrent identifications *play*' and that the text may on occasion achieve its effect precisely through the element of uncertainty.

Or, perhaps, aniconism. That tawhid is the defining and primary religious message, attitude and duty of Islam is undisputed. We wish to demonstrate that opposition and duality is the *sine qua non* of tawhid, its 'other half' as it were. And in mentioning the idea of this other half we are reminded of the original meaning of the word symbol itself, from the Greek *symbolon*:[24]

> that broken object, the two halves of which bear witness, for those holding them, to old bonds between themselves or their families; but it also signifies sign, contract, a signification that is undecipherable without its counterpart . . . its complement and support, its bestower of meaning.

Paradoxically, this message of duality further enhances and emphasises the message of oneness that is the focus and task of tawhid. This, in itself, is another example of duality and opposition. Such opposition, and the even more important automatic tension pointing to its resolution, is a key element in the remarkabe hold the Quran has upon those who experience it. Furthermore, this topos or figure – this enantiodromia – is distributed, or perhaps more accurately, circulates throughout the Quran so that it figures in narratives, prayers and laws; it covers the spectrum from abstraction to the concrete, from divine attributes to elements of the natural world. It is an element of the Quran's 'text grammar'[25] and it describes a vast spectrum of relative intensities between frequently recurring polarities (partially detailed below).

Thus, part of the experience of the Quran entails a heightened suspense based upon the evocation of opposition and duality and whatever tension may be created, expressed or alluded to thereby. If the basic structure of human consciousness is indeed binary, then we know and order our experience by virtue of a comparison of theoretical (if not perceived) polarities: hot ≠ cold; up ≠ down; good ≠ evil. With regard to the Quran, we see the same basic assertion attested to repeatedly. Such a preoccupation has affected all subsequent, Quran-derived or -influenced Islamicate discourse. To give a prime example, a preoccupation with duality, opposition and reversal achieves a zenith, if not apotheosis, in the work of Ibn Arabi, the emblem and embodiment of the confluence and synthesis of classical and early medieval Islamic intellectual culture.[26] This, in turn, continues to pulse through the work of his vast audience, whether followers or detractors. The robust verve of such enantiodromia is formed and fuelled by the basic Quranic material, but it eventually blossoms and flowers in Islamicate literary culture, for example in the quite productive and distinctive hermeneutic pair *zahir/batin* (exoteric/esoteric) and other, more mutually exclusivist religio-social categories such as 'the commonality and the elite' (*al-'awamm/al-khawass*).

In the case of the Quran itself, the basic Islamic desideratum of tawhid may be thought to be emphasised and acquire meaning in the context of the binary nature of consciousness ceaselessly and, one might say, musically invoked throughout that work.[27] Linguistically, the lexical parallel opposite of tawhid or unity is *tashrik*, but it was another verbal form that would come to stand for the notional opposite: *shirk*, 'assigning partners to God/violation of tawhid'. It seems clear, in the context of the message of the Quran, that the numerous references to *shirk* are meant as a foil to the all-important message of unity, and not the other way around, in the same way that references to divine wrath are meant as a foil for divine mercy.[28] Thus the otherwise purely theological topic of tawhid may be brought into direct relation with the omnipresent obbligato-type motif of duality and opposition that is heard and read throughout the Quran.

Dualities pervade the Quran from the merely quotidian up ≠ down, north ≠ south, night ≠ day, hot ≠ cold, to the downright Wagnerian eschatological emblems of the beginning and the end, hell and heaven, including those anonymous and mysterious groups, the Party of God (*hizb Allah*), the Party of Satan (*hizb al-Shaytan*), the People of the Right Hand, the People of the Left Hand and so on. It would become the task of exegesis to identify such groups as the *ashab al-yamin/al-maymana, ashab al-mash'ama* and *al-sabiqun*, a third category identified by the Quran as those brought near (*al-muqarrabun*), Q56:11–14.[29] Night ≠ day; heaven ≠ earth; private ≠ public; hidden ≠ seen; moon ≠ stars; sun ≠ moon; fire ≠ water; air ≠ earth; male ≠ female; mountain ≠ plain; road ≠ wilderness; shade ≠ sun are frequently invoked features of the natural world found mentioned throughout the Quran. They appear to have something in common with similar pairs of opposites, near-opposites and other pairs of ethical moral religious values and qualities invoked in and found also throughout the Quran: guidance/salvation ≠ perdition; faith ≠ unbelief; good ≠ evil; obedience ≠ rebelliousness; lying ≠ truth-talking; violence ≠ peace; patience ≠ impatience; kindness ≠ brutality; frivolity ≠ seriousness; knowledge ≠ ignorance; civility ≠ barbarism. These in turn have something in common with the oppositions that designate the last things such as: heaven ≠ hell; reward ≠ punishment; delight ≠ suffering; peace ≠ torment. Finally, these oppositions and dualities resonate with those thought special because they designate names of God Himself: the Manifest ≠ the Hidden; the First ≠ the Last; the Merciful ≠ the Wrathful; the Rewarding ≠ the Punishing; the Angry ≠ the Clement.[30]

Norman O. Brown made the important remark that it does not matter where you open the Quran, one can start reading it anywhere and find that one is 'in the right place'[31] as it were:[32]

> It does not matter in what order you read the Koran; it is all there all the time; and it is supposed to be there all the time in your mind or at the back of your mind, memorised and available for appropriate quotation and collage into your conversation or your writing or your action.

The theme and/or 'device' – surely it is with this figure that structure and content are most perfectly melded – of opposites and duality in the Quran helps account for the truth of Brown's observation. In short, it is at least partly due to duality and opposition that the Quran can be read as 'making sense' despite its notoriously fragmented, almost adamantly anti-narrative structure and content (these two are oppositions as well: narrative/anti-narrative). To repeat: duality and opposition is a prominent element of the Quran's text grammar.[33] The consistent presence of duality and opposition compensate, to some extent, for the lack of (apparent or explicit) linear narrative continuity, unity or cohesion in the Quran (the Quran is a book unlike other books). As structural and semantic constants they lend coherence to the text: the interplay of oppositions and dualities is a thread that runs through the text. Duality and opposition, in fact, may be thought to provide something of a narrative spine or stream connecting uninterruptedly throughout the Quran from the 'beginning' to the 'end'.

So prominent a feature of the Quranic landscape is, it would seem, worthy of the kind of treatment Van Duzer has given the Homeric epics.[34] This study has identified the structure of duality as being particularly operative in what the author has called 'saving devices'.[35] Insofar as the epic genre has been given definition, at least in the Western imagination, by Homer's great poems, this duality can thus be seen as a key element of that genre. Here are obvious implications for the study of the Quran as epic, something that has not really attracted the attention of contemporary scholarship. This is so, certainly, because the Quran is profoundly concerned with salvation through an epic struggle. In terms of culture, such a struggle is described by the journey from ignorance to knowledge. At the individual level, in the person of the prophet or messenger, the struggle, as was shown in Chapter 1, is against such ignorance in the form of opposition and persecution.

The dualities, oppositions, pairs and symmetries in the Quran appear in at least two ways: 1) explicit; 2) implicit. Explicit dualities such as heaven and hell or the heavens and the earth occur throughout the Quran in numerous passages. As such, they may be thought categorical, given. In their elements there is no room for changing the terms of the symmetries or dualities thus announced. Dualities also appear implicitly, as when the word 'heaven' may appear without its mate and the mind is drawn to complete a conceptual syzygy or duality through its own 'fluent logic'. In such an instance, there may be one or several mental responses to the original code word 'heaven'. This could be 'hell' it could be 'earth'. Or it could be only partly conceptualised, as when the mind is not immediately forced to contemplate or otherwise engage with some 'concrete' and explicit pair of dualities or oppositions.[36] Other terms such as 'belief' simply cannot occur to the 'Quranised' consciousness without summoning the opposite value of 'unbelief'. When the task of completing the duality is left to the reader, then, the dynamic may be thought more purely 'literary' than doctrinal and as a result more profound and pervasive: the reader, in a way, becomes the conduit of the revelation in a decidedly direct manner by virtue of this autonomous and disciplined participation.[37] In such a relationship the distance between subject and object is obscured and confused: the reader, now the object, is actually read by the Quran, now the subject.[38] Thus we have another apocalyptic reversal of dualities and oppositions and one which must surely help account for the passion and intensity of the 'Quranic experience'. In addition, it may also help us understand such epithets of personification as 'the wise Quran' in addition to such 'supra-rational' references in the tradition to the Quran as 'the brother' of the Prophet.[39]

Years ago Izutsu, building on the edifice of structuralism, drew our attention to the semantic and semiotic importance of what he termed 'key Quranic terms', defined as terms which have as a mate a polar opposite, such as: *zann ≠ yaqin*; *kufr ≠ iman*; *jahl ≠ islam*.[40] Izutsu was intrigued by the historical period bridging the Islamic Age and the *jahili* Age of Ignorance or Barbarism; 'the period ... illustrates the semantic phenomenon in which the key terms forming a system are disintegrated, transformed in their connotative structure, modified in their combinations, and, with the addition of a number of new key terms, finally integrated into an entirely different system'.[41] So, apart from their function as an index of the apocalyptic, the dualities and oppositions also generate positive, discursive 'logocentric' 'theological' meaning. It is precisely at this nexus or literary feature that the miraculous power (*i'jaz*) of the Quran may be explained or at least hinted at in articulable terms as the site where primitive/pagan meets its opposite, civilised/monotheist. This is a function of opposition or duality as a 'natural' noetic site where magic, poetry, religion, philosophy and mysticism simultaneously perform their various respective tasks. Here both synaesthesia and synthesis (*jam'*) feature as effects of 'reading the Quran'. And, perhaps most interestingly, in this way Islam, as the polar opposite of *jahl* comes to be understood as 'recognition' rather than unqualified submission. Such oppositions provide limits – and therefore psychic relief – to an otherwise insupportably vast and overwhelming spectrum of consciousness.[42] Thus the reading of the Quranic text gives wings to the soul at the same time as it anchors it, another coincidence of oppositions.[43]

It is surely interesting to observe in this context that an astonishing number of literary, poetic and rhetorical figures depend for their efficacy upon dualism/opposition/'twoness'. This points us in the direction of what might be termed the 'master duality' of the Quran, at least in terms of religious ideas. The Quran's main 'theological' teaching is divine oneness (the mystical tradition in Islam will insist that the adjective here is redundant – all oneness is divine), and one of the reasons the faithful reader of the Quran never tires of affirming this oneness is because it has been read and experienced throughout the text in an almost infinite number of literary contexts through explicit mention or, more frequently, as an unstated (aniconic) presence opposite the various contrarities, dualities and pairs that are explicitly mentioned in the text.[44] These appear in a potentially infinite array of different gradations of intensity, light and shadow, colour and tonality, by virtue of all the multifarious dualities that this same text also enshrines and valorises. Outside the enchanted circle of this reading of a virtually infinite field of interlocking and mutually reinforcing dualities and oppositions, such enthusiasm for the doctrine of oneness is not understood. If we add to the juxtaposition of the idea of divine oneness against and with the many examples of its first immediate opposite (that is twoness, and then by extension opposition and duality themselves) the variety of the music upon which is carried this sacred idea (or sacred silence),[45] we can perhaps learn to appreciate something seriously important about the living Quran and the way it is read. Then we may begin to grasp how the verb 'to read' becomes a synonym for the verb 'to believe' or 'to serve' in the key of 'bearing witness'. Despite and because of the incessant invocation of opposition and duality, then, the central notion of oneness shines forth certainly as a theological principle; but from the literary point of view, if this were all there were to be said, the richness of the message of the Quran would be poorly served. The challenge of the text – the experience that awaits the reader from just beyond the borders of discourse is the one indicated in the celebrated statement attributed to Abu Saʿid al-Kharraz (899 or 890): 'I know God by means of the bringing together of opposites.'[46]

So the pattern established in the minds of the 'children of the Quran' is indeed, to use Nwyia's apt characterisation a 'Quranisation' of consciousness – what has perhaps come to be referred to more recently in religious studies as 'soul formation' – heavily dependent upon the always-tending-towards a somewhat Manichean apocalyptic drama of opposition and duality. Things are black or white, *din* or *dunya*, at one level of this consciousness and black and white, *din* and *dunya*, at another level. For Ibn Arabi 'the world is He/not He'.[47] Eliade's apperception that the coincidence of opposites represents the apocalyptic motif par excellence is suggestive for the way the Quran has been read not only in the upper floors of the library but also among common or garden practising human beings.

The leitmotif of duality and opposition also helps us read those dual usages which we are 'Quranically' conditioned to read as yet another miraculous meaning event involving twoness as the polar opposite of sacred oneness. The enigmatic 'two gardens' (Q55:46 and Q55:62), the 'two Easts and the two Wests' have elicited much commentary.[48] However, before commentary can begin there must be an assent to the dignity of the text. That is, it must be deemed 'worth the effort'. It may be that these otherwise mysterious and enigmatic dualities are seen as 'worth the effort' precisely because of the continuous occurrence throughout the rest of the Quran of multifarious dualities and oppositions. So, the grammatical dual figure here is taken quite readily to the bosom of the exegetical exercise, if not by every single *mufassir*, as another divine meaning event, even if it is perhaps a bit more opaque than others.[49]

For Ibn Arabi 'one' is not a number: God is certainly single (*fard*), but this is a singleness beyond numeration. According to Ibn Arabi the first single (odd) number is three, not one. 'One' is the source of numeration, whence all numbers from two upwards are derived. Creation depends upon knowledge and therefore involves *tathlith*, or conceptual 'triangulation': there is the thing, its opposite, and the space between that allows one to see the difference between the two.[50] This syzygy of two and one wrought and uttered in such an epical key is responsible for our experience of the Quran as a deeply religious and simultaneously ungothic or antigothic book because the basic initiatory vehicle of the operative revelatory duality is precisely the natural world on the earthly horizontal, *afaqi* plane. To say this is not to imply that the Quran is uninterested in 'heaven' or the unseen realm. On the contrary, belief in the unseen (*al-ghayb*) is a requirement the Quran itself stipulates for its reader (Q2:3). Rather, to say such a thing is more to emphasise what Fazlur Rahman referred to as the nondualistic nature of the Quran, for which the characteristically Quranic theme of 'signs' is the logical coordinate. This is not necessarily 'nature mysticism' but rather a revelation of the true status and meaning of what the unitiated call "nature", in line with the much-quoted verse and our epigraph: 'In time We shall make them understand our signs in nature, and in their own souls, until it becomes manifest to them that this is the Truth' (Q41:53).

The universe, the cosmos, and everything in it are created phenomena. The life of the human soul and, of course, the Quranic revelation itself, are, according to the Quran, signs that point beyond themselves to their true source and meaning: the transcendent oneness of God. Thus, the paradox of monotheism[51] finds its Quranic expression in the fact that a thing is both itself and something ultimately and unimaginably greater than itself: He/not He.[52]

To sum up the discussion of duality and opposition:

1. Duality and opposition are, by virtue of their strong presence, one of the distinguishing features of the Quran. Here it should be added that because of their elemental and universal nature, they are easily translated into other languages and cultures.

2. Duality and opposition present a conceptual 'stream' or 'spine' uniting and giving coherence and form to the Quran in the absence of a strong unbroken narrative line from 'beginning' to 'end'. Thus, this interplay of an apparently infinite number of interlocking pairs and oppositions is an element in what has aptly been referred to as the 'Quranisation of consciousness' among the believers/readers of the text.

3. Such pairs and oppositions evoke the existence of an overall, master opposition, in line with the theological perspective of the Quran. The virtually ceaseless invocation of 'twoness' (whether positive, negative or mixed) evokes its opposite, namely one-ness. Thus, duality and opposition are a mode of the aniconic tawhid so characteristic of the Quranic theophany and Islamic thought in general.

4. Duality, thus accordingly a feature of the text grammar of the Quran, may also be at work in the numerous instances of another literary device trailing clouds of apocalyptic glory: typological figuration.

CONCLUSION

In the previous chapter, we pointed out that the Quran is not without a centre of narrative gravity despite its notoriously challenging narrative flow. There, based on the work of Zwettler and others, we also described the functioning of typological figuration in the Quran with particular reference to the sura of Joseph and the implications this has for an understanding of its epic character. In this chapter, we have suggested that, in addition to other specific tasks or meanings they may have, duality and opposition provide continuity to the text and now we would like to recall that typological figuration also provides such continuity. Typological figuration works with duality and symmetry to achieve a coherent vision which may be thought to culminate in the identification of Muhammad's mission with that of Joseph and every other prophet and messenger and to identify his audience with their followers and rejecters. This may be thought the great moment of recognition or revelation.

In 'Mantic Manifesto', Zwettler concentrated not on *Surat Yusuf*, but on the sura of the Poets (*al-Shu'ara'*) (Q26) to make his point. He demonstrated that it actually functions as a catalogue of prophetic types (*zawj*) and their opposites (in this case precisely not antagonists, but rather antitypes or reflections of the original type) in order to show how Muhammad ibn Abd Allah is one of their number. To be sure, he does address the problem of the antagonist or 'enemy' of the prophet. It is not Iblis or Shaytan or even the Quraysh, at least not on the literary level. Rather it is the poet. And here is where Zwettler brings home another important insight. The Quran is not poetry. But this is not because it is not 'poetic' or aesthetically compelling. It is because the Prophet Muhammad was not a poet. The social function of the poet was utterly different and in many ways antithetical to the social function of the prophet. The poet was the champion of the status quo at best, insofar as we are familiar with his pre-Islamic avatar. The prophet was the champion of change. The poet's talents were for hire, he was not expected to enunciate a moral or ethical code, much less exemplify one,[53] and most importantly, the source of his inspiration was not God through an angel, rather it was any one of a number of lesser pneumatic beings, jinn or gods, the acceptance of which entailed the unforgivable sin identified by the Quran as *shirk*. By ranging the whole history of monotheistic prophecy against the concerns of the institution of Arabic poetic culture, the Quran identifies the experience of Muhammad with the experience of earlier prophets from Adam to Jesus. As is well known, so congenial was such a typological argument that later Islamic tradition posited the existence of 124,000 prophets to account for the whole sweep and progress of earthly human history, even if the history of humanity, according to the Quran, has its beginning in a much more mysterious realm.[54]

A concise and persuasive example of the centrality of typological figuration may be seen in the comparison and ultimate identification of Muhammad's mission with that of the prophet Salih. The journey from history to myth to apocalypse and the return to history is charted in the typological relationship established between Salih and Thamud and the Prophet Muhammad and his community. Jaroslav Stetkevych has illuminated the way in which Islam sees Muhammad's mission as a simultaneous identification with and fulfilment of Salih's mission in his discovery of the golden bough that was buried in the apocalyptic ruins of the Thamud tribal home al-Hijr, today's Mada'in Salih.[55] The great apocalyptic scream (*al-sayha*) here represents the totality of the drama of prophecy and its rejection in one near-synaesthetic gesture. Al-Tha'labi's version of the cataclysm is instructive:[56]

> There came upon them a scream from heaven, in which there was the sound of every thunderbolt and the voice of every thing on earth that has a voice, and it cut through their hearts and breasts, and they all perished, young and old.

Such a dramatic image seems to transcend, by virtue of its power and intensity, the usual 'common sense' boundaries of time and space. The action and event of this scream is such that it may have had a beginning, but it certainly has not ended. It offers a clear example of a 'law of perception' articulated in one of the more formative and powerful explorations of apocalypse published seventy years ago by another literary scholar, this time from beyond the borders of Islamic studies – Northrop Frye:

> It would perhaps be difficult to prove completely the axiom that objects do not cease to exist when we have stopped looking at them. Yet it is hard to see how we could maintain a consistent sense of reality without assuming it, and everyone does so assume it in practice and would even assert it as the first article of common sense. For some reason it is more difficult to understand that events do

not necessarily cease to exist when we have stopped experiencing them, and those who would assert, as an equally obvious fact, that all things do not dissolve in time any more than they do in space are very rare. [57]

Typology requires symmetry. Symmetry requires duality. Duality is a *sine qua non* of typological figuration. By virtue of compelling symmetry and therefore sacred meaning, the scream, which according to the logic of narrative occurred in the past, continues to be heard behind the music of every Quranic *aya* through the transformative power of the apocalyptic imagination. It is this looming divine presence which conditions the experience of the Quran.

Frye has also offered the very helpful observation, with regard to typological figuration, that it is more powerful than logical argumentation precisely because its rhetorical verve is felt to derive from some supra-logical region. There is a similarity between 'causality' and 'typology'. Both are rhetorically effective. The main difference is that causality is dependent upon ratiocination, investigation of phenomena and the 'scientific' method. As such, it is concerned mainly with the past 'on the principle that the past is all we genuinely or systematically know.' Typology does relate to the future, and the faculties by which it is enlivened are 'faith, hope and vision'. Logical, causal thinking functions in one 'tense', whereas typological thinking assumes a future, and can even transcend time itself. Though I am not aware of Frye actually saying this, typological figuration deploys, exploits and ultimately unites such 'vulgar illusions' as past, present and future. To the apocalyptic imagination, time is that which keeps everything from happening all at once. Typological thinking bespeaks a desire to awaken from the 'nightmare of history' and is 'essentially a revolutionary form of thought and rhetoric'.[58] This inspiring and lucid reading of the biblical code provides a largely unused key for unlocking the secret of the celebrated, so-called 'licit magic' (*sihr halal*) of the Quran and a means of elevating the reading dynamic above the plane of politics and history with the hope of revealing something distinctive, instructive and at the same time universal about the text and its ways. As we saw above, Frye uses the image of waking from sleep to describe the workings of typological figuration.[59]

So, to (temporarily) conclude this exploratory meditation on the apocalyptic nature of the Quran, it seems clear that while duality and opposition provide a skeleton, typological figuration puts the flesh on that skeleton, and that when this happens the apocalyptic or revelatory reality is truly born. The apocalypse enters history once again with the experience and preaching of Muhammad, who is both the symbol and exemplar of all previous prophetic types. This constant recurrence of the pervasive figure of typology, not just in *Surat al-Shu'ara* but throughout the Quran, provides a dramatic counterpart to the narrative stream or spine supplied and mirrored by continuous and mutifarious enantiodromia. Here we are reminded of Hanson's analysis, quoted earlier, in which one of the purposes of apocalypse is to deny the apparent superior position to the enemies of the apocalypticist and to provide comfort for the apocalyptic community.[60]

The narrative resonance enhances and intensifies the interplay of dualities and oppositions with the personification or 'embodiment' of this in the typological iteration or rendering of Muhammad's prophethood. As such, two modes of enantiodromia are joined together, both pointing to the erasure of time and history – or perhaps even time and space[61] – in a persuasive and compelling gesture of the apocalyptic imagination.

In this chapter we have tried to stress the value and importance of looking at the Quran as a distinctive, powerful and effective instance of imaginative communication. That is to say, a bridge between the known and the unknown, presented as a linguistic performance in a particular time and place. The power and efficacy of this performance are such that the universality of its message and the universality of the techniques by means of which this message is communicated indicate that it is the proper literary heritage of humanity in general and Islam in particular. We have attempted to look at the Quran quite detached from theological or doctrinal preoccupations and suppositions to examine the more purely figurative and poetic elements of the text. All of this has been in aid of a single primary question: how does the Quran continue to live such an extraordinarily robust life as a source of moral values, religious commitments, aesthetic orientations and information? The answer we have arrived at is, we think, quite clear. Such an answer helps us also to understand one of the more intriguing functions of prophethood as acknowledged by the Islamic tradition: the prophet as translator (*mutarjim*) of the workings of the sacred imagination.

Chapter 5

Water and the Poetics of Apocalypse

Have not the ungrateful then beheld that the heavens and the earth were once a single thing all sewn up, and then We unstitched them and of water fashioned every living thing? (Quran 21:30)

In this chapter, in an exploration of wrath and mercy in Islam, we will restrict ourselves largely to the Quranic data in an attempt to let Islam speak for itself and minimise authorial intervention, distortion, manipulation and interpretation. Much of what follows, therefore, is actual quotation from the Quran inasmuch as the Quran is that which permeates the Islamic worldview and regulates the actions and thinking of the followers of Muhammad to an exceptionally high degree – probably unparalleled in the other world religions. Authorial presence (mine) may be detected in the emphasis placed here on the relationship between these two divine attributes and the way in which the Quran uses water imagery to communicate their reality and function, their drama.

Allah is by far the most characteristic designation of the utterly transcendent (Q112) yet infinitely close and intimate (Q50:16) creator and master of the cosmos. Its etymology, like the etymology of the English word 'God' is somewhat foggy and/or elliptical. Being composed of two elements, the standard Semitic definite article and the Arabic word for 'god' the usual rendering is '*The* one and only god deserving of allegiance and obedience.' This understanding reflects the *Sitz im Leben* of the original revelation in its polytheistic context, a context in which the supreme god Allah was not unknown, but was not the sole focus of attention or spiritual and religious concentration. The task of the Prophet was to demonstrate and argue in this milieu that Allah was in fact 'the only god worthy of the name', or more simply God.[1] In this chapter, God and Allah will be used interchangeably when referring to the master of creation and 'Lord of all worlds', by whose grace, providence and solicitude for humanity the Quran was revealed. (See Q2:121–2; 6:153, 157; 7:63; 11:118–19; 17:86–7; 18:65; 36:5–6.)

Both God and the Quran are designated and alluded to by many different epithets and substantives throughout the sacred text. Whether this is a related development out of the polytheistic milieu: 'only one God, but numerous names', cannot be ascertained. We do know that Arabic loves words and their concomitant distinctions, nuances and differences. And, we owe to this general love of words – what sometimes appears to the uninitiated as mere pleonasm – the distinctive and culturally significant literary aesthetic that produces the wonderful variety and richness of descriptions of God and the book, frequently employing synonyms and near synonyms. It should be added immediately that the great learned tradition, which may in some ways be seen as issuing from a study of the Quran, did not, in spirit or theory, recognise the existence of pure synonyms. Each Quranic word must have its own meaning, its own *raison d'être*. Thus, a sub-theme to the general theme of God's nature and description arose, namely the organisation and categorisation of those special words that are seen as divine names and attributes.[2] The somewhat popular doctrine of the so-called Ninety-Nine Beautiful Names (*al-asma al-husna*) is a feature of this sub-theme. It developed from the contemplation of such Quranic verses as: 'To God belong the most beautiful names so call upon Him with them' (Q7:180) or: 'Say: Beseech Allah or beseech al-Rahman. Unto whichsoever you cry (it is the same). His are the most beautiful names' (Q17:110).

The word 'muslim' has as its primary meaning or intention 'one who is wholly committed to God'. This commitment may take several forms, but the basic and elementary intention is generally understood to be commitment and obedience – 'submission', if you will – to the divine law as revealed in the Quran and as indicated in the blessed example of the Prophet Muhammad. This example is preserved in that other highly venerated compendium of Islamic religious teaching known as the Hadith, frequently referred to as Tradition. Because of space constraints, we will restrict our discussion and observations mainly to the Quran, its form and contents. However, it must not therefore be lost sight of that alongside the wealth of material on the topic of wrath and mercy to be found in the Quran there is an additional storehouse of information, teaching and lore contained in Hadith. Any exhaustive study of this question will of course take into consideration both sources of Islamic belief and teaching.

In one of the more lucidly argued modern studies of the Quran, Fazlur Rahman notes that of the several major themes of the book, the description and nature of God must come first in both importance and thematic sequence, because it is only in the shadow of the Quranic 'theory of God' that the rest of the book can properly be understood.[3] 'Who is the God of the Quran?' is therefore the first question we must try to answer in our exploration of divine wrath and mercy. There is no topic better suited for an introduction to the 'mind of the Quran' – which for Muslims is also in some way or another, a window into the 'mind of God' – than a close examination of the theme of divine mercy ceaselessly proclaimed and invoked throughout its six thousand-plus verses (Arabic *ayat*; lit. 'miraculous signs'). By comparison, the theme of anger may be seen as a foil against which the mercy of God is made manifest. Such a window into the mind of God is thought to provide access to and understanding about a divine plan for humanity, whether this humanity be expressed in, through and as society or in, through and as the individual.

The central importance of divine mercy in the Quran and in Islam in general may be illustrated by a brief reference to the thought of the thirteenth-century spiritual and literary virtuoso, Ibn Arabi. His synthesis and elaboration of the basic elements of Islamic religious thought – known eventually as the Unity of Being (Arabic *wahdat al-wujud*) – would influence, whether positively or negatively, all Islamicate religious discourse after him. Here mercy is not only a defining attribute of the otherwise utterly unknowable God, it is also the answer to the question, 'Why is there something rather than nothing?' For Avicenna (Ibn Sina, 1037) this same question would be answered with reference to the central and somewhat abstract notion of Being (Arabic *wujud*) and for Suhrawardi (1191, *al-Maqtul*, 'the Executed one') the same question is answered with the much less abstract but still comparatively cold, remote and impersonal notion of Light. Ibn Arabi insists that the foundational ontic category is none other than divine mercy. Rather than say God created the universe, or God existentiated the universe, or God 'fulgurated' the universe, it is most apposite and useful to think in terms of God's having 'mercified' the universe.[4] The universe or cosmos is therefore simultaneously a manifestation of divine mercy and composed of the substance of this mercy. Things have not been merely 'created' they have been 'mercified' into being. The major source for

Ibn Arabi's distinctive and quite imaginative thought was, as is now firmly established, the Quran itself which he obviously internalised to such a high degree that his consciousness and conscience were suffused with and structured on its various patterns of meaning, literary and otherwise.[5]

Divine wrath, while certainly of profound importance in the worldview of Muslims and Islam, is by comparison best thought of as an absence of clemency or mercy, or even more helpfully, as the foil against which the drama of divine mercy is carried out. But even here, there are several celebrated and beloved instances of mercy masquerading as wrath or anger. The prime example comes in the sura of the Cave in the Quranic depiction of the sojourn of Moses with his unnamed servant and the mysterious stranger they are destined to encounter (Q18:59–82). Moses is strongly attracted to the spiritual knowledge that seems to emanate from the stranger and so Moses asks to accompany him on his journey. The stranger warns Moses that he is likely to be shocked and scandalised by the stranger's actions, who will appear to perform cruel and heartless acts. Moses insists that he will obey and acquiesce if only allowed to accompany him. The stranger agrees with one proviso: Moses is not permitted to question any of his doings. Then in quick succession there occurs a series of what appear to Moses unjust, irrational, destructive and violent acts against innocent or otherwise blameless people: 1) the stranger sinks a ship without cause, putting its passengers in harm's way; 2) the stranger kills a young man for no apparent reason; 3) in a town where the small party (the stranger, Moses and Moses' servant) have been treated inhospitably, the stranger, for no apparent reason or compensation decides to repair one of the town walls that was on the verge of collapse. As the stranger had warned, Moses was unable to bear the incongruity and mystery of these actions, two of which were clearly violent and destructive and could have been interpreted as a gesture of unjust divine anger, since the stranger was clearly a representative of God. Exasperated by Moses' lack of patience and his breaking his vow not to question the stranger about his actions, the stranger then explains his actions, only after issuing the resounding and heartbreaking 'Now is the parting between me and thee' (Q18:78, Arabic *hadha firaq bayni wa baynika*). As Abdel Haleem translates the verse: 'He said, "This is where you and I part company. I will tell you the meaning of the things you could not bear with patiently."'

The stranger, whom tradition, not the Quran, identifies as Khadir or Khidr (Persian *Kezr* 'The Verdant One') then explains that he sank the ship because there was a tyrannical king who was confiscating all of the

seaworthy vessels in the land for his own purposes and if he saw this particular ship which was owned by poor men who had no other means of
gaining a livelihood, they would be utterly bereft. So the stranger scuttled
it knowing that once the danger had passed the owners could raise the
ship and repair it. In the second case of apparent cruelty meted out by
this mysterious servant of God, the stranger explains that had this youth
lived his parents, who were faithful believers, would be tested and pained
by his rebelliousness. Thus, he killed this son that he might be substituted
for a more virtuous son in the future and the parents come to no grief, a
son who would be 'better in purity and closer in affection' (Q18:81) than
the one the stranger had killed. Although the final act of the stranger is
apparently the opposite of wrath, anger and destruction, the solution to
the puzzle of why the stranger would perform an act of such charity for a
city that had been so inhospitable is explained to the impatient Moses. The
stranger tells him that because he knew there was a buried treasure under
this unstable wall and that this treasure was the legal inheritance of two of
the city's orphans, he repaired the wall so that the rightful owners of the
treasure could actually retrieve the legacy their deceased father had buried
under it. This story illustrates the famous hadith 'God's mercy exceeds – (or
in some versions – "precedes, outstrips") His wrath.'[6] In the case of the
mysterious stranger, it is important to remember, especially in the present
context, that he is introduced in the following verse: 'So they met one of
Our servants on whom We had bestowed mercy (*rahma*) from Ourselves
and whom we had taught knowledge from Our own presence' (Q18:65).

The Quran conceals the central lesson of this engaging story in the
single word 'mercy' (*rahma*), indicating from the outset that whatever
the mysterious stranger says or does would be a manifestation of divine
mercy.[7] In what follows, we will explore first the topic of wrath or anger
as it appears in the Quran in a series of the most characteristic words.
Then we will look at the subject of mercy. By way of comparison, we will
explore the clear relationship that obtains in the 'divine poetics' of the
Quran between these two 'theological' categories and their counterparts
in the images of water in the Quran. This will permit us to see something
very essential about the Quranic theophany, namely the way in which the
'paradox of monotheism' is resolved through the compelling language
and poetics of the Quran. Thus, the remote and abstract notions of mercy
and wrath are given something like what T. S. Eliot called, in discussing
another literary work, an 'objective correlative', a topic to which we will

return. Finally, the reader of/listener to the text will have no doubt about either the quality of divine mercy, identified with pure, sweet, life-giving water or the quality of divine wrath, identified with vile, poisonous, or destructive and life-threatening waters used to illustrate the reality of divine anger and punishment.

DIVINE WRATH

It is best to deal with this topic first inasmuch as while it is clearly an important Quranic theme, by comparison with mercy it occupies less prominence in the book and may be seen, frankly, as an ancillary or component of mercy, rather than its diametric and equal opposite. The Quran, as has been observed repeatedly, is adamantly non-dualistic. Despite the numerous and incessant invocations of various dualities and opposites throughout the Quran, it is never doubted that God is one, undivided, simple and the sole master of the universe.[8] While the devil certainly has a role to play, it is as the enemy of man not God.[9] The divine nature, will and decree are all of the same seamless reality (Arabic *al-haqq*), and the various words and adjectives are given to us by God in accordance with our capacities to understand and articulate our own experience.[10] God's anger is referred to several times throughout the Quran.[11] In the very first sura, The Opening (or Overture: *al-Fatiha*), God's mercy and anger are brought together in this most frequently invoked of all prayers.[12]

> In the name of God, the Lord of Mercy, the Giver of Mercy!
> Praise belongs to God, Lord of the Worlds,
> the Lord of Mercy, the Giver of Mercy,
> Master of the Day of Judgment.
> It is You we worship; it is You we ask for help.
> Guide us to the straight path:
> the path of those You have blessed, those who incur no anger and
> who have not gone astray. (Q1:1–7)[13]

As in many questions Quranic, the *Fatiha* provides a reliable guide to the form and contents of the message. Note here that in addition to the repetition of divine mercy in four separate places, the word 'Lord' is also invoked in the Arabic *rabb*. The meaning of this word refers to caring, nourishing, education and guidance. The idea of wrath or anger occurs almost as a grace note to set off and emphasise the overwhelming mercy of God.

Quranic Arabic words that may be translated as wrath or anger are derivative of the following triliteral roots: *gh-d-b*; *l-'-n*; *s-kh-t*: *n-q-m*; *r-j-s*; *s-a-f*. With regard to the most frequent and characteristic word used by the Quran to refer to God's wrath, *gh-d-b*, this third person singular verb is predicated of Allah five separate times in the Quran with the meaning of 'God was angry at him/them'. One interesting instance of this verb, in the third person plural, applies to humans, indicating that among those who are on the right path are those who, when moved to anger, readily forgive (Q42:37). To the degree that the pattern of divine attributes in the Quran is ultimately as much, if not more, about human potential and the development of 'god-like qualities' as it is about the nature of the unknowable God, this verse suggests that one of the god-like qualities human beings would do well to emulate is precisely forgiveness (Arabic *ghufran*), an attribute applied to God dozens of times throughout the Quran. To return to anger and wrath, the nominal form (*ghadb*) is also associated with the divine only thirteen times throughout the Quran. This same word, or its derivative, is also used to describe the anger or wrath of Moses (Q7:154; 20:81–2) and Jonah (Q21:87). A companion word to *ghadiba* is construed on the Arabic root *l-'-n* and occurs several times as a near synonym. Taken by itself it is frequently translated as the verb 'to curse/reject/damn' or the noun 'curse' or the object 'accursed'. This root occurs forty-one separate times throughout the Quran. We will indicate its presence in the following quotations.[14]

Another Quranic root that denotes anger or wrath is *s-kh-t*. Derivations, which also can be translated as 'condemnation' or its derivations, occurs four separate times in the Quran, three of these refer to God. A related concept is found in the term 'vengeance' (Arabic *naqma*). This important Quranic idea occurs in referring to the vengeance of God, in the formulaic phrase: 'We exacted retribution from them' (Q7:136; 15:79; 30:47; 43:25; 43:55, compare also Q5:95). The related form occurs in the several passages that describe God as 'capable of retribution' (Arabic *dhu intiqam* x4: Q3:4; 5:95; 14:47; 39:37). The recipients of God's retribution, wrath and vengeance (*muntaqimun*) are singled out in three separate verses (Q32:22; 43:41; 44:16). It seems important here to point out that this word is also used to describe the wrath of the unbelievers as well (compare for example, Q9:74). As is common to the style of the Quran, God is shown to be more able, even in vengeance and wrath, than the humans who reject His signs.[15]

One key example of God's anger from the Quran is in the case of the unjust taking of human life:

> If anyone kills a believer deliberately, the punishment for him is Hell, and there he will remain: God is angry (*ghadiba*) with him, and rejects him (*la'ana*), and has prepared a tremendous torment for him. (Q4:93)

Another example of the expression of God's anger is in the context of those who worship other gods:

> Say, 'Shall I tell you who deserves a worse punishment from God than [the one you wish upon] us? Those God distanced from Himself, was angry with (*la'ana*), and condemned (*ghadiba*) as apes and pigs, and those who worship idols: they are worse in rank and have strayed further from the right path. (Q5:60)

Bearing false witness also elicits divine anger:

> As for those who accuse their own wives of adultery, but have no other witnesses, let each one four times call God to witness that he is telling the truth, and, the fifth time, call God to reject (*la'ana*) him if he is lying; punishment shall be averted from his wife if she in turn four times calls God to witness that her husband is lying and, the fifth time, calls God to reject (*ghadiba*) her if he is telling the truth. (Q24:6–9)

People of the Book (*ahl al-kitab, passim*), those who have received revelation in the past and who now follow their scripture, are frequently praised by the Quran. But, they may also fall foul of the divine and incur God's wrath:

And, unless [the People of the Book] hold fast to a lifeline from God and from mankind, they are overshadowed by vulnerability wherever they are found. They have drawn God's wrath upon themselves. They are overshadowed by weakness, too, because they have persistently disbelieved in God's revelation and killed prophets without any right, all because of their disobedience and boundless transgression. (Q3:112)

Remember when you said, 'Moses, we cannot bear to eat only one kind of food, so pray to your Lord to bring out for us some of the earth's produce, its herbs and cucumbers, its garlic, lentils, and onions.' He said, 'Would you exchange better for worse? Go to Egypt and there you will find what you have asked for.' They were struck with humiliation and wretchedness, and they incurred the wrath (*ghadab*) of God because they persistently rejected His messages and killed prophets contrary to all that is right. All this was because they disobeyed and were lawbreakers. (Q2:61)

Those who took to worshipping the calf will be afflicted by their Lord's wrath, and by disgrace in this life. This is the way We repay those who invent such falsehoods, but your Lord is most forgiving and most merciful towards those who do wrong, then repent afterwards and truly believe. (Q7:152–3)

Again, the idolaters, polytheists, deniers and hypocrites are singled out for God's wrath:

And to torment the hypocritical and idolatrous men and women who harbour evil thoughts about God – it is they who will be encircled by evil! – who carry the burden of God's anger, whom God has rejected (*wa ghadaba Allahu 'alayhim wa la'anahum*) and for whom He has prepared Hell, an evil destination! (Q48:6)

He said, 'You are already set to receive your Lord's loathing (*rijs*) and anger (*ghadab*). Are you arguing with me about mere names you and your forefathers invented, names for which God has given no sanction? Just wait; I too am waiting.' We saved him, and those who were with him, through Our mercy; We destroyed those who denied Our revelations and would not believe. (Q7:71–2)

Have you not seen [Prophet] those who give their loyalty to people with whom God is angry (*ghadiba*)? They are neither with you nor with them, and knowingly swear to lies. God has prepared a severe torment for them: what they do is truly evil. They have used their oaths to cover up [their false deeds], and barred others from the path of God. A humiliating torment awaits them – neither their wealth nor their children will be of any use to them against God – they will be the inhabitants of Hell, where they will remain. (Q58:14–17)

Low indeed is the price for which they have sold their souls by denying the Godsent truth, out of envy that God should send His bounty to any of His servants He pleases. The disbelievers have ended up with wrath upon wrath (*ghadab 'ala ghadab*), and a humiliating torment awaits them. When it is said to them, 'Believe in God's revelations,' they reply, 'We believe in what was revealed to us,' but they do not believe in what came afterwards, though it is the truth confirming what they already have. Say [Muhammad], 'Why did you kill God's prophets in the past if you were true believers? Moses brought you clear signs, but then, while he was away, you chose to worship the calf – you did wrong.' (Q2:90–2)

Can the man who pursues God's good pleasure be like the man who has brought God's wrath (*sakht*) upon himself and whose home will be Hell – a foul destination? (Q3:162)

Eat from the good things We have provided for you, but do not overstep the bounds, or My wrath (*ghadabi*) will descend on you. Anyone on whom My wrath (*ghadabi*) descends has truly fallen. (Q20:81)

How will they feel when the angels take them in death and beat their faces and their backs because they practised things that incurred God's wrath (*ma askhata Allah*), and disdained to please Him? He makes their deeds go to waste. (Q47:27–8)

You who believe, do not take as allies those with whom God is angry (*ghadiba*): they despair of the life to come as the disbelievers despair of those buried in their graves. (Q60:13)

As for those who argue about God after He has been acknowledged, their argument has no weight with their Lord: anger (*ghadab*) will fall upon them and agonizing torment awaits them. (Q42:16)

With the exception of those who are forced to say they do not believe, although their hearts remain firm in faith, those who reject God after believing in Him and open their hearts to disbelief will have the wrath (*ghadab*) of God upon them and a grievous punishment awaiting them. (Q16:106)

Believers, when you meet the disbelievers in battle, never turn your backs on them: if anyone does so on such a day – unless manoeuvring to fight or to join a fighting group – he incurs the wrath of God, and Hell will be his home, a wretched destination! (Q8:15–16)

DIVINE MERCY

If the word Allah is the most characteristic of the numerous names and attributes of God mentioned in the Quran it is only so by a thin margin. In the ranking of the numerous divine names it is generally accepted that they are 1) Allah; 2) *al-Rahman*; and 3) *al-Rahim*. These two other names, names which bear directly on the present theme, are in fact equally important in Islamic piety and 'God theory': as the Quran itself has it, whatever can be said of Allah can be said of *al-Rahman* (Q17:110 quoted above). These Arabic nouns of description and agency are derived from the same Arabic root: *r-h-m*.[16] The central meaning of this root is kindness, beneficence or an act of kindness and favour.[17] This word occurs 114 times in the Quran and in all but three instances, relates such kindness and beneficence to God alone. It is important to point out that the earliest lexicographers saw the deep connection, on the etymological level, between this word and the Arabic word for 'womb', *rahim* (plural *arham*). Thus, it is not without some interest that we note a similar connection between two of the most important and most frequently invoked names of God, *al-Rahman* and *al-Rahim* with the qualities of motherhood, nurturance and unconditional love. Perhaps we have here a species of agape love, if it is possible to conceptualise this form of love without the Christocentric sacrificial element.

On a strictly statistical level, the word Allah occurs most often (x 2811). Its persistent and repeated association and identification with the qualities of mercy and compassion is, however, quite clear. The otherwise remote, abstract and infinitely aloof Allah is thus given 'form' by its identification with the more familiar and worldly notions of mercy and compassion. And, to repeat, this is the most frequent and intense 'gloss' of Allah throughout the Quran. The ideas of mercy, love and compassion carried by each of the words *al-Rahman* (x 170), *al-Rahim* (x 227) – both of which are in the *basmala* or invocation that heads 113 of the 114 suras of the Quran – are ceaselessly used to 'flesh out' this otherwise utterly transcendent Being. There are of course other attributes ascribed to and associated with God.[18] But there is no question that the quality of mercy is the most important not only with regard to the mere fact of frequency of occurrence but more importantly by taking into consideration what has been called the 'élan' of the Quran.[19] However abstract, remote or 'mathematical' the concept of Allah might otherwise seem to us,[20] its identification with these two words ameliorates and modulates such existential distance. After all, this same Allah, as the Quran tells us, is somehow a creator and infinitely close: 'We created man – We know what his soul whispers to him: We are closer to him than his jugular vein' (Q50:16).

The essential point to be made here is that attempting to speak about particular verses (*ayat* = divine signs) of the Quran that privilege the idea of mercy is also a little bit like trying to look at the forest and the trees at the same time. We have seen how every sura (but one) is introduced with an invocation of divine mercy and how the particular idea of loving mercy (*rahma*) permeates the Quran and surfaces in an astonishing number of contexts. In addition, for the pious believer/reader/listener, every single letter of the revelation is a symbol, harbinger and bearer of this same mercy. It may even be said that the space against which the words of the Quran itself are written or heard are also reminders of the central theme of the Quran, God's mercy, through the wondrous reversal of figure and ground that occurs in reading, meditation and audition. Thus, to some extent, to simply list verses that mention mercy is somewhat redundant and unnecessary, unlike the case with divine wrath. Rather, let us proceed to the next section of our study, a short introduction to the way in which the Quran's distinctive expressive style, its poetics, may be seen to function with regard to wrath and mercy.

WRATH, MERCY AND WATER

In the brief amount of space available, it is best to try to make the key point as succinctly as possible. We return to the idea introduced above, 'the objective correlative'. This term, coined originally in the 1840s, was used by the literary critic and poet, T. S. Eliot, to refer to one of the ways in which literature operates. Specifically, he wished to discuss the way in which emotion is expressed and represented in literature:

> [T]he only way of expressing emotion in the form of art is by finding an 'objective correlative'; in other words, a set of objects, a situation, a chain of events which shall be the formula for that particular emotion; such that when the external facts, which must terminate in a sensory experience, are given, the emotion is immediately evoked.[21]

Here we would like to apply this literary insight to the manner in which an otherwise abstract or theoretical divine 'emotion' such as wrath or mercy is made 'sensible' and concrete to the audience of the Quran. A reasonable objection to this method might be offered on the grounds that since it is a matter of doctrine, based on the statements in the Quran itself, it cannot be considered poetry. However, Quranic studies of the last fifty years or so have loosened to a considerable degree such strictures and impediments to the understanding and appreciation of what is likely the most read and quoted book on the planet. Not least of these is the fine research of Navid Kermani, *Gott ist schön* (referred to below). And there are others. Most pertinent to the present context is the recent masterful study by Zwettler in which the poetry question is most satisfactorily analysed and elucidated. It is now clear that the Quran was condemning, in the first place the poets and soothsayers who were responsible for the compositions. This condemnation was pointed directly at the source of their inspiration, which was never Allah, but rather the mysterious entities know as jinn or even other inhabitants of the invisible realm. Thus their 'revelations' were tainted. The Prophet Muhammad was not a poet, but this does not mean that the revelation that came through him was not poetic.[22]

A careful reading of the Quran will disclose that while divine revelation as such is largely restricted to prophets and messengers (*anbiya* and *rusul*), all of creation is portrayed as the grand instrument of the divine will. Indeed, in one famous passage, God tells us that the natural world is guided by the same kind of divine inspiration (*wahy*) through which His messengers receive revelation.

> And your Lord inspired the bee, saying, 'Build yourselves houses in the mountains and trees and what people construct. Then feed

on all kinds of fruit and follow the ways made easy for you by your Lord.' From their bellies comes a drink of different colours in which there is healing for people. There truly is a sign in this for those who think. (Q16:68–9)

Thus, the natural world is an expression of the mercy, guidance and generosity of God. A primary symbol of the natural world in the Quran is the all-important element of water. It is mentioned several times in key contexts where it is made clear that just as water is essential for biological life, divine water, revelation as mercy, is necessary for spiritual life. The two are symbols of each other. There are several distinct words used dozens of times throughout the Quran to describe water and its various functions and forms as an instrument of the divine. A few of these characteristic passages are offered here, but they must be seen as only a sampling from the vast sea of Quranic water references and imagery – a topic clearly worthy of a separate study.[23] Among the many Quranic words which designate water or its various forms and related activities or objects we may list the following: water/rain, *ma'* (x 63); rain, *ghayth* (x 3); *wadqa* (x 2); to ask for rain, *istaghatha* (x 1); to rain, *matara/amtara* (x 15); spring, running water, *ma'in* (x 4); torrential rain, *midrar* (x 3); hail, *barad* (x 1); cloudburst, *sayyib* (x 1); and rainclouds, *ghamam* (x 4); *muzn* (x 1); *sahab* (x 9); *mu'sirat* (x 1); *'arid* (x 2).[24] There are also the several designations for bodies of water: sea, river, river bed: *bahr* (x 41); *yamm* (x 8); *nahar/anhar* (x 54); *wadi/awdiya* (x 10); rivulet, *sariy* (x 1); spring, fountain, *'ayn/'uyun* (x 21 see also *ma'in* above); *yanbu'/yanabi'* (x 2); watering place, *wird* (x); pool, *lujja/lujji* (x 2). In addition, there are also several mentions of various objects associated with or identified in the context of water of some kind or another: pearls, *bayd* (x 1); *lu'lu'* (x 6); cup/goblet, *ka's* (x 6); fish, *hut* (x 5); ship, *fulk* (x 23); *jara* (x 1); *safina* (x 4). In addition to verbs, such as 'to rain', mentioned above, there are also many usages of several other action words (or words directly derived from them) which have to do only with water in some form or another: to give to drink, *saqa'* (x 25); to come to or bear water, *warada, warid* (x 4); to drink, *shariba* (x 39), to sail on the water, to flow, *jara'* (x 64); to cascade, *thajjaj* (x 1); to weep, *baka* (x 6); tears, *dama'a* (x 2); *ibyaddat 'aynahu min al-huzn* (x 1). Specific types or qualities of water are also mentioned: sweet to drink, *furat* (x 3); salty to drink, *milh* (x 2); vile (actually 'pus') to drink; *sadid* (x 1); boiling to drink, *hamim* (x 14); pleasant mixture, *mizaj* (x 3) of, respectively, perfume, *kafur*, ginger, *zanjabil*, and spiritually exhilarating musk, *tasnim*. To close this brief and incomplete catalogue of Quranic water imagery we must mention the rivers and springs of paradise, such as those named (*salsabil, kawthar*) or those not named but which flow perpetually with wine (*khamr, rahiq*), with milk (*laban*), with honey (*asal*) or sweet water (*furat*).[25] In this connection, even the frequent Quranic references to fruit would find a place in a thorough discussion inasmuch as fruit, among other things, is a natural and efficient means for preserving and transporting water. Quranic words that would come under this category include those having to do also with fruit/fructify (*thamara/athmara*, x 24; *fakiha*, x 14; *jana*, x 2; *nabata*, x 28). Such references also frequently occur in a moral, spiritual and even eschatological context.

There is clearly no need here to emphasise the logicality and efficacy of this general poetic conceit, this 'objective correlative', given the geographic realities of the *Sitz im Leben* of the rise of Islam and the revelation of the Quran. Water in the Quran is clearly the most precious thing in the material world and frequently the search for it was the chief occupation of the Arabs. It is thus no accident that the Quran uses water to teach about the spiritual and sometimes intangible things of God. The word *shari'a* means, after all, 'path to the water spring'. What follows is simply a series of a few of the most dramatic examples of the Quranic use of water as emblem and 'objective correlative' of both divine wrath and mercy. We will begin with those verses in which water in some form or another is representative of divine wrath and anger. The first quotation is a succinct and powerful reminder to all humanity that it is God who is in control of the natural realm as well as the spiritual realm. The image here is the ability of God (contrasted with the inability of humanity) to supply water, the source of all life. 'Say, "Just think: if all your water were to sink deep into the earth who could give you flowing water in its place?"' (Q67:30).

WATER AS SYMBOL OF WRATH AND DIVINE CHASTISEMENT

The flood and other natural calamities

And so We let loose on them the flood, locusts, lice, frogs, blood – all clear signs. They were arrogant, wicked people. (Q7:133)

When Our command came, and water gushed up, We said, 'Place on board this Ark a pair of each species, and your own family – except those against whom the sentence has already been passed – and those who have believed,' though only a few believed with him. He said, 'Board the Ark. In the name of God it shall sail and anchor. My God is most forgiving and merciful.' It sailed with them on waves like mountains, and Noah called out to his son, who stayed behind, 'Come aboard with us, my son, do not stay with the disbelievers.' But he replied, 'I will seek refuge on a mountain to save me from the water.' Noah said, 'Today there is no refuge from God's command, except for those on whom He has mercy.' The waves cut them off from each other and he was among the drowned. Then it was said, 'Earth, swallow up your water, and sky, hold back,' and the water subsided, the command was fulfilled. The Ark settled on Mount Judi, and it was said, 'Gone are those evildoing people!' (Q11:40–4)

Noah said, 'My Lord, help me! They call me a liar,' and so We revealed to him: 'Build the Ark under Our watchful eye and according to Our revelation. When Our command comes and water gushes up out of the earth, take pairs of every species on board, and your family, except for those on whom the sentence has already been passed – do not plead with me for the evildoers: they will be drowned – and when you and your companions are settled on the Ark, say, "Praise be to God, who delivered us from the wicked people."' (Q23:26–8)

Use of water as an instrument or symbol of divine disfavour

We took the Children of Israel across the sea. Pharaoh and his troops pursued them in arrogance and aggression. But as he was drowning he cried, 'I believe there is no God except the one the Children of Israel believe in. I submit to Him.' (Q10:90)

There are, in the land, neighbouring plots, gardens of vine-yards, cornfields, palm trees in clusters or otherwise, all watered with the same water, yet We make some of them taste better than others: there truly are signs in this for people who reason. (Q13:4)

The only true prayer is to Him: those they pray to besides Him give them no answer any more than water reaches the mouth of someone who simply stretches out his hands for it – it cannot do so: the prayers of the disbelievers are all in vain. All that are in heaven and earth submit to God alone, willingly or unwillingly, as do their shadows in the mornings and in the evenings. (Q13:14–15)

If only, when you entered your garden, you had said, 'This is God's will. There is no power not [given] by God.' Although you see I have less wealth and offspring than you, my Lord may well give me something better than your garden, and send thunderbolts on your garden from the sky, so that it becomes a heap of barren dust; or its water may sink so deep into the ground that you will never be able to reach it again. And so it was: his fruit was completely destroyed, and there he was, wringing his hands over what he had invested in it, as it drooped on its trellises, and saying, 'I wish I had not set up any partner to my Lord.' He had no forces to help him other than God – he could not even help himself. In that situation, the only protection is that of God, the True God: He gives the best rewards and the best outcome. Tell them, too, what the life of this world is like: We send water down from the skies and the earth's vegetation absorbs it, but soon the plants turn to dry stubble scattered about by the wind: God has power over everything. (Q18:39–45)

But the deeds of those who disbelieve are like a mirage in a desert: the thirsty person thinks there will be water but, when he gets there, he finds only God, who pays him his account in full – God is swift in reckoning. Or like shadows in a deep sea covered by wave upon wave, with clouds above – layer upon layer of darkness – if he holds out his hand, he is scarcely able to see it. The one to whom God gives no light has no light at all. [Prophet], do you not see that all those who are in the heavens and earth praise God, as do the birds with wings outstretched? Each knows its [own way] of prayer and glorification: God has full knowledge of what they do. Control of the heavens and earth belongs to God: and to God is the final return. Do you not see that God drives the clouds, then gathers them together and piles them up until you see rain pour from their midst? He sends hail down from [such] mountains in the sky, pouring it on whomever He wishes and diverting it from whomever He wishes – the flash of its lightning almost snatches sight away. (Q24:39–43)

Eschatology

Say, 'Now the truth has come from your Lord: let those who wish to believe in it do so, and let those who wish to reject it do so.' We have prepared a Fire for the wrongdoers that will envelop them from all sides. If they call for relief, they will be relieved with water like molten metal, scalding their faces. What a terrible drink! What a painful resting place! (Q18:29)

Hell awaits each one; he will be given foul water [oozing pus] to drink, which he will try to gulp but scarcely be able to swallow; death will encroach on him from every side, but he will not die; more intense suffering will lie ahead of him. (Q14:16–17)

Here is a picture of the Garden promised to the pious: rivers of water forever pure, rivers of milk forever fresh, rivers of wine, a delight for those who drink, rivers of honey clarified and pure, [all] flow in it; there they will find fruit of every kind; and they will find forgiveness from their Lord. How can this be compared to the fate of those stuck in the Fire, given boiling water to drink that tears their bowels? (Q47:15)

In the Name of God the Merciful the Compassionate

Have you heard tell about the Overwhelming Event? On that Day, there will be downcast faces, toiling and weary, as they enter the blazing Fire and are forced to drink from a boiling spring, with no food for them except bitter dry thorns that neither nourish nor satisfy hunger. On that Day there will also be faces radiant with bliss, well pleased with their labour, in a lofty garden, where they will hear no idle talk, with a flowing spring, raised couches, goblets placed before them, cushions set in rows, and carpets spread. Do the disbelievers not see how rain clouds are formed, how the heavens are lifted, how the mountains are raised high, how the earth is spread out? So [Prophet] warn them: your only task is to give warning, you are not there to control them. As for those who turn away and disbelieve, God will inflict the greatest torment upon them. It is to

Us they will return, and then it is for Us to call them to account.
(Sura 88, The Overwhelming Event (*al-Waqi'a*), 24 verses)

WATER AS SYMBOL OF MERCY

A few of the many Quranic verses in which water may be identified with divine mercy are now presented. To begin with, there are verses that speak of water in connection with creation, cosmogony and ontology. It is precisely such verses that have helped inspire the theory of the ontic ground as mercy, referred to above.

It is He who created the heavens and the earth in six days. His Throne extends over the water too – so as to test which of you does best. Yet [Prophet], if you say to them, 'You will be resurrected after death,' the disbelievers are sure to answer, 'This is clearly nothing but sorcery.' (Q11:7)

Are the disbelievers not aware that the heavens and the earth used to be joined together and that We ripped them apart, that We made every living thing from water? Will they not believe? (Q21:30)

And God created each animal out of water: some of them crawl on their bellies, some walk on two legs, and some on four. God creates whatever He will; God has power over everything. (Q24:45)

It is He who released the two bodies of flowing water, one sweet and fresh and the other salty and bitter, and put an insurmountable barrier between them. It is He who creates human beings from water, then makes them kin by blood and marriage: your Lord is all powerful! (Q25:53–4)

In the following series of verses, the symbolic role of water as mercy is highlighted:

People, worship your Lord, who created you and those before you, so that you may be mindful [of Him] who spread out the earth for you and built the sky; who sent water down from it and with that water produced things for your sustenance. Do not, knowing this, set up rivals to God. (Q2:22–3)

[Prophet], give those who believe and do good the news that they will have Gardens graced with flowing streams. Whenever they are given sustenance from the fruits of these Gardens, they will say, 'We have been given this before,' because they were provided with something like it. They will have pure spouses and there they will stay. (Q2:25)

Remember when Moses prayed for water for his people and We said to him, 'Strike the rock with your staff.' Twelve springs gushed out, and each group knew its drinking place. 'Eat and drink the sustenance God has provided and do not cause corruption in the land.' (Q2:60)

Even after that, your hearts became as hard as rocks, or even harder, for there are rocks from which streams spring out, and some from which water comes when they split open, and others which fall down in awe of God: He is not unaware of what you do. (Q2:74)

In the creation of the heavens and earth; in the alternation of night and day; in the ships that sail the seas with goods for people; in the water which God sends down from the sky to give life to the earth when it has been barren, scattering all kinds of creatures over it; in the changing of the winds and clouds that run their appointed courses between the sky and earth: there are signs in all these for those who use their minds. (Q2:164)

[Prophet], say, 'Would you like me to tell you of things that are better than all of these? Their Lord will give those who are mindful of God Gardens graced with flowing streams, where they will stay with pure spouses and God's good pleasure – God is fully aware of His servants. (Q3:15)

It is He who sends the winds, bearing good news of His coming grace, and when they have gathered up the heavy clouds, We drive them to a dead land where We cause rain to fall, bringing out all kinds of crops, just as We shall bring out the dead. Will you not reflect? Vegetation comes out of good land in abundance, by the will of its Lord, but out of bad land only scantily: We explain Our Revelations in various ways to those who give thanks. (Q7:57–8)

We divided them into twelve tribes [as distinct] communities, and, when his people asked him for water, inspired Moses to strike the rock with his staff [so that] twelve springs gushed out. Each tribe knew its own drinking place; We gave them the shade of clouds and sent down to them manna and quails [saying], 'Eat the good things We have provided for you.' They did not wrong Us; it was themselves they wronged. (Q7:160)

Remember when He gave you sleep as a reassurance from Him, and sent down water from the sky to cleanse you, to remove Satan's pollution from you, to make your hearts strong and your feet firm. (Q8:11)

With this brief introductory exploration and listing of key Quranic verses, we see that divine wrath and mercy are major Quranic themes and that some of the Quran's distinctive character may be understood by observing how these otherwise somewhat abstract, theoretical or even theological ideas are rendered powerfully intelligible to the reader/listener/believer. Indeed, this exploration and discussion may be considered an example of what the great classical Muslim philosopher, al-Farabi (950) meant when discussing the nature of prophethood and its relation to intellect, imagination and philosophy. Known to Muslim intelligentsia as 'the second teacher' (after Aristotle, who was the first), his task was, in some sense, to coordinate the insights and axioms of Greek philosophy with the form and contents of the Islamic religion. Naturally, he was led to compare the role of the philosopher king with the prophet legislator and concluded that the ability to render philosophical (metaphysical and theological) truths and values into cognisable images that the untrained could understand, was among the greatest abilities and distinguishing characteristics of a prophet.[26]

In closing, we may express the hope that while the subject of divine mercy certainly serves as a suitable topic with which to introduce that vast religious, social and cultural complex known as Islam, we now also have some notion of how this same Islam, with its deep and rich scriptural affiliations and decidedly spiritual vocation, may serve as a place from where to view the question of divine mercy in a distinctive and instructive light. With regard to the suggestion that the drama of mercy and wrath is reflected in the Quranic use of water imagery, much more could be said. We have not, for example, touched upon the important role of actual physical water; ablutions, general hygiene, funeral procedure, irrigation laws and so on, where the central place which water as mercy holds in the book is also reflected. Nor have we touched upon the uniquely Islamicate notion of the cosmogonic, noetic and ontic category of later Islam known as the

World of Images (*alam al-mithal*), the door to which is said to be located at, among other places, the reflective surfaces of water.[27] The ablutions for the prayer codified in the *shari'a* 'path to the watering pool' reminds the believer of the symbolic and non-symbolic value represented by Quranic water.[28] Ablutions at prayer and washing the dead and all of the other many religious instructions and rites involving water attest to this fact: that in Islam, water as an essential, life-giving element is symbolic of a spiritual reality otherwise veiled from the senses.

Chapter 6

Chaotic Cosmos and the Symmetry of Truth

> Symmetry, in any narrative, always means that historical content
> is being subordinated to mythical demands of design and form.
> Northrop Frye, *The Great Code*[1]

The somewhat playful title of this chapter alludes first to the long tradition of seeing the Quran, at least upon first encounter, as a disordered 'chaotic' collection of intermittent, random or casually arranged pericopes, which have been put in some kind of 'order' by the early generations of redactors and editors as a scripture for the Islamic religion and Muslims. Research over the past few years, however, has clearly demonstrated that the present form of the Quran represents a number of interconnected logics of structure, content, performance, imagery, textual grammar, vocabulary and poetics.[2] Thus, while from the 'outside' the Quran appears to lack those essential features of 'the book', namely a beginning, middle and end, recent scholarship has remarked about and elucidated the many ways, some more subtle than others, in which the Quran reveals its textual secret of unity and consistency.[3] True, the Quran is not like other books, but despite this, in reading the Quran one is never in doubt about its 'centre of narrative gravity'.[4]

The second half of the title of this chapter refers to the *Sitz im Leben* of the Quranic revelation, the conditions of life, the social matrix, the notion, or its absence, of history and the general malaise we are told by sources that seemed to permeate daily life, at least in some quarters: meaninglessness, despair, anarchy and nihilism as these were felt and expressed in the Arabian Peninsula on the eve of the rise of Islam, a mood and ethos frequently denoted by the Arabic word *jahl*, ignorance, barbarity, injustice (about which more below). However chaotic and brutal this pre-Islamic period was, the Islamic ethos is confident that it was part of a larger scheme, a higher and broader inscrutable sense of order, and that without it Islam as we know it would not have distinguished itself. The juxtaposition of chaos and order is intended to evoke the creative tension that may be seen to have been resolved, or at least addressed, in the Quran and its later interpretation. Here, we are concerned only with the Quran.

However chaos is defined or however it functions, there is no getting away from the fact that one of its main tasks is to affirm and support the terribly human experience of (or ineluctable predilection for), symmetry.[5] It is, moreover, clearly no accident, and less an oversight, that not only is there no entry for chaos in the massive *Encyclopaedia of the Quran*, the word itself seems not to occur more than once anywhere in its nearly four thousand pages.[6] While in the Quran and Islam there are a number of 'chaoses' (apparently there is no real plural) acknowledged, whether obliquely, by inference, allusion or metaphor, and as such presumed, the familiar one of a pre-creational chaos of emptiness and/or uncontrolled water as the starting point of a cosmogonic process is virtually absent (see a possible exception below).[7] By contrast, in the Quran water is always firmly connected to the ultimately rational (if currently inscrutable and mysterious) will of God. Even when there is an apparent irrational and violent or chaotic deluge, it is clear that the water is under the ultimate control of God, and is an instrument of God's rational will. Thus, it may be used to mirror or dispense divine mercy and wrath, as seen in the previous chapter, and it may even represent an apocalyptic cataclysm,[8] but it does not stand for the nothingness or void which is at a core meaning of chaos and which may be, in other traditions, coeternal or coeval with God.[9]

A number of vestigial references to primordial chaos may be read in a series of Quranic words and verses. For example, it is possible that *al-tammat al-kubra* in Q79:34, usually understood as an eschatological eventuality, may indeed reflect, at least in its etymology, the great dragon *ti'amat* and thus an interesting cosmogonic – and also apocalyptic reversal: chaos comes at the end of creation as paradoxical affirmation of the truth of Islam. Note, in this connection, such words as – *al-dukhan* 'the great smoke' in Q41:11 and 44:10, the crumbling of mountains (Q101:5), the splitting of the moon (Q54:1) and so on. The exegetes have confidently placed these emblems of terrestrial chaos and disorder at the end of time.[10]

One notable exception where primordial disintegration plays an important role may be in Q21:30:

> Do not the unbelievers see that the heavens and the earth were joined together (as one unit of creation), before we clove them asunder? We made from water every living thing. Will they not then believe?

Such a verse could, in fact be read to support the view that creation is precisely not tinged by disorder of any kind. The original state was unitary. And such a view would be very much in line with the cardinal Islamic doctrine of tawhid, the commitment to the oneness of God, as distinct from and opposed to *shirk* or polytheism. What splitting or apparent disorder one might see is actually the result of God's creative will, a will that is presented as being pre-eminently orderly, reasonable and harmonious.

The significant primordial event in the Quran is referred to in the literature as the Day of the Covenant, *yawm al-mithaq*. Because of the distinctive events described in Q7:172–4, it is also universally known as the Day of Alast: the day of 'Am I not [your Lord?]'. The Quran reads as follows:

> [Prophet], remember when your Lord took out the offspring from the loins of the Children of Adam and made them bear witness about themselves, He said, 'Am I not your Lord? and they replied, 'Yes, we bear witness.' So you cannot say on the Day of Resurrection, 'We were not aware of this,' or, 'It was our forefathers who, before us, ascribed partners to God, and we are only the descendants who came after them: will you destroy us because of falsehoods they invented?' In this way We explain the messages, so that they may turn [to the right path].

This scenario is universally understood as having transpired prior to actual creation and, in fact, represents 'the beginning' in the great universal histories, such as that of al-Tabari, produced during the heyday of Abbasid power. Long recognised as having important influence in the realm of purely religious, theological and spiritual thought, recent research indicates that this Quranic vignette reflects something salient and irreducible about the Islamic view of the world and its place in history. We mention it as the only pre-creational scenario in the Quran and one that would seem to reflect and emphasise certain key features of the Islamic religion, especially as they might pertain to the question of chaos, and its conceptual twin, order. Indeed, the primordial, 'pre-creational' Day of the Covenant radiates order, meaning, justice and harmony. The idea that all future souls are somehow present in Adam is familiar from Augustine.[11] God's act of creation, as we are informed by the Quran, seems to be a species of *creatio ex nihilo,* although some have argued persuasively that however striking the frequent and characteristic Quranic phrase may be (see below), it cannot be demonstrated, on the available evidence, that the Quran therefore holds that God 'was existing with absolutely nothing else'.[12] This mode of creation is nonetheless clearly and powerfully expressed in nine separate contexts throughout the Quran with some variation on the basic idea: when God wishes to create something he merely says to it 'Be', and it is. A representative example is the one that occurs earliest in the Quran text:[13]

> He is the Originator of the heavens and the earth, and when He decrees something, He says only, 'Be,' and it is (*kun fa-yakunu*). (Q2:117)[14]

This is possibly akin to the creation described in Genesis, where the forms of life are spoken into existence.[15] Such ensures that whatever chaos and void might have existed prior to creation as such, it could not have been coeval with God. Thus, the Quran and Christian understanding of the Hebrew Bible would seem to share the same basic point of view. Again, the notion of order emerging from primordial chaos is not present. The analogue of this may be thought to be, as suggested above, the apocalyptic chaos described and indicated numerous times throughout the Quran. Here 'smoke' or 'deluge' or all images of uncontrollable nature are organised in an eloquent and frightening symmetrical scenario of the coming Hour (*al-sa'a*) or Event (*al-waqi'a*). As disturbing and cataclysmic as these obviously are, the Quran never hesitates about them being the result of God's justice and will. So, they are controlled chaos, or paradoxical chaos. We frequently find this notion attested to and expressed in some of the more powerful, shorter Quranic suras, such as the Chapter of the Chargers (Q100, *Surat al-'adiyat*) or the Chapter of the Clatterer (Q101, *Surat al-qari'a*), to name only two. In these instances, the powerful apocalyptic energies of destruction and confusion are in some sense simultaneously tamed and intensified by the compelling verbal artistry of the actual Arabic.[16]

There is one more interesting example, or possible example, of a kind of chaos. The famous Light verse, Q24:35 esteemed as one of the more beautiful and compelling passages in the Quran, has recently been compared with the *Paradiso* vision of Dante.[17] The verse is as follows:

> God is the Light of the heavens and earth. His Light is like this: there is a niche, and in it a lamp, the lamp inside a glass, a glass like a glittering star, fuelled from a blessed olive tree from neither east nor west, whose oil almost gives light even when no fire touches it – light upon light – God guides whoever He will to his Light; God draws such comparisons for people; God has full knowledge of everything. (Q24:35)

The image of undifferentiated, perhaps blinding light presents us with the interesting paradox or irony that the first principle of order and knowledge is a powerful symbol for the unknowableness and inaccessibility of God, in line with other similarly apophatic pronouncements (for example Q112). The beauty of this divine 'chaos of light' is almost immediately counterbalanced by a true image of ignorance, disbelief and confusion. Indeed, the uncontrollable effulgence of the divine light acquires an immediate intensification of meaning by the comparison with darkness (and vice versa):

> But the deeds of those who disbelieve are like a mirage in a desert, the thirsty person thinks there will be water but, when he gets there, he finds only God, who pays him his account in full – God is swift in reckoning. Or like shadows in a deep sea covered by wave upon wave, with clouds above – layer upon layer of darkness – if he holds out his hand, he is scarcely able to see it. The one to whom God gives no light has no light at all. (Q24:39–40)

If we wish to find real disorder and chaos in the Quran, we must turn, then, to a different realm, one that is under the immediate control not of God, but human beings. A few Quranic terms explicitly denote social disorder, disruption or even cataclysm. For example, *fitna*, a word that occurs thirty times in this nominal form, strongly connotes disorder on a social scale, its root meaning is 'test' or 'temptation'. It is frequently translated as 'civil war' and is used to refer to the great, apparently irreparable breach in the unity of the Muslim community that issued in what we now refer to as Sunni and Shiʿi Islam. Here, the understanding is that there was an inability to withstand the temptation for which the unity of the Muslim community was sacrificed.[18] The word in the plural (*fitan*) refers to those later 'intramural' skirmishes, struggles and battles in which the idea of religious authority was at stake and derives special meaning to the degree that it engages with the apocalyptic topos of the Hour (*al-saʿa*) so frequently mentioned in the Quran.[19] Another pair of terms, *tafawut* (fault, disharmony) and *futur* (flaws, fissures) occurs in one of dozens of verses espousing a distinctive Islamic teleological argument as heard in Q67:2–5:

> He is the Mighty, the Forgiving; who created the seven heavens, one above the other. You will not see any flaw (*tafawut*) in what the Lord of Mercy creates. Look again! Can you see any flaw (*futur*)? Look again! And again! Your sight will turn back to you, weak and defeated. (Q67:205)[20]

Nonetheless, the dialectic of such oppositions and dualities as 'chaos and order' – even if this particular pair is not mentioned in the sacred text – is a very strong sub-theme throughout Islamicate literature beginning with the Quran. Here we will touch on how this dialectic functions in Quranic discourse by focusing on three different categories: scripture, society and history. The various and multiple interconnected symmetries of the Quran may be thought of as representing two banks of a river through which the central epic theme of Quranic sacred history (which is the only kind) flows. Such symmetry, as was seen earlier in Chapter 4, is present, either explicitly or implicitly, in every verse – of which there are just over six thousand.

Among the many pairs of opposites used in this way throughout the Quran, one is of particular interest for thinking about chaos and order in Islam: *islam ≠ jahl*. A brief examination of the semantic value of these two words will illustrate why it is perhaps not necessary for the Quran to either posit or even contemplate primordial cosmogonic chaos in order to supply a foil or mate for its opposite. The interesting question, whether such an absence represents an inter-confessional apologetic, is enticing but will not be explored here.[21] We will begin with the second term. *Jahl*, from the Arabic root *j-h-l*, means in the first instance 'ignorance'. It is, according to the way in which the root and its derivations occur in the Quran, an ignorance of far-ranging consequence and influence. In keeping with the 'myth of symmetry', so important to the Quran and Islamic religiosity, later commentators and theorists divided historical time into two major periods: the period of ignorance, known as *al-Jahiliyya* in the Quran, and its polar opposite, *al-Islamiyya*. The word is used to describe the condition most frequently exemplified by the Arabs of the Hijaz and environs prior to the revelation of Islam. It is in this context that the two terms, though one contains two syllables, may be thought to function as an ideational 'minimal pair'. The root occurs twenty-four times. A related term, and one which is expressive of a strictly moral chaos and corruption of the type that obtained during the *jahili* period, is represented by the Arabic word *fasad,* which occurs no less than fifty times in some form or another in the Quran. As observed by the author of the article on creation in the *Encyclopedia of the Quran*: 'The universe has been organized into a cosmos rather than a chaos and humanity is accordingly warned to introduce no human disorder into the divinely ordained arrangement of the physical world: Do not sow corruption in the earth after its ordering (Q7:56).'[22] In this instance, what might be thought the linguistic accident of rhyme and homophony obtaining between the words *islah* (order, well-being) and *islam* is, in the context of the seamless vision of the Quran, a most happy one. Thus, *jahl* and *fasad*, as diametric opposites of *islam* shed light on the meaning of that word in the process of supplying a symmetrical counterweight to it.

It will be useful to reproduce here all the twenty or so verses in which the word in some form or another actually appears in the Quran. These verses will be arranged according to the grammatical form of the root in mushafi order,[23] the first being the nominal *jahiliyya,* which occurs four times.

After sorrow, He caused calm to descend upon you, a sleep that overtook some of you. Another group, caring only for themselves, entertained false thoughts about God, thoughts more appropriate to pagan ignorance (*jahiliyya*), and said, 'Do we get a say in any of this?' [Prophet], tell them, 'Everything to do with this affair is in God's hands.' They conceal in their hearts things they will not reveal to you. They say, 'If we had had our say in this, none of us would have been killed here.' Tell them, 'Even if you had resolved to stay at home, those who were destined to be killed would still have gone out to meet their deaths.' God did this in order to test everything within you and in order to prove what is in your hearts. God knows your innermost thoughts very well. (Q3:154)

Do they want judgment according to the time of pagan ignorance (*jahiliyya*)? Is there any better judge than God for those of firm faith? (Q5:50)

Stay at home, and do not flaunt your finery as they used to in the pagan past (*jahiliyya*); keep up the prayer, give the prescribed alms, and obey God and His Messenger. God wishes to keep uncleanness away from you, people of the [Prophet's] House, and to purify you thoroughly. (Q33:33)

While the disbelievers had fury in their hearts – the fury of ignorance (*jahiliyya*) – God sent His tranquility down on to His Messenger and the believers and made binding on them [their] promise to obey God for that was more appropriate and fitting for them. God has full knowledge of all things. (Q48:26)

The second instance of the root to be noticed here is *jahala*. It also occurs four times in the Quran:

But God only undertakes to accept repentance from those who do evil out of ignorance (*bi-jahala*) and soon afterwards repent: these are the ones God will forgive, He is all knowing, all wise. (Q4:17)

When those who believe in Our revelations come to you [Prophet], say, 'Peace be upon you. Your Lord has taken it on Himself to be merciful: if any of you has foolishly (*bi-jahala*) done a bad deed, and afterwards repented and mended his ways, God is most forgiving and most merciful.' (Q6:54)

But towards those who do wrong out of ignorance (*bi-jahala*), and afterwards repent and make amends, your Lord is most forgiving and merciful. (Q16:119)

Believers, if a troublemaker brings you news, check it first, in case you wrong others unwittingly (*bi-jahala*) and later regret what you have done. (Q49:6)

Thus, the two forms are used to express, respectively 1) a general period of ignorance, whose chief characteristic we eventually learn is the absence of strict monotheistic worship as revealed to Muhammad and 2) specific cases of ignorance or foolishness which although they need not have the greater theological implications of the first usage, nonetheless enhance its meaning by elaborating a broader semantic field. By far the most numerous occurrences of the root *j-h-l* are found in the fifteen verses in which it appears in verbal or participial form. These related, various forms demonstrate and dramatise the meanings thus far encountered. We will list the verbal instances first:

> Even if We sent the angels down to them, and the dead spoke to them, and We gathered all things right in front of them, they still would not believe, unless God so willed, but of this most of them are ignorant (*yajhaluna*). (Q6:111)
>
> We took the Children of Israel across the sea, but when they came upon a people who worshipped idols, they said, 'Moses, make a god for us like theirs.' He said, 'You really are foolish people (*tajhaluna*).' (Q7:138)
>
> My people, I ask no reward for it from you; my reward comes only from God. I will not drive away the faithful: they are sure to meet their Lord. I can see you are foolish (*tajhaluna*). (Q11:29)
>
> How can you lust after men instead of women? What fools you are (*bal antum qawm tajhaluna*)! (Q27:55)
>
> He said, 'Only God knows when it will come: I simply convey to you the message I am sent with but I can see you are an insolent people (*arakum qawman tajhaluna*)'. (Q46:23)

With the verbal form we acquire a new appreciation for the active dimension of *jahl*, 'ignorance' or 'savage brutality'. It is something perpetrated and performed. Even though it may seem to represent a passive or negative quality, such as ignorance or foolishness, it nonetheless requires a kind of existential or individual conscious decision to be 'deployed'. It may be forgiven, as we saw above in verses Q6:54 and Q16:119. But repentance is necessary – an equally authentic conscious act, it would seem. The notion of individual choice in the matter of *jahl* is most clearly drawn in these following verses that use the active participle *jahil*: 'one who does *jahl*'. This can occur in singular or plural:

> Remember when Moses said to his people, 'God commands you to sacrifice a cow.' They said, 'Are you making fun of us?' He answered, 'God forbid that I should be so ignorant (*min al-jahilin*).' (Q2:67)

[Give] to those needy who are wholly occupied in God's way and cannot travel in the land [for trade]. The unknowing (*al-jahil*) might think them rich because of their self-restraint, but you will recognize them by their characteristic of not begging persistently. God is well aware of any good you give. (Q2:273)

If you find rejection by the disbelievers so hard to bear, then seek a tunnel into the ground or a ladder into the sky, if you can, and bring them a sign: God could bring them all to guidance if it were His will, so do not join the ignorant (*al-jahilina*). (Q6:35)

Be tolerant and command what is right: pay no attention to foolish people (*al-jahilina*). (Q7:199)

God said, 'Noah, he was not one of your family. What he did was not right. Do not ask Me for things you know nothing about. I am warning you not to be foolish (*min al-jahilin*).' (Q11:46)

[Joseph] said, 'My Lord! I would prefer prison to what these women are calling me to do. If You do not protect me from their treachery, I shall yield to them and do wrong (*wa'akun min al-jahilina*).' (Q12:33)

He said, 'Do you now realize what you did to Joseph and his brother when you were ignorant (*idh antum jahiluna*)?' (Q12:89)

The servants of the Lord of Mercy are those who walk humbly on the earth, and who, when the foolish address them (*al-jahiluna*), reply, 'Peace.' (Q25:63)

Whenever they hear frivolous talk they turn away, saying, 'We have our deeds and you have yours. Peace be with you! We do not seek the company of ignorant people (*al-jahilina*).' (Q28:55)

Say [O Muhammad to the disbelievers], 'Do you order me to worship someone other than God, you foolish people (*al-jahiluna*)?' (Q39:64)

Linguistic studies of this word *jahl* have made it clear that however much the term may be in some ways correctly considered a semantic opposite of the Arabic word for 'knowledge' or 'knowing' (viz, *'ilm*) its meaning in the context of the evolution of an Islamic semantic worldview is more to be found as a polar opposite of another, perhaps more revealing concept. As was demonstrated so clearly by Goldziher, who in the process of his explanation revised a millennium of thinking about the semantics of the term *jahl*, the proper opposite is not 'knowledge' or 'knowing' – but, precisely *hilm*,[24] a well-attested pre-Islamic concept and virtue described as 'the moral reasonableness of a civilized man . . . thus *jahl* in the sources had the 'primary semantic function' of referring to the 'implacable, reckless temper of the pagan Arabs'.[25] Building on this research, Izutsu, nearly fifty years ago, revised further the understanding of the term by demonstrating that the semantic field of *islam*, understood as designating the master ethos of the religion that goes by this name, is profoundly entwined with all of those virtues and moral qualities subsumed in the term *hilm*: forbearance, patience, generosity, compassion, slowness to anger and humility. Izutsu further argued that in fact the word '*islam*' stands for a religious and moral recital of all of those qualities understood by the word *hilm*.[26] As a result of this painstaking research by both Goldziher and Izutsu it becomes clear that in an Islamic context the opposite of the word *jahl* is precisely *islam*, as indicated in the above gloss on verses Q25:63 and Q28:55, where the linguistic crux of the problem is eloquently expressed. Thus, if *jahl* means ignorance it is the opposite of the kind of 'knowledge' denoted by the Spanish notion of *educado* or the English notion of 'cultivated' and the Arabic notion of *adab*. To quote Izutsu:

> All things considered, it will be clear by now that in the semantic category of *jahl* there is [according to the Quran] comprised the central notion of a fierce, passionate nature which tends to get stirred up on the slightest provocation and which may drive a man to all sorts of recklessness; that this passion tends to manifest itself in a very peculiar way in the arrogant sense of honor characterizing the pagan Arabs, especially the Bedouin of the desert; and lastly that in the specifically Quranic situation the word refers to the peculiar attitude of hostility and aggressiveness against the monotheistic belief of Islam, which was to the minds of most of Muhammad's contemporaries, too exacting ethically and which, moreover, called upon them to abandon their time-honored customs and their idols.[27]

In such a context, Islam then comes to stand for the opposite of barbarity, savagery, brutality and vainglory as well as standing for the opposite of ignorance and polytheism. 'Submission' thus becomes understood as obedience to an ethical norm which, if put into practice, will allow the greatest variety of human communities to live together peaceably. Such a vision has been associated with the 'Constitution of Medina', in which numerous tribal and religious groups are identified and called upon to obey the law of Islam. In such a context, then, Islam – through the Quran – may be seen as having raised the notion of civilisation to the level of religious value. In the process, and as a result of the distinctive Islamic view of history and its profound relationship to prophecy, the prevailing 'chaos of religions' obtaining at the time of the prophet Muhammad, could, under the guidance of distinctively Islamic insights and teachings, be understood as equal partners in the spiritual and religious journey of humanity, *al-nas*. The mindless fate (*dahr*, compare Q45:24 and Q76:1) of the pre-Islamic *jahili* mindset is transformed under the pressure and immediacy of Muhammad's revelation into a symmetrical and rational account of communities whose respective histories are determined by their obedience to or deviation from their own particular revelation. As the Quran says:

> We sent a messenger to every community, saying, 'Worship God and shun false gods.' Among them were some God guided; misguidance took hold of others. So travel through the earth and see what was the fate of those who denied the truth. (Q16:36)

The Quran insists that it teaches a divine and perennial wisdom. The twenty-five prophets it names in its pages and the 124,000 prophets recognised by Islamic tradition are all related as emissaries of a consistent, harmonious and supremely rational and ordered divine message. It is with such an extensive 'alphabet of prophets' that the language of the Quranic ethos came to be spoken and understood over a heretofore unimaginably vast cultural and geographic range. Thus, the Quran demonstrates through the orchestration of an equally vast number of interlocking and mutually reinforcing symmetries a heretofore unrecognized sacred and luminous order of enlightenment and plan.

At the deeper levels, each symmetry is connected to all others by virtue of its symmetry. Taking as the central and defining metaphor of Islamic religious orientation the notion of tawhid, it may be argued that far from being a mere abstract 'theological' idea, it is – in addition to this – a metaphor or emblem of a social transformation which took place in the wake of Muhammad's powerful religious experience, the revelation, for which one cognate is the word apocalypse, the evidence for which is known as the

Quran. Thus, each key term of the Quranic worldview is determined and understood by an opposite or companion term.[28] So, tawhid 'affirming or making one' is contextualised by its conceptual opposite, the unforgivable sin in Islam, *shirk* 'violating divine oneness'.[29] It is perhaps for this reason that the final respective verbal forms of these two central concepts have acquired their permanence in the discourse.

A CHAOS OF RELIGIONS

The Quran may be slyly speaking of itself, when in sura 12, the remarkable *Surat Yusuf* (Joseph), Pharaoh's benighted advisers dismiss the sequence of images that came to the royal sleeper as 'jumbled dreams' (*adghath ahlam*, Q12:44). These are the same dreams that will soon be interpreted by the young, imprisoned prophet Yusuf and thereby achieve the status of divine revelation. Moreover, it is the public act of properly reading and interpreting these Pharaonic dreams that wins Yusuf his release from prison and elevates him to a powerful royal position. In short, Yusuf's reading of the dreams causes his up until now secret status as prophet to be revealed along with the true meaning of the heretofore coded or 'jumbled' message of Pharaoh's dream. Meaning emerges from apparent chaos and meaninglessness. This is a key feature of the Quranic apocalypse: revelation occurs through interpretation. In the first place, and perhaps the most obvious, this interpretation occurs when the Quran understands all previous religious history as leading to its own vision. From one somewhat cynical point of view, this is the all-too-familiar 'imperial device' known in countless contexts and periods of human experience. From another angle it solves the problem of the 'chaos of religions' confronting both Muhammad and his community, transforming this disorder into order through narrative and interpretation. Here, both intellectual or spiritual and social chaos are the atemporal "starting point" for the Islamic worldview as this is expressed in the Quran text. There is no cosmogonic or ontological equivalent. This is perhaps unsurprising and 'as it should be' in a religion for which the primary spiritual and doctrinal value is oneness and its affirmation.

Islam does not teach an original sin, there is nonetheless a Fall. The distinctive Islamic Fall is understood not as the result of sin as such but the result of forgetting the original covenant mentioned above. Indeed, in order to make this point some commentators, beginning with the so-called 'father of exegesis', Ibn Abbas (687), have derived the word for humanity, *al-nas* not from its etymologically sound root *uns* ('conviviality') but as homily from *nasiya* 'forgetfulness'.[30] And just as Islam acknowledges a Fall without original sin, there seems also to be a Creation without previous chaos. According to Islam, chaos lurks beneath the surface of civilisation and is actually always a threat, even though historically the *jahiliyya* period is given a specific date. Such historicisation would seem to be more for convenient reference to remind the believer of the true character of *jahl* so that it may be recognised and resisted whenever it is encountered.

> [J]āhilīyah was conceived by Muhammad and his companions not as a period of time that had now passed away, but rather as something dynamic, a certain psychological state apparently driven away by the new force of Islam, but surviving secretly in the minds of the believers, ready to break in at any moment upon their consciousness; and that this was felt by the Prophet to be a standing menace to the new religion.[31]

Islam thus means, in addition to 'submission', order, self-discipline and enlightenment in the context of its own chronotope, where it sees itself as ringed round by chaos, temporally (the historic *age of ignorance*), spatially (the medieval *abode of war*), and existentially (*jahiliyya* as a constant inner pressure). Islam as such emerges as a refuge of order and meaning, precisely an *abode of refuge* (*dar al-hijra*). In this refuge, symmetry and morality reflect the oneness of God. In the community, the *umma*, social and political justice and equity (of the type delineated, for example, in the Constitution of Medina) also reflect divine oneness. So, it emerges that another possible synonym for *jahl* is the unforgivable sin mentioned above, *shirk* 'polytheism'. As the opposite of *islam* and tawhid there can be no doubt that these two key words from the Quran bespeak a chaos that is more dangerous and threatening than the cosmogonic void of *tohubohu*; dangerous because it threatens to break through at all times and, it would seem, is not the sole responsibility of the merciful God who speaks through the Quran. Perhaps the single most eloquent argument or statement against chaos, nihilism, meaninglessness, vanity and emptiness (for which a frequent Quranic term is *batil* – the diametric opposite of the Quranic term for truth or reality in the highest possible degree, *al-haqq*)[32] is the theory of signs found in those several verses thought of as elaborating and constituting a distinctive Quranic theme. The most frequently quoted is the one in which it is made clear in no uncertain terms that human consciousness is 'imprisoned' in a cosmos of meaning from which there can be no escape. The key term here, *aya*, singular (*ay/ayat*, plural), is also the distinctive term by which a Quranic verse is known (verses of 'mere' poetry are called *bayt/abyat*). It is equivalent to the Hebrew *oth,* and the Aramaic and Syriac *atha*. In the Quran and Islamic usage it should be further nuanced as 'miraculous sign', 'portent', or perhaps even 'meaning event'.[33] As such, the term may have something in common with the *semeia* of the Gospel of John.[34] In any case, it has provided countless generations of Muslim intellectuals with guidance, confirmation and inspiration in their attempts to reconcile the twin sources of knowledge recognised by their tradition: revelation and reason. The verse runs as follows:

> We shall show them Our signs in every region of the earth and in themselves, until it becomes clear to them that this is the Truth. (Q41:53)

Thus the entire creation is a cosmos of order, beauty and, most importantly, meaning. Each created thing (and all 'things' – *ashya'* – are by definition created) is a 'sign', a meaning event. Such signs appear in every region (*fi 'l-afaq*, lit: 'in the horizons', 'in the external realm', 'in the macrocosm') and in the souls of human beings: 'in themselves' (*fi anfusihim*, lit.: 'in their souls', 'in the interior realm', 'in the microcosm' or 'among themselves'). All of these various occasions or events of meaning are to be understood by the aid of those textual 'signs' of the Quran, the divine verses themselves. According to the Quran, it was not a cosmogonic creation of a perfect world out of primordial chaos that is responsible for such order, rather it is the birth of consciousness identified with the Day of the Covenant mentioned above. The difference between *jahl* and *islam,* savagery and civilisation, chaos and order is determined by the ability to read aright the signs of God wherever they may be encountered, and they are encountered everywhere.

Is this an apocalyptic vision? Recent scholarship has advanced the study of apocalypse by refining a definition of the genre. Such refined definitions are based upon the identification of several motives and categories frequently found in such texts. Of the several literary and religious textual features thus isolated and characterised it is important to note that many, if not all, occur in the Quran. Such has implications for the study of Islam and comparative scripture. This research could help to refine our thinking about the relationship between the Quran and an apocalyptic cultural and literary landscape out of which it may have arisen. These striking literary qualities are what seem to set the Quran text apart from other scriptures. Simultaneously, they also provide evidence for the ebbing of an apocalyptic imagination. Such a study helps us approach the question, using terminology from other traditions, of how in Islam heresy became orthodoxy. The apocalyptic themes so prominent in the Quran are, during the classical age, pressed into the service of dividing the world into two mutually exclusive domains: the so-called *dar al-islam*, 'the abode of Islam' and the *dar al-harb*, 'the abode of strife'. It is difficult not to associate these two categories with the parallel notions of cosmos and chaos.

Chapter 7

Joycean Modernism in
Quran and Tafsir

We are the first generation in the West able to read the Koran, if we
are able to read *Finnegans Wake*.
　　　　　Norman O. Brown, *Apocalypse and/or Metamorphisis*[1]

INTRODUCTION

Numerous structural, thematic and reception parallels exist
between two otherwise quite incommensurable literary
works. The one is James Joyce's well-known, controversial
and vastly influential *Ulysses*, generally considered the first major work
of the modernist movement in European literature. The second, entitled
Qayyum al-asma',[2] is the virtually unknown, unpublished and unread
yet highly distinctive and unusual commentary on the twelfth sura
of the Quran by the Iranian prophet Seyyed Ali Mohammad Shirazi
(1819–50), better known to history as the *Báb*, an Arabic word meaning
'gate' or 'door'. By suggesting the existence of parallels and similarities
between these two works it is not also suggested that there is any sort
of connection between them or their authors, genetic, social, historical or otherwise. But, both wrote at specific and intense moments of
cultural crisis and change in their respective socio-historical situations.
And each was profoundly and acutely aware of the particular centrality
of the literary tradition in which they wrote and the literary weight of

the sources and models for their respective compositions. In the case of Joyce and *Ulysses*, the weight and authority of this literary history is represented by *The Odyssey* and Joyce's appropriation (and simultaneous celebration and critique) of the epic tradition, through his rewriting of the Homeric epic. In the case of the Bab and his *Qayyum al-asma'*, the quite considerable and truly unique weight and authority of his tradition is represented by the Quran, on which this ostensibly exegetical work is modelled.[3] In actuality, with this composition, which is better thought of as being in the cloak of exegesis, the Bab is claiming the same authorial independence and originality claimed by the Quran itself. The adoption of the similarly monumental and sacrosanct genre of scriptural exegesis (*tafsir*) for this disguise is only a little less daring than the Quran imitation that it 'hides'. Our author, a merchant by profession and milieu, came from outside the typical learned class and was indeed unschooled in the Islamic sciences according to prevailing standards. He was also only twenty-five years old at the time of writing and would have thus been regarded as far too immature, even were he of the scholarly class, to attempt such a work. The grandiosity and brashness of presuming to compose a new Quran is analogous to Joyce's hubris in rewriting the epic in his *Ulysses*, but actually outstrips it in terms of outrageousness because of the Quran's unique place in Islamic religious scholarship and culture. In both authors their work is simultaneously a literary fiction paying homage to tradition and an authentic occasion for unprecedented – if not shocking – originality. This is the primary structural analogy: both *The Odyssey* and the Quran (and its traditional exegesis) occupy monumental and epic space in their respective cultural contexts, and both will appear to be deeply violated and disfigured by our authors. Such innovative, thoroughgoing and self-conscious imitation and improvisation on these venerable symbols and metonyms of culture had not been previously achieved or attempted to the degree we have in these two works.[4] (See Figures 1 and 2 on p.140 and 144–5.) In what follows, we will give some brief introduction to the generally well-known life and celebrated works of James Joyce, and some necessarily more extended introduction to the much less well-known life and works of the Bab. Then we will focus on a comparison of the two works to illustrate formal and thematic similarities. This comparison will focus on a few major topics: 1) the formal structure of the two works and 2) the thematic concerns of the two works, such as a) time, b) polarities or oppositions and their resolution, c) the relation between form and content, d) the prominence of epiphany, manifestation, advent and apocalypse, e) the theme of heroism, reading and identity.

JAMES JOYCE AND HIS WORK

James Joyce (1882–1941) was born in Dublin, acquired from the Jesuits a thorough education including the classics and theology, excelled as a scholar of modern languages at university, and at the young age of twenty-two left Ireland, more or less for good, in 1904. He is considered *the* father of literary modernism because of his two major books, *Ulysses* and *Finnegans Wake.* Both works represent radical innovations in the art of the novel and changed forever the way literary art was construed and practised. The works were also highly controversial, attracting censorship, ban, derision and condemnation on the grounds of obscenity and general structure and style of which the famous (or infamous) 'stream of consciousness' (perfected by Joyce) was a major feature and which challenged the reader in ways no earlier work of literary art had done. Today, Joyce has been vindicated and recognised as a great literary genius. No less an authority than Northrop Frye deems his *Finnegans Wake* a uniquely powerful example of literary art in our time.[5] The library of Joyce scholarship is massive, with commentaries, concordances, dedicated journals, analyses, appreciations, imitations, criticism and *explications de texte* seemingly without number. During his life he struggled with poverty, ill-health and family crises, and is distinguished by his heroic dedication to his art – which he never abandoned, even momentarily.[6] In the case of the author of the older Arabic work, there is really no reason to believe most readers should have even the barest notion of who he was. In fact, one of the somewhat ironic facts that the present comparison records is that, in the case of *Ulysses*, a daring literary experiment resulted in universal renown (and/or infamy), celebrity and veneration, highly productive literary influence and a continuous tradition of scholarship devoted to the study of Joyce and his works; with the Bab the situation could not be more different.[7]

THE BAB AND HIS WORK

The daring literary experiments of the Bab resulted in the opposite: obscurity, disregard, and ultimate imprisonment and death by firing squad.[8] The literary innovations of the text were not pursued or emulated by later authors because of such extra-literary and extra-artistic factors as the deeply embastioned cultural and religious attitudes towards the Quran as inimitable and final revelation. It will be of some useful interest to provide a very brief outline of this author's life and career before continuing further with the more purely literary comparison of the two works, *Ulysses* and the *Qayyum al-asma*'. 'The Bab' is an Anglicisation of the Arabic *al-bab*, the usual word for 'door' or 'gate' in that language. In the present instance, it functions as a title with a very long history, especially in Shi'i Islamic religious literature. The general understanding is that the word designates one who represents the twelfth or hidden imam of *Ithna-'ashari* (so-called Twelver) Shi'ism, even though it is clear that the word has frequently indicated statuses other than mere representative to suggest the imam and the Prophet himself. It is also true that in the Islamic philosophical tradition the intellect was frequently termed 'the gate' (to knowledge).[9]

The Bab was born in Shiraz in 1819 into a family of merchants. His precocity and piety caused remark and anxiety among his family, and teachers were challenged by his intellect and originality. The time, according to Shi'i sacred history, was propitious and pregnant with eschatological event, it being one thousand years since the disappearance of the long-awaited hidden imam. In his early twenties, the Bab abandoned the life of a merchant to join the circle of a prominent millenarian teacher based in the holy shrine cities of Iraq. This teacher, Seyyed Kazem Rashti (1793–1843), was a learned Persian mulla and mujtahid, and successor to the Arab polymath, philosophical theologian and mujtahid Shaykh Ahmad al-Ahsa'i (1753–1826). These two teachers had, on the brink of the Twelver Shi'i eschaton, attracted a large following especially of young seminarians, because of their creative and compelling interpretation of the standard topics of Shi'ism, including the idea of the return of the hidden imam, the imminent resurrection and Day of Judgment (*qiyama*), or rising of the Qa'im who, as Mahdi ('rightly guided one'), would lead an army of spiritual warriors against the forces of darkness at the end of time. This following, which burgeoned throughout Iran during the middle half of the nineteenth century, came to be known as the *Shaykhiyya* – 'the Shaykhis' – an eponymous reference to the above-mentioned Shaykh Ahmad al-Ahsa'i. The main thrust of the eschatological teaching of the first two masters of the Shaykhi School was that while the return of the hidden imam is assured, the end of time and creation is not. Rather, what ends is a cycle of prophecy that will be replaced by a new cycle of fulfilment.[10] They furnished a vocabulary and method for thinking about and perhaps domesticating the potentially unruly and mysterious forces that were gathering at the time and would issue in profound social and historical change. In short, they provided a discourse for the emergence of a distinctive Qajar modernity from its traditional past.[11] There was also much about the form and content of the Shaykhi doctrine that appealed to an Iranian audience; not least, was the way in which the masters of the school combined the mystical with the rational in the interest of solving the many supra-rational problems confronting Shi'i religion. In addition, the prolific writings of the first two teachers are characterised by a strong literary and poetic aesthetic very much in keeping with the general élan of Islamicate scholarship in which style is as important as substance. In the case of the Shaykhis, their technical terminology, deriving from the broader Islamic philosophical and mystical tradition, is at times transmuted into a kind of poetry of metaphysics. Thus, one may also be justified in thinking of it as a liter-ary movement as well as a theological movement in which theological connections and resonances have literary *value* and literary connec-tions and resonances have theological *implications*. Such a movement and such a discourse was evidently irresistible for our author, Seyyed Ali Mohammad Shirazi, soon to become known as the Bab. And he, accordingly, abandoned his career as a merchant to study at the feet of Seyyed Kazem Rashti. At the time of composition of the work at hand, his beloved teacher had recently died and his followers were left to search or wait for the realisation of the Shi'i eschaton: the return of the hidden imam, the promulgation of the true Quran, the establishment of justice throughout the world through the defeat of the forces of dark-ness and the establishment of the rule of the Mahdi. At the time, this doctrine had generated numerous interpretations and was teeming with a variety of possibilities including 1) the appearance of a general age of enlightenment, as distinct from 2) the actual triumph of an individual messianic figure, or 3) a combination of both.[12]

COMPOSITION OF THE *QAYYUM AL-ASMA'*

We have precise, if enchanting, details of how the Bab came to compose his revelatory exegesis, the *Qayyum al-asma'*. As these circumstances are inseparable from the resulting literary form of the work, it is important briefly to relate them. The actual composition began during a meeting with one of the senior students of the recently deceased Kazem Rashti, the young and talented mulla, Hoseyn Boshru'i (1813–49). Upon the death of Rashti, he, together with a few companions, set out from Karbala in quest of the long-awaited advent: the manifestation of the hidden imam and the beginning of the new cycle of fulfilment. Their search had taken them to Shiraz where Boshru'i encountered the young merchant, Ali Mohammad (the Bab), whom he had apparently known from his Karbala sojourn. The year was 1844 and our author was twenty-five years old. He invited Mulla Hoseyn to his home and there, in discussions about how the hidden imam was to be identified, the Bab is said to have suggested that he himself could be the promised one as he fulfiled many of the descriptions outlined in the traditions. Mulla Hoseyn, nonplussed by what he took as unwonted arrogance and perhaps thinking to quench the impudent and impertinent messianic pretensions of his host, remembered that their teacher, Seyyed Kazem Rashti, had added to the list of requirements and physical attributes that would identify the promised one another more purely literary requirement: the promised one would compose a commentary of the Quran's sura of Joseph. At this point, so the story goes, the Bab, apropos of apparently nothing, announced that it was now time for him to reveal the commentary on the sura of Joseph and then proceeded to write the first of the 111 chapters of this highly unusual work, the *Surat al-mulk*, the Chapter of Divine Dominion or Ownership.[13] So important is this literary event in the mind of the author, its date is fixed in Babi and Baha'i scripture: 22 May 1844, corresponding to the early evening of the Islamic date 5 Jumada I 1260, almost exactly one thousand (lunar) years since the assumption of the imamate by the 'hidden' twelfth imam, Muhammad ibn al-Hasan al-Askari in the year 874. In addition, the actual astro-chronological moment for the beginning of the new cycle is fixed by the Bab, in a later work, at two hours and eleven minutes after sunset on that date.[14] Amanat is doubtless correct when he suggests that this striking precision in timing the beginning of the long-awaited resurrection, the Day of Judgment, represents the moment when Mulla Hoseyn assented to the Bab's claim.[15]

The author of the completed commentary, which he tells us was composed over a forty-day period, eventually attracted a large and active messianic following, known to Iranian religious history as the Babi religion. Announcing that with these new revelations the new cycle of fulfilment had been inaugurated and the *qiyama*, the resurrection and Day of Judgment, were now in play, it was now necessary to recognise the Bab as the source and focus of all religious authority, the word for which in Islamic theological terminology is *walaya/wilaya* (Persian *valayat/velayat*). His mission would last nearly six years until he was executed in Tabriz for blasphemy and heresy on 9 July 1850. The remnants of his movement eventually formed the Baha'i religion in which followers saw the fulfilment of prophecies found in the remarkably voluminous writings of the Bab. These writings may be briefly summarised as an attempt to reorient and recast the sacerdotal and political hierarchical authority in the social imagination of Shi'i Iran in which the main elements were: the Prophet and the imams (including Fatima, the daughter of Muhammad and wife of the first imam Ali); the royal family, the Qajars, their retainers and officials; the religious estate, comprising the classically educated religious classes, and others, unevenly divided between scripturalists and rationalists; and of course the general population of believers, the Shi'i community.[16]

An attempt to clarify lines of authority in a culture, it has been suggested, is also intimately related to the perennial problem of and quest for identity, which presents a single and powerful literary theme in world literature and one of the main themes of the epic genre as such.[17] The writings of the Bab may be thought an attempt to provide orientation in a highly turbulent period during which standard and traditional notions of identity, authority and allegiance were in flux and were being debated in various quarters throughout Iranian society, from the very highest levels of courtly life, to the religious seminaries, to the bazaar and its environs. Another similar attempt may be discerned in the decisive developments at this time in understanding the 'sacerdotal' office of universal authority for the Shi'i community, the *marja' al-taqlid* (authoritative exemplar), closely related to what came to be known after the Second World War as the office of Grand Ayatollah, a relatively recent religious innovation.[18] However much the literary activities of the Bab were fraught with profound and dramatic religious and theological implications, in the present somewhat experimental exploration, I am studying the Bab's writings from the point of view of artistic and literary considerations. Although it was thought important to provide some theological background as context, in what follows, I will, as much as possible, avoid theological and religious questions, even though there is an obvious deep connection between the artistic/aesthetic and the religious in Islamicate culture in general, Iranian Islamic culture more specifically, and the life and the work of the Bab himself as heir to these cultural realities and predispositions. In the case of the Bab, the seamless interplay between the artistic/aesthetic and what might be thought the more purely 'religious' dimensions of his life and ministry has been noted from the very beginning.[19]

FORM AND STRUCTURE OF THE *QAYYUM AL-ASMA'* AND *ULYSSES*

The form and structure of both works suggests a veneration or sacralisation of the past and a simultaneous desire to replace the old with the new. The following tables illustrate to some degree the way in which each work is structured by its author to represent a reworking of two culturally central texts, *The Odyssey* and the Quran. And because these structures are themselves so symbolically meaningful, their adoption has implications for thematic and narrative content.

Joyce himself made two different tables illustrating the close relationship between his *Ulysses* and *The Odyssey*.[20] The chart on the next page was prepared in 1921 for his friend Stuart Gilbert and demonstrates how Joyce simultaneously took great liberties with and venerated *The Odyssey*, rearranged it and recast its stories and myths, which in the original take place over a twenty-year period (a generation), in order to fit it all within a single day in the life of Dublin: 16 June 1904.[21] Further, the events and narrative flow of Joyce's epic are, according to his schema, intricately coordinated with numerous other factors and elements. Thus, the first episode, not marked off in the actual published novel, may be identified with Telemachus, the name of Odysseus' son who searches for his father and awaits his return back home in Ithaca. There is in *Ulysses* a correspondence between this and the opening scene and the time of day. Joyce also assigns to this episode a

Joyce's own diagram of the structural and thematic correspondences between *Ulysses* and *The Odyssey* (this example is transcribed from Wikipedia: http//en.wikipedia.org/wiki/Gilbert_schema_for Ulysses)

TITLE	SCENE	HOUR	ORGAN	COLOUR	SYMBOL	ART	TECHNIC
Telemachus	The Tower	8am	–	White / gold	Heir	Theology	Narrative (young)
Nestor	The School	10am	–	Brown	Horse	History	Catechism (personal)
Proteus	The Strand	11am	–	Green	Tide	Philology	Monologue (male)
Calypso	The House	8am	Kidney	Orange	Nymph	Economics	Narrative (mature)
Lotus Eaters	The Bath	10am	Genitals	–	Eucharist	Botany / chemistry	Narcissism
Hades	The Graveyard	11am	Heart	White / black	Caretaker	Religion	Incubism
Aeolus	The Newspaper	12pm	Lungs	Red	Editor	Rhetoric	Enthymemic
Lestrygonians	The Lunch	1pm	Oesophagus	–	Constables	Architecture	Peristaltic
Scylla and Charybdis	The Library	2pm	Brain	–	Stratford / London	Literature	Dialectic
Wandering Rocks	The Streets	3pm	Blood	–	Citizens	Mechanics	Labyrinth
Sirens	The Concert Room	4pm	Ear	–	Barmaids	Music	*Fuga per canonem*
Cyclops	The Tavern	5pm	Muscle	–	Fenian	Politics	Gigantism
Nausicaa	The Rocks	8pm	Eye, nose	Grey / blue	Virgin	Painting	Tumescence / detumescence
Oxen of the Sun	The Hospital	10pm	Womb	White	Mothers	Medicine	Embryonic development
Circe	The Brothel	12pm	Locomotor apparatus	–	Whore	Magic	Hallucination
Eumaeus	The Shelter	1am	Nerves	–	Sailors	Navigation	Narrative (old)
Ithaca	The House	2am	Skeleton	–	Comets	Science	Catechism (impersonal)
Penelope	The Bed	–	Flesh	–	Earth	–	Monologue (female)

particular colour and science or art (theology) and literary technique (narrative). Each of the following seventeen sections of the novel is similarly structured. Thus, the famous, if not notorious, Joycean stream of consciousness disguises an almost unbelievably and meticulously structured work of art. But apart from this, we may discern in this vast system of connections, correspondences and resonances what might be thought – and surprisingly in this modernist literary experiment – a somewhat medieval certitude about the essential meaningfulness and interconnectedness of life, the kind of sanguine certitude that such totalising devices as 'The Great Chain of Being' or 'The Diapason' bespeak.[22] In sum, Joyce takes great liberties with *The Odyssey* while at the same time remaining faithful to it. Such has been characterised as Joyce's 'art of mediation', an art that seeks to negotiate the space between two apparently diametrically opposed elements, in this case the opposites are innovation and tradition.[23]

The interplay between tradition and the new is also the main focus of the Bab's *Qayyum al-asma'*, whether from the point of view of structure or content. That we find a similar web of correspondences in the Bab's work is, perhaps, to be expected given the medieval ontological and mystical presuppositions of his tradition and his audience. So we see in his writing a vast grid of correspondences (even if a complete table illustrating them has yet to be made), in which climates, prophets, heavenly spheres, colours, hierarchical levels of being, types of individuals and so on, provide both the flesh and the skeleton of his compositions.[24] For example, many of these compositions exploit to a very high degree the traditional *abjad* system of numerology, in which every word has a numerical value to be read and considered in a given context.[25] If we remain at the level of literature in comparing both compositions we see that they embody to an astonishing degree a great deal of exquisitely and intricately designed literary 'hanging together', much of which has to do with the relationship of their respective works to their monumental and epic exemplars. In Joyce's case this model is *The Odyssey*. In the Bab's case, it is the Quran.[26]

THE SACRAMENTAL DAY

The Bab, like Joyce, goes to great lengths to innovate and improvise while also preserving and honouring the sanctity of tradition. In this, one could also refer to his art as the 'art of mediation'. The central narrative at the core of the Bab's work, the story of Joseph son of Jacob, is the epic quest of a son for his father and a father for his son after separation. The structure of the work, which is divided into suras (chapters) and ayas (verses), is explicitly patterned on the Quran, a feature many would, did and do consider shocking and heretical.[27] At the same time, it is clear that the Bab is also concerned with a single day, that day outside time and space when all humanity – 'Adam's children' – were gathered in God's presence. This is the day referred to at Q7:172 and known to the Islamic tradition as the Day of the Covenant. In mythic terms, it symbolises for the Islamic tradition the birth of both consciousness and history.[28] In Quranic terms, it is the essential prelude for the crea- tion of the world as told, for example, in the biblical book of Genesis. Evidence of the Bab's deep concern for this mythic event is woven into the very structure of his composition, through versification (explained below) and in innumerable explicit textual references. The covenant and its renewal is the central concern of the work because it supplies a sacred paradigm for the Josephian theme of separation and reunion through the cyclicism mentioned earlier. For the moment, suffice it to remark that the Day of the Covenant involves also another day, the Day of Judgment. According to the Quran, all humanity was gathered in the presence of God on the Day of the Covenant at a time and place before actual creation so that they would have no excuse on the Day of Judgment for not having obeyed God and his prophets. It is clear that the *Qayyum al-asma'* is also a new rendition or performance of the Day of the Covenant.[29] When Mulla Hoseyn Boshru'i accepted the claims of the Bab, the momentousness of the act was enshrined in its exact time being recorded in the Bab's later book of laws, the *Persian Bayan*. Such momentousness resides in its making present the drama of the original primordial covenant mentioned in the Quran. Here the Bab, from the literary (metaphorical) perspective is God – or more accurately the face or aspect of God (*wajh allah*) and Mulla Hoseyn – is Adam/Muhammad. And to the degree that the work is concerned with the journey between affirmation of the covenant and judgment it may be thought to assume a circular form where the two ends of the composition are indicated in each other. This is of course one of the more prominent features of Joyce's *Finnegans Wake*: its end is its beginning and its beginning is its end, what Joyce calls 'Doublends Jined' (*FW* 20).[30] Such points to the multilayered meaning of the title: revelation/awareness, resurrection (*Wake*), cyclical repetition (Man [*finn*] again), and the concomitant circular nature of history, the wake of human activity. Such continuity and stability as is represented in this totalising design, whether of the *Qayyum al-asma'* or *Ulysses*, seems to offer solace and assurance for chaotic times, in the promise of a new day that is simultaneously and mysteriously ancient. For Joyce's day, we have a compression of thousands of days (the twenty years of the original *Odyssey*) into a single twenty-four-hour period. In the case of the Bab's day, it is the opposite. Rather than a compression of time, here we have an expansion of a single moment, an expansion that fills all time and history. In musical terms, it may be thought of as the melismatic cantillation of an originary act, suffusing all subsequent ages and generations through verses, words and syllables, as when God merely says to a thing 'Be!' and it is (Q6:73; 19:35; 36:82; 40:68). The original and originating power of that mysterious and momentous day (or moment) of the covenant represented by the word *bala* – Yes! – is intoned by all created things by virtue of their having been created. The power is somehow felt to be circulating through all time, uniting it in a single transcendent moment. Thus, the considerable spiritual energy of the myth of the Day of the Covenant is joined with that of the day of resurrection and represents a perfect fusion of epic and apocalypse and is, of course, more than a mere literary trope. The Quranic revelation continuously calls upon believers to remember or call to mind, the Day of the Covenant. This is the practice instituted in Sufism known as *dhikr* (Persian *zekr*).[31] In this way also the original (and originating) moment is present in every other ensuing moment.[32] One of the many important titles by which the Bab refers to himself in this work is precisely '*the* Remembrance' (*al-dhikr*) – embodiment or personification of the spirit of the Day of the Covenant. Both the Bab and Joyce offer an implicit commentary on and radical interpretation of the idea of time and history in relation to the nature of consciousness. They demonstrate in their respective works the subjectivity, malleability, and shape-shifting quality of time and what the otherwise commonplace notion 'day' can possibly mean. For both authors, the extraordinary enchanted quality of the epiphany is in contrast to the humdrum and mundane occasion of its

A provisional Table of Contents for the Bab's *Qayyum al-asma'* the *Tafsir surat Yusuf*. The first column shows the sura (chapter) number, the second the title of the sura and the third shows the mysterious disconnected

#	Sura	Disconnected Letters	#	Sura	Disconnected Letters	#	Sura	Disconnected Letters
1	al-Mulk	none	41	al-Kitāb	K-H-Y-ʿ-Ṣ	81	al-Kāf	A-L-M-B-ʿ
2	al-ʿUlamāʾ	A-L-M	42	al-ʿAhd	A-L-M-R-A	82	al-Aʿẓam	A-L-M-Ḥ
3	al-Imān	Ṭ-H	43	al-Wāḥid	A-L-M-ʿ	83	al-Bāʾ	A-L-M-F
4	al-Madina	A-L-M-Ṭ-H	44	al-Ruʾyā	Ṭ-M-R-A	84	al-Ism	A-L-M-R-A
5	Yūsuf	A-L-M-ʿ	45	Huwa	K-H-Y-ʿ-Ṣ	85	al-Ḥaqq	A-L-M-Ṭ
6	al-Shahāda	A-L-M-S	46	al-Mirʾāt	Ṭ-H	86	al-Ṭayr	A-L-R-A
7	al-Ziyāra	Ṭ-S	47	al-Ḥujja	A-L-M-ʿ-Ṣ-R-A	87	al-Nabaʾ	A-L-R-A
8	al-Sirr	A-L-M-Ṣ	48	al-Nidāʾ	A-L-H-L	88	al-Iblāgh	A-L-M-Ṣ-ʿ
9	al-ʿAmāʾ (i)	A-L-M-N	49	al-Aḥkām (i)	Ṭ-H	89	al-Insān (ii)	A-L-M
10	al-ʿAmāʾ (ii)	A-L-M-Gh	50	al-Aḥkām (ii)	A-L-M-Ṣ	90	al-Tathlīth	A-L-M-ʿ-Ṣ
11	al-Musaṭṭar	Ṭ-H-ʿ	51	al-Majd	Ṭ-H	91	al-Tarbiʿ	A-L-M-R
12	al-ʿĀshūrāʾ	K-S-N	52	al-Faḍl	none	92	al-Mujallal	A-L-M-ʿ-Ṣ
13	al-Firdaws	Ṭ-H-M	53	al-Ṣabr	K-H-M	93	al-Naḥl	K-H-M-ʿ
14	al-Quds	A-L-M-Ṭ	54	al-Ghulām	A-L-M-ʿ-Ṣ	94	al-Ishhār	A-L-M-R-A
15	al-Mashiyya	Ṭ-H-Ṣ	55	al-Rukn	K-H-ʿ-Gh	95	no title	Ṭ-B-ʿ
16	al-ʿArsh	A-L-M-Q	56	al-Amr	Ḥ-M-R-A	96	al-Qitāl (i)	A-L-M-Ṣ
17	al-Bāb	A-L-M-ʿ-R-A	57	al-Akbar	Ḥ-M-R-A	97	al-Qitāl (ii)	A-L-M-S
18	al-Ṣirāṭ	K-H-Y-ʿ-S	58	al-Ḥuzn	A-L-H-L	98	al-Jihād (i)	A-L-M-ʿ-Q
19	al-Saynāʾ	A-L-M-R-A	59	al-Afida	K-H-ʿ-Ṣ	99	al-Jihād (ii)	A-L-M-R-A

letters chosen to head the sura. I am grateful to Dr Omid Ghaemmaghami for assistance in preparing this table. An Arabic version is included as an appendix.

No.	Name	Letters
100	al-Jihād (iii)	A-L-M-ʿ-H-L
101	al-Qitāl (iii)	A-L-M
102	al-Qitāl (iv)	K-H-Y-ʿ-Ṣ
103	al-Ḥajj	A-L-M-ʿ
104	al-Ḥudūd	Ṭ-H
105	al-Aḥkām (iii)	A-L-M-ʿ-R-A
106	al-Jumʿa	A-L-M-Ṣ
107	al-Nikāḥ	A-L-M-Ḥ
108	al-Dhikr (ii)	ʿ-L-Y
109	al-ʿAbd	M-Ḥ-M-D
110	al-Sābiqīn	A-L-M-Ṭ-ʿ
111	al-Muʾminīn	A-L-M

No.	Name	Letters
60	al-Dhikr (i)	Ṭ-H-Ṣ
61	al-Ḥusayn	K-H-N
62	al-Awliyāʾ	K-H-Y-L
63	al-Raḥma	Ṭ-N
64	al-Muḥammad	none
65	al-Ghayb	A-L-M-Q
66	al-Aḥadiyya	A-L-M-Ṣ-R
67	al-Inshāʾ	none
68	al-Raʿd	A-L-M-Ṣ
69	al-Rajʿ	K-H-Y-ʿ-Ṣ
70	al-Qisṭ	A-L-M-R-A
71	al-Qalam	A-L-M-Ṣ
72	al-Baʿīr	A-L-M-ʿ
73	al-Kahf	A-L-M
74	al-Khalīl	none
75	al-Shams	A-L-M-R-A
76	al-Waraqa	Ḥ-M-R-A
77	al-Salām	A-L-M-Ṭ-S
78	al-Ẓuhūr	A-L-M-ʿ-S
79	al-Kalima	A-L-M-Ṭ
80	al-Zawāl	K-H-Y-ʿ-Ṣ

No.	Name	Letters
20	al-Nūr	A-L-M-Y
21	al-Baḥr	A-L-M-Ṣ
22	al-Māʾ	T-Ẓ-L
23	al-ʿAṣr	A-L-ʿ-M
24	al-Qadr	A-L-M-Ṣ
25	al-Khātam	A-L-M-ʿ-S
26	al-Ḥall	A-L-R-A
27	al-Anwār	A-L-M-Q
28	al-Qarāba	A-L-M
29	al-Ḥūriyya	K-H-Y-ʿ
30	al-Tablīgh	A-L-M-ʿ
31	al-ʿIzz	A-L-M-Ḥ
32	al-Ḥayy	K-H-Y-ʿ-Q
33	al-Naṣr	A-L-M-H-Ṣ
34	al-Ishāra	Ḥ-M-R-A
35	al-ʿUbūdiyya	A-L-M
36	al-ʿAdl	Ṭ-H
37	al-Taʿbīr	F-ʿ-S-N
38	al-Fāṭima	Ṭ-H
39	al-Shukr	A-L-M-R-A
40	al-Insān (i)	Ṭ-H

occurrence.[33] Both the *Qayyum al-asma'* and *Ulysses* in some ways turn time into a literary trope, or, express concern with the unity and literary significance of time in interesting and innovative ways, demonstrating that both authors seem intrigued by the recurrence of character types and cycles in the wake of which normal historical and chronological time becomes transmuted into something approaching sacrament.

Ulysses came at a time in the history of the English novel when traditional notions of literature and authorial vocation were in flux. The Babi movement also arose during a transition period in which the nature of orthodoxy and religious authority was being negotiated. In the first case we use the term modernism as signal and 'symptom' of the change.[34] The Bab and his audience used the word *qiyama*: resurrection and judgment (Persian *rastakhiz*). The Bab takes even greater liberties with the Quran than Joyce did with *The Odyssey* in composing this new work, one that he explicitly presented as an emblem of the arrival of the resurrection, namely the true Quran that had been in the safekeeping of the hidden imam during his occultation.[35] The tables above give some indication of the Bab's iconoclastic desire to compose a 'new Quran'. Note here the pervasive use of the uniquely Quranic literary device of the mysterious disconnected letters (*al-huruf al-muqatta'at*) that appear in various combinations at the beginning of 29 of the 114 suras of the Quran.[36] As can be seen, in the Bab's composition the disconnected letters are used in all but four of his new suras, that is, in almost all 111 of them.[37] We will return to some of the other ways in which the Bab's work imitates the Quran and in some senses 'out-Qurans' the actual Quran. Suffice it to say, that the implications of such an unprecedented outrage were not lost on his contemporaries. Even during the Bab's lifetime, a combined Sunni and Shi'i court of Islamic jurists was convened in Baghdad to deliberate on the legality of the provocative composition. Their joint fatwa condemning the author of the *Qayyum al-asma'* for composing an imitation of the holy Quran demonstrates how a contemporary audience would be scandalised by such a daring and shocking literary event.[38] As is well known, Joyce's work was repeatedly challenged in the courts, most frequently for obscenity. While there is nothing that could be construed as obscenity in the Bab's composition, the religious scandal his writings provoked was, in the context of this cross-cultural comparison, analogous in the intensity of the outrage it provoked.

EPIC, MONOMYTH AND EPIPHANY

Both artists rethink and reconstrue their respective 'monomyths' – a word coined by Joyce in *Finnegans Wake* as a near synonym for the epic telling of collective humanity's genealogical, historical and mythic experience. Joyce wants us to understand the epic dignity and value of the mere quotidian: the grand interconnectedness of the ordinary. The Bab wants us to understand something similar, but in reverse, if you will. All time and history is a perpetual and continuous performance of a single day, the Day of the Covenant. In both Joyce and the Bab, the idea of the day acquires a distinctive sacramental value: the day looms as a central integer and quantum of experience, revelation/epiphany and being.

The epic, whether Homeric or Quranic, seeks, among other things, to demonstrate or imitate the interconnectedness and therefore meaningfulness of experience, consciousness and history. Such interconnectedness may be thought a given of the Bab's religious perspective. Joyce, forging a new understanding of the existential and psychological realm, has Stephen contemplate 'the ineluctable modality of the visible', the realm in which Stephen is called upon to read 'the signatures of all things'.[39] The implication is, of course, that there is much else besides the visible and the sensible to which this visible is somehow connected, even if it is only connection itself. And, we know that much more than connection itself is indicated, namely the great unseen and unknown inner world of the psyche or soul to which access is gained precisely through the epiphany and which would remain incompletely known without it.[40] Such an attitude towards the natural, visible world has a great deal in common with the Bab's logocentric universe, where the true believer is really a true reader who has been charged with reading and contemplating the 'signs of God' that have, according to Islamic teaching, been placed in the Quran, the physical universe and the souls of human beings:

> We shall show them Our signs in the horizons and in themselves,
> till it is clear to them that it is the truth. (Q41:53 Arberry)

Creation, whether divine or artistic, has profound literary implications. The Bab wishes to emphasise the interconnectedness of being-as-such (*wujud*) symbolised by the central notion of spiritual and worldly authority (*walaya*) that circulates through these three distinct 'modalities': the readable book, the visible cosmos and the invisible soul. *Walaya*, the word for this authority, has a special charisma as the all-important Quranic divine attribute which stands for religious (and, for that matter, secular) authority, allegiance, guardianship, friendship, intimacy, sanctity, love and being. Here, the Bab, like Joyce, wishes to read 'the signatures of all things'. The Prophet Muhammad and the imams were bearers of this divine quality and as such are the sources of all authority in the cosmos (which was, in fact, created for them), whether construed as secular and political or spiritual and religious. The Bab, as representative of the hidden imam, would also be a bearer of this authority. Joyce's profoundly creative authorial licence may be considered something of an analogue. Ultimately, *walaya* may be understood as a metaphor for consciousness itself: that through which all things are connected and thus endowed with or acquire meaning. Recall that it is really *walaya*, God's guardianship, that is set in play on the mythic Day of the Covenant described at Q7:172. As 'divine friendship', the notion is pre-eminently participatory and renders even the most ordinary thing or event holy or sacred through a distinctly Islamicate version of communion.[41]

Coincidentia Oppositorum

Both Joyce and the Bab may be thought, therefore, to explore the possibilities of what is sometimes referred to these days as an enchanted reality. Nowhere is concern for such enchantment more palpable than in the way both authors contemplate and demonstrate the essential fundamental unity or resolution of oppositions – the *coincidentia oppositorum* of the Scholastics, including the alchemists.[42] This ancient philosophical theme has enjoyed a similar life in both Christian European and Islamic Middle Eastern thought where it is frequently encountered in writers of a more mystical orientation. More than any other conceit or trope, it speaks of the paradoxical nature of reality and calls into question such manmade notions as 'good' and 'evil', 'justice' and 'tyranny'. This is the apperception behind Blake's 'fearful symmetry'. As a frequent feature of paradox, the *coincidentia oppositorum* has, as it were, one foot in the realm of philosophy and theology and one foot in poetics and the art of literature. There is an ongoing debate in Joyce Studies, as to which preponderates in his thought and work. One argument suggests that he took the idea from Bruno's theological work and adapted it to a more or less purely literary usage.[43] Others suggest that Joyce's interest in and use of the *coincidentia oppositorum* goes deeper than this, that it indicates a faith that true knowledge rises above such 'logical entanglements' as result from a slavish devotion to the epistemic value of such notions as saved and damned, heaven and hell, up and down, here and there, past and present, day and night and so on. Joyce's interest in the 'figure' has been studied with regard to the final chapter of *Ulysses*, the Penelope episode.[44] 'Penelope' begins and ends with the word 'yes', emblematic of the circularity of lived experience, the circle being a representation of the resolution of polarities. The resolution of opposites is also evident in the character Molly Bloom whose heroic response 'yes' to the otherwise unjustifiable and perhaps unbearable contradictions and defeats offered by life is the goal to which the entire novel has been travelling on its epic journey. For Joyce, the greatest man in literature was Odysseus whom he had encountered for the first time as a schoolboy through Charles Lamb's retelling of the story.[45] Lamb highlights how Odysseus was saved from Circe by the intervention of the god Hermes/Mercury, who gave him, as a magical protection, the ugly and black-rooted plant with the beautiful white flower (and the instructions how to use it) called, as it happens, *moly*. The entire passage deserves to be quoted:

But neither [Mercury's] words nor his coming from heaven could stop the daring foot of Ulysses, whom compassion for the misfortune of his friends had rendered careless of danger: which when the god perceived, he had pity to see valor so misplaced, and gave him the flower of the herb *moly*, which is sovereign against enchantments. The moly is a small unsightly root, its virtues but little known and in low estimation; the dull shepherd treads on it every day with his clouted shoes; but it bears a small white flower, which is medicinal against charms, blights, mildews, and damps. 'Take this in thy hand,' said Mercury, 'and with it boldly enter her [Circe's] gates; when she shall strike thee with her rod, thinking to change thee, as she has changed thy friends, boldly rush in upon her with thy sword, and extort from her the dreadful oath of the gods, that she will use no enchantments against thee; then force her to restore thy abused companions.' He gave Ulysses the little white flower, and, instructing him how to use it, vanished.[46]

In a recent study of duality in *The Odyssey* (having nothing directly to do with Joyce or Joyce Studies) it has been suggested that the magical power of the *moly* comes from none other than its joining the opposites of mortal and divine, ease and difficulty, black and white, root and flower in its very biological and botanical structure. It was this structure and composition that rendered it a 'saving device' for Odysseus.[47] In short, the magical plant, the *moly*, is a *coincidentia oppositorum*. Molly Bloom is also a *coincidentia oppositorum* and may also be thought to embody a kind of salvific function. She is: Madonna and whore, mother and daughter, good and evil, beautiful and ugly, joyful and sad, tender and scold, dismissive and loving, jealous and faithful; she 'saves' (gives meaning to) the epic of *Ulysses* with her affirmative engagement with life.[48]

Joyce's interest in the *coincidentia oppositorum* as something of a foundation for his personal religious and spiritual vision was, as is well known, deeply influenced by his great admiration for the sixteenth-century heretic Giordano Bruno (1548–1600). It is from the trope or device of the coincidence of opposites that the much-studied Joycean epiphany emerges out of the 'ineluctable modality of the visible (at least that if no more)' (*U* 37). This background is useful for coming to terms with Joyce's highly personal relationship with the numinous, as distinct from his relationship with the Catholic church.[49] It also provides a firm basis upon which to proceed with the comparison of the two otherwise literally incomparable works examined in this essay. This basis is none other than the ontological presuppositions from which and because of which the *coincidentia oppositorum* and its expressive power emerges as both literary trope and philosophical axiom. The coincidence of opposites speaks to the possibility of a noetic experience with creation (viz. epiphany) as the 'device' through which God's presence as immanent in matter is encountered or at least witted. It bespeaks an adamantly non-dualistic view in which 'flesh' is no longer the enemy of 'spirit' but one half of a syzygy that comprehends both and rises above 'logical entanglements'– precisely, Blake's 'fearful symmetry'. And the description of Joyce's epiphanic experience resonates beautifully and harmoniously with the Islamic apophatic mysticism that was the central pillar of the Bab's religious universe in which Absolute Being and Reality were frequently considered synonyms, if not 'improvements', for the word Allah or God vis-à-vis the type of 'entity' those words were meant to indicate.[50] Pointing out that Bruno himself was deeply influenced by the pre-modern 'father of the *coincidentia oppositorum*', Nicholas of Cusa

(1401–64), Voelker quotes from one of Joyce's favourite books about his martyr hero on the topic of Being:

> Knowledge is posterior both in time and in value to Being, or Reality, of which it is at best a copy or sign, hence Reality can never be wholly comprehended by it. Every human assertion is at best a 'conjecture,' a hypothesis or approach to truth, but never the absolute truth itself. Only in the Divine spirit are thought and reality one; the divine thought is at the same time creative, human only reflective, imitative, thus the Ultimate Being is and must remain incomprehensible.[51]

At *U* 782 Molly says 'well who was the first person in the universe before there was anybody that made it all who ah that they dont know neither do I so there you are' – in perfect demonstration of Brunonian apophaticism. Molly is also singled out as expressing most perfectly the metaphysical and poetic implications of this same Brunonian existential monism and its influence on the young Joyce who, in a 1903 review of the then new book on Bruno by Lewis McIntyre, wrote:

> As an independent observer, Bruno . . . deserves high honour. More than Bacon or Descartes must he be considered the father of what is called modern philosophy. His system by turns rationalistic and mystic, theistic and pantheistic is everywhere impressed with his noble mind and critical intellect . . . In his attempt to reconcile the matter and form of the Scholastics . . . Bruno has hardly put forward an hypothesis, which is a curious anticipation of Spinoza . . . It is not Spinoza, it is Bruno, that is the god-intoxicated man. Inwards from the material universe, which, however, did not seem to him, as to the Neoplatonists the kingdom of the soul's malady, or as to the Christians a place of probation, but rather his opportunity for spiritual activity, he passes, and from heroic enthusiasm to enthusiasm to unite himself with God.[52]

Inhabited or possessed by God, the literal translation of the word 'enthusiasm', is the sense one has of Molly in the closing pages of *Ulysses*. The Penelope episode represents a crescendo of the meeting of contraries and contradictions in the person of Molly who was, as it happens, born on the Feast of the Virgin, 8 September.[53] The following underlines what might be thought, for want of a better term, the 'sacramental value' of the *coincidentia oppositorum* in *Ulysses*[54] and its apotheosis in Penelope and the character of Molly who therefore emerges as something of simultaneous (living) martyr saint to and high priestess of Joyce's powerful spiritual or mystico-poetic vision:[55]

> God of heaven theres nothing like nature the wild mountains then the sea and the waves rushing then the beautiful country with the fields of oats and wheat and all kinds of things and all the fine cattle going about that would do your heart good to see rivers and lakes and flowers all sorts of shapes and smells and colours springing up even out of the ditches primroses and violets nature it is as for them saying theres no God I wouldnt give a snap of my two fingers for all their learning why dont they go and create something I often asked him atheists or whatever they call themselves (*U* 781–2)

This passage is revealing on another level. It provides yet another entrée into the comparison between Joyce and the Bab. In Bruno, as in the Quran and the Islamic philosophical tradition, nature is not the opposite of the divine but a vehicle for its expression and encounter. To one familiar with the Quran, a decidedly non-dualistic book,[56] it is impossible to read the above lines without thinking of such verses as:

> Hast thou not seen how that God sends down out of heaven water, and therewith We bring forth fruits of diverse hues? And in the mountains are streaks white and red, of diverse hues, and pitchy black; men too, and beasts and cattle – diverse are their hues. Even so only those of His servants fear God who have knowledge; surely God is All-mighty, All-forgiving. (Q35:27–8; see also, for example Q67:19; Q24:43; Q24:45; Q13:2–4; Q13:13; Q16:48; Q16:68–9)

Such exemplifies a cardinal presupposition of Islam, universally applicable regardless of which Islamic community we are studying, Sunni, Shi'i, Sufi, traditional or modern. This is the theory (or 'doctrine') of signs, briefly detailed above, in which everything other than God is in fact a sign or portent; precisely 'epiphany' of God. This applies to the verses of the Quran, the material universe including nature and its constituents, or to the ideas, thoughts and feelings that compose the interior of the individual. Thus the Quran and eventually, but not exclusively, the mystical philosophers of Islam, such as Ibn Arabi anticipate the theology of Eckhart (1260–1328), Cusanus (1401–64) and Bruno, and such modern spirits as Berdayev (1874–1948).[57]

The Bab was fully at home in and indeed celebrated this deeply mystical and religious existentialism. In addition to the centrality of Q7:172 in the Bab's composition, the above verse (Q41:53), much beloved by the Islamic tradition as a whole, is quoted or alluded to literally hundreds of times in the *Qayyum al-asma'* as well as in other of his works.[58] The two authors, Joyce and the Bab, may have much more in common than thought possible.[59]

CHAOSMIC EPIC AND READER AS HERO

All this seems to suggest that Joyce knew the Quran, and of course this is true, as Atherton, McHugh and Yared have convincingly demonstrated.[60] Whether or not this specific passage is the direct result of such knowledge is not possible to confirm at this time. However, the idea that joining, reconciling or resolving the nearly infinite instances of opposition and duality encountered during mundane lived experience in the sublunary realm provides the modality or occasion for epiphany is one held both by Joyce, as has been demonstrated, and by the Bab, especially in the work at hand, the *Qayyum al-asma'*.[61]

Ulysses emerges as a critique, an interpretation and a typological re-presentation-cum-appropriation of the traditional epic. It is also a representation and critique or commentary on social reality. It is massive, creative, inventive, very rich and difficult to read. The modern world is, in Joyce's word, 'chaosmic'.[62] Neither purely chaos nor cosmos, it is both together and it represents serious problems for the thinking and feeling individual who would like to make sense of it all. The task of making sense of it all, in the case of *Ulysses,* is most definitely left to the reader in much the same way the aware individual must reconcile the oppositions and contradictions of lived experience to perceive the truth of their revelatory message. The relationship between the reader and the text here is a microcosmic example of the relationship between the individual and the world. Apart from the epic tasks of the main characters in *Ulysses* (Leopold Bloom, Stephen Dedalus and Molly Bloom), the work is also an epic that the reader accomplishes through the heroic feat of reading and understanding.[63] In the nineteenth century, the 'outside' third-person narrator was in complete control of everything that went on in the novel. Even if the novel was problematic and difficult and chaotic, the narrator saved us at the end by being in control and solving the problems, answering the questions. Joyce, Virginia Woolf, T. S. Eliot and their 'progeny' say it is not like this any more (if it ever was). And this is a hallmark of modernity and many works of literary modernism.[64] In the end, Joyce, through *Ulysses*, specifically through the voice of Molly Bloom, affirms a hopeful and life-affirming response to the chaotic 'nightmare' of history[65] and modern life with her famous series of twelve yesses that end the novel and which transforms the chaos into not cosmos but 'chaosmos'.[66]

There is also an epic at the centre of the Bab's composition, the Quran.[67] This is the story of God's relationship to humanity from the beginning on the Day of the Covenant, to the end, on the Day of Judgment. The Bab's composition is based on the sura of Joseph, the Quranic model of narrative continuity and coherence as a result of which it is frequently known by its other name: The Best of Stories, a self-descriptive epithet found at Q12:2. The sura of Joseph may be thought the narrative core of the Quran because it sets out the terms of the paradigmatic Quranic 'monomyth' in clear and consecutive detail. By choosing the sura of Joseph, the Bab demonstrates that he is alive to the special place of this sura in the Quran as the best and most complete iteration of the distinctively Islamic monomyth and as simultaneous emblem of the entire Quran: divine revelation.[68] It is not without significance that the story of Joseph, like *Ulysses,* entails a quest of a father for a son and a son for a father. The Bab recast the story to make the audacious and startling observation that the Day of the Covenant – the father, and the Day of Judgment – the son, both occur at the same time in apocalyptic reunion and renewal. Here we have a clear instance of the mythic motif of uroburos, what Joyce would refer to in *FW* as "Doublends Jined" symbolizing the circular or cyclical structure of of life and art.

Ulysses is a retelling of or commentary on *The Odyssey*. It is an imposition of the Odyssean template on the events and character of modern life in Dublin, and so is simultaneously very old and completely new. In Islamic terms, Joyce confuses or disturbs an easy understanding of the difference between revelation (*tanzil*) and interpretation (*ta'wil*). In both *Ulysses* and the *Qayyum al-asma'*, differences and relationships and reversals between content and form are privileged and explored. In the case of the Bab's composition, his commentary proceeds without

the use of the typical and universally employed technical exegetical con-
nectives such as 'this means' (ya'ni) or 'the intention of the text here is'
(al-murad), devices used frequently in his earlier tafsir and also used in
some of his later work. Rather, here the commentary is the composition
and the composition is the commentary. Another aspect of Ulysses that
is most suggestive of comparison with the Qayyum al-asma' is the way it
highlights and problematises the relationship between text ('father') and
commentary ('son'). Their 're-union' in the Qayyum al-asma' is indicated
in the device of paraphrase offering an excellent comparative example of
the way in which form and content exchange roles in this work.

This finds a parallel in those episodes in the first half of Ulysses in which
the character, say Bloom, is the episode (as in Lestrygonians) through
the replacement of a typical nineteenth-century-type narrator with
Joyce's original and newly crafted technique of stream of consciousness
and 'interior monlogue'. We do not read about Bloom, we read Bloom
directly. The Circe episode, in the latter half of the novel, is written as a
play precisely because everything in the brothel is speaking, everything has
a tongue. All things are connecting themselves while speaking themselves
into existence. Again, a Quranic resonance may be seen in the fact that its
main topic there is precisely revelation, discourse and communication:
form and content are a perfect generative unity.[69] This Quranic 'conceit'
is continued and intensified in the Bab's Qayyum al-asma'. In Ulysses the
form becomes content in the Oxen of the Sun, which functions also as
a chrestomathy of English prose styles in forty sections (the number
of weeks for human gestation), or in the chapter Aeolus in which the
advertising and newspaper layout is the content. Both works embody a
resounding and unambiguous – if quite avant la lettre – demonstration
of McLuhan's 'the medium is the message'.[70]

By its structure, the Bab's composition has much in common with
the literary rupture represented by Joyce's Ulysses. The Tafsir surat
Yusuf (another name by which the Qayyum al-asma' is known) is, as we
saw, the work through which he proclaimed his messianic mission. In
this title we see, perhaps, some Joycean mischief with the word tafsir, a
technical term meaning 'scriptural commentary', and always indicating
the long tradition of Muslim scholasticism that produced it.[71] In reality, this work has virtually nothing in common with that tradition and
is as much unlike a standard work of tafsir as it could possibly be. It is,
however, a reconfiguration of the Quran and a rewriting of the Quran,

in the same way that Joyce's *Ulysses* is a creative reconfiguration of *The Odyssey*. That Joyce did not have to resort to such a disguise for his work and could proclaim openly that it was an imitation of *The Odyssey* says something about the differences in the respective cultural settings and the differences between the two texts, *The Odyssey* and the Quran and their respective functions.

The word *al-qayyum* comes from the Quran (Q2:255; Q3:2; Q20:111), where it always appears as a divine attribute in tandem with *al-hayy*, 'the everliving'. It is frequently translated as 'self-subsisting'. Its choice as part of the title of this work is related to its numerical (*abjad*) value,[72] a gematric iteration of the name Yusuf: both *qayyum* and Yusuf have the same numeric value (156) and are therefore read as equivalent in the deep 'unseen' structure of the language. Additionally, the word *qayyum* is derived from the same Arabic root as the key messianic terms *qa'im* (resurrector) and *qiyama* (resurrection/judgment). So, the figure of Joseph is understood and presented in a messianic and eschatological mood. The prominence of the word, which tends to elude a crisp translation, especially in the title of the work *Qayyum al-asma'*, is explained by its connotative function as symbol of the resurrection and Day of Judgment through articulating the same sounds of the words *qa'im* and *qiyama* and bearing the central semantic value of the triliteral Arabic root *q-w-m*.

In the *Qayyum al-asma'*, there are a 111 chapters designated by the author 'suras'.[73] Each sura is composed of verses designated by their author as ayat, usually translated as 'divine signs'. A wordier though accurate translation is: 'miraculous portents of God's transcendent oneness'. They are miraculous in the first place because the Prophet Mohammad, by whom they were first spoken, was an unschooled merchant[74] and because any description of God is, according to the Quran, paradoxically fraught because of 'His' utter unknowability (Q112). The word aya/sign reflects something of the idea in the New Testament's 'signs and wonders' (John 4:48; Romans 15:9), without the negativity implied in the John passage. Here it is the author, Ali Muhammad Shirazi, who uses the term *tafsir* in the opening words of the first sura. But the composition in reality takes the form of a 'new' Quran or more accurately, from the mythopoeic point of view, it is the 'true' Quran that had until now been in hiding with the hidden imam.

God has ordained the coming forth [from concealment] of this book in explanation (*fi tafsir*) of the Greatest of Stories directly from Muhammad bin al-Hasan bin 'Ali bin Muhammad bin 'Ali bin Musa b. Ja'far b. Muhammad b. 'Ali bin al-Hasan b. 'Ali b. Abi Talib upon his servant [that is the Bab: Sayyid 'Ali Muhammad] a conclusive and eloquent proof of God from the Remembrance unto all the worlds. (QA3, *Surat al-mulk*, 9)

Each verse of the 111 verses of the *Surat Yusuf*, becomes the lemma for each of the suras in this work, the topic-heading under which the commentary is generated. The first chapter of the Bab's composition, as mentioned earlier, is entitled the *Surat al-mulk*. After this first element of a given sura, comes the *basmala* – that is the ubiquitous Islamic short prayer and invocation: 'In the Name of God, the Merciful the Compassionate', a formula that heads all but one of the Quran's 114 suras and which is also used throughout Islamic culture on countless other occasions, literary, liturgical and social as blessing or prayer. After the *basmala* comes, in the spirit of the 'occasions of revelation' genre of Quranic sciences,[75] and in imitation of Qurans which typically list the number of verses at the head of each sura, the following statement: 'this was revealed in Shiraz in forty-two verses'. All this constitutes the title section of a given sura and is standard throughout.

As in *Ulysses*, so in the *Qayyum al-asma'*, there is a pervading sense of affirmation, assent, acceptance and commitment. The number forty-two, the total number of verses for each sura, the Bab himself points out, is the numerical equivalent of the word *bala* 'Yes!' which is, as mentioned earlier, the answer of humanity to the question posed by God on the Day of the Covenant, the Day of Alast: 'Am I not your Lord?' This 'Yea verily' – which in the Quranic chronotope represents the beginning of consciousness and history – finds an unexpected yet powerful resonance in Molly Bloom's future directed affirmation in Penelope, the last chapter of *Ulysses*, ending the entire novel with 'yes I will I will Yes.' And just as chaos and cosmos are combined in Joyce's modernist literary masterpiece, by making each of his new 111 suras 42 verses in length lends a heretofore unimaginable regularity to the form of 'Quran' which is distinguished by the large variety of chapter or sura lengths. But, as we saw, the number 42 is not accidental (even if the number

111 in *Finnegans Wake* is), encoding how form becomes content in this remarkable work by the Bab. It should be thought that this primordial 'yes' flows through the 'veins' of the entire work, all 4,442 verses, as the Bab himself explicitly says.[76] Casting new verses, braiding direct quotations from the Quran with his own words and words and phrases from Hadith in a seamless new verse, the author regulates it all with the familiar – and here unvarying – Quranic rhymed prose, *saj'*. There can be wide variation in the length of the individual verse in the Bab's composition, just as there is in the original Quran, from the shortest, for example a set of disconnected letters, to the longest (the 15 lines of verse 8 of the *Surat al-abd*, (QA109:225–6). The Bab combines commentary with text, audience with performance, revelation with interpretation. In terms of European literary history, such may certainly be considered a modernist gesture.

Following this first section of a given sura, comes the citation of the Quranic verse from the *Surat Yusuf* that is to be the object of commentary – the lemma – for the particular chapter. Then come, for all but four suras, the disconnected letters (some Quranic, some new). After the disconnected letters, comes the third section of the commentary. It is difficult to characterise this third section satisfactorily because it can be so different from sura to sura and sometimes highly variegated within each sura. In many of the suras, this third section represents a further level of paraphrase, gloss and commentary. For example, the Bab's composition from suras 80 to 91,[77] in addition to offering a commentary for the Quranic verses 12:79 to 12:91 (as would be expected following the structural logic of the work) also presents a running paraphrase of a long series of verses in Quranic order that takes into account the bulk of the actual Quran from suras 10 to 16. The final or fourth section or division is the return to the actual verse from the *Surat Yusuf* under which the new sura has been written. Here authorial creativity assumes the character of pure paraphrase. The verse itself is recast to reflect the concerns of the writer. These concerns are largely to do with the appearance of the hidden imam and the inauguration of the return, the *qiyama* and the Day of the Covenant and the Day of Judgment all in one literary moment. In comparison with *Ulysses*, this final section may be thought a similarly life-affirming response to the challenges and 'nightmare' of history – in short, an awakening, a revelation. In order to illustrate what might otherwise be difficult to visualise, reproduced here is a translation of the opening of chapter 109 of the Bab's

Qayyum al-asma', the sura of the Servant. Here the Quranic form will be quite apparent in the opening invocation, the mention of the number of verses and the place of revelation, and perhaps most importantly, the close relationship between commentary and text in which it is very difficult to discern at times where the Quranic material ends and the Bab's so-called commentary begins. In order to illustrate this aspect of the work I have employed the typographical expediency of showing the verbatim Quranic passages and words in small capitals.

The Sura of the Servant[78]
Forty-two verses, revealed in Shiraz
IN THE NAME OF GOD THE MERCIFUL THE COMPASSIONATE
NOR DID WE SEND BEFORE THEE [AS MESSENGERS] ANY BUT MEN
WHOM WE DID INSPIRE – [MEN] LIVING IN HUMAN HABITATIONS.
DO THEY NOT TRAVEL THROUGH THE EARTH, AND SEE WHAT WAS
THE END OF THOSE BEFORE THEM? BUT THE HOME OF THE HERE-
AFTER IS BEST, FOR THOSE WHO DO RIGHT. WILL YE NOT THEN
UNDERSTAND? (QURAN 12:109)

Verse 1
Mim Ha Mim Dal [= 'Muhammad' when connected in script]

Verse 2
O People of the THRONE! Listen to the CALL of your Lord, THE
MERCIFUL, He who THERE IS NO GOD EXCEPT HIM from the tongue
of the REMEMBRANCE, this YOUTH son of THE SUBLIME (*al-'ali,* also
the first name of the Bab: Ali), the Arab to whom [God has] in the
MOTHER BOOK testified.

Verse 3
Then LISTEN TO WHAT IS BEING REVEALED TO YOU FROM YOUR
LORD: VERILY VERILY I AM GOD, OF WHOM THERE IS NO GOD
BUT HIM. NOTHING IS LIKE UNTO HIM while He is God, Lofty
(*ali*) Great.

Verse 4
O People of the Earth! HEARKEN to the CALL of the BIRDS upon
the TREES leafy and perfumed with the CAMPHOR of Manifestation

describing this YOUNG MAN descended from the Arabs, from MUHAMMAD, from Ali, from Fatima, from Mekka, from Medina, from Batha, from Iraq with what the MERCIFUL HAS MANIFESTED upon their leaves, namely that he is THE SUBLIME and he is God, MIGHTY, PRAISED.

Verse 5

This YOUTH most white in colour and most beautiful of eye, even of eyebrow, limbs well formed like gold freshly cast from the two springs, soft of shoulder like pure malleable silver in two cups, sublimely awesome in appearance, like the awe-inspiring appearances of the Elders, and outspreading his MERCY as the two Husayns spread mercy over the land, the centre of the sky (that is the sun) has not seen the like of the justice of the two justices, and in grace like the two Lights joined in the two names from the most lofty of the two beloveds and the ISTHMUS between the two causes in the SECRET of al-Tatanjayn, the abider like the *Alif Rising Upright* (*al-alif al-qa'im*) between the two scrolls at the centre of the two worlds, THE JUDGE, BY THE PERMISSION OF GOD in the two later births, the SECRET of the two 'Alawis and the splendour of the two Fatimis and an ancient fruit from the BLESSED TREE encrimsoned by the FIRE of the Two Clouds and a group of those of the sacred veils pulsating with shimmering light, the abider around the FIRE in the TWO SEAS the glory of heaven unto the causes of the two earths and a handful of the clay of the earth over the people of the two – these two GARDENS of DARK GREEN FOLIAGE over the point of the TWO WESTS and those SECRET two names in the creation of the TWO EASTS born in the two Harams and the one looking towards the two Qiblas beyond the two Ka'bas, the one who prays over the incandescent THRONE twice a possessor of the two causes and the Pure Water in the two gulfs, the speaker in the two stations and the knower of the two imams, the Letter 'B' that circulates in the water of the two groups of letters and the Point Abiding over the DOOR of the Two Alifs revolving around God in the two cycles and the one made to speak on the authority of God in the two cycles, the SERVANTS OF GOD and the REMEMBRANCE of His PROOF. This

YOUNG MAN CALLED, because his grandfather is ABRAHAM, THE SPIRIT in the forerunners and he is the Gate, after the two later gates. And PRAISE BE TO GOD THE LORD OF ALL THE WORLDS. And he is God, indeed the one who comprehends everything concerning ALL OF THE WORLDS.

Such literary activity, in the guise of exegesis, may be understood partly as excavating or carving out of the mass and luminous chaos of "Light upon Light" a heretofore inconceivable regularity in which the pre-existing irregular and the frequently non sequitur narratological aspect of Quranic suras become as formally structured as sonnets (even if the actual language, as we have just seen, can be challenging in the extreme). In the context of the return of the hidden imam with the true Quran, this could suggest that the irregularity of the Uthmanic codex – the basis for all published Qurans – was a result of textual violence on the part of the breakers of the covenant. Whatever the implications of this new orderly Quran text might be, it is clear that the resulting composition mirrors the confidence of the author in claiming the authority to do such an otherwise unimaginable and heretical thing: to rearrange and rewrite the Quran. It may be that Joyce's design, to collapse the twenty-year-long story of Odysseus into the confines of a single day in the life of Dublin bespeaks a similar desire to exercise control over the 'nightmare of history' of which Stephen Dedalus so famously spoke (*U* 34). Thus, the name of the first sura written by the Bab: *mulk*, or (divine) ownership, may be read as his ownership and mastery of the Holy Quran, reorganising it, making it regular, in a sense making it 'rational', while at the same time announcing and declaiming through a torrential storm of language pregnant with fulfiment, anticipating a kind of Joycean 'chaosmos'. It should be recalled, as well, that the composition can be seen as a melding together of innumerable fragments of scripture making the resulting composition simultaneously old and new – another *coincidentia oppositorum*.

A similar storm is experienced in *Ulysses* but is even more manifest and intense in *Finnegans Wake*: a riot of language, which eventually emerges as quite deliberately and meticulously orchestrated – and this to a nearly unbelievable degree.[79] Eventually emerges, that is, after the heroic effort of the reader has succeeded in discerning the art and craft sometimes otherwise obscured by these two extraordinary compositions, *Ulysses* and the *Qayyum al-asma'*, in which the epic adventure of language, namely, to extend the resources and significance of language itself, is central.

We do not need to emphasise how shocking and scandalous – unthinkable even – such an imitation of the Quran was and is. But such extreme scandal – though in a different 'key' – also relates to the literary act of Joyce seventy-five years later, when he takes ownership of and participates quite fully in the culturally sacred aura and dignity of the epic tradition, and appropriates its authority for himself in refiguring it according to contemporary Irish life in all its 'chaosmic' plenitude, from the sublime preoccupations of Stephen, to the fatherly and husbandly quest and the attendant peripeties of Bloom and the ultimate salvific affirmation of Molly. The life is told in the – at that time – scandalous graphic depiction of sexual and other intimate bodily acts and functions, in the roiling, sometimes tawdry and racist encounters in Dublin pub life, in the private tenderness that occurs between various characters. Furthermore, the language is frequently quite non-standard and colloquial, not to say vulgar. There is also pointed criticism of the hypocrisies and paralysis Joyce saw in Roman Catholicism. He makes *The Odyssey* his own in order to express his own particular artistic vision, a vision that entails a significant Brunonian 'mystical' noetic. The Bab does the same thing with the Quran. He tacitly says, 'this is mine. I am now demonstrating how I am taking ownership of it. And, I am reorganising it and rewriting it according to the exigencies of the moment.' Thus the Bab also interrogated, disturbed and problematised the relationship between revelation (*tanzil*) and its interpretation (*ta'wil*), in the life-affirming hope to awaken from the nightmare of history marked most dramatically at his time by the mutual and frequently quite virulent heartbreaking enmity among various Muslim communal identities all of which traced their genesis to the gospel of divine unity originally preached by Muhammad. As a son of Shi'i Islam the Bab's awareness of such disunity was particularly acute.

When the *Qayyum al-asma'* was first brought to the attention of 'Orientalism' in the nineteenth century, people said it is meaningless; the man was insane; there is no sense to this; 'it is an unintelligible rhapsody'; the grammar is bad.[80] This response is of course very similar to the kind of thing that was said about *Ulysses* when it inaugurated literary modernism in 1922. However, neither the *Qayyum al-asma'* nor *Ulysses* is nonsense. Both are very clearly and intricately structured, even if the warp and woof of this structure is frequently overwhelmed by torrential linguistic virtuosity. It is worth noting that by the time the Bab was writing, Shiʿi philosophy had established an interesting discourse in which the hidden imam could be identified with an individual internal spiritual or existential reality, in addition to the expected advent of history, as in a Protestant transposition of the return of Jesus to the inner realm of the individual soul. The Bab reorganised the words and verses of the Quran to apply specifically to the appearance of the hidden imam and his own role as the gate to the hidden imam. Thus, the hidden imam serves in some ways as a poetic reference for the 'new' individual as such, in addition to being an ever-living symbol of radical historical change, which seeks to resolve the problems tradition poses to the current moment in Iranian society. This would seem to be clearly indicated in the Bab's much recited short prayer, called in English 'The Remover of Difficulties'.[81]

> Is there any remover of difficulties save God? Say: Praised be God, He is God. All are his servants and all abide by His bidding.[82]

An equally accurate translation, and one which acquires a certain immediacy in the exceptional context of the Shiʿi eschaton or *qiyama* (during which time the Bab composed his various works), would alter the translation of the last five words (which in Arabic are *wa kullun bi-amrihi qaʾimun*) to 'and each is a *qaʾim* in God's cause'. In Twelver Shiʿism, the *qaʾim* is typically held to be the hidden or twelfth imam who had, until the time of his divinely ordained return, been in occultation (*ghayba*). So, in another rendering of the original Arabic prayer a 'modern' notion of the individual emerges: 'Is there any remover of oppression apart from God? Say: All praise be to God! He is God. All others are His servants and are to arise (*qaʾim*) in obedience to His holy cause (*amrihi*).' This indicates also that the time for waiting for a saviour is over. In the new cycle, the cycle of fulfilment, maturity and resurrection, all members of the human race are potentially *qaʾim*s, arisers in the cause of God. Naturally, it is also quite within the bounds of accepted usage to understand both meanings as complementary to each other.

Here, we see another point of comparison with Joyce and the Bab and another feature of the epic dimension of both *Ulysses* and the *Qayyum al-asmaʾ* (and of course of the Quran itself): in some ways the most salient aspect of their epic qualities becomes apparent in the epic struggle of the reader to 'complete' the journey. The individual becomes singled out as the centre of narrative gravity and comprehension. Understanding is heroic. The reader is an autonomous and creative participant without whom the composition would not exist. Revelation is cast in the language of the recipient:

> And We have sent no Messenger save with the tongue of his people, that he might make all clear to them; then God leads astray whomsoever He will, and He guides whomsoever He will; and He is the All-mighty, the All-wise. (Q14:4)

Related to the idea of 'reader as hero' is the quest for identity, emblematised in the search of son for father in both works. It is the grand monomythic theme of literature as such.[83] This theme emerges in both *Ulysses* and the *Qayyum al-asma'* through revelation, recognition (anagnorisis) or epiphany (*zuhur, kashf*), the Greek word for which is, of course, apocalypse. Both *Ulysses* and the *Qayyum al-asma'* are dealing in revelation. For *Ulysses*, this is intensely encountered in Penelope. For the *Qayyum al-asma'* the intensity of the encounter is maintained at a remarkable level throughout the entire work. Revelation, for the Bab, springs from the *coincidentia oppositorum*, which entails all created phenomena in order to demonstrate that there is something beyond logic and sense perception that shines through the 'clash' of apparent oppositions. And in both the Bab and Joyce this is demonstrated over and over again through the epic adventure of language in which the *coincidentia oppositorum* has a simultaneous poetic or literary function and a philosophical or mystical function.[84]

The literary fiction, that the book was given to the Bab by the hidden imam, asserts of course an important 'religious' credential, namely that he is the 'official' representative of the hidden imam and so the focus and locus of all the power in the universe (viz. *al-walaya al-mutlaqa*). But the actual work establishes an even more important 'literary' credential. Certainly, the earliest followers of the Bab made much of his verbal artistry and prodigious literary abilities as a proof of his claims to be in touch with the hidden imam. Without the hidden imam there is, of course, no Twelver Shiʿism; without the idea of the absence or the discussion about the hidden imam's representative, there is also no Twelver Shiʿism. But, there are certain clues throughout the text that the Bab himself is actually this same hidden imam, clues that *he himself is the one from whom he himself received the book*.[85] What might be thought clear and unambiguous indication of this is found in the titles of suras 108 and 109. The disconnected letters for these two chapters, *Surat al-dhikr* (QA 108) and *Surat al-abd* (QA 109), are respectively *'a-l-y* (*'ayn-lam-ya*) and *m-h-m-d* (*mim-ha-mim-dal*). Neither set of disconnected letters occurs in the Quran and must be thought original – as disconnected letters – with the Bab (as are many other sets of disconnected letters in this work). Further, these two sets, when looked at as *not* disconnected but as spelling a word, are seen to be the names 'Ali and Mohammad. These are the names, in reverse order, of (according to Shi'i Islam) the first two bearers of divine authority in Islam: 'Ali ibn Abi Talib (661) cousin and son-in-law of the Prophet Muhammad (632). That these are also the names – in correct order – of the author of the *Qayyum al-asma'* is obviously no accident, making the point that history is cyclical and is repeating itself in the revelation of the Bab. They are inserted here in an artistic, nearly playful manner to underscore that he is indeed responsible for this text as its author. (See illustration below.) The name of the author 'Ali Muhammad (viz. Shirazi – the Bab) is thus camouflaged in these not too mysterious, 'disconnected' letters, which are clearly not disconnected at all.[86] And, most importantly, with this assertion of authorship, the Bab complicates and challenges a traditional understanding of divine revelation.

The *Qayyum al-asma'* is the very embodiment of high seriousness and earnestness. No irony, no comedy or humour. These 'disconnected letters' are striking evidence of authorial presence and an artistic gesture that combines the Bab's inborn temperament and preoccupations with his unconventional, even iconoclastic, religious ideas. These concerns are channelled through a traditionally pietistic religious modality: the Quran and its exegesis. The Quran is the raw material out of which issues this work, just as *The Odyssey* is the raw material out of which *Ulysses* emerges as Joyce's expression of his own unorthodoxy. Both are works that by their very nature ask questions about the relationship between tradition and change, narrative and authorial creativity, and the role of the reader. In the Bab's composition, the relationship between revelation and interpretation is privileged. This may be thought emblematic of the basic presupposition of a distinctively Shi'i hermeneutic in which the angel of revelation is also the angel of interpretation.[87]

This is of course where it parts company to some degree with *Ulysses*. *Ulysses* is not terribly religious in the traditional institutional sense of that word, although Joyce was himself saturated in Roman Catholicism, and

Opening lines of *súrat al-dhikr* (QA 108, pp. 223-5).

٢٢٣

اللهالحيوندكان سورة الذكر | اثنتان واربعون ايات فأم الكتاب شديد
لــــــــــــــــمراللهالرحمن الرحيم ٠ مثل هذه سبيلى ادعوا الى الله على حمة
انا ومن اتبعنى وسبحان الله وما انا من المشركين ٠ عكي ٥ هو الله الذى لا اله الا هو رب
والسماء وهو الله كان عليا عظيماه هو الذى نزائل الاسرار فى اسط بين الارض والحق

Opening lines of *súrat al-'abd* (QA 109, pp. 225-9).

المآء مشهودآه وسبحان اللهالحق الذى لا اله الا هو وهو الله كان بكل شئ قديرا
وهو الله نمكا سورة العبد ٠ لــــــــــمراللهالرحمن الرحيم اثنتان واربعون عن العالمين
وما ارسلناس قبلك الا رجالا نوحى اليهم من اهل القرى افلم يسيروا فى الارض فينظروا كيف كا
عاقبة الذين من قبلهم ولدار الاخرة خير للذين اتقوا افلا تعقلون ٠ محمده ٠ ياأهل
العرب اسمعوا نداء ربكم الرحمن الذى لا اله الا هو من لسان الذكر هذا النقى ابن العلى العربى

The Bab's signature masquerading as disconnected letters

much of his language and much of his point of view was formed by his early education and his conflicts coming up against Catholicism in the modern world. It is indisputable that he rejected Catholicism. But, we have seen how Joyce's 'religious faculty' was attracted to and stimulated by the mystical philosophy of thinkers like Bruno. It is not accurate to call *Ulysses* secular precisely because of its epic structure and élan, its seriousness, which may be thought highlighted and accentuated by the fluent, obbligato-like leitmotif of humour and its revelatory observation of the hallowed interconnectedness of all things. *Ulysses* has the gravitas of scriptural purpose and the solemnity and nobility of the epic. Just as the Quran is concerned with a universal human experience – an epic which it casts in terms of *din* – sacred responsibility or 'religion', *Ulysses* locates sacred responsibility in Bloom's search for a son (Rudy), Stephen's search for a father, and Molly's exuberant and somehow also highly devout affirmation of life. We can never imagine the Bab saying anything like Joyce's: 'How I hate God and death! How I like Nora.'[88] However, in the opening chapter of his work, the *Surat al-mulk*, the sura of dominion, he says with similar vehemence and commitment that all power, explicitly that of the shah and that of the ulema, has now been returned to its rightful place . . . the hidden imam (that is, himself). And though the Bab's *bala* 'Yes indeed!' is a different affirmation than Molly's series of twelve yesses that end the book, both adverbial affirmatives assent to the power of life to endure, abide, flourish in order to provide the 'modality' out of which more life can be created and renewed. Earlier, it was suggested that the Quranic word *qiyama* may in some ways reflect and indicate Qajar modernist energies and intineraries. Another word, much used in the Bab's writings and by later Baha'i writers, is *badi'*, which may be translated as 'wondrously new'. It is wondrous because it indicates a quality that is simultaneously new and eternal or ancient. It is the word used, for example, to indicate the new calendar constructed by the Bab and followed by Baha'is. This same tension uniting the old and the new is clearly present in *Ulysses*.

Thus does literary modernism, in the cloak of Iranian religiosity, anticipate by seventy years or so a much more well-known and recognised epochal literary shift whose emblem is James Joyce's *Ulysses*.[89] Whether this has relevance for theorising about the relationship between such literary creativity and the more purely historical problem of the relationship between the modern and whatever its opposite might be, is a question unasked here. But for the moment, we can perhaps allow ourselves a little latitude to ask in closing whether we might not be somewhat justified in thinking of *Ulysses* as a case of Qajar literary modernism in a twentieth-century European masterpiece. Indeed, all of the Bab's literary works were condemned and demonised by the broader culture as heretical. Thousands of the Bab's followers were slaughtered by the shah's forces, at the behest of the clerical estate. Those who might otherwise have been attracted to and inspired by the literary achievements of the Bab had much more at stake than mere literary success or failure. But the comparison of the two works is suggestive on the level of literature precisely because of the structural and thematic parallels, the similarities between the two texts as scandalous, outrageous and 'difficult', the respective authors' sense of themselves as revolutionising their own particular literary cultures and their singular and heroic dedication to their respective visions. From the point of view of the centrality of rupture, scandal and shock and the signal that something new (and old) was happening embodied by both works, there is much to commend the comparison and it is difficult to ignore their obvious similarities.

Conclusion

EPIC AND THE DOMESTICATION OF APOCALYPSE

C an the Quran really be the hero of its own epic? An 'incomplete' epic? Or, is it a text through which an epic journey, quest and struggle is refracted in original, compelling and challenging ways? To the degree that these questions are reasonable, it is also reasonable to pursue and attempt to delineate the distinctive features of the Quran's epic voice as we have done in Chapters 1, 3 and 7. Again, it is important to emphasise that the epic form and content of the Quran functions in various ways. It comes into sharpest relief when we consider the Quran as a new telling of the story of humanity as a whole. From this perspective, the epic voice of the Quran also offers a critique of other competing, more narrowly ethnic or national epics. The Quran thus calls forth a universal human identity through its insistence on the originary Day of Alast, on the certitude that all human communities have received divine guidance from the same unique and only God, and that all humanity is participating, consciously or not, in a process of civilisation, an epic journey from ignorance to knowledge or enlightenment. And finally, it says that all humanity will be judged on how the challenge was met, the challenge to live in peace, unity and prosperity. We have also seen that the centrality of the epic form applies to the concerns of the individual whose epic task it is to engage with the Quran, to read it, embody it and understand it, to travel the straight path which leads to knowledge and finally recognition that God has spoken directly to the individual and the community and charged both with recognising a common humanity. This would prove to have been a particularly apt 'paradigm shift' when, on the cusp between late antiquity and the age of a new universalism ushered in by the venture of Islam, numerous forces, whether historical, economic, environmental, political and religious – to use sometimes very inadequate terminology – would gather and produce a new world, a new modernity. It is very difficult to read the Quran and not find these themes either explicitly stated or alluded to with a continuous and distinctive frequency from the beginning of the *mushaf* to the end. The epic vision of the Quran teaches a gospel of unity, harmony, prosperity and judgment. This vision or message is contrapuntal to the other master genre of the Quran, apocalypse.

As was argued, especially in Chapter 2, there seems to be a perfect fit between contemporary theories of apocalypse and the Quran text. The Quran is as much – if not more – about revelation as it is about God or his prophets, so it may be viewed as a kind of meta-apocalypse, one that is conscious of itself as the main character of the revelatory communication, one for which the Quran's various subjects and themes, whether epic or apocalyptic, serve as occasions for revelation: God's speaking to humanity. In the Quran, several interrelated sub-themes are markers of the apocalypse as a literary genre. Perhaps the most important is the agency of the angel in the process of revelation. Some others include the interplay of duality and opposition (the enantiodromia of the church fathers), revelation, glory, justice, history and its periodisation, story, otherworldly beings and paradise. Typological figuration is a potent Quranic literary device by which the apocalyptic character of the Quran is expressed, whether in relation to itself and its immediate audience or through taking account of previous religious history to demonstrate that Muhammad's mission is of the same order of authority and vision as previous messages. And the pervasiveness of typological figuration gives a distinctive mood to the Quran's epic narrative in which all prophets are somehow the same through trial and tribulation and ultimate triumph, just as their communities are alike with regard to acceptance or rejection of the divine messenger. That this is communicated through the apocalyptic mode of typological figuration adds the non-negotiable and uniquely powerful element of eternal religious truth to the epic – an epic for which awareness, recognition and illumination are an essential part of the story. In this way, also, the Quran functions as a commentary on previous scripture in much the same way that the New Testament functions as a commentary on the Old Testament. Apocalypse thus involves an overall mood or voice of urgency and intensity that characterises both the delivery and reception of the revelation – the sense of being on the verge of something, as if waking from a dream, when the supra-logical device of typological figuration engages with the imagination of the audience. Time collapses, the voice of the Quran is heard as the message of all prophets, and the impending reckoning is one more in a historical sequence.

Late Antique Modernity

This consecutive pattern of revelation is demonstrated in the Quran through the stories of several previous prophets and their communities. An excellent example, contextualised in Chapter 2, is in the Quran's narrative about the people of Ad, their community Thamud and their prophet Salih. In this story, there occurs a great mysterious scream or cry that is heard by Ad, symbolising the irruption of the divine into the world to call it to account. It dramatises the nearness of the overwhelming divine power that is 'closer than the jugular vein' (Q50:16) yet simultaneously utterly remote: 'its like is not comparable to anything' (Q42:11; 112:4). In a fine example of serene self-consciousness, the Quran calls this the divine presence (*sakina*, see Chapter 2), a complex notion involving tranquillity and the occasional aid of invisible hosts. The Quran identifies twenty-four other historic instances of apocalypse, along with its acceptance or rejection, associated with the remaining prophets and messengers it calls by name. It also leaves ample room for other such events when it says there have been prophets whose names are not mentioned (Q40:78). Thus Islamic tradition posits the figure 124,000 as the number of all divine messengers that have come to humanity in order to understand the Quran's insistence that every human community has received divine revelation (Q10:47). This divine presence "descends", as we saw with the chanting of the Quran, and it is seen to have much in common with the descent of other powers and energies, such as the angels and the spirit mentioned in connection with the Night of Power (Q97). The Quran presents an articulation and dramatisation of all the themes and phenomena associated with the genre of apocalypse, and this category of religious expression and action was not only an integral part of the mission of the Prophet and the life of his movement but also a particular language that was very well-known indeed in the late antiquity of the land of Islam's birth.* Apocalypse and messianism, as a distinctive feature of the Quranic epic, are frequently in close proximity. This specific combination would also become a characteristic feature of various historical Islamic or Islamicate communities' and movements' defining forms of thought, social rhythms, and political and spiritual institutions. In short, the culture produce by Islam, the civilisational modalities and assumptions it inculcates, was firmly plotted along the coordinates of epic time and apocalyptic space, coordinates that had become during the long course of late antiquity familiar tools or concepts for understanding why there is something rather than nothing, why we are here, why we suffer and why we die. The Quran's answer proved compelling and irresistible for that new world about to be born.

Epic and apocalypse characterise much of the literature, oral or written, of late antiquity and it is therefore not surprising to find characteristic elements and features of these genres in the Quran, whose first audience was, of course, firmly ensconced in what has proved to have been a highly distinctive and productive transitional period of human history. It is as if the Quran wished to sacralise, in no uncertain terms, the idea of epic and to harness and control the considerable sacred energy of apocalypse in the form of a scripture suited to the demands of a looming modernity in which the world, beginning with the Nile to Oxus region and soon to stretch beyond these boundaries, would be thrown together as the centre of a new burgeoning and ramifying system of trade, communication, creativity, conflict and identity. The epic confidence of the Quran supplied the stability upon which culture thrives, apocalypse provided the essential imaginative and experiential élan. This combination of what may at first appear to be incompatible opposites actually may be seen to represent two modes of knowing, sometimes referred to as reason and revelation or causality and poetry.

The 'end' of the world may denote its disappearance or its purpose, a telos. Certainly, history bears witness to the fact that no matter how compelling the Quran's warnings about the Hour or the Day, or the Command of God, the world did not end and life carried on. Indeed, life flourished. The apocalyptic music of the Quran enlivens and continues to make urgent the Quran's vision of a just community living in harmony with the will

---

* See Hoyland, Shoemaker and Neuwirth in *Roads*.

of God in peace and prosperity. So closely do the two forms of epic and apocalypse harmonise with each other in the Quran that a very interesting and engaging dynamic between figure and ground occurs. It is indeed the case that they may be seen to exchange roles, that the epic vision of enlightenment and unity acquires the verve and poetry of apocalypse while the otherwise fleeting or ephemeral occasions of divine revelation somehow become the permanent substance of reality. The shift from a tribal or national epic to a universal epic represents a parallel transformation in the religious expectations of late antiquity, one that commands our respect and engages our sense of wonder because it tells us who we are as human beings in a language simultaneously old and new, familiar and strange.

Abbreviations

ACAE	J. M. Foley (ed.), *A Companion to Ancient Epic*, Oxford: Blackwell Publishing Ltd., 2008.
Bihar	Majlisi, Muhammad Bāqir. *Bihar al-anwar*, 111 vols, Beirut: Muʿassasat al-Wafāʾ, 1403/1983.
Boullata	Boullata, Issa J. (ed.), *Literary Structures of Religious Meaning in the Qurʾān*, Richmond: Curzon, 2000.
Brown	Norman O. Brown.
BSOAS	Bulletin of SOAS, London.
Burhan	al-Bahrani, Hashim, *Kitāb al-Burhān fī tafsīr al-Quran*, 4 vols, Tehran: Chapkhānah-i Aftab, 1375/1955.
Collins	John J. Collins, *The Apocalyptic Imagination*.
Corbin	Henry Corbin, *En Islam Iranien: Aspects Spirituels et Philosophiques*, 4 vols, Bibliothèque Des Idées, Paris: Gallimard, 1971.
Dharīʾa	Agha Buzurg al-Ṭihrani, Muhammad Muḥsin, *al-Dharīʾa ilā taṣānif al-shīʾa*, 25 vols, Tehran and Najaf, 1355–98/1936–78.
EA	Collins, John Joseph, Bernard McGinn and Stephen J. Stein (eds), *The Encyclopedia of Apocalypticism* (3 vols). Volume 1: *The Origins of Apocalypticism in Judaism and Christianity*, ed. by J. J. Collins; Volume 2: *Apocalypticism in Western History and Culture*, ed. by B. McGinn; Volume 3: *Apocalypticism in the Modern Period and the Contemporary Age*, ed. by S. J. Stein, 3 vols, New York: Continuum, 2000.
EI1	*Encyclopaedia of Islam*, ed. M. Th. Houtsma et al., 4 vols, Leiden: E. J. Brill, 1913–36, repr. 1987.
EI2	*Encyclopaedia of Islam*, ed. P. J. Bearman et al, 12 vols, Leiden: Brill, 1960–2004.
EI3	*Encyclopedia of Islam Three*, K. Fleet et al. (eds), Leiden: Brill online 2009.
EIr	*Encyclopedia Iranica*.
EQ	Jane Damen McAuliffe (ed.), *The Encyclopedia of the Qurʾān*, 6 vols, Leiden: Brill, 2001–6.
ER2	Jones, Lindsay (ed.), *Encyclopedia of Religion*, 2nd edn, 15 vols, Detroit: Macmillan Reference USA, 2005.
ETCW	Beissinger, Margaret, Jane Tylus and Susanne Wofford (eds), *Epic Traditions in the Contemporary World: The Poetics of Community*. Berkeley, Los Angeles and Oxford: University of California Press, 1999.

FW	James Joyce, *Finnegans Wake.*
GAL	Brockelmann, Carl, *Geschichte der arabischen Litteratur*, Leiden: E. J. Brill, 1937–49.
IJMES	International Journal of Middle Eastern Studies
Ikmāl	Ibn Babawayh, Muhammad ibn Aliī, *Ikmāl al-dın wa-itmām al-ni'ma fī ithbāt al-raj'a*, Najaf: al-Maṭba'a al-Ḥaydariyya, 1970.
JAAR	*Journal of the American Academy of Religion*
JAL	*Journal of Arabic Literature*
JAOS	*Journal of the American Oriental Society*
JQS	*Journal of Qur'ānic Studies*
JRAIns	*Journal of Royal Anthropological Institute (new series)*
Kafi	al-Kulayni, Muhammad ibn Ya'qub, *al-Uṣūl min al-Kāfī*, 2 vols, ed. Alī Akbar al-Ghaffārī, Tehran: Dār al-Kutub al-Islāmiyya, Maṭba'at al-Ḥaydarī, 1374/1954.
Mafatih	al-Qummī, Abbās, *Mafātīḥ al-jinān wa-yalahu Kitāb al-Bāqiyyāt al-ṣāliḥāt*, Beirut: Dar al-Adwa', 1407/1987.
Mir'at	al-Āmili-Isfahani, Abu l-Hasan, *Tafsīr mir'āt al-anwār wa-mishkāt al-asrār*, Tehran: Matbaat al-Aftab, 1374/1954.
MUSJ	*Mélanges de l'Université Saint-Joseph* 50: 443–75.
MW	*The Muslim World*
Nur	al-Huwayzi, Abd Alī, *Kitāb Tafsīr nūr al-thaqalayn*, 8 vols, ed. Alī Āshur, Beirut: Mu'assasat al-Ta'rikh al-Arabi, 1422/2001
QA	*Qayyūm al-asmā'*
RII	Todd Lawson (ed.), *Reason and Inspiration in Islam: Theology, Philosophy and Mysticism in Muslim Thought*, London: I. B. Tauris, in association with the Institute of Ismaili Studies.
Roads	Günther, Sebastian and Todd Lawson (eds), *Roads to Paradise: Eschatology and Concepts of the Hereafter in Islam* (2 vols). Volume 1: *Foundations and Formation of a Tradition, Reflections on the Hereafter in the Quran and Islamic Religious Thought*; Volume 2: *Continuity and Change, The Plurality of Eschatological Representations in the Islamicate World*. 1st edn, Islamic History and Civilization 136, Leiden and Boston: Brill, 2017.
U	James Joyce, *Ulysses.*
WLL	Arbel, Daphna and Andrei A. Orlov (eds), *With Letters of Light: Studies in the Dead Sea Scrolls, Early Jewish Apocalypticism, Magic, and Mysticism; in Honor of Rachel Elior*, New York: Walter de Gruyter, 2011. http://uclibs.org/PID/130450/10435727.
Zwettler	Michael Zwettler, 'Mantic Manifesto'.

Glossary

Abu Bakr (*Abū Bakr,* 634) The first caliph.

Aeneas (Greek Αἰνείας) Hero of the epic by Horace, the Aeneid, who is cast there in the role of founder of Rome after fleeing his war-torn homeland Troy.

Afaqi (*āfāqī*) Adjective derived from Q43:51 referring to the macrocosm, the natural realm. Literally it means 'of the horizons'.

Ahl al-Kitab (*ahl al-kitāb* Q *passim*) People of the Book, a Quranic designation generally understood to apply to Jews and Christians but frequently expanded to followers of other religions.

Ahsan al-qasas (*aḥsan al-qaṣaṣ*) Q12:3. 'The best of stories' a designation of the story of Joseph, sura 12 of the Quran. It also became one of the titles of the Báb's composition also known as *Qayyúm al-asmā'* discussed at length in Chapter 7.

Al-Lat (*al-lāt*) Name of a goddess worshipped by pre-Islamic Arabs according to Q53:19.

Al-Uzza (*al-'uzzā*) Name of a goddess worshipped by pre-Islamic Arabs according to Q53:19.

Aletheia (Greek ἀλήθεια) Truth, disclosure, unconcealed, not dead or asleep.

Ali (*'Alī*) Name of the first imam of the Shi'a.

Allah (*allāh*) Q *passim*. God.

Alphabet of Prophets. The totality of prophets and divine messengers mentioned in the Quran (25) subsequently supplemented by the Islamic tradition (+ 124,000), the recognition of which makes human history and variation understandable.

Amr (*amr*) Qx166. Cause (of God), command, thing.

Anagnorisis (Greek ἀναγνώρισις) In a literary work a moment of recognition, discovery thus akin to revelation and apocalypse.

Apocalypse (Greek ἀποκάλυψις) Revelation, disclosure; an important genre of religious literature. Related words: apocalyptica, apocalyptist, apocalypticism.

Aya/Ayat (*āya/āyāt*) Qx382. Sign/signs; Quranic word (*passim*) for unit of communication of divine reality and truth. All created things, that is, all things other than God, are signs and portents of their creator, God.

Babiya (*bābiyya*) Gatehood, technical term from the lexicon of Shiʻi religious thought and philosophy more broadly. Refers to that which gives access to God, the hidden imam or truth as such.

Bahira (*baḥīrā*) Monk who recognized the signs of prophethood in the young Muhammad during a caravan journey through al-Shām (Syria).

Basmala (*al-basmala*) The phrase: *In the name of God the Merciful the Compassionate*. It introduces all but one of the 114 suras of the Quran and is used in Islamicate culture to begin letters, speeches and other important and weighty events or activities.

Batal (*al-baṭal*) An Arabic word for hero (extra-Quranic).

Batil (*al-bāṭil*) A Quranic word meaning 'false, vain, empty' (*passim*) the direct opposite of Haqq, on which see below.

Bayan (*al-bayān* from *B-Y-N*) Qx3. Quranic word (*passim*) for revelation, explanation, explication, eloquence. All forms, verbal, nominal, prepositional, of this triliteral root carrying cognate meanings are found 523 times in the Quran.

Chiasmus, ring composition. Features of the compositional structure of many Quran suras. Generally indicates that the point or meaning of a discourse is to be found in its centre and not at its end.

Coincidentia Oppositorum. The coincidence, sometimes harmonisation, of opposites.

Companions (*ṣaḥāba*) The early group of Muslims who lived during the prophet Muhammad's lifetime. The triliteral root occurs frequently in the Quran.

Covenant (*ʻahd*) Qx29. A Quranic word or concept that denotes God's agreement with humanity arrived at on the Day of the Covenant mentioned at Q7:172 before creation had occurred. A companion term *mīthāq*, pact, agreement, occurs 25x.

Daʻwa (*al-daʻwa*) The Islamic call, summons or invitation to recognise Islam and become believers, a cognate of the Greek kerygma (κῆρυγμα). Q *passim*. Can also mean prayer.

Dar al-Harb (*dār al-ḥarb*) Abode or region of war.

Dar al-Islam (*dār al-islām*). Abode or region of Islām.

Dar al-Kufr (*dār al-kufr*) Abode of Ingratitude and Unbelief.

Day of Alast (*yawm a'last*) The Day of the Covenant, mentioned above.

Dhi intiqam (Q39:37) Avenger, a name of God.

Dhikr (*al-dhikr*) (Q *passim*) Remembrance, mention, reminder of God, the covenant, divine oneness and one's commitment to these.

Dhukhan (*al-dhukhān*) A Quranic word (Q41:11; 44:10) meaning intense smoke as one of the signs of the prophesied Hour (*al-sāʻa*) or Day (*al-yawm*) (Q *passim*).

Din (*dīn*) Qx92. What one owes to God, judgment of God, frequently inadequately translated as 'religion'.

Dunya (*al-dunyā*) Qx115. The world below, in contrast to the heavenly realm. Dunyawi is the adjectival form.

Enantiodromia. The dynamics between oppositions, sometimes denoting the changing of something into its opposites, sometimes denoting only interrelationships between opposites.

Epic (from Greek ἔπος: word, story, poem) Refers to the stories a culture regards as sacred or definitive, involving a sacred or quasi-sacred hero, a journey, difficulties, persecution, return and triumph.

Fasad (*al-fasād*) Qx11. Moral and spiritual corruption.

Fasiq (*al-fāsiq*) Qx37. One who is disobedient, wicked.

Ghadb (*al-ghaḍb/ghaḍiba* etc.) Qx24. Divine anger, wrath.

Ghayb (*al-ghayb*) Qx58. The unseen, the spiritual realm, hidden, absent.

Ghufran (*al-ghufrān*) Qx234. Forgiveness. In this intensive form (Q2:285).

Glory motif. The theme of the appearance of the divine as luminosity, grandeur and power. An important element in the genre of apocalypse.

Grand Ayatollah. A supreme clerical rank in Imami Shīʿism which did not exist prior to the late nineteenth century and became more widespread after the founding of the modern Qom seminary (*ḥawza*) in 1922.

Hadith. Capitalised it refers to the large body of literature collected between the seventh and tenth centuries by Muslim scholars. It forms the second major scripture in Islam, the first being the Quran. In lower case, it refers to one formerly oral report now transcribed as part of the Hadith corpus. A single hadith has two parts: an *isnād* or 'chain of transmission' and a matn, main text of the transmission or report.

Hal (*ḥāl*) Sufi terminology. A spiritual, mystical or noetic state of experience or awareness.

Harb (*al-ḥarb*) War. It occurs four times as such in the Quran.

Hayat al-dunya (*ḥayāt al-dunyā*) Quran *passim:* 'the life of the world' – that which leads or tempts away from the right path.

Heilsgeschichte (German) 'Salvation History' or Sacred History: the story that tells of God's historical plan of redemption beginning, for example in the Hebrew Bible and continuing through the New Testament.

Hikaya, Haki, Mahki ʿanhu (*ḥikāya, al-ḥākī, al-maḥkī ʿanhu*) The first means story or imitation (mimesis), the second is the storyteller or actor/imitator, the third is that which is told or imitated.

Hilm. Forbearance, justice, tolerance, moderation, dignity, leniency, self-control. The opposite of spontaneous and reactionary anger or violence. A mark of the civilised human. In the Quran the form *Ḥalīm* is a divine attribute for God the ever forbearing one (Q *passim*).

Iman (*al-īmān*) Qx45. Security, safety, faith.

In medias res (Beginning) in the midst of things, in contrast to beginning at the start of the events the story is telling. A frequent feature of epics in which the actual beginning is alluded to or described later in the poem or work through flashbacks and allusions.

Injil (*al-injīl*) Q *passim*. The Gospel, the New Testament, the holy book of Christians.

Insan (*al-insān/al-ins*) Qx91. Mankind, human beings, humankind, humanity, a man.

Islah (*al-iṣlāḥ*) Qx6. Reconciliation, setting things right, promoting wellbeing.

Jamʿ (*al-jamʿ*) Q *passim*. Joining together, assembly.

Kāfir (*al-kāfir*) Q *passim*. One who is ungrateful for divine guidance, an unbeliever.

Kashf (*al-kashf*) Qx20 in derived usages. Removal of hardship, covering or obscurity; apocalypse, revelation.

Kerygma (Greek κῆρυγμα) Preaching, the role of the church, cognate of Arabic *daʿwa* (see above).

Khadija (d. 620) Beloved first wife of the Prophet Muḥammad.

Kitab (*al-kitāb*) Qx260. Writing, book or scripture.

Kufr (al-*kufr*) Qx27; related usages x498. Unbelief, ingratitude, infidelity, covering.

Majus (*al-majūs*) Q22:17. Magicans/Zoroastrians.

Malak (*malak/malāʾika*) Qx88. Angel/angels.

Manat (*manāt*) Name of a goddess worshipped by pre-Islamic Arabs according to Q53:20.

Marjaʿ taqlid (*marjaʿ al-taqlīd*) Lit. 'example to be imitated'. Exemplar. Role of Shīʿī religious scholar/jurist as one whom the faithful should imitate in their religious thought and practice.

Melisma. A group of notes sung on one syllable of text, as in Gregorian chants.

Metalepsis (Greek μετάληψις) The concatenation of verbal figures in writing or speech in which figurative usages are used to construct new figurative usages.

Miʿraj. The ascension of the Prophet Muhammad through the seven heavens during his celebrated Night Journey (*al-isrāʾ*) which, according to traditional exegesis, is alluded to at Q17:1.

Mount Hira. Mountain near Mecca where, in a cave, the Prophet Muḥammad first received divine revelation.

Muʾmin (*al-muʾmin*) Qx202. One who has faith (*īmān*) and is secure in Islam.

Mufassir. An exegete, commentator on the Quran. One who does *tafsīr* (see below).

Munafiqun (*al-munāfiqūn*) Qx27. Hypocrites, sing. Munafiq (*al-munāfiq*) does not occur in Q.

Munazzah. Transcendent, said of God.

Muse. An inspirational goddess of Greek arts and sciences. In mythology there were nine muses who were custodians of epic poetry, history, music and song, love poetry, tragedy, hymns, dance, comedy, astronomy.

Mushaf (*al-muṣḥaf*) This technical term designates the current form, order and arrangement of the Quran text as it is found in all manuscripts and editions throughout the Muslim world. It is also known as the ʿUthmānic codex. The word *muṣḥaf* is used to distinguish this 'edition' of the text from the chronological order – *tanzīl* (see below) – which almost perfectly reverses the order of the text in the *muṣḥaf*.

Mushrik (*al-mushrik*) Qx44. One who commits the unforgivable sin of *shirk* (see below).

Muslim (*al-muslim*) Qx39. One who is committed to Islam, its ideals, morality, laws and *Heilsgeschichte*. The feminine plural form is *al-muslimāt* (Q33:35).

Mutawatir (*al-mutawātir*) Technical term from the discipline of hadith studies. Widely attested; said of, for example, a hadith report that has many corroborative chains of transmission and is therefore virtually beyond doubt.

Nabi (*al-nabīy*) Qx75. Prophet of God, and related words such as *al-nabā'* announcement, warning, divine message Qx131.

Naqizin (*al-nāqiḍīn*) Breakers of the divine Covenant in extra-Quranic polemic. Does not occur in the Quran; it is formed on the Quranic root *n-q-ḍ* (Qx9) where it refers to the breaking of the divine covenant or another agreement five times.

Nas (*al-nās*) Qx241. Humanity, humankind, people, men.

Nasara (*al-naṣāra/al-naṣrāni*) Qx15. Christians.

Nasiya (*al-nasiya*) Qx45. Forgetting. Used in homiletic etymologies – even though it springs from a completely different tritliteral root – to explain that while humankind is not burdened with original sin, the Arabic (*al-nās*) indicates that humanity is described by God as having an inborn tendency to forget, precisely the originary covenant mentioned at Q7:172. This is why it is necessary to send new prophets and messengers from time to time.

Nasr (*al-naṣr*) Qx143, including derivatives. Help, divine assistance and therefore victory.

Paraenesis (Greek παραίνεσις) Advice, counsel, exhortation.

Peripeteias (Greek περιπέτεια) Reversal of fortune, the trials, tests, tribulations, betrayals a hero or his/her people suffers in the course of an epic.

Qa'im (*al-qā'im*) Qx17. Standing, supporting.

Qamis (*qamīṣ*) Q12:18, 25, 26, 27, 28, 93. The shirt of Joseph.

Qari'a (*al-qāri'a*) Qx5. Disaster, calamity prophesied in the Quran in suras 69 and 101.

Qawm (a*l-qawm*) Qx383. A people, a nation, a folk.

Qiyama (*al-qiyāma*) Qx70. Literally: arising. Resurrection. May refer to bodily resurrection on the Day of Judgment, or the Day of Judgment, especially in Shi'ism for which the Qa'im 'the one who arises' is the central emblem as the return of the hidden imam.

Qiyas (*al-qiyās*) Analogy. One of the four sources of jurisprudence in classical Sunni legal theory. The other three are Quran; Sunna, the example of the Prophet Muhammad, his close companions, or a given community; *Ijmā'*, consensus variously construed.

Rahim (*al-rahīm*) Q *passim*. The Compassionate, name of God.

Rahman (*al-rahmān*) Q *passim*. The Merciful, name of God.

Ring composition. A technique for narrative composition characteristic of oral literature in which the composition forms a ring around the central point of the story, rather than privileging that point or purpose by placing it at the end of the oral performance/text. It has been identified in several suras of the Quran. See above, Chiasmus.

Risala (*al-risāla*) Qx3 and other related derivative words Qx510. Divine message, messenger (*al-rasūl*) Qx332, sent message. See above Nabi.

Road, Path, Way, Travel. A central, defining theme in the Quran expressed in various Arabic words, some of which are: *al-sabīl* (x176), *al-minhāj* (x1), *al-sayra* (x27), *dhahaba* (x56), *al-sunna* (x16), *al-ṣirāṭ* (x45), *al-ʿaqaba* (x2), *al-sharīʿa* (x1).

Sabians (*al-ṣābi'ūn*) Qx3. An ill-defined ritual group mentioned in the Quran identified in classical exegesis with various historic communities.

Sakhita (*sakhiṭa*) Qx4. To be wrathful. Associated with the wrath of God.

Sakina (*al-sakina*) Qx6. The divine presence, comfort, peace, aid. Cognate of the Hebrew *Shekhina*/שכינה.

Salih (*Ṣāliḥ*) Qx9. Name of a Quranic prophet.

Samad (*al-ṣamad*) Q112:2. Attribute or name of God: the Eternal.

Sayha (*al-ṣayḥa*) Qx13. Apocalyptic scream, warcry, shout.

Shahada (*al-shahāda*) Qx23. Testimony, the Muslim creed: *There is no god but God and Muhammad is the prophet of God.* Martyrdom largely in extra-Quranic usage.

Shahid (*al-shahīd*) Qx56. Witness/martyr.

Shirk (*shirk*) Polytheism, idolatry. "Joining partners with God". Esteeming there to be more than one source of life, power, knowledge, and so on, in the cosmos. Then unforgivable sin of Islam (Q4:48) The notional opposite of tawhid, see below.

Sihr halal (*sirr ḥalāl*) Legal magic: the Quran.

Sirat mustaqim (*al-ṣirāṭ al-mustaqīm*) Qx14, including Q1:5. The straight or righteous path Islam teaches.

Sunna (*al-sunna*) See above, Road, Path, Way, Travel.

Symbol from symbolon (Greek σύμβολον) meaning two broken pieces of an original medallion or other item that when rejoined together make a perfect object and generates meaning of various kinds.

Synaesthesia. Stimulation of multiple sense perception from one sensory stimulant: seeing music, hearing colour.

Tafsir (*al-tafsīr*) Most common designation for Quran exegesis/commentary.

Taghut (*al-ṭāghūt*) Qx8. Idols, false gods.

Tammat al-Kubra, al- (*al-ṭāmmat al-kubrā*) Q79:34. The great disaster.

Tanzil (*al-tanzīl*) Qx15. A common alternate name for the Quran. Refers to its descent or revelation to the Prophet Muhammad and by extension, its chronological order. See above, Mushaf.

Tashrik (*tashrīk*) Not in the Quran. Used here as a symmetrical opposite of Tawhid, on which see below.

Tawhid (*al-tawḥīd*) To make or consider as one, also not in Quran. Obligatory attitude towards the divinity in Islam. It is the opposite of *Shirk*, on which see above.

Tawrat (*al-tawrāt*) Qx18. Torah, Pentateuch, holy book of Jews.

Theophany (Greek θεοφάνεια) Appearance of a divinity or a god.

Totum simul (Latin) Everything at once.

Trope of intensity. Term used to describe the powerful Quranic references to the events associated with the Hour, or the Cause of God.

Umma (*al-umma*) Qx64. Community. Generally understood to refer to the community in which Islam is the guiding ethos.

Uthmanic ('*uthmānī*) Adjective applied to the final arrangement of the Quran (see below *muṣḥaf*) which happened during the caliphate of '*Uthmān ibn 'Affān* (656), the third Sunni caliph.

Wadd (*al-wadd* and derived words) Qx29. Love, affection, wish.

Wahda (*al-waḥda*) Unity, divine or otherwise, though the idea of unity automatically carries special charisma in Islam.

Waqi'a (*al-wāqi'a*) Qx2. The Event, identified with the Hour and other similar tropes of intensity.

Yahūd (*al-yahūd*) Qx20. Jews.

Zabur (*al-zabūr*) Qx9. Psalms of David, scriptures, written records, Qx9.

Zann (*al-ẓann* and derivatives) Qx69. To assume, surmise, speculate. The opposite of certitude, *al-yaqīn,* Qx28 in various derivations.

Acknowledgements

This book took a number of years to achieve its present form. During that time my thinking about the Quran has benefited from exchanges with a wide variety of teachers, friends, colleagues and students. I would like to mention them all with gratitude for their learning and thoughtfulness and respect for their dedication to the study of Islam, the Quran and the literary imagination. I am sure I will not succeed and I hope that persons who should be mentioned here but are not will forgive the lapse.

Hanna Kassis was the first person I heard speak about the Quran, its beauty, its wisdom and the love and devotion it claimed from its auditors and readership. His deep engagement with the Quran at the linguistic, spiritual and poetic levels, his own obvious and distinctive love of 'the Recitation' and the way in which he communicated this had a great impact on me and I will never forget the special excitement of those classes I was privileged to attend and for which I am forever grateful. I would also like to record a debt of thanks to Antony N. Grobovsky for his friendship, ideas, essential encouragement and moral support in the early years. And, I would like to thank Mahnaz Butt, my undergraduate student at the University of Toronto who, many years ago, raised the simple (if unprecedented) question during class: Is the Quran an epic?

It is a great pleasure here to thank Helen Blatherwick, editor with the *Journal of Qur'ānic Studies,* for her unfailing perspicacity, patience and technical expertise in the original editing of what have become Chapters 1 and 4 of this book. Peri Bearman of the *Journal of the American Oriental Society* was a valued reader and patient, knowing, careful editor and guiding sensibility for what is now Chapter 3. In this connection, I would like to thank also the anonymous reviewers, who kindly gave their time and effort to both journals, for their suggestions and discomfitures. I would also like to thank Johannes Haubold and Oliver Taplin for suggestions concerning current scholarship on the epic genre.

All the chapters in this book began life as conference presentations and so I am grateful to institutions, organisers and participants who are simply too many to mention. I am grateful to the University of Toronto, especially the Department of Near and Middle Eastern Civilizations and its Chairs, Jim Reilly, and especially Tim Harrison, for support over the years. I am also grateful to the Social Sciences and Humanities Research Council of Canada for its support. Other colleagues, particularly Sebastian Günther, Franklin Lewis, Leonard Lewisohn, Mustafa Shah, Devin Stewart and Stefan Winter, offered helpful suggestions and corrections. Rebekah Zwanzig and Omid Ghaemaghami have both helped in various, invaluable ways as research assistants, proof-readers and sensible judges. Special thanks go to my colleague Robert Holmstedt for calling attention to the possible relevance of the 'canon issue' for Quranic studies. I would like to thank Professor Issa Boullata for his warm encouragement and interest over the years. Elisabetta d'Erme generously provided invaluable feedback, corrections and questions on the article that has become Chapter 7: 'Joycean Modernism in a 19th Century Quran Commentary'. Her knowledge, criticism and sympathetic reading of a challenging comparative study helped me more than I can say. In connection with this same chapter, I would like to mention two other people especially: Ennio Ravasio, whose brilliant study of the philosophical and theological background of Joyce's work he kindly shared with me in pre-publication form was inspiring and reassuring. Houchang Chehabi expended epic effort in editing the original article to begin with and I thank him most heartily. I have benefited greatly from Robert Denham's deep and wide knowledge of all things Northrop Frye, particularly the spiritual or religious aspects, through his many published studies, email conversations, the generous gift of several publications, and through the very kind hospitality he and his wife Rachel offered us in the spring of 2012 when we spent a weekend with them in their beautiful mountain home. Dear friends, colleagues and students who have wittingly or unwittingly contributed to this book are: Wadad al-Qadi, John J. Collins, Ingrid Hehmeyer, Munir Jiwa, James Morris, Maurice Pomerantz, Christian Mauder, Florentina Badalanova Geller, Christopher Buck, Jeffrey Einboden, Arsheen Devji, Soraya Hajjaji-Jarrah, Jamel Velji, Shawkat Toorawa, Peter Wright, Jonah Winters, Stephen Lambden, Sholeh

Quinn and Kathy Van Vliet. McGill librarian, Steve Millier, who died far too young, made numerous generous contributions to this book. His worthy successor, Dr. Eliza Tasbihi, has continued the tradition and I am deeply grateful to her. Karen Ruehrdanz and Christiane Gruber kindly offered suggestions and information for the cover art of the book. Burhan Zahra'i provided the beautiful calligraphy of Q41:53 for the epigraph.

Oneworld, beginning with Novin Doostdar, have been unfailingly encouraging and supportive from the beginning until the end. I would like to thank Jonathan Bentley-Smith, Paul Nash, Laura McFarlane and Elizabeth Hinks for their expertise, exemplary professionalism – and patience.

This statement of gratitude is also meant to absolve all and sundry – but me – of any responsibility for this book's final form and contents.

Barbara Lawson, my wife (an inadequate word), has been the guiding light for this and related projects over the last forty-plus years. During that time she has, in addition to much else, read, listened to, suggested further reading for, criticised, argued about and laughed at various expressions of the ideas in this book (and their precursors). Any merit in these pages is frequently largely in her unrepayable debt. I am not inclined to absolve her of anything.

Notes

The book's epigraph is my translation of Quran 41:53. The beautiful calligraphy of the Arabic on the facing page is by Burhan Zahrai.

Parts of the Introduction and Conclusion were published in 'The Quran and Epic', in *JQS* 16.1 (2014), pp. 58–92; 'Le Coran et l'imaginaire apocalyptique' (trans. G. Rivier), in *Religions et Histoire* 34 (2010), pp. 48–53; 'Apocalypse', in G. Böwering et al. (eds), *PEIPT*, pp. 38–9.

Chapter 1 was originally published as: 'The Quran and Epic', in *JQS* 16.1 (2014), pp. 58–92.

Chapter 2 was originally published as: 'Paradise in the Quran and the Music of Apocalypse', in *Roads* 1 (2017), pp. 93–135.

Chapter 3 was originally published as: 'Duality, opposition and typology in the Qur'an: the apocalyptic substrate', in *JQS* 10.2 (2008), pp. 23–49.

Chapter 4 was originally published as: 'Typological figuration and the meaning of "spiritual": The Quranic story of Joseph', in *JAOS* 132.2 (2012), pp. 221–44.

Chapter 5 was originally published as: 'Divine Wrath and Mercy in Islam: Their Reflection in the Quran and Quranic Images of Water', in Reinhard G. Kratz and Hermann Spieckermann (eds), *Forschungen zum Alten Testament*, 2nd series (Tübingen, 2008), pp. 248–67.

Chapter 6 was originally published as: 'Coherent chaos and chaotic cosmos: The Quran and the symmetry of truth', in P. Gemeinhardt and A. Szgoll (eds), *Weltkonstruktionen: Religiose Weltdeutung zwischen Chaos und Kosmos vom alten Orient bis zum Islam* (Tübingen, 2010), pp. 177–93.

Chapter 7 was originally published as: 'Joycean Modernism in a Nineteenth-century Qur'an Commentary? A Comparison of the Bab's *Qayyūm al-Asmā'* with Joyce's *Ulysses*', in *Erin and Iran: Cultural Encounters between the Irish and the Iranians*, ed. H. E. Chehabi and Grace Neville (Washington DC and Boston), pp. 79–118.

INTRODUCTION

1. As in the case of Northrop Frye's three studies of the Bible, *The Great Code: The Bible and Literature*; *Words with Power: Being a Second Study of the Bible and Literature*; and *The Double Vision: Language and Meaning in Religion*. On the usefulness of Frye's approach for Quranic studies, see Waldman, 'Review: Islamic Studies', pp. 546–7; Stetkevych, *Zephyrs*, p. 333; Arkoun, 'Contemporary Critical Practices and the Quran'; Lawson, 'Seeing Double', p. 69.

2. Wansbrough, *Quranic Studies*, p. 1; Neuwirth, 'Referentiality and Textuality'.

3. On the notion of an open-ended, encyclopaedic, cornucopian text, see the study of Erasmus, Rabelais and others in Cave, *The Cornucopian Text*, esp. pp. 332–4. The comparison with the 'secular' writings of French humanists is not impertinent. Rather, it is directed by Frye's observation that: 'In the mythical mode, the encyclopaedic form is the sacred scripture . . . In the mythical mode [the] central or typical episodic product is the oracle. The oracle develops a number of subsidiary forms . . . Out of these, whether strung loosely together as they are in the Koran or carefully edited and arranged as they are in the Bible, the scripture or sacred book takes place' (Frye, *Anatomy of Criticism*, p. 56).

4. See, for example, the excellent collection of articles in *ACAE*, edited by John Miles Foley. A similarly excellent collection focused on the question of the continuing hold of the epic on the contemporary imagination is in *ETCW*. It should be added that in neither of these two recent collections – which may be considered something of a *status quaestionis* for epic studies – is the Quran the topic of discussion and analysis. I am applying the results of this and other epic scholarship to the Quran by means of the venerable (if controversial) intellectual tool known as *qiyas* (analogy). It is hoped that the correspondences thus arrived at will stimulate further discussion and research.

5. Haubold, 'Greek Epic'.

6. Martin, 'Epic as Genre', p. 18.

7. See above, note 1, for the titles of the three most important books by Frye on the Bible and literature.

8. Frye himself was quite candid about his approach and perspective: 'For my purposes the only possible form of the Bible that I can deal with is the Christian Bible, with its polemically named "Old" and "New" Testaments. I know that Jewish and Islamic conceptions of the Bible are very different (*The Great Code*, p. xiii). Further, he does not wish to discuss theological or dogmatic issues, but rather wants to relate the Bible 'to imaginative rather than doctrinal or historical criteria' (*The Great Code*, p. xxii). He is thus interested in the 'literary unity' of the Bible (*The Great Code*, p. xiii) as we are interested in the literary unity of the Quran. For a merciless and frequently reasonable critique of Frye's method in this and other of his biblical studies, see Alter, 'Northrop Frye between Archetype and Typology'.

9. Boullata, *Literary Structures of Religious Meaning*.

10. Reda, *The al-Baqara Crescendo*.

11. Ernst, *How to Read the Quran*, p. 38.

12. The pertinent literature is vast and controversy remains, but see as examples, Sanders, *Canon and Community*; Mays, 'The Question of Context in Psalm Interpretation'. For an overview of the general topic, see McDonald and Sanders, *The Canon Debate*; also the modern classic, Cross, *From Epic to Canon*.

13. This is the English original of, Lawson, 'Le Coran et l'imaginaire apocalyptique', pp. 48–53, combined with portions of my article 'Apocalypse' in *PEIPT*, pp. 38–9.

14. Lawson, in *PEIPT*.

15. This quotation is also from J. J. Collins, this time from his article 'Apocalypse: An Overview' in *ER2*. 'This definition has attained wide consensus' (Jonathan Z. Smith, 'Cross-cultural Reflections on Apocalypticism', in Adela Yarboro Collins (ed.), *Ancient and Modern Perspectives on the Bible and Culture* (Atlanta: Scholars Press, 1998), pp. 281–5). See also Jonathan Z. Smith, 'Wisdom and Apocalyptic', in Birger A. Pearson (ed.), *Religious Syncretism in Antiquity: Essays in Conversation with Geo Widengren* (Missoula: Scholars Press, for the American Academy of Religion and the Institute of Religious Studies, University of California, Santa Barbara, 1975), pp. 131–56.

16. Collins, Introduction to Vol. 1, in *EA*, p. xiii.

17. The incomparable richness of the paradise theme is now studied in great detail in *Roads*. See also C. Lange, *Paradise*.

18. Cf. e.g. *EA* which consists of three volumes. While *Volume 1* contains an index of ancient sources (Hebrew Bible, New Testament, Dead Sea Scrolls, pseudepigrapha, Rabbinic texts, Classical authors, Christian authors, Persian texts and so on), there seems to be no room for anything to do with the Quran, even by way of comparison. As such the Quran appears to represent a perhaps unconscious *terminus ad quem* for *Volume 1*. Thus we hope for a fuller treatment in *Volume 2*, but nothing approaching an adequate preliminary discussion is to be found. The author, a prominent sociologist of Islam, spends all of four pages (*Vol. 2*, pp. 239–44) on the Quran within a larger chapter entitled 'Islamic Apocalypticism in the Classical Period'. Here the main focus is on religio/political conflicts (*fitan/malahim*) and although the author promises to pay full attention to the place of apocalypticism in this article there seems to be no interest in the advances made in the study of the genre over the last several years. It is symptomatic of the mysterious problem that not even the editors of the publication, many of whom are responsible for these advances, felt it necessary to correct this or intervene. At the very least, we are now in a position to begin a discussion on whether or not the Quran belongs in such a volume. The question is skirted here. The name Muhammad (the Prophet) does not even occur in the index. In the final volume there is, of course, due attention to movements within Islamic history. But once again, the *sui generis* imaginative expression that may be seen as the literary or imaginative ground (*l'imaginaire*) for all of these movements, i.e. the Quran itself, is neglected.

19. Hanson, *Dawn*, p. 433.

20. J.J. Collins in *Semeia* 14, p. 28.

21. Lawson 'Apocalypse', in *PEIPT*.

CHAPTER 1: THE QURAN AS EPIC

1. See the pioneering article on the epic dimension of the *Sira* by Stefan Sperl, 'Epic and Exile'. The Arabic word *sira* has become a near equivalent for the Greek derived term 'epic'. But it is not the only one: *hamasa* ('valour', 'bravery', 'heroism') is also found – thus the use of *hamas* ('zeal') as the acronym for *harakat al-muqawama al-Islamiyya*, 'the Islamic Resistance Movement'. Others use *shi'r malhami* ('heroic poem', 'poem about fierce battle'); cf. also the related *batal* ('hero') from *batula* ('to be brave', 'to be a hero'). Matta b. Yunus (328/940) could not think of an Arabic equivalent for the Greek ποποιία and merely used the (nonexistent) Arabic *afi*. See Pellat, 'Hamasa' see also the very interesting comments regarding the relationship between the Quran and epic motifs in classical Islamic historiography in Wansbrough, *Quranic Studies*, pp. 4–5.

2. Niditch, 'Epic and History in the Hebrew Bible'; Niditch, 'The Challenge of Israelite Epic'; and Cross, *From Epic to Canon*. See also the foundational study by Gordon, 'Homer and Bible'.

3. Davidson, 'Persian/Iranian Epic'.

4. On the epic hero in the *Mahabharata*, see the comments and references in Nagy, 'The Epic Hero', esp. pp. 85–6.

5. See the several studies by Dwight Reynolds. The most recent is 'Epic and History in the Arabic Tradition'; also the brilliant pioneering discussion in Hamori, *On the Art*, esp. Ch. 1; and the extended and substantial studies of pre-Islamic Arab heroism in Bravmann, *The Spiritual* pp. 39–122 and pp. 254–87.

6. Such would appear to be part of the task in Northrop Frye's three last books, all of which were on the Bible: *The Great Code, Words with Power* and *The Double Vision.* But this task was already set in his very first book, *Fearful Symmetry,* as Denham has suggested in *Northrop Frye,* p. ix.

7. The articles in the *EQ* in which the word epic occurs are: 'Ararat' (x1 in title of work in the bibliography); 'Epigraphy' (x1: re *Shahnameh*), 'Literature and the Quran' (x1: 'ancient Hindu e.'); 'Material Culture and the Quran' (x1: re 'e. struggle' against nineteenth-century colonialism); 'Satanic Verses' (x1: 'epic prophetic biography'); 'South Asian Literatures and the Quran' (x6: various indigenous literatures are epic inspired by the Quranic Joseph story); 'Turkish Literature and the Quran' (x6: re pre-Islamic Turkish e., romantic e. as gloss for '*hikaye*', and the remarkable mix of Quranic piety with worldly culture); and 'Yemen' (xl: the epic cycle of Abu Karib). The word 'epic' has not merited an index entry in the more recent comprehensive source book Neuwirth, Sinai and Marx (eds), *The Quran in Context.*

8. Badalanova Geller, *Quran in Vernacular.* My thanks to the author for this deeply learned, illuminating study.

9. DeWeese, *Islamization and Native Religion in the Golden Horde.*

10. There is of course a large bibliography, especially on the *Shahnameh.* But reference to the Quran as a possible kernel for the more elaborate poetry is very meagre indeed.

11. Not least of which is the incisive critique of Bakhtin's celebrated and influential study, 'Epic and Novel: Toward a Methodology for the Study of the Novel', Ch. 1 in his *The Dialogic Imagination.*

12. Revard and Newman, 'Epic. I. History (Revard) and II. Theory (Newman)'. The following excerpt is lightly adjusted for readability by removing encyclopaedic cross-references.

13. Eco, *The Open Work*; see p. 11 for a reference to a relationship between epic performance technique and 'openness'.

14. Cuypers, *The Banquet.* This is an English translation of the original work of Cuypers, *Le Festin,* summarised in Ernst, *How to Read the Quran.*

15. See below, Ch. 4.

16. On the uneasy and colourful career of Quranic rhyme in the Islamic intellectual tradition see the various articles by Devin Stewart, starting with the most recent 'Divine Epithets and the *Dibacchius*' and 'Poetic License in the Quran'. See especially his groundbreaking 'Saj' in the Quran', reprinted in Turner (ed.), *The Koran,* Vol. 3, pp. 74–111, and in Rippin (ed.), *The Quran,* pp. 213–51. See also his 'The Mysterious Letters and Other Formal Features'.

17. The other arts and their corresponding muses were: history (Clio), love poetry (Erato), song and elegy (Euterpe), tragedy (Melpomene), hymns/praise (Polyhymnia), dance (Terpsichore), comedy (Thalia) and astronomy (Urania).

18. *Zwettler.*

19. The term *ab ovo* ('from the egg') was coined by Horace in his ideal description of the epic, which – according to him – should not begin at the very beginning, in this case the egg from which Helen (of Troy) was born. Rather, a good epic should put us in the middle of the action from the very start *(Ars Poética or Epistle to the Pisos,* A.S. Kline translation, pp. 119–52).

20. See below Ch. 3, p.61.

21. Brown, 'The Apocalypse of Islam', p. 167 (see here also a reference to the similarity between the Quran and Eco's 'open work').

22. On the epic simile, see below. Some of the words for 'road' or 'path', 'journey', and 'travel' in the Quran are: *imam, manakib, minhaj* (cf. *nahj*), *sabil, aqaba, sawaa', shari'a, shir'a, rashada, sirat, sunna, tariq, tariqa, yabas*; journey (n): *rihla, safar*; journey (v): *daraba, sara, saha, sata, sara, za'anar*; traverse: *abara, qata'a*; steep road:

aqaba. It is not accidental that many of these words have become veritable emblems of Islamic identity, e.g. *sunna, shariʿa, imam.*

23. Corbin, 'De l'Épopée héroïque à l'Épopée mystique', reprinted in Corbin, *Face de Dieu, face de l'homme,* pp. 175–243.

24. Lawson, *Gnostic* p. 102. The hadith continues: and everything in the *Fatiha* is in the *basmala.* 'Everything in the *basmala* is in the first letter "b" and everything in the "b" is in the point under it. And I am that point.'

25. They are traditionally numbered as ninety-nine, plus the frequently unknown or still hidden Greatest Name (Böwering, 'God and His Attributes').

26. Al-Suyuti, *al-Itqān,* Vol. 1, pp. 50ff.

27. *Zwettler,* pp. 106–9. See below, Ch. 5, pp. 106.

28. Most translations, sometimes slightly adapted, are from Abdel Haleem, *The Quran.*

29. For a fuller discussion of this textual feature, see Wansbrough, *Quranic Studies,* pp. 2–4.

30. Günther, 'Literacy'.

31. Hallaq, 'Law'.

32. Cuypers, *The Banquet,* pp. 30–2. See also the remarks on sura 5 in Hallaq, 'Law'.

33. See the related stimulating discussion in Bray, 'Lists and Memory'.

34. For a pioneering (if not always satisfactory) discussion of the Quran in connection with the Parry-Lord thesis and related questions, see Dundes, *Fables of the Ancients.* Here Dundes points out that while much important work on the oral composition of pre-Islamic Arabic poetry has been done (mentioning James Monroe and Michael Zwettler), by comparison little on the actual poetics of the Quran exists. Since then, however, the sources on this topic have multiplied. In addition to another 'pioneering' article, Gluck, 'Is There Poetry in the Quran?', the work of Cuypers (see above note 32), and the works of Devin Stewart (see above note 16), much of the writing of Mustansir Mir, Angelika Neuwirth and her colleagues at the Corpus Coranicum project, in addition to numerous excellent discussions of the poetic power of the Quran, such as Soraya Hajjaji-Jarrar's 'The Enchantment of Reading', have helped fill a serious and deep lacuna in Quranic studies. (Incidentally, Boullata's groundbreaking *Literary Structures of Religious Meaning,* in which this article occurs, appears not to have been known to Dundes.)

35. Mir, 'Names of the Quran'.

36. Revard and Newman, 'Epic. I. History (Revard) and II. Theory (Newman)'.

37. Cf. Gordon, 'Homer and Bible', pp. 62–3, 68, 77, 92–3.

38. See below Ch. 5.

39. See Ch. 2 below, pp. 42.

40. Chronotope is the technical term developed by Bakhtin to refer to the time/space continuum of a given work.

41. See below Ch. 6.

42. 'Epics . . . produce a vision of aesthetic and cultural order which shapes historic time at the expense of representations of the multiple contexts and competing intentions that bear on historical moments' (Wacker, 'Epic and the Modern Long Poem', p. 126).

43. Revard and Newman, 'Epic. I. History (Revard) and II. Theory (Newman)'.

44. *Zwettler,* pp. 108–9.

45. See below Ch. 6, pp. 129–30.

46. Carlyle, *Heroes and Hero-Worship* ('Lecture II: The Hero as Prophet. Mahomet Islam. Friday 8 May 1840'), pp. 60–110.

47. Campbell, *The Hero with a Thousand Faces,* pp. 28–37. Campbell, originally a Joyce scholar, borrowed a neologism from *Finnegans Wake* as a technical term for the heroic process he saw functioning in human societies ancient and new, Eastern and Western: 'monomyth'. As we observed earlier, *Sira* is a word that easily can be, and often is, translated as 'epic'.

48. A highly suggestive first exploration of the *Sira* as epic is Sperl, 'Epic and Exile'.

49. Ibn Hisham/Ibn Ishaq, *al-Sira al-nabawiyya*, Vol. 1, pp. 112–34.

50. Caves are classic and widely attested scenes for the inception of a heroic vocation. See e.g. Hcyden, 'Caves'.

51. Ibn Hisham/Ibn Ishaq, *al-Sira*, Vol. I, pp. 167–73.

52. As when the Quraysh charged Muḥammad with *bidʿa*/innovation: breaking the unity of the community, challenging the existing 'religion' (*din*) and ethos (*ahlam*) Ibn Hisham/(Ibn Ishaq, *al-Sira al-nabawiyya*, Vol. 1, pp. 192–5).

53. See also Gordon, 'Homer and Bible', pp. 69–70, for parallels with the Hebrew Bible.

54. Cf. the epithet 'Odysseus the Cunning' with the assertion in the Quran that 'God is the best of schemers' (Q3:54 and Q7:30, cf. also *makr, passim* in, e.g. Q7:99; Q8:30; Q10:21; Q13:42).

55. Hodgson, *The Venture of Islam*.

56. Gordon, 'Homer and Bible', p. 93.

57. Cf. Gordon, 'Homer and Bible', pp. 70–1. It is instructive to note those epic elements listed by Gordon in this article, such as the frequent embarrassment of the gods by humans, p. 94. On the other hand, animals speak, p. 95 in the Quran as they frequently do in hero myths (cf. Q27:16; Q18; Q22–6 and Q82).

58. For more on glory as apocalyptic motif, see below Ch. 2; see also Gordon, 'Homer and Bible', p. 101.

59. Gordon, 'Homer and Bible', p. 102. Note that shifts in person (a frequent Quranic phenomenon) in the epic have been noted as characteristic (Gordon, 'Homer', p. 103).

60. 'The image of the Prophet as the universal political hero takes its place alongside his presence as the spiritual centre of the universe. More progressively, there is some evidence that the vitality of the traditional patterns persists in modern reformulations' (Tayob, 'Muhammad').

61. Bowra, *Heroic Poetry*, pp. 351–3: 'In 1934 Milman Parry encountered a bard in Southern Serbia, a Moslem called Avdo Mededović aged about sixty, who would sing for two hours in the morning and for another two hours in the afternoon, resting for five or ten minutes every half-hour. To sing a long song took him two weeks with a week's rest in between to recover his voice. The result was an epic poem . . .

62. Frye, *The Great Code*, pp. 62–3.

63. McDonald and Sanders, *The Canon Debate*.

64. Lawson, *The Crucifixion and the Quran*, p. 70. See now, however, the pioneering study of Bukhari by Stephen Burge, *Reading Between the Lines*. I am grateful to the author for an unpublished typescript dealing with the same important question (Burge, *Fragmentation*). Such pioneering and persuasive studies ultimately ask us to re-evaluate how we understand the category: *tafsir bi'l-ma'thur* and to appreciate more acutely the authorial nature of 'mere' arrangement, in this case of hadith. Obviously, one might apply these new insights to any text in which arrangement is a factor, including the Quran.

65. See the analytical overview in Waltke, 'A Canonical Process Approach', pp. 3–18.

66. Kawashima, 'Verbal Medium and Narrative Art'.

67. '[Epic] is, very importantly, a genre that is performed before an audience. While individual performers of epic (each with varying levels of creativity) are appreciated, anonymity and collective involvement surround authorship per se . . . literary epic, unlike oral traditional epic, is usually seen as the creation of a single author, immersed in literacy and everything that literacy brings with it. Literary epic is created with artistic perfection in mind, not expediency of performance . . .' (*ETCW*, pp. 7–8).

68. '[W]ritten epic often twists uncomfortably on the dilemma of whether the poet should emphasize submersion in a collective voice or an individual poetic voice and authority' (Beissinger, Tylus and Wofford (eds), *ETCW*, p. 9), And; 'It is perhaps only historical accident, but again and again one encounters poets in the tradition of literary epic who likewise write from the margins and whose poems thereby hinge on the thematics of exile and estrangement: Dante writing his *Commedia* in exile from Florence, Milton writing *Paradise Lost* during the Restoration, the composer of the *Chanson de Roland* – perhaps – in figurative exile at the English court. In such ways, the social and economic vulnerabilities to which oral poets continue to be subject have left their mark, however mediated, on the legacy of written epic as well' (Beissinger, Tylus and Wofford (eds)., *ETCW*, p. 9).

69. Hastings (ed.), *Encyclopaedia of Religion and Ethics*, Vol. 6, p. 633. The two related books by J. Renard, *Islam and the Heroic Image* and *Friends of God* support, by their titles alone, the equivalence: *Wali/*[epic] hero. A comprehensive overview of what I have referred to as the 'institution' of *Walaya* is H. Landolt, 'Walāyah'.

70. Corbin, 'De l'Épopée héroïque', p. 234. There is, of course, another sense in which the reader achieves the status of hero, and this is by virtue of having 'understood' the challenging text through which they have journeyed.

CHAPTER 2: THE QURAN AS APOCALYPSE

1. Madigan, *Self-image*. This Quranic self-awareness is unique in world literature and may be related to the very interesting phenomenon of its personification in the hadith literature, as when the Quran appears as a person at the end of time.

2. This was first emphasised in Koch, *Rediscovery* (*Collins*, pp. 9–11); see also W. R. Cook, 'Glory'. For glory in the Islamicate cultural sphere see e.g. the works of Shihab al-Din al-Suhrawardi, *al-Maqtul* (1191) in general and his commentators, including the essential studies of Henry Corbin. For the recognition of a glory motif in the Quran, Lawson, 'Duality'. An interesting connection between the literary motif and material culture is suggested by a reading of Winter, 'Radiance'.

3. Here one is inspired by Northrop Frye and his desire to see and explain how 'Biblical imagery and narrative had set up an imaginative framework . . . within which Western culture had operated down to the eighteenth century and is to a large extent still operating', Frye, *Great Code*, p. xi.

4. See below for a discussion of the relevant Quranic terminology.

5. '[T]he word *apocalypse* is often associated with the end of the world, or with some great catastrophe. This analogous usage of the word apocalyptic is inevitably imprecise, as resemblance is a matter of degree . . . The expectation of an "end" of history, or of a new era of radical change, has been enormously important in Christian tradition, but also in Judaism and Islam, and while it is often the subject of a vision or a revelation, it can also be communicated in other ways.' J. J. Collins, 'Apocalypse: An overview', 410b.

6. My thanks to C. Mauder for this and several other important refinements.

7. Smith, 'On the History', p. 14.

8. Ibid., p. 18: '. . . what was the source from which both it and Paul derived this somewhat unlikely term for such material?'

9. Such is an implication of the existence of the traditional Quranic auxiliary study of the media or occasions of revelation (*'ilm asbab al-nuzul*).

10. Murphy, *Fallen*, pp. 48–55.

11. Hanson, *Dawn*, p. 433, quoted above p. 00.

12. Cf. Smith, 'On the history', p. 12.

13. Ibid., p. 13 (*ad* Ezekiel 33:32). On the reality effect see Barthes, *Rustle*, pp. 141–8.

14. Bull, 'The end', p. 661. See also the remarks in Smith, 'On the history', p. 18, suggesting that the popularity of the term as the name of a literary genre grew especially in pagan circles in the third and fourth centuries CE. It is also the case that the word began to be substituted by translators of Jewish texts after about the second century CE when, for example, the vision in Daniel 10 came to be called an apocalypse, where the earlier Greek of the Septuagint used a different word.

15. Even a brief account of this intellectual history is beyond the space limitations of the present chapter. In the Bibliography and the Notes the reader will find reference to some of the most important works in modern apocalypse studies. One of the purposes of this chapter, and one of the points I hope to be forgiven for repeating from time to time, is that studies of the Quran, in the first place, and Islamic-related literature and groups in the second, are virtually completely absent from this monumental and impressive library of scholarship. Exceptions are noted below.

16. Such non-theologians as Francis Bacon (1626) and Isaac Newton (1727), however, devoted much energy to a study of Revelation. Force and Popkin (eds), *Newton, passim* and pp. 216–20.

17. *Collins*, pp. 1–2.

18. *EA*, p. vii.

19. Arjomand, 'Classic', in *EA2* pp. 239–44 for the section on the Quran; Amanat, 'Modern'.

20. See, for example, the comments in D. Cook, *Studies*, pp. 269–74.

21. All of the above comments and observations pertain to so-called Western scholarship (an odious formulation). The problem of the study of the apocalyptic nature of the Quran in the Islamic tradition is another matter entirely and is only infrequently referred to here .

22. Collins, *Dead Sea Scrolls*, p. 150 (apocalypse as a genre receives a good discussion at pp. 45–7).

23. As embodied in *EA*

24. Baukham, 'Rise'. An early version of such a grid appears in J. J. Collins (ed.), *Apocalypse: The Morphology of a Genre, Semeia*, 14, p. 28.

25. As in A. Y. Collins (ed.), *Early*. See now Shoemaker, *Death*.

26. Hanson, *Dawn*, p. 429.

27. Casanova, *Mohammed*, pp. 68–83.

28. 'Die Methode Casanovas stellt alles, was Goldziher und Snouk Hurgronje muhevoll erarbeitet haben, direkt auf den Kopf' (Becker, 'Islam', p. 544).

29. Snouck Hurgronje, *Mohammedanism*, pp. 25–8.

30. Shoemaker, *Death*, pp. 121–36. See now also Cuypers, *Une apocalypse coranique*.

31. Shoemaker, *Death*, p. 136.

32. Numbers in parentheses here and elsewhere refer to the number of times the given word or root occurs in the Quran.

33. Kinberg, 'Paradise', pp. 12–15.

34. For recent discussions of Quranic eschatological terminology see also several contributions in Part 1 of *Roads* in general, and those by M. Abdel Haleem and J. Hameen-Anttila in particular.

35. On the issue of myth in the context of Islamic apocalypses, see Lange in *Roads 1*, pp. 341–70 and his reference to Beltz's important book on the mythology of the Quran, *Sehnsucht nach dem Paradies*.

36. Cf. also the relevant passages from the Old Testament, e.g., Isaiah 11–12, 24–27, 35, 60–66; Daniel 7; Amos 9:7–15; Micah 4–5.

37. D. Cook, 'Moral'.

38. Ch. 3 below.

39. 'Symmetry, in any narrative, always means that historical content is being subordinated to mythical demands of design and form', Frye, *Great Code*, p. 43. Indeed the interplay of duality is another distinctive feature of the Quran not found to the same degree in other scriptures of the Abrahamic tradition. See below Ch. 3. See Abdel Haleem and Neuwirth in *Roads* and Neuwirth, 'Symmetrie'.

40. Nwyia, *Exégèse*, p. 178.

41. Neuwirth, 'Symmetrie'.

42. Koch, *Rediscovery*, pp. 28–33, isolated glory among seven other features.

43. Weinfield, 'Presence', provides an excellent overview of the relationship between presence and glory in the Hebrew Bible. For glory as apocalyptic motif, see Koch, *Rediscovery*, pp. 28–33; *Collins*, pp. 9–11. See also Kugel, *God*; W. R. Cook, 'Glory'; Arbel and Orlov (eds), *Letters*; Merkur, 'Cultivating'; Fox, 'Glory'. A fascinating study of the phenomena in early Islam is van Ess, *Youthful*. For Quranic studies of glory outside the Quran but within Islamic intellectual history, see e.g. Corbin, *Man*.

44. Specifically Ezekiel 10:6–13.

45. Padwick, *Devotions*, p. 19.

46. Attar in *Roads*.

47. Arberry translation and versification.

48. Arberry translation and versification.

49. Abdel Haleem translation.

50. Abdel Haleem translation, Arabic transliteration added.

51. Returning to the question of pre-Islamic 'glory' before leaving this too brief discussion of Quranic glory, it is of some interest to note its function in the *Burda* poem of Ka'b b. Zubayr where it may be thought to represent the question at hand: In line 48 of the poem as given by Ibn Ishaq, the Prophet is presented as a light from which illumination is sought. In the an alternate reading, the Prophet is a sword from which illumination is sought. However, it is important to note that in both readings it is the illumination that is the centre of attention, its essence is untouched by the place, manner or mode of appearance. In an important study, Stetkevych demonstrates that glory as illumination and presence was very much a part of the poetic resources of pre-Islamic Arabic poetry. (Stetkevych, *Mantle*, pp. 70–150). This calls to mind the renowned story surrounding the conception of the Prophet Muḥammad. When his father, Abdallah b. Abi Mutallib was on his way to the home of Amina bt. Wahb (the Prophet Muhammad's mother), a light was seen shining from his brow. After the conjugal visit during which the Prophet was conceived the light was no longer visible. (Ibn Hisham/Ibn Ishaq, *Sīra* i, pp. 115–16). Thus the Quran's concern with light as supernatural glory is a natural theme common to its time and place. (See also, for example, Annus, 'Mesopotamian precursors', and Winter, 'Radiance', for related discussions of other pre-Islamic phenomena.) It is therefore no wonder that it is such a prevalent expectation of the Quran's audience.

52. Goppelt, *Typos*; Auerbach, 'Figura'.

53. *Zwettler*; Stewart, 'Understanding'. See below Ch. 3.

54. A notable exception is Isaiah 19:25b: 'Blessed be Egypt my people, and Assyria the work of my hands, and Israel my inheritance.'

55. Hardie, 'Metamorphosis'.

56. Cf. the Quranic Maryam, e.g. at sura 19. 'Christian commentators on the Koran naturally say that this is ridiculous, but from a purely typological point of view from which the Koran is speaking, the identification makes good sense' (Frye, *Great Code*, p. 172, see now Abboud, 'Mary').

57. Kreuzer, 'Ark'.

58. Fairbairn, *Typology*, p. 126.

59. *Zwettler.*

60. Indeed, exegesis as such is a well-attested method for the apocalypticist: *Collins*, pp. 205–10; Lawson, *Gnostic*, pp. 1–20.

61. Frye, *Great Code*, pp. 82–3.

62. *Collins*, p. 215; Goppelt, *Typos*; Auerbach, 'Figura'; Frye, *Great Code*; Collins, *Dead Sea Scrolls*, p. 204.

63. Note the words used to refer to the two previous scriptures in Arabic: *al-ahd al-qadim* = 'the older or former testament/covenant' and *al-'ahd al-jadid* = 'the new testament/covenant', cf. e.g. *al-Kitab al-Muqaddas ay kutub al-'ahd al-'qadim wa-l-'ahd al-jadid* ('The Holy Book, namely the books of the old or former testament/covenant and the new testament/covenant').

64. Wansbrough, *Sectarian*. This is taken up below in Ch. 4.

65. The trope of intensity was first suggested as a characteristic of the Quran as apocalypse in Lawson, 'Duality', p. 25.

66. For a recent comprehensive study of what emerges as *the* central mytheme of the Quran and Islam, see al-Qadi, *Primordial*.

67. As it is universally known in the Islamic world, the day of 'Am I not' echoes the sacred question from Q7:172: *a-lastu bi-rabbikum* = Am I not your Lord?

68. Cf. Stock, *Augustine*, pp. 32–42.

69. Something of the idea is captured in Rosenthal, 'History' p. 430, quoted below in Ch. 3, p. 59.

70. See Introduction.

71. Melisma is a prominent distinguishing feature of Arabic music even as it has fallen out of favour in other cultural contexts. This bespeaks the profound appreciation of the relationship in Arabic literature and poetics between sound and sense and its continued vitality. The type of ideational melisma suggested here is a natural implication of this and the kind of characterisations found, for example, in Scholem, *Major Trends*, pp. 130–5, in discussing the kabbalistic contemplations of Abu Lafia as structured on a 'music of pure thought'. On the pervasive feature of melisma in Arabic music in general and in Quran recitation in particular, see Nelson, *Art*, pp. 127, 128, 132, 148, 235. My thanks to Prof. G. Sawa for valuable discussion on this topic.

72. Levitin, *Your Brain*, p. 6. See also Jarret, *Drifting*. The question is not so much how the Quran itself might have changed from one generation to the next – from pre-canonical or pre-exegetical or 'pre-critical'. Rather, the revealing question concerns how and in what ways the audiences from generation to generation changed. How did their 'musical expectations' both differ from and relate to the expectations of the Quran's first hearers. For the example of *al-sakina* see Goldziher, 'La Notion', p. 11.

73. See *Roads, passim* and Brown's astute comment quoted above (p. 84) petitioning the idea of the *totum simul* and Frye's remark about the 'freezing' of a verbal structure, above p. 21.

74. Cf. G. Böwering, 'Time' (*EQ*), pp. 286–7.

75. Al-Qadi, *Primordial*; *Zwettler*; Frye, *Fearful Symmetry*; Auerbach, 'Figura'; Lawson, 'Duality'.

76. G. Böwering, 'Ideas of time in Persian Sufism', in *Iran* 30 (1 January 1992), pp. 77–89; Stowasser, 'Time Sticks'.

77. Ch. 4 below.

78. In addition to *Collins*, see Funkenstein, *Perceptions*.

79. See Baumgarten, *Apocalyptic Time*; Funkenstein, *Perceptions*; Garcia Martinez, 'Apocalypticism'; VanderKam, *Calendars*; Rosenthal, 'History'.

80. Frye, *Great Code*, pp. 6–17 and his discussion of the phases of language. See also the numerous supportive examples in Günther (ed.), *Ideas* and Neuwirth et al. (eds), *Myths*.
81. Because it is "made of" consciousness.
82. Ravasi, *Crypt*, p. 38.
83. With regard to the move away from such 'mythic thinking' in Western intellectual history, the following comment is suggestive: 'Leibniz believed in the *Prisca Theologia* just as much as Newton did, but he could envision submarines, airplanes and all kinds of things absent from ancient texts. For that matter so could Roger Bacon and Leonardo da Vinci. Past perfect and future perfect only began to be separated during Newton's lifetime. It would take the eighteenth century to accomplish this separation, at a cost well documented by Romantics and conservatives of every subsequent generation' (Coudert, 'Newton', p. 42).
84. Wilson, *Red*, p. 128.
85. See below Ch. 3, p. 59, the long quotation from Rosenthal.
86. Goldziher, 'La Notion'; Fahd, 'Sakina'.
87. Abdel Haleem translation, Arabic transliteration added.
88. Ryan, 'Descending'; see also Ghaemmaghami's chapter in *Roads*.
89. For a masterful article on this, see Hajjaji-Jarrah, 'Enchantment'.
90. Hallaq, 'Law', p. 150.
91. VanderKam, *Calendars*; cf. also the Dead Sea scroll entitled 'Community Rule'; J. J. Collins, 'Was the Dead Sea Sect'; Roth, *Dead*.
92. Kinberg, 'Paradise', pp. 18–9.
93. Ibid., p. 19.
94. Furuzanfar, *Aḥādīth-i mathnawī* #222.
95. Günther, 'Paradiesevorstellungen', pp. 44–9.
96. For an excellent introduction to the numerous ways the story has been received and understood see Gruber and Colby (eds), *The Prophet's Ascension*.
97. On importance of chiasmus in the Quran, see Cuypers, *Le Festin*; Ernst, *How to Read*. The allusion to Ezekiel's wheel of glory is unintended but apposite.
98. See Nagel, in *Roads*.
99. Cf. the holy descent of the banquet in the Dead Sea Scrolls. It is a symptom of the current state of our studies that there is no reference at all to Qumran in Cuypers' magnificent and truly groundbreaking study of the fifth sura, *The Banquet*. See, with caution, Gallez, *Messie*.
100. As such a term is used to refer, for example, to Qumran. See Collins, 'Was the Dead Sea sect'; Collins, *Dead Sea Scrolls*, pp. 45–7 and 130, where he characterises both the Essenes and the early church as apocalyptic communities. See also *Collins*, p. 145 and *passim* Vermés, *Jesus*. On Qumran see also the more recent VanderKam, 'Apocalyptic Tradition'.
101. Hodgson, *Venture* i, p. 367.
102. Kinberg, 'Paradise', p. 12. Kinberg continues that such statements 'transcribed by Jews in Hebrew characters and translated from Arabic into Latin, taught the Spanish Christians how to fight Islam in the most vigorous and harsh way'.
103. Cook, *Studies*.
104. Cuypers, *La Composition*; Cuypers, *Une apocalypse*; Cuypers, *Le Festin*; Ernst, *How to Read*.
105. As in Chapter 1, above.
106. Neuwirth, 'Negotiating'; Lawson, 'Duality'; Ernst, *How to Read*.
107. See Günther, in *Roads*.
108. Yuccsoy, *Messianic*.
109. Cook, *Studies*; Rubin, 'Apocalypse'.

110. Fleischer, 'Lawgiver'; Fleischer, *Mahdi*.
111. Quinn, *Historical*, pp. 63–9; Babayan, *Mystics*.
112. Bashir, *Messianic*.
113. Lawson, *Gnostic*; Amanat, 'Resurgence'.
114. Friedmann, *Prophecy*; Valentine, *Islam*.
115. Filiu, *Apocalypse*. See Introduction.

CHAPTER 3: THE EPIC OF JOSEPH, APOCALYPSE OF REUNION

1. Goppelt, *Typos*. For Lamb of God, Suffering Servant and Jonah as typological prefigurations of Jesus as antitype, see pp. 189 and 72–3, respectively. See also Goppelt's near contemporary: Auerbach, 'Figura'. On repetition, see Kierkegaard, *Repetition*.
2. Funkenstein, *Perceptions*, pp. 74–87.
3. 'In the Quran, descriptions of the hereafter appear in relation to the arrival of a day, "the hour" *(al-sa'a)*, "reckoning day" *(yawm al-hisab)*, "the day of judgment" *(yawm al-din)'*, "the last day" *(al-yawm al-akhir)*, or "the day of resurrection" *(yawm al-qiyama)'*, Kinberg, 'Paradise', p. 12a.
4. Frye, *Great Code*, p. 80.
5. Frye, *Fearful Symmetry*, p. 272.
6. Corbin, *History*, p. 5.
7. Rosenthal, 'History', p. 4. See below, Ch. 4, p. 91 for a related observation from Frye *Fearful Symmetry*, 247. Compare William Faulkner's famous line in *Requiem for a Nun*: 'The past is never dead. It's not even past.'
8. Sells, 'Sound'.
9. Frye, *Great Code*, pp. 80–1.
10. Ibid., pp. 82–3, see above p. 60.
11. As in the title of *Collins*.
12. Such a radical mode of reading has been identified by Auerbach, ('Figura', p. 42), vis- à-vis Augustine: 'Even though Augustine rejects abstract allegorical spiritualism and develops his whole interpretation of the Old Testament from the concrete historical reality, he nevertheless has an idealism which removes the concrete event, completely preserved as it is, from time and transposes it into the perspective of eternity.'
13. The other is the constant interplay of duality, symmetry, and opposition, namely Quranic enantiodromia. See below, Ch. 4.
14. Waldman, 'Approaches', p. 55.
15. Mir, 'Quranic Story'.
16. Hanson, *Dawn*, p. 433, quoted above p. 22
17. See below Chs 5 and 6. Note the implication such movement or 'return to the beginning' has for the power of the Joseph myth to gather the heretofore scattered energies and resources of 'Israel'. In such a way does the Quran's Joseph have implications for consolidation and individuation on both the communal, societal level and the individual, existential level. Frye's discussion of the myth of *sparagmos* may be suggestive here: (*Fearful Symmetry*, esp. pp. 394–7 and 287; see also pp. 289, 403). On the distinctive and characteristic understanding of history in the Quran, see Neuwirth, 'Two Views'; Rosenthal, 'History'. See now also the recent discussion by Stewart, 'Prophecy'.
18. *Badi'* means, in a passive sense, 'innovated, discovered' but because it also evokes God the Originator/Innovator par excellence – one of the so-called ninety-nine names

(see Q2:117; 6:101) – it denotes ancientness, timelessness and pre-eternity. The rhetorical and literary *coincidentia oppositorum* in this word is possibly one reason the virtuoso Abbasid poets used the term to describe – and not in a self-effacing way – their own poetry. Consult, for example, Khalafallah, 'Badi''.

Again, Auerbach's words are apposite:

> These two comparisons, with allegory on the one hand and with the symbolical, mythical forms on the other, disclose figural prophecy in a twofold light: youthful and newborn as a purposive, creative, concrete interpretation of universal history; infinitely old as the late interpretation of a venerable text, charged with history, that had grown for hundreds of years (Figura, p.58).

19. See below Ch. 6.

20. Pellat, 'Ḥilm', quoting Goldziher, *Muhammedanische*, 1: 319 ff.

21. The juxtaposition of the duality of experience and the universality of truth is a major preoccupation of the complex and singular polymath, Muḥammad b. ʿAbd al-Karim al-Shahrastani (1153) in his Quran commentary, *Mafatih al-asrar*, recently beautifully explicated and analysed in Mayer, *Keys*, pp. 25–35.

22. Neuwirth, 'Symmetrie, p. 454.

23. This calls to mind Umberto Eco's (1994: 508) widely quoted comment: 'I would define the poetic effect as the capacity that a text displays for continuing to generate different readings, without ever being completely consumed.'

24. This is a question that arises from viewing the text from a particular perspective. Viewed from another angle, there is neither beginning nor end.

25. This very feature was one of the reasons it was rejected as being an authentic part of the Quran by a faction of the Kharijites, according to al-Shahrastani. The Ajarida, the followers of ʿAbd al-Karim b. Ajrad, and especially, it seems, the subgroup of the Ajarida called the Maymuniyya (followers of Maymun al-Qaddah), rejected the sura of Joseph on the grounds precisely that it was a complete, consistent narrative ('a [mere] story') and a love story at that.

26. A question awaiting a satisfactory answer is just how it came to be that most of the other clear and characteristic attributes of the Quranic Joseph seem to dissolve into insignificance in the presence of his beauty. The picture presented by the Quran is one of a very powerful, independent and pious mind capable of controlling an entire society. Yet it is beauty that emerges as the most important of his many qualities, according to the tradition. This is the case with many of the Quranic prophets: one key trait, at the expense of many others, becomes identified with this or that specific prophetic figure. See Tottoli, *Biblical*.

27. It has been observed (Waldman, 'Approaches') that Muḥammad can serve, simultaneously, as the antitype for both Joseph and Jacob. See the very suggestive comments by Frye, *Code*, p. 196. I am not addressing here the many ways in which Joseph functions as a type for Jesus, the antitype.

28. *Zwettler*. See below Ch. 4.

29. It is a puzzle why Eliade in *Myth of the Eternal Return* did not pay more attention to Islam.

30. See Introduction.

31. Note the role of Tahep in Samaritan theology, a theology in which Joseph has a prominent role. Macdonald, *Theology*, pp. 332–44. On anagnorisis in Arabic literature in general and in the Joseph sura in particular see now Kennedy, *Recognition*.

32. *Pace* Wansbrough, who analyses the commentary on sura 12 by Muqatil ibn Sulayman (765). Wansbrough, *Quranic*, p. 131, maintains that, notwithstanding the claim of narrative consistency by exegetes, the story of Joseph is 'elliptic, often

unintelligible without exegetical complement'. It should be noted that Wansbrough paid no attention to the aural dimension of the story.

33. Brinner, *Lives*, p. 646. See now Brinner and Thackston for translations of al-Tha'labi and al-Kisa'i.

34. According to the usual numbering of verses, sura 21 has 112 verses, while suras 17 and 12 both have 111 verses. No sura has 114 verses, the number that corresponds exactly to the total number of suras in the Quran.

35. By devoting discrete works of exegesis to this sura alone.

36. Reda, *Crescendo*.

37. Ibn Arabi, *Fusus*, 1, pp. 99–106. See also Ibn Arabi, *Bezels*, pp. 119–27. For the importance of the figure of Yusuf and his ordeal with Potiphar's wife in early Sufi *tafsir*, see Böwering, *Mystical*, p. 256.

38. Al-Ghazali , *Tafsir*.

39. See *GAL* S I, p. 747 for a list of several manuscripts of this work with the name *Sirr al-'allamayn fi tafsir surat Yusuf*.

40. *GAL* mentions this work in several places.

41. See *GAL* II, pp. 204, 437; S II, p. 135.

42. *GAL* S II, p. 589. The catalogue in question is *Fihrist kitābkhāna-yi madrasa-yi Sipahsālār*, 1, p. 128. *Dharī'a* appears to be the source of this error in *GAL*, see below.

43. *GAL* S II, p. 853.

44. Momen, *Introduction*, p. 145.

45. *GAL* S II, p. 984.

46. de Prémare, *Joseph*; Goldman, *Wiles*; Fatoohi, *Prophet*; Kugel, *Potiphar* (and the translation into English of Bajouda, *Joseph*). See also several references in later works by Annemarie Schimmel to a monograph in progress entitled *The Shirt of Joseph* (Schimmel, 'Yusuf', p. 45 n. 1; Schimmel, *Deciphering*, p. 109 n. 5). As far as I know, it was never completed. Of course, Joseph is tremendously important to the Christian tradition as well, as is evidenced, inter alia, by Thomas Mann's self-described masterwork, *Josef und seine Brüder*, composed in four separate substantial books between the years 1926 and 1943. His artistic rendering has recently become the focus of such scholars as Assman, *Thomas Mann*, and Bal, *Loving*. Of interest also is McGaha, *Coat*.

47. Macdonald, 'Joseph', pt 1 and 2; Waldman, 'Approaches'; Abdel Haleem, 'Story'; Bernstein, *Stories*.

48. Beeston, *Baidawi's*; Keeler, *Sufi*, esp. pp. 278–309.

49. Johns, 'Joseph'; Rendsburg, 'Literacy'; Morris, 'Dramatizing'.

50. Neuwirth, 'Zur Struktur'; Waldman, 'Approaches'; Mir, 'Quranic Story' and 'Irony'.

51. Lawson, *Gnostic*, Ch. 4; Schimmel, 'Yusuf'; Subtelny, 'Visionary'.

52. Johns, 'Joseph'.

53. See the resumé of much of this work in Renard, *Seven*, pp. 259–72 and the comprehensive Firestone, 'Yusuf'.

54. Amanat, *Resurrection*, p. 202.

55. *Dharī'a*, 1, p. 288.

56. *Dharī'a*, 4, pp. 344–6.

57. See below Ch. 7.

58. Amanat, *Resurrection*, pp. 190–1.

59. On the myth and motif of the hostile brothers in classical and modern Arabic literature, see Günther, 'Hostile'.

60. On this, see, for example, Amir-Moezzi, 'Notes'; see also Lawson *Gnostic*, Ch. 2.

61. Strothmann, 'Takiya', p. 562. See now also Amanat, *Resurrection*, pp. 200–1; Clarke, 'Rise'.

62. *Burhan,* 2, p. 270 no. 7 (from *Kāfī*).

63. *Burhan,* 2, p. 271 no. 12 (from Qummi's *tafsir*).

64. *Burhan,* 2, p. 272 no. 23.

65. *Ikmal,* p. 18.

66. *Ikmal,* p. 613. Elsewhere it is mentioned that the Qaʿim will announce his message to the 'east and west' that he is *baqiyyat allah* (*Bihar,* 52, pp. 191–2 no. 24).

67. *Mirʿat,* p. 105.

68. *Bihar,* 52, p. 347 no. 97.

69. *Bihar,* 53, p. 36.

70. *Ikmal,* p. 621.

71. *Ikmal,* p. 620.

72. *Bihar,* 52, p. 394.

73. Al-Ahsaʾi, *Sharh,* 3, p. 75. The actual commentary on this verse begins on p. 48 and ends on p. 101. Much of this is taken up with the quotation of and ancillary commentary on the notoriously long apocalyptic hadith transmitted by Mufaddal from al-Sadiq.

74. Ricks, 'Garment', p. 203. See also Bernstein, 'Story'.

75. Note the etymological relationship between *ʿarf,* one word for 'scent', and *ʿirfan/maʿrifa* 'recognition, knowledge, gnosis, intuition'.

76. Classen, *Color,* esp. p. 60.

77. This is not to suggest, however, that the Islamicate meaning of 'spiritual' is exhausted by the literary device of typological figuration. But it is certainly one important component of the broader category of 'spiritual'. Other layers of the notion would include ethics, comportment and learning itself, as represented by the categories *adab* and *akhlaq,* which rescue the idea of 'spiritual' from pertaining solely to abstract intellectual constructs, tying it to practise in the here and now. But this is not the subject at hand.

78. Mir, *Quranic Story.*

79. Lawson, *Gnostic,* Ch. 4.

80. The Quran ends the story of Joseph on a note of 'happily ever after' to emphasise the wisdom and salvific value of obedience and tawhid. After all, this was not just any family who was thus rescued, but the 'holy remnant' of Abrahamic monotheism of which Islam is the most recent dispensation. Thus, it is also representative of the rescue of 'true Islam'. Later, of course, in this specific historical circumstance, the fortunes of the children of Israel in Egypt take a turn for the worse. Again, Israel (and therefore ultimately the future Islam) is rescued by the prophet Moses. This is doubtless part of the contemporary reception of the sura of Joseph: the audience (i.e. Muhammad's audience) is led to see themselves as the heroes of the Abrahamic line and the guardians of Islam. As mentioned earlier, typological figuration applies to both the prophetic figures and their communities. On the importance of Joseph to the identity of Israel, see Kugel, *Potiphar,* esp. pp. 13–27: 'Indeed, relatively early in the biblical period, the figure of Joseph came to be profoundly affected by political change . . . if there nevertheless remained a hope that "the Lord, the God of hosts, may be gracious to the remnant of Joseph" (Amos 5:15), this hope became dimmer and dimmer' (p. 17). But it did not die. Joseph's coffin was carried by Moses and his fellow exiles from Egypt to the Promised Land. But first they had to find it. On this, see Benin, 'Jews', p. 32.

81. As in Philo or the Sunni Sufi Ala al-Dawla Simnani (1336), whose influential theory of the interior prophets of the individual soul is studied in Corbin, *Man,* pp. 121–31, and generally by Elias, *Throne.*

82. For an exceptionally lucid analysis, which emphasises the important fact that typlogical figuration flows in two directions, see the recent discussion in Stewart, 'Prophecy'.

83. For a general comparison between prose writing and musical improvisation, see Jarrett, *Drifting*.

84. This point is made, somewhat incompletely, in Stern, 'Muhammad'.

85. 'Narreme' is a technical term in the relatively recent science of 'narratology'. It is defined as a self-standing unit of a narrative composition on the model of 'morpheme' or 'mytheme'. For a narratological approach to the Quranic story of Joseph, see Gasmi, 'Narrative' and 'Les Reseaux'.

86. That the woven fabric represents a 'manifestation' of the coincidence of opposites (warp ≠ weft) may also be of interest.

87. *Corbin*, 4: index, 'amphibolie, *iltibās*'. A cognate perspective is found in William Blake as discussed by Frye, *Fearful Symmetry*, pp. 381–2:

> This is the power of seeing the physical appearance as the covering of the mental reality, yet not concealing its shape so much as revealing it in a fallen aspect, and so not the clothing but the body or form of the mental world, though a physical and therefore a fallen body or form. If we try to visualize this development of the 'clothing' symbol, we get something more like a mirror, a surface which reveals reality in fewer dimensions than it actually has.

88. While it may reasonably be questioned whether such a subtle occurrence of the root *w-l-y* here in Q12:84 can be so significant, it should be remembered that in Shiʻi *tafsir* such otherwise apparently 'weak' occasions may serve the exegete in surprising ways. This has been amply demonstrated in Lawson, 'Akhbari', pp. 163–97.

89. When used to speak about Islam, *Heilsgeschichte* must always be understood to emphasise the entering of divinity or holiness into actual history through the agency of prophecy. Thus it may also be translated as 'divine history', which in some ways may actually be closer to the German, where 'salvation' is actually *Erlösung*.

90. See above, p. 64.

91. As far as the heavenly origin of the shirt is concerned, there is no disagreement across sectarian boundaries (Lawson, 'Typological' pp. 235-6.)

92. Meier, 'Aspects', p. 421. See now also Greifenhagen, 'Garments'.

93. See the *hadith al-kisaʼ*, related on the authority of Fatima, daughter of Muhammad, in *Mafatih*, pp. 386–9, with its specific reference to the 'sweet fragrance' (*raʼiha tayyiba*) of the Prophet's mantle (lit. 'Yemeni cloak', *al-kisaʼ al-yamani*). Here, Hasan and other members of the *ahl al-bayt* exclaim in turn upon entering Fatima's house, 'I detect something like the fragrance of my grandfather.' The spiritual reality of the cloak and the physical reality of the Prophet have become one. My thanks to Arsheen Devji for suggesting the importance of this in the present context. See also Momen, *Introduction*, p. 14.

94. Corbin, *Cyclical*, p. 75.

95. In the early exegetical work *Kitab Asas al-taʼwīl*, by the Ismaʻili *daʻi* Qadi al-Nuʻman (974), the interesting comment is made to the effect that the 'front' and 'back' of the shirt refer to exoteric and esoteric knowledge respectively (p. 144). The *qamis* in verse Q12:93 is seen as representing *imama* (p. 163).

96. Böwering, *Mystical*, p. 256.

97. The same phrase occurs one other time, in Q18:84, where it is used to describe how God gave 'security throughout the land' to Dhu l-Qarnayn, frequently identified with Alexander the Great in *tafsir*.

98. Sufi literature on the initiatory *robe (khirqa)* speaks of its heavenly origin also, and mentions the *qamis* of Joseph (with which the *khirqa* is compared) as that which protected Abraham from the fire. Al-Suhrawardi, 'Awarif', pp. 95–102. For a broader survey of Sufi writers on the robe, see Elias, *Sufi* and now the useful article 'Joseph' by Dadbeh et al. in *EIr*.

99. *Nur,* 2: 462 no. 187. The compiler adds that a similar tradition is found elsewhere as follows: 'When the Qāʾim comes forth, the shirt of Joseph will be on him, and he will have the staff of Moses and the ring of Solomon.' The heavenly origin of this shirt was also taught by the early exegete al-Kalbi (150/767) in what Wansbrough (*Quranic,* p. 134) termed 'a reflex of Rabbinic descriptions' of the robe in Genesis.

100. *Mirʾat,* p. 110.

101. As in the famous title of Ibn al-Jawzi's *Talbīs Iblīs - "The Devil's Disguise".*

102. *Mirʾat,* pp. 294–5. In discussing the connotations of 'deception' that the word carries, this author refers to Q6:72 ('those who do not clothe their faith in darkness'), and says that this refers to those who did not confuse *the walaya* with the *walaya* of 'so-and-so and so-and-so'.

103. Rashti, *Sharh,* p. 68.

104. The fascinating relationship, typological and otherwise, between the celebrated mantle or *burda* of the Prophet Muhammad is, unfortunately, not pursued here due to lack of space. See the recent study of the poetry in Stetkevych, *Mantle Odes,* where Joseph (but not his shirt) appears on pp. 96, 130, 172.

105. Ibid.

106. Lawson, 'Akhbari', p. 164; see also Lawson, *Gnostic,* Ch. 4 and appendices for a closer look at the Bab's commentary.

107. On Abraham as model and exemplar, see Firestone, *Journeys;* see also Paret, 'Ibrahim'. On Islam/Muhammad's similar esteem for Moses, see now Wheeler, *Moses.* See also the very interesting discussion by Moreen, 'Moses'.

108. Al-Ghazali, *Tafsir,* p. 198.

109. Classen et al., *Aroma,* p. 60. See also the suggestive study of the 'anthropology of air, scent, and wind', Parkin, 'Wafting'. Scent also distinguishes itself from other senses by acting directly on the brain without intermediary.

CHAPTER 4: THE APOCALYPTIC SUBSTRATE: DUALITY AND OPPOSITION

1. For a useful differentiation of these terms as they are used in the study of the problem outside scholarship on Islam, see Hellholm, 'Introduction', in *Apocalypticism,* pp. 1–5. See also Hanson, *The Dawn of Apocalyptic.* In this chapter we will be using such terms according to their understanding in contemporary biblical and literary scholarship: 1) apocalypse is the thing itself (as is sometimes apocalyptic in its nominal intention); 2) apocalypticism is the activity, either social, intellectual/literary or a combination of both; 3) apocalyptic is the adjective that may refer to either or both of the first two. (See below for the working definition of apocalypse as a literary genre.) A more recent usage, also adopted here, that indicates all three modes is the anglicised form of the original Greek: ἀποκάλυψις < apocalypsis.

2. D. Cook, *Studies.* In this particular instance the noteworthy observation is made that among the early Islamicate apocalyptic works (e.g. Nuʿaym ibn Hammad al-Marwazi's (844) *Kitab al-fitan*), very little of the Quran is found either referred to or quoted. There is another type of historical study of interest here, namely one that examines the way in which the Muslim community and Islam was viewed 'from the outside' as a sign of the apocalypse expected by other groups. See for example R. Hoyland, *Seeing.*

3. A most suggestive and useful methodological tool fashioned by Angelika Neuwirth, in one of the earlier numbers of this journal: 'Negotiating Justice', pp. 25–41 and 2:2, pp. 1–18; also Neuwirth, 'Referentiality and Textuality. Finally, the term is used by Neuwirth again in 'Orientalism'.

4. J. J. Collins, '"Response" in the panel discussion organized by T. Lawson.
5. Cook, *Studies*, pp. 270–4. These are identified in order: *al-sa'a* (the Hour [of Judgment]), *amr, fitna, ajal* and *yawm*.
6. Cook, *Studies*, p. 301, quoting Andrew Rippin, in Stefan Wild (ed.), *The Quran as Text* (Leiden: Brill, 1996), pp. 125–36 (quotation from p. 125). Cook also refers to an unpublished study by Fred Donner.
7. But see F. Leemhuis, 'Apocalypse': 'as a prophetic, revealed message, the Quran is to a large extent apocalyptic yet there are parts of it that carry this theme in a more intense manner'.
8. One is reminded here of the sagacious observation: 'the story of scholarly error is largely one of questions wrongly put because their presuppositions were wrong; correspondingly, the story of scholarly achievement can almost be summed up in successive refinements of terminology.' (Hodgson, *The Venture of Islam*, Vol. 1, p. 46.
9. E.D. Hirsch Jr., *Validity* pp. 68–102. This assumption is also heavily relied upon in *Collins* p. 6.
10. Some of these are: 'history', 'prophecy', 'law', 'fable', 'prayer', 'psalm', 'oaths' and so on. See, for example, A. T. Welch, 'al-Ḳurʾān', in *EI2*. Mohammed Arkoun has criticised Welch's approach in his *Lectures* where he commends the study of Jalal al-Din al-Suyuti's *al-Itqan* as a starting point for an appreciation of the complexities and artistry of the Quran.
11. Casanova, *Mohammed*.
12. See above, Ch. 2.
13. Cf. the classic by C.K. Ogden & I.A. Richards, *Meaning*
14. Cf. the remark in H. Corbin, *Annuaire* pp. 236–7, 'this closed circuit [of oppositions] is its own justification, because by its very existence, its opposite, that is absolute transcendence, is indicated.' (my translation)
15. Neuwirth, 'Symmetrie', pp. 443–75. This article should be read by every student of Islam and the Quran. Fortunately, many of its insights are now part of the author's recent 'Paradise as a Quranic Discourse'. Neuwirth acknowledges a debt to the earlier groundbreaking exploration of the afterlife in which pertinent and lucid observations on the role of duality in the Quranic worldview were offered, possibly for the first time in modern scholarship: S. Saleh, *La Vie* published a doctoral dissertation written in 1954 under the guidance of Louis Massignon. However, the topic is left comparatively undeveloped. See now the more recent article by M. A. S. Abdel Haleem 'Context' See now also the excellent discussion by S. Schmidtke, 'Pairs and Pairing', in *EQ*.
16. M. A. S. Abdel Haleem, 'Introduction', in *The Quran* pp. ix–xx. The author continues in harmony with our general thesis: 'This sense of balance in the text is continued in passages where the Prophet is instructed to say, "*Now the truth has come from your Lord: let those who wish to believe in it do so, and let those who wish to reject it do so*" (Q18:29) and "*There is no compulsion in religion: true guidance has become distinct from error*" (Q2:56) (one of the many names the Quran gives itself is *al-Furqān* – "the book that distinguishes [right from wrong]" Q25:1). Here the author refers to a work by A. Nawfal, *al-Iʿjāz al-ʿadad li'l-Quran al-karim* (Cairo: n.p., 1976), in which duality and numeration is studied. Unfortunately, I have been unable to locate it.
17. This patristic word should be taken here in the sense which comes in from the Greek *enantiodromein* 'something running in the opposite direction', meaning in this context the 'play of opposites'. This meaning should be contrasted with the perhaps more familiar Jungian usage adapted to the concerns of individuation in which the oppositions inherent in the undifferentiated *massa confusa* tend to become each other. See the comments in C. O'Regan, *Gnostic* pp. 40, 247. Obviously, this interplay of opposition ceaselessly expressed throughout the Quran would have serious implications for the

form and contents of all Islamicate mystical discourse, and in some of these subsequent contexts one may perceive something of a more purely Jungian enantiodromia. Here we are concerned solely with the Quran.

18. This is a reference to *Collins*.

19. Mircea M. Eliade, 'La Coincidentia' pp. 195–236, p. 234.

20. A 'weak' example of such eradication may be seen in the philological opinion that the two gardens of Q55 should be understood as a figure for one vast garden (Neuwirth, 'Symmetrie', pp. 460–1). A 'strong' example would be the conceptual joining (*ijtima '*) referred to in Abu Sa 'id's remark (see below p. 87). In either case, what Neuwirth so perfectly characterises as the 'deeply connected logic of the imagination' (*fortlaufender Logik der Imagination*) ('Symmetrie', p. 454) is obviously in operation in either instance.

21. In what may be referred to as the 'mystical perspective', time and history cease when they are perceived as illusory.

22. *Collins*, p. 12.

23. *Collins*, p. 13, citing Paul Ricoeur, 'Preface' to A. Lacocque, *The Book of Daniel* (Atlanta: John Knox, 1979), pp. xxii–xxiii.

24. Kristeva, *Tales,* p. 70.

25. On this term, see T. van Dijk, *Some*.

26. For a fine introduction to the role of 'enantiodromia' (though I think the word is never used by her) in Ibn Arabi, see S. Murata', *The Tao*.

27. 'Work' may conjure, through the accident of etymology, the idea of opera and raises the very interesting question about the operatic aspects of the Quran, its recitation (performance) and audition (reception), its power to hold, transport and explain or at least contextualise the great mysteries and deep sufferings of life. A suggestive study that would certainly be of use in such an exploration is the recent L. & M. Hutcheon *Opera and the Art of Dying*. The guiding insight is that audiences of opera are 'participating in a ritual of grieving or experiencing their own mortality by proxy . . . they can feel both identification and distance as they – safely – rehearse their own (or a loved one's) demise . . . death is made to feel logical or somehow right' (pp. 10–11).

28. Schmidtke, 'Pairs and Pairing'.

29. It is interesting to observe here the type of attributes that are never used to designate God, e.g. happy, gay, laughing and so on. See also the interesting observation in Schmidtke, 'Pairs and Pairing', pp. 5–6, on those pairs of divine names that are in fact not opposites, what she refers to as 'double divine epithets'.

30. This may be thought the literary equivalent or analogue of one of Nicholas of Cusa's favorite philosophical and theological maxims: 'God is a sphere whose center is everywhere' (in J. Hopkins, *Nicholas of Cusa* pp. 33, 56). We know, though, that Nicholas of Cusa (1464) got this image from his reading of Meister Eckhart (1328). On the history of the metaphor see K. Harries, 'The Infinite Sphere' pp. 5–15.

31. The passage continues: 'hence the beautiful inconsequentiality of the arrangement of the Suras: from the longest to the shortest. In this respect the Koran is more avant-garde than *Finnegans Wake*, in which the over-all organization is entangled in both linear and cyclical patterns which it is trying to transcend' (Brown, 'The Apocalypse' p. 166). We do not believe that the arrangement of the suras is inconsequential.

32. Brown goes on to say: 'the rejection of linearity involves a rejection of narrative. There is only one decent narrative in the Koran: sura 12, "Joseph", acclaimed by condescending Western Orientalists: for once Muhammad overcame his temperamental incoherence and managed to do it right. The strict sect of the Kharidjis, on this point and on others the voice of strict Islamic consistency, condemned sura 12 on the ground that narrative has no place in revelation. The Koran breaks decisively with that alliance between the prophetic tradition and materialistic historicism – "what actually happened" – which set in with the materialistically historical triumph of Christianity. Hence the strangely abortive and incoherent character of the pseudonarratives in sura 18. Something happened, but this strange revelation manages not to reveal what or why' (Brown, 'The Apocalypse' p. 166). Brown was not aware of the importance of ring structure and chiasmus when he wrote this. But then neither was the vast field of historical Quranic sciences.

33. Van Duzer, *Duality and Structure*.

34. The prime example offered (Van Duzer, *Duality and Structure* pp. 6–7) is that of the moly, given by Hermes to Odysseus to protect or save him from the wiles of Circe. The moly has a black root and a milk-white flower. Hermes is, as it happens, the god of interpretation (cf. hermeneutic), so it is likely that the giver is as important as the gift. In any case, the moly represents the joining together of two absolute and otherwise diametrically opposed elements (black ≠ white); this is analogous to the way in which dualities seem to function in the Quran if the realisation of oneness may be thought to stand for a kind of Islamic salvation. The moly represents such a *coincidentia* not just from the opposition of colours. It shows that upper and lower (flower and root), mortal and divine, and ease and difficulty, are all combined in the symbol. We will encounter the moly again in Ch. 7 below. The classic study of the conjunction of oppositions is of course C. G. Jung, *Mysterium Conjunctionis*, Jung's last booklength work.

35. Cf. Arabic: *zawj*, 'one of a pair or the pair itself'. See below for the importance of this term in the discussion of typological figuration, which here is seen to emerge and develop from the incessant Quranic deployment of polarities, opposites and dualities.

36. In addition to the oft-cited notion of the 'coranization du conscience' from Paul Nwyia, *Exégèse coranique et langue mystique* p. 178, the following succinct quotation from Cragg makes the same point in a slightly different way: 'It has also conditioned the mentality of those generations and their patterns of emotion. *Hifz* [memorisation of the entire Quran] has effectively Quranized the instincts of mind in Islam to a degree which could not have been the case if the Scripture had been only a written court of appeal. Further, the habit of recital in strict sequence fixed the juxtaposition of Quranic incidents and phrases, endowed them with a sort of sacred logic. Adjacence became significant of meaning and sense was linked strongly with proximity. To have a literature thus scrupulously by heart is to think instinctively in its idiom and its content' (Kenneth Cragg, *The Mind of the Quran* (London: Allen & Unwin, 1973), p. 26).

37. For example, such an experience is described by Plotinus through the parable of the reader who forgets they are reading. See Elmer O'Brien (tr. and commentary), *The Essential Plotinus: Representative Treatises from the Enneads* (Indianapolis: Hackett, 1981), p. 30.

38. As mentioned in Michel Chodkiewicz, *Seal of the Saints: Prophethood and Sainthood in the Doctrine of Ibn Arabi*, tr. Liadain Sherrard (Cambridge: The Islamic Texts Society, 1993), pp. 37, 71. Such personifications may be thought part of the subtext evoked in the striking but apt title of the recent book on the Quran by Bruce Lawrence, *The Quran: A Biography* (London: Atlantic, 2006).

39. Izutsu, *Ethico-religious Concepts*. Surely it is partly due to the success of his discussion here that the Quran has been called a 'structuralist's dream', as in A. Rippin, 'The Quran as' pp. 38–47, p. 38.

40. Something of a linguistic apocalypse; Izutsu, *Ethico-religious Concepts*, p. 251.

41. Akin to what Frye in another, but possibly related, context refers to as 'the tyranny the idea of unbounded space exerts on the mind' (Frye, *Fearful Symmetry*, p. 261).

42. The term 'opposition' as used here does not automatically denote antagonism. It does denote one thing being 'placed across' or 'in front' of another. Obviously, it can also mean antagonism.

43. As may be apparent, oneness can also be considered the opposite of any expression of multiplicity. We are experimenting here with the notion of duality.

44. Bernard P. Dauenhauer, *Silence, the Phenomenon and its Ontological Significance* (Bloomington: Indiana University Press, 1980).

45. After which he is reported to have recited Q57:3, *He is the First, the Last, the Manifest, the Hidden*. See also Ibn Arabi, *Fusus*, p. 77 and T. Lawson, 'The Hidden Words' pp. 427–47.

46. It is not impertinent to mention the drama of the Androgynes in the Symposium. 'The audacious wish of these total beings was to scale heaven and set upon the gods; therefore they were punished, the gods cut them in two – and that division was a sexualization. Henceforth each one seeks the part of which it has been deprived, and that quest is the true impetus of action as well as love' (Kristeva, *Tales*, p. 69).

47. See works of Abd al-Haleem and Neuwirth et al. mentioned above.

48. See Neuwirth, 'Symmetrie', and her discussion and analysis of the pertinent classical works of Arabic philology, pp. 460–2.

49. R. A. Nicholson, *Studies*, p. 151.

50. This is the title of one of the more important later books of Henry Corbin.

51. W. Chittick, *The Sufi*.

52. This is certainly not to suggest that Arabic poetry – pre-Islamic or otherwise – was devoid of concern with ethics or morality. Rather, it is to point to the difference between the social role of the prophet as distinct from, and frequently opposed to, that of the poet. The chief distinction here is that no matter how concerned with morality or ethics a particular poet might have been, he was never expected to be a moral exemplar. The prophet was expected to practice what he preached. *Zwettler* here, esp. pp. 76–84, is quite useful. The upshot of all of this is that the Quran is not poetry because Muhammad was not a poet, at least not according to the social construction of that role in his own *Sitz im Leben*. But the Quran 'as literature' is certainly poetic from another point of view. See, for example, *Boullata, passim*.

53. I am referring here to the mythopoeic function of Q7:172, the Day of the Covenant or Day of Alast. The classic treatment of the motif in sufism is Böwering's *The Mystical Vision*. On this central theme see now the recent masterful article by al-Qadi, 'The Primordial Covenant'.

54. Stetkevych, *Muhammad*.

55. Stetkevych, *Muhammad*, translating al-Tha'labi, *Kitab qisas al-anbiya'* For the scream, see Q11:67; Q11:94; Q15:73; Q15:83; Q23:41; Q29:40; Q36:29; Q36:49; Q36:53; Q38:15; Q50:42; Q54:31; Q63:4.

56. Frye, *Fearful Symmetry*, p. 247.

57. Frye, *Great Code*, pp. 82–3.

58. Frye, *Great Code*, pp. 82–3, quoted above p. 42.

59. Hanson, *Dawn*, p. 433, quoted above p. 22.

60. Blake, for example, relying on the myth of Atlantis, which during the 'flood of Tharma' was drowned and 'covered', prophesies that the 'Sea of Time and Space' will dry up completely in the apocalypse and Atlantis will once again be revealed (Frye, *Fearful Symmetry*, p. 280).

CHAPTER 5: WATER AND THE POETICS OF APOCALYPSE

1. As has noted, this bespeaks the 'paradox of monotheism', H. Corbin, Le Paradoxe.

2. The interested reader is directed to the excellent specialised articles in the three

editions of *EI*. On this topic they would be C. Gilliot, 'Attributes of God', in *EI3*; L. Gardet, al-Asmā' 'al-Husna' (The Most Beautiful Names), *EI2*; see also L. Gardet, 'Allāh ', in *EI2*.

3. F. Rahman, *Major Themes.*

4. Ibn Arabi, *Fusus*. Cf. also the title of Ibn Arabi's biography by S. Hirtenstein, *The Unlimited Mercifier.*

5. M. Chodkiewiczs, *Un océan.*

6. This well-known and oft-repeated idea occurs in two forms as a Hadith Qudsi: 'Truly, My mercy prevails over My wrath.' or 'My mercy outstrips My wrath.'

7. See the comparison of this Quranic tale with the Alexandrian romance in Brown, 'The Apocalypse. On Khidr/Kezr in general, see the comprehensive study by P. Franke, *Begegnung.*

8. See above, Ch. 4.

9. Wensinck and Gardet., 'Iblīs', *EI2*.

10. See Gardet, 'Allāh', *EI2*.

11. Other Quranic figures also express anger. These include the believers themselves, enemies of the Prophet Muḥammad, other prophets such as Moses and Jonah. In this chapter we are restricting the discussion to God, even though prophets may be understood as instruments of the divine. See Bashir, 'Anger', *EQ*.

12. M. Ayoub, 'The prayer of Islam' (on *Sūrat al-Fātiḥa*), in: *JAAR*, 47 (1979), pp. 635–47.

13. On the English translation of this all-important sura see the excellent article by S. Toorawa, 'Referencing', in addition to Ayoub above and B. Lawrence, *The Koran* pp. 15-16, 201-2. M. Sells, *Approaching* is, of course, indispensible.

14. Indeed *ghadab* itself may be translated as 'curse', as in Q24:9. See below.

15. Other words that may be translated in specific contexts as divine anger or wrath are: *ba's* (x2: Q4:84; 40:29); *rijs* (x3 Q6:125; 7:71; 10:100), *asafa* (x1: Q43:55).

16. There are numerous other roots from which are derived verbs and nouns in the Quran to refer to such specific divine names and attributes as tenderness, kindness (*h-n-n*; *l-t-f*; *r-'-f*), generosity (*h-w-sh*; *k-r-m*; *w-h-b*), lovingness (*h-b-b*; *w-d-d*), graciousness (*n-'-m*), friendship, clemency (*h-l-m*; *'-f-w*), forgiveness (*gh-f-r*; *'-f-w*), faithful (*'-m-n*), helper (*n-s-r*), guardian (*h-f-z*; *w-k-l*; *w-l-y*), educator, teacher, parent (*r-b-b*), solicitous, one who turns to the needy and unrepentant (*t-w-b*). These are merely a few of the dozens of word forms that are used throughout the Quran to refer to God's loving kindness and merciful qualities. See the truly invaluable reference work prepared especially for the English reader by H. Kassis, *A Concordance.*

17. Gimaret, 'Raḥma', *EI 2*.

18. Gilliot, 'Attributes of God', *EI3*.

19. Rahman, *Islam and Modernity*, p. 19.

20. For example, note the frequently suggested etymology that the word Allah actually represents the ligature of two northern proto-Semitic words, both of which may be derived from the definite article yielding a possible translation for *allah*: 'The the'. Gardet, 'Allāh', in *EI 2*.

21. Eliot, *Selected Essays*, pp. 144–5.

22. *Zwettler.*

23. See the recent brief but important discussion in M. A. S. Abd al-Haleem, Ch. 3: 'Water in the Quran', pp. 29–41. See also the same author's, 'Water in the Quran'. A more sustained consideration of the water symbolism of the Quran is in the recent report by M. L. Bouguerra, 'Water: Symbolism and culture', in *Les Rapports de l'Institut Veolia Environment*, no. 5, available at: www.institut.veolia. org/en/cahiers/water-symbolism/. References here are to the downloaded version of the issue, especially pp. 31–45: 'Water in the Quran: Symbolism and foundations

of a water culture'. See also the important philosophical exegesis on water in the Quran by Mulla Sadra Shirazi (ca. 1635), cited *Corbin* 1, pp. 315–16. The recent excellent study of Quranic aesthetics, by N. Kermani, *God is Beautiful*, surprisingly pays scant attention to this topic. Finally, the narratological approach to a reading of the elements in the Quran is presented in H. Toelle, *Le Coran revisité*.

24. Note, the related phenomenon of shade (*zalil, zill/zilal*) and cloud shadow (*zullah*) used many times (24) throughout the Quran as a metaphor for God's mercy. Unfortunately, there is no space here to consider those other essential 'waters' mentioned in the Quran: blood, tears, wine, honey, milk and so on.

25. A thorough discussion of what might be called 'Quranic hydrology' (if the term were not so unappealing) would, of course, include other words and concepts, such as *yabisa* (x4) that indicate the absence, withholding or drying up and withering of nature because of a lack of water and the divine name *al-samad* – usually translated as 'the Eternal Refuge' – said by lexicographers to denote in its original meaning a great solid boulder which may be used to protect inhabitants of a cul-de-sac river bed in times of flood.

26. M. Mahdi, 'Farabi, Abu Nasr'. *EIr*, 9: 228.

27. In the premodern period, the World of Images became a commonplace of philosophical speculation. Its history begins with Avicenna and Suhrawardi and reaches an apogee in the work of the Safavid philosophers. Henry Corbin and Fazlur Rahman have written pioneering works on this topic, they are referred to in T. Lawson, 'Ahmad Ahsa'i'.

28. Bouguerra, pp. 37–41.

CHAPTER 6: CHAOTIC COSMOS AND THE SYMMETRY OF TRUTH

1. Frye, *Great Code,* p. 43.

2. Of this recent scholarship amongst the most engaging is that of Angelika Neuwirth, Navid Kermani, Mustansir Mir and Mathias Zahniser, in addition to the seminal collection of studies in *Boullata* to which each of the above has contributed. See also the work of Muhammad Abdel Haleem, Daniel Madigan, and Anthony Johns. There are now many other scholars following this leading work on the literary power of the Quran.

3. See, for example, Reda, *Crescendo*. In addition to the new insights it offers on the dynamics of inclusios, keywords, *iqtisas* and intertextuality in the Quran, it also provides a very useful overview of the earlier scholarship referred to above.

4. This phrase is borrowed from D. C. Dennett, 'The Self' as a Center of Narrative Gravity', in F. Kessel, P. Cole and D. Johnson (eds) *Self and Consciousness: Multiple Perspectives* (Hillsdale, NJ: Erlbaum, 1992), pp. 103–14.

5. Apparently humans are not the only ones with this 'problem'. Bees, for example, are said to be guided to the flower neither by its scent nor its colour but rather by its symmetry.

6. *EQ.* A search for 'chaos' performed on the electronic version through the University of Toronto interface, 7 September 2009. Nor does the word occur as a translation of an Arabic original H. Kassis, *A Concordance*. There are numerous non-Quranic words in modern standard Arabic that are used for some aspect of chaos: *fawda* (disorder, *tohubohu*); *haba'* (formless dust); *harjala* (confusion, muddle); *hayula* (primordial matter); *idtirab* (disarray, commotion); *tashwish* (confusion); *ikhtilat* (mixture, hodgepodge); *khawa'* (emptiness, confusion of elements before creation).

7. Gunkel, *Creation and Chaos*. The pioneering study of this chaotic water we owe, of course, to Hermann Gunkel.

8. As in Q79:34: 'When comes the most great overwhelming'. An interesting exception may be read in the famous Hadith of the Cloud, *al-'ama'*. In it the prophet Muhammad is asked 'Where was God before he created the heavens and the earth?' Muhammad responded: 'He was in a cloud (*al-'amā*) above which there was no air and below which was no air.'

9. N. J. Girardot, 'Chaos', *ER2*.

10. I am pleased to express my thanks to Professor Emerita Wadad al-Qadi for suggesting the significance of this for the present discussion (personal communication, September 2009).

11. On this see M. Suchocki, 'The Symbolic'.

12. Peterson quoting Averroës, 'Creation', *EQ*, 1: 475–6.

13. Recall, this means later in the chronology of the actual composition of the Quran.

14. Other Quranic verses which repeat some version of this formula are: Q3:47; 3:59; 6:73; 16:40; 19:35; 25:7; 36:82; 40:68.

15. On this phenomenon, see the interesting discussion by Frye, *Great Code*, pp. 104–16. The asexual creativity of God (of a type found also in the Quran) is, accordingly, a critique of nature cosmogonies and ontologies.

16. Unfortunately, there is no space here to explicate this artistry. An excellent discussion is S. Hajjaji-Jarrah, "Enchantment".

17. S. Attar, 'An Islamic Paradiso'.

18. A good general but brief discussion is L. Gardet, '*Fitna*', *EI2*.

19. E.g. Nu'aym ibn Hammad (843), *Kitāb al-fitan*, studied at length in Cook, *Studies*.

20. See also a similar meaning in the Arabic plural *furuj* at Q50:6.

21. T. Hoffman, 'From the Chaotic to the Chaordic'. See also T. Hoffman, 'Koranisk', (unavailable to me).

22. Peterson, 'Creation', *EQ*, 1:474.

23. We will leave to one side the very interesting Verse of the Trust: 'We offered the Trust to the heavens, the earth, and the mountains, yet they refused to undertake it and were afraid of it; mankind undertook it – they have always been inept and foolish (*jahul*)' (Q33:72).

24. Goldziher, *Muhammedanische studien*, Vol. 1 pp. 319ff; Toshihiko Izutsu, Chaper VIII, in *God and Man in the Koran* (Tokyo: Keio University, 1964), pp. 216–53; Izutsu, *Ethico-religious Concepts*, pp. 28–36.

25. Izutsu, *Ethico*, p. 28.

26. Izutsu, *God,* Ch. 8.

27. Izutsu, *Ethico-Religious Concepts*, p. 35. My sincere thanks to Prof. B. R. Lawson of Celaya for the Spanish equivalent.

28. Izutsu, *Ethico*.

29. 'God does not forgive the joining of partners with Him: anything less than that He forgives to whoever He will; but anyone who joins partners with God has concocted a tremendous sin' (Q4:48).

30. Arnaldez, 'Insan', *EI2*.

31. Izutsu, *Ethico-religious Concepts*, p. 29.

32. *Batil* occurs 31 times in some form or another; *al-haqq* occurs 227 times. They are presented as diametric opposites at Q2:42; 3:71; 8:8; 13:17; 17:81; 18:52; 21:18; 22:62; 31:30; 34:49; 40:5; 40:78 (verbal); 42:24.

33. A. Jeffery, 'Aya', *EI2*. See, for example, A. Schimmel, *Deciphering*.

34. A useful source for such a comparison would be W. H.Salier, *The Rhetorical Impact*.

CHAPTER 7: JOYCEAN MODERNISM IN QURAN AND *TAFSIR*

1. 'The Apocalypse', p. 168.
2. 'Sustainer of the Divine Names'. There are two other titles for this extraordinary composition: *Commentary on the Chapter of Joseph* (Quran 12), *Tafsīr sūrat Yūsuf* and *The Best of Stories, Aḥsan al-qaṣaṣ. Qayyūm al-asmā'* – though difficult to translate properly – is probably the most common. See T. Lawson, *Gnostic*, p. 77.
3. T. Lawson, 'Interpretation'.
4. On epic as metonym for culture see Martin, 'Epic as Genre', pp. 9–19.
5. 'This is the only twentieth century book that I find myself living with, in the way that I live with *Tristram Shandy*, Burton's *Anatomy*, Dickens, and the greater poets. It is an inexhaustible word hoard of humor, wit, erudition, and symbolism; it never, for me, degenerates into a mere puzzle, but always has on every page something to astonish and delight', N. Frye, in *The American Scholar* 30.4 (Autumn 1961), p. 606. (My thanks to Robert Denham for this reference.)
6. The standard biography is R. Ellmann, *James Joyce*.
7. It is very difficult to choose a single title for a comprehensive study of Joyce, his art and influence, however the interested reader will be handsomely rewarded by the recent *James Joyce in Context*, ed. John McCourt (Cambridge University Press, 2009).
8. The work may be thought to have had quite considerable influence from another angle, inasmuch as it was the first announcement of a powerful if short-lived messianic movement in Iran which ultimately led to the rise and worldwide expansion of the Baha'i faith. But this is not literary influence as usually understood.
9. T. Lawson, 'The Terms'.
10. A specifically Viconian cyclicism eventually would be adopted by Joyce, not in *Ulysses*, but rather in his last work, *Finnegans Wake*. However, cyclicism is not absent from *Ulysses*, as will be seen.
11. A. Amanat, *Resurrection*; M. Bayat, *Mysticism* J.R. Cole, *Modernity and the Millennium* D. MacEoin, 'Orthodoxy' T. Lawson, 'Orthodoxy'.
12. T. Lawson, *Intimacy*, Ch. 5.
13. N. Zarandí, *The Dawn-Breakers*; D. MacEoin, *The Sources*; D. MacEoin, *The Messiah of; J. R. I. Cole, Modernity*; J. R. I. Cole, 'Individualism'; Nader Saiedi, *Gate*; T. Lawson, *Gnostic*.
14. The Bab, *Bayán-i Fársí*, vahid II, bab 7, pp. 30–1: INBA62 (Tehran: Azali Publication, 1946). Reprinted, East Lansing, MI: H-Baha'i, 1999, pp. 30–1. Cited in A. Amanat, *Resurrection*, p. 170. See also N. Zarandi, *Dawn-Breakers*, pp. 62–5.
15. A. Amanat, *Resurrection*, p. 170.
16. In his Epistle on Spiritual Wayfaring, the Bab delineates the levels of authority and application of religious truth and allegiance (God, the Prophet, the Imams and the Shiʿa) and says that they are all dependent on each other. See T. Lawson, 'The Bab's Epistle', pp. 231, 237, 241. For a discussion of these factors from a socio-historical perspective, see A. Amanat, *Resurrection*.
17. Frye, *Words with Power*, p. 125.
18. On the various ways in which this quest for authentic identity were debated and contemplated, see L. Walbridge (ed.), *Most Learned*.
19. For a recent comprehensive discussion of the Bab's artistic nature and aesthetic preoccupations see M. Momen, 'Perfection'.
20. N. A. Fargnoli and M. P. Gillespie, *Critical*, pp. 392–93 for a reproduction from Hugh Kenner's finished composite of Joyce's two schemata for his friends and colleagues Linati and Gilbert.

21. This Joycean conceit may be thought to have been anticipated by the ancient Arabian poetic tradition, which saw in the idea of 'the day' – *al-yawm* (pl. *ayyam*) – a certain epic dignity and challenge as in 'the days of the Arabs *(ayyām al-ʿarab)*', where the word connotes battle and the heroic resources required to survive the day through struggle for survival. The Quran's (and the Bible's) a 'day with thy Lord is as a thousand years' would also seem to resonate: Q22:47; Psalms 90:4; 2 Peter 3:8. See Günther, 'Day, Times of', in *EQ* 1: 499-504, and Mittwoch, 'Ayyām al-ʿArab', *EI2*.

22. U. Eco, *The Aesthetics*.

23. D. Weir, *James Joyce*.

24. V. Rafati, 'Colours'. Lawson, *Gnostic*.

25. Here, we follow Frye's insight about the function of 'numerology' in the book of Revelation in such topoi as 'the seventh seal' and the 144,000 companions of the Lamb of God, where we understand that the first function of such occult-esque passages in the Bible is, in fact, a literary one – one which helps the reader to experience coherence and cohesiveness in the text, to experience, in Frye's simple phrase, how the words 'hang together'. Frye, *Great Code*, p. 60; R. Denham, *Northrop Frye*, p. 227.

26. For the epic dimension of the Quran see above Ch. 1.

27. The words sura 'chapter' (Arabic plural *suwar*) and aya 'verse' (Arabic plural *ayat*) are only used for the Quran. Tradition forbids their use to describe the corresponding elements of any other work.

28. As discussed above in Ch. 2.

29. Lawson, *Gnostic*, pp. 6, 29, 36, 90–1.

30. On the Quranic resonances in this circularity see A. Yared, '"In the Name of Annah"', pp. 401–38 (408, 410). It has also been argued that a similar structure is discernible in *Ulysses*, in which the last letter – 's' – of the first word of the text is the last letter of the all-important last word of the book: 'Yes!'

31. *Dh-k-r*, the triliteral root upon which the word remembrance is formed, occurs 292 times in the Quran. Of these, the majority of occurrences indicate the obligation and command to remember God and the Day of the Covenant. Remembrance is thus a major theme of the Quran (as it is in Plato). For the specifically mystical aspects of the institution of the covenant, see Böwering, *Mystical Vision of Existence*.

32. During the Iranian revolution and the protracted and tragic war between Iraq and Iran, the battlecry was frequently heard, in both Persian and Arabic: 'Every day is the day of resurrection *(kullu yawm qiyama)*' and 'Every day is Ashura', the day on which the martyr-hero par excellence of Islam, Husayn, the son of ʿAli, was massacred along with his family. It is a nationally sanctioned holy day in Iran and observed elsewhere throughout the Muslim world.

33. M. Beja, 'Epiphany', 1984), pp. 707–25 (p. 719).

34. J. Aubert, 'Lacan'.

35. Lawson, *Gnostic* p. 4.

36. See the recent discussion of their importance in the Sunni tradition in M. Nguyen, 'Exegesis'.

37. It is possible that this figure will change once all the 15 or so known manuscripts of the work have been properly collated.

38. M. Momen, 'The Trial'.

39. *U*, 1961, p. 37.

40. Weir, *Mediation*, p. 39.

41. On the prominence of the topic in the Bab's writings, see Lawson, *Gnostic*; on *walaya* see Landolt, 'Walayah'.

42. On *coincidentia oppositorum* see the major study by C. G. Jung, *Mysterium.*

43. N. Frye, 'Cycle', p. 371.

44. J. C. Voelker, '"Nature It Is"'; R. McHugh, *The Sigla*, 1976), pp. 27–31.

45. C. Lamb, *The Adventures of Ulysses.* According to Joyce himself, from this time on he was preoccupied with *The Odyssey*; R. Ellmann, 'The Backgrounds', p. 341. See also R. Ellman, *James*, p. 46; Z. R. Bowen and J. F. Carens (eds), *A Companion*, p. 43: Joyce advised several people who complained of the obscurity of *Ulysses* to read Lamb's *Adventures* for guidance and clues to the text.

46. Lamb, *The Adventures of Ulysses*, p. 18.

47. Van Duzer, *Duality*, pp. 4–6.

48. J. Van Dyck Card, '"Contradicting"', pp. 17–26, 20–1. See the impressive litany of opposites in J. Van Dyck Card, *An Anatomy*, pp. 50–2 and 66–7. It should be remarked, in passing, that Card makes no substantial mention of Voelker's insights in this book and seems to have no interest at all in the Brunonian substrate of Joyce's writing. Neither Voelker nor Card observe that Molly, whose birth name was Marion Tweedy, may be thought to take her 'heroic' or 'initiatic' name from the magical plant known in *The Odyssey* as the *moly*.

49. G. Lernout, *Help.*

50. Lawson, *Gnostic*, pp. 75–92.

51. J. Lewis McIntyre, *Giordano*, 1903), pp. 142–43.

52. J. Joyce, *Critical*, pp. 133–4.

53. Card, 'Contradicting', pp. 17–26, 21. Incidentally, Card points out that the roses mentioned in this passage, 'Id love to have the whole place swimming in roses' (*U* 782, and elsewhere in *U*) may allude to the ecstatic religious vision in Dante symbolised by the multifoliate rose. See W. Y. Tindall, *The Literary*, pp. 199–202 and William York Tindall, *A Reader's*, pp. 91–2. Joyce himself had quite early on expressed his interest in the 'history of religious ecstasies', *Joyce, Critical* p. 134.

54. The existence, function and form of the *coincidentia oppositortum* thus explicated by Voelker, it is clear that the figure occurs not only in Penelope with Molly, but on almost every page of the novel. G. Balsamo, *Joyce's*. See now the highly illuminating *Il Padre di Bloom e il Figlio di Dedalus:* by E. Ravasio. (My profound thanks to the author for sharing with me a prepublication draft of the English translation of this book.)

55. On the poetry in this passage see Card, *Anatomy*, p. 80.

56. Rahman, *Major,* p. 12.

57. See above, Ch. 4. It should be remarked that the question of Bruno's indebtedness here to Cusanus has recently been questioned: L. Catana, 'The Coincidence'.

58. Lawson, *Gnostic, passim.*

59. Another evidence of Joyce's exposure to the Quran may be read in Molly's rhetorical question 'why dont they go and create something I often asked him atheists or whatever they call themselves' (*U* 782), which is also remarkably similar to the so-called challenge verses in the Quran. These are five passages which have been read traditionally as a response to the sceptics and cavillers who doubted Muhammad's mission. One will suffice: 'And if you are in doubt concerning that We have sent down on Our servant, then bring a sura like it, and call your witnesses, apart from God, if you are truthful. And if you do not – and you will not – then fear the Fire, whose fuel is men and stones, prepared for unbelievers' (Q2:23–4).

60. J. S. Atherton, *The Books*; R. McHugh, 'Mohammad', pp. 51–8; Yared, 'In the Name of Annah'; A. Yared, 'Introducing'. It would appear to be no accident, given the interest in Islam and the Quran evident in his *Newslitter* article mentioned above that McHugh in *The Sigla*, had devoted an entire chapter to the topic of the *coincidentia oppositorum*.

In addition, there are a number of studies dealing generally with Joyce and the Middle East and/or the Saidian theory of 'orientalism' in the special edition of the *James Joyce Quarterly*, 'ReOrienting Joyce', mentioned above. In addition to the excellent article there by Yared, see also those by Bouazza, Bowen, Ehrlich, Harris, Kershner, King and Shloss. Another related publication is S. Bushrui and B. Benstock (eds), *James Joyce*. See here, especially, the article by Bushrui, 'Joyce in the Arab World', pp. 232–7. (The possibility that Dante also transmitted Islamic and Quranic influence to Joyce has not been noted.) See the interesting comment, available online, in a blurb for F. Dumas' 'Funny in Farsi', which discusses the censorship issues surrounding her best-selling memoir in Iran. She says: 'A translation of James Joyce's *Ulysses* has been with censor's office for seventeen years!' www.randomhouse.com/highschool/RHI_magazine/pdf3/ Dumas.pdf

In addition, there are a number of studies dealing generally with Joyce and the Middle East and/or the Saidian theory of 'orientalism' in the special edition of the *James Joyce Quarterly*, 'ReOrienting Joyce', mentioned above. In addition to the excellent article there by Yared, see also those by Bouazza, Bowen, Ehrlich, Harris, Kershner, King and Shloss. Another related publication is S. Bushrui and B. Benstock (eds), *James Joyce*. See here, especially, the article by Bushrui, 'Joyce in the Arab World', pp. 232–7. (The possibility that Dante also transmitted Islamic and Quranic influence to Joyce has not been noted.) See the interesting comment, available online, in a blurb for F. Dumas' 'Funny in Farsi', which discusses the censorship issues surrounding her best-selling memoir in Iran. She says: 'A translation of James Joyce's *Ulysses* has been with censor's office for seventeen years!' www.randomhouse.com/highschool/RHI_magazine/pdf3/ Dumas.pdf

61. T. Lawson, '*Coincidentia Oppositorum* in the Qayyum al-Asma'.

62. Eco, *Chaosmos*; see also M. P. Gillespie, *The Aesthetics*.

63. Frye, *Cycle*, p. 366, discussing *FW*.

64. Virginia Woolf's *Mrs Dalloway* (1925), and to some extent *To the Lighthouse* (1927), follows the example of Joyce's meditation on the 'wonders' of the epic quality of a single day in *U*. But both may be thought anticipated in the search for the epic in the otherwise drear diurnal by Baudelaire, who famously observed in 1845: '[T]he heroism of modern life surrounds and presses upon us . . . There is no lack of subjects, nor of colours, to make epics. The painter, the true painter for whom we are looking will be he who can snatch its epic quality from the life of today and can make us see and understand, with brush and pencil, how great and poetic we are in our cravats and our patent-leather boots. Next year let us hope that the true seekers may grant us the extraordinary delight of celebrating the advent of the new', Charles Baudelaire, 'The Salon of 1845', pp. 31–2.

65. 'History, Stephen said, is a nightmare from which I would like to awake' (*U* 34).

66. Not only are these rarely remarked twelve yesses prominent in the closing lines of Ulysses, but if we scan the pages carefully, reading with the ear, we find other yesses hiding in the foliage of the vocabulary. Quite apart from the fact that the title of the book itself, Ulysses is composed of Ul + ysses (= yesses), such words in the final lines as 'yellow houses', 'Jessamine', 'cactuses', 'kissed', 'eyes', 'breasts', all echo the sound of the affirmative English adverb.

67. See above Ch. 1.

68. See above Ch. 3.

69. Madigan, *The Qur'an's*.

70. M. McLuhan, *Understanding*, pp. 7–21.

71. *Tafsir* symbolises the sacred authority of tradition in Islam the same way the word *midrash* does in Judaism.

72. *Abjad* refers to the system by which each Arabic letter has a numerical value. This is a common – and ancient – phenomenon in the alphabets of many Middle Eastern languages, perhaps related to the need for a computational system in a trade-oriented culture. The numerical value of words is part of their esoteric meaning in much mystical and theological writing throughout the history of Islamic letters.

73. Inexplicably, this is the same number of suras mentioned in *FW*. Atherton, *Books*, p. 203 (see however some inconsistency in Atherton on this subject at pp. 45 and 172). The proper number of Quranic suras is 114. There is no reason to believe that Joyce had any knowledge of even the existence of the Bab's writings although he did have knowledge of the Quran and Islamic history and was also in some ways consciously trying to 'rewrite' the Quran. (See Yared above in note 60.) Atherton's view (p. 203) is that Joyce's 111 is a veiled condemnation of or expression of 'hostility towards' the Quran because it is also an allusion to a condemnatory sura (Q111) in which the arch villain of early Islamic history, Abu Lahab, is roundly condemned to hell. I do not agree that Joyce was hostile to the Quran.

74. On Muhammad's so-called 'illiteracy' see S. Günther, 'Muhammad, the Illiterate Prophet. On the parallels between the life of the Prophet Muhammad and the biography of the Bab, see S. Lambden, 'An Episode'.

75. On this topic see A. Rippin, 'Occasions of Revelation', in *EQ*, 3: pp. 69–73.

76. See below the translation from the *Qayyūm al-asmā'*: 'the Letter "B" that circulates in the water of the two groups of letters'. 'Two groups of letters' is a poetic way of referring to all language. The letter 'B' is, among other things, the first letter of the word *bala*: Yes!!

77. QA *suwar al-zawal, al-kaf, al-a'zam, al-ba', al-ism, al-ḥaqq, al-tayr, al-naba', al-iblāgh, al-insān* (ii) and *al-tathlith.* (See Appendix.)

78. This is very slightly adapted from T. Lawson, 'The Súrat al-'Abd'. This excerpt with footnotes and other indications removed from the original, is from pp. 127–8.

79. There are numerous works of scholarship devoted to decoding the otherwise extremely daunting *FW* and revealing its intricate logic and structure, we mention here only five, beginning with the oldest: J. Campbell and H. M. Robinson, *A Skeleton*; A. Glasheen, *A Census*; C. Hart, *A Concordance*; J. Atherton, *The Books*; J. Bishop, *Joyce's Book.*

80. Lawson, *Gnostic*, pp. 46–7, 82.

81. The Arabic original is found in *Muntakhābāt*, p. 156. For an English translation, see *Selections*, p. 217.

82. *Bahá'í Prayers*, p. 106.

83. On reader as hero: Frye, *Anatomy* pp. 323–4; on losing and regaining identity as the central concern of the 'monomyth': N. Frye, *The Educated*, p. 55.

84. 'The juxtaposition of opposites, however, is thematic at least as much as it is structural', Card, *Anatomy*, p. 52.

85. Lawson, *Gnostic*, p. 117. A similarly self-reflexive process is studied in O. Ghaemmaghami, 'A Youth'.

86. While I am unaware of any of the sets of actual Quranic disconnected letters being identified as proper names, the reverse is certainly true. Sets of these mysterious letters have frequently been given as proper names in Islamic societies, e.g. Ta Ha (from sura 20) and Ya Sin (from sura 36).

87. *Corbin* 3: 292–300.

88. James Joyce, from a letter to Nora dated about 1 September 1904, in R. Ellmann (ed.), *Selected Letters*, p. 27.

89. The present exploration is not the first time the unique oeuvre of the Bab has been likened to modernist European literary developments. For details see T. Lawson, 'Joycean', p. 117, n.92.

Appendix

#	السورة	الحروف المقطعة
١	سورة الملك	
٢	سورة الظماء	الم
٣	سورة الإيمان	طه
٤	سورة الحديقة	المطه
٥	سورة يوسف	الحم
٦	سورة الشهادة	المص
٧	سورة الزيارة	طس
٨	سورة السر	المص
٩	سورة العماء (i)	المر
١٠	سورة العماء (ii)	المص
١١	سورة المبطر	طعس
١٢	سورة المطهر	كهعص
١٣	سورة العاشوراء	طعه
١٤	سورة القدس	المط
١٥	سورة المشية	طعس
١٦	سورة المرثن	المق
١٧	سورة الباب	المحر
١٨	سورة الصراط	كهيعص
١٩	سورة السيناء	المر
٢٠	سورة النور	المحي
٤١	سورة الكتاب	كهيعص
٤٢	سورة العهد	المر
٤٣	سورة الوحيد	المح
٤٤	سورة الرؤيا	طهر
٤٥	سورة هو	كهيعص
٤٦	سورة المرات	طه
٤٧	سورة الجنة	المختصر
٤٨	سورة النداء	الم
٤٩	سورة الأحكام (i)	طه
٥٠	سورة الأحكام (ii)	المص
٥١	سورة الحج	طه
٥٢	سورة الفضل	
٥٣	سورة الصبر	كهع
٥٤	سورة الفلاح	المحص
٥٥	سورة الركن	كهيع
٥٦	سورة الأمر	حم
٥٧	سورة الأكبر	حم
٥٨	سورة الحزن	الم
٥٩	سورة الأفئدة	كهيعص
٦٠	سورة الذكر (i)	طعس
٨١	سورة الكهف	المح
٨٢	سورة الأعظم	الح
٨٣	سورة الباب	المث
٨٤	سورة الاسم	المر
٨٥	سورة الحق	المط
٨٦	سورة الطير	الر
٨٧	سورة النبأ	الر
٨٨	سورة الإبلاغ	المحص
٨٩	سورة الإنسان (iii)	الم
٩٠	سورة التأنيث	المحص
٩١	سورة التبديع	الر
٩٢	سورة المجتل	المحص
٩٣	سورة النحل	كهيع
٩٤	سورة الإشهار	الحز
٩٥	سورة الاختيار	طعه
٩٦	سورة القتال (i)	المحص
٩٧	سورة القتال (ii)	المحي
٩٨	سورة الجهاد (i)	المحي
٩٩	سورة الجهاد (ii)	الحز
١٠٠	سورة الجهاد (iii)	المحقل

#	سورة		#	سورة		#	سورة	
٢١	سورة البحر	المهيمن	٦١	سورة الحسين	كهيعص	١٠١	سورة القتال (iii)	الم
٢٢	سورة الماء	طططل	٦٢	سورة الأولياء	كهيعل	١٠٢	سورة القتال (iv)	كهيعص
٢٣	سورة العصر	النجم	٦٣	سورة الرحمة	طس	١٠٣	سورة الحج	التح
٢٤	سورة القدر	التحنى	٦٤	سورة المحمد	التحق	١٠٤	سورة الحدود	طه
٢٥	سورة الخاتم	التحنى	٦٥	سورة الغيب	المحصر	١٠٥	سورة الأحكام (iii)	التحنى
٢٦	سورة الحل	النون	٦٦	سورة الأحدية	المحصر	١٠٦	سورة الجمعة	التحس
٢٧	سورة الأبرار	الحق	٦٧	سورة الإنشاء	المحص	١٠٧	سورة النكاح	التح
٢٨	سورة القربة	الم	٦٨	سورة الرعد	كهيعص	١٠٨	سورة النكر (ii)	على
٢٩	سورة القرابة	كهيعص	٦٩	سورة الحج	الر	١٠٩	سورة العبد	محمد
٣٠	سورة التبليغ	الحى	٧٠	سورة القسط	التحس	١١٠	سورة المنافقين	المطح
٣١	سورة العر	الحج	٧١	سورة الفتح	التحص	١١١	سورة المؤمنين	الم
٣٢	سورة الحى	كهيعق	٧٢	سورة الكبير	التح			
٣٣	سورة النصر	التحنى	٧٣	سورة الكهف	ال			
٣٤	سورة الإشارة	حمرا	٧٤	سورة الخلل	الر			
٣٥	سورة العبودية	الم	٧٥	سورة الشمس	الر			
٣٦	سورة العدل	فصحسن	٧٦	سورة الورقة	حمرا			
٣٧	سورة التكبير	طه	٧٧	سورة السلام	المحص			
٣٨	سورة الفاطمة	طه	٧٨	سورة الطهور	التحس			
٣٩	سورة التذكر	الثور	٧٩	سورة الكلمة	التحط			
٤٠	سورة الإنسان (i)	طه	٨٠	سورة الزوال	كهيعص			

Todd Lawson, Joycean Modernism in the Bāb's Tafsīr Sūrat Yūsuf (Approaches to the Qur'an in Contemporary Iran), 3 September 2013.

Bibliography

'Āmilī-Isfahānī, A. H. (1954/1374) *Tafsīr mir'āt al-anwār wa-mishkāt al-asrār*, Tehran: Chāpkhānah-yi Āftāb.

Abboud, H. (2014) *Mary in the Qur'ān: A Literary Reading.* New York: Routledge/ Taylor & Francis.

Abdel Haleem, M. A. S. (2010) *The Qur'ān: English Translation and Parallel Arabic Text*, Oxford: Oxford University Press.

_____ (2004) 'Introduction' in *The Qur'ān: A New Translation*, Oxford: Oxford University Press, ix–xx.

_____ (1993) 'Context and Internal Relationships: Keys to Quranic Exegesis – A Study of *Sūrat al-Rahmān* (Quran Chapter 55)', in *Approaches to the Quran* ed. G. R. Hawting and Abel-Kader A. Shareef, London: Routledge, 71–98.

_____ (1990) 'The story of Joseph in the Qur'ān and the Old Testament', in *Islam and Christian-Muslim Relations* 1: 171–91.

_____ (1989) 'Water in the Qur'ān', *Islamic Quarterly* 33.1: 34–50.

Ahsā'ī, Shaykh Ahmad ibn Zayn al-Dīn, al- (1999/1420) *Sharh al-ziyāra al-jāmi'a al-kabīra*, 4 vols, Beirut: Dār al-Mufīd.

Alter, Robert (2002) 'Northrop Frye between Archetype and Typology', in *Semeia* 89: 9–21.

Amanat, A. (1999) 'The Resurgence of the Apocalyptic in Modern Islam', in *The Encyclopedia of Apocalypticism*, iii, *Apocalypticism in the Modern Period and the Contemporary Age* ed. S. J. Stein, New York: Continuum, 230–64.

_____ (1989) *Resurrection and Renewal: The Making of the Babi Movement in Iran, 1844–1850*, Ithaca: Cornell University Press.

Amanat, A. and M. T. Bernhardsson (eds) (2002) *Imagining the End: Visions of Apocalypse from the Ancient Middle East to Modern America*, London and New York: I. B. Tauris.

Amir-Moezzi, M. A. (2010) 'al-'Āmilī al-Isfahānī, Abū l-Hasan', *EI3*.

_____ (2002) 'Notes à propos de la *walāya* imamite (Aspects de l'imamologie duodecimaine, X)', *JAOS* 122: 722–41.

Annus, A. (2011) 'The Mesopotamian Precursors of Adam's Garment of Glory and Moses' Shining Face', in *Identities and Societies in the Ancient East Mediterranean Regions: Comparative Approaches; Henning Graf Reventlow memorial volume*, ed. T. R. Kämmerer, Munster: Ugarit-Verlag, 1–17.

Arbel, D. and A. A. Orlov (eds) (2011) *With Letters of Light: Studies in the Dead Sea Scrolls, Early Jewish Apocalypticism, Magic, and Mysticism in honor of Rachel Elior*, New York: Walter de Gruyter.

Arjomand, S. A. (1999) 'Islamic Apocalypticism in the Classic Period', in *EA* 2: 238–83.

Arkoun, M. (2001) 'Contemporary Critical Practices and the Qur'ān' in *EQ*.

_____ (1982) *Lectures du Coran*, Paris: G.-P. Maisonneuve et Larose.

Assman, J. (2006) *Thomas Mann und Ägypten: Mythos und Monotheismus in den Josephsromanen*, Munich: C. H. Beck.

Atherton, J. S. (1974) *The Books at the Wake: A Study of Literary Allusions in James Joyce's Finnegans Wake*, Mamaroneck, NY: P. P. Appel.

Attar, S. 'An Islamic Paradiso in a Medieval Christian Poem? Dante's Divine Comedy Revisited', in *Roads* 2: 891–921.

Auerbach, E. (1984) 'Figura', trans. Ralph Manheim, in *Scenes from the Drama of European Literature*, 11–78. *Theory and History of Literature*, Vol. 9, Manchester: Manchester University Press.

Ayoub, M. (1979) 'The Prayer of Islam' (on *Sūrat al-Fātiha*), in *JAAR* 47: 635–47.

Bab, The (2007) *Muntakhābāt āyāt az āthār Hadrat Nuqtah-yi Ūlā*, Chandigarh: Carmel Publishers.

_____ (1976) *Selections from the Writings of the Bab*, Haifa: Bahá'í World Centre.

Bab, The et al. (1982) *Bahá'i Prayers: A Selection of Prayers Revealed by Bahá'u'lláh, The Báb, and 'Abdu'l- Bahá*, Wilmette, IL: Baha'i Publishing Trust.

Babayan, K. (2002) *Mystics, Monarchs and Messiahs: Cultural Landscapes of Early Modern Iran*, Cambridge, MA: Harvard University Press.

Badalanova Geller, F. (2008) *Qur'ān in Vernacular: Folk Islam in the Balkans*, Max Planck Preprint 357, Berlin: Max-Planck-Institut für Wissenschaftsgeschichte.

Bahrānī, Hāshim -al (1955/1375) *Kitāb al-Burhān fī tafsīr al-Quran*, 4 vols, Tehran: Chāpkhāna-yi Āftāb.

Bajouda, H. (1992) *Joseph in the Quran: Thematic Unity*, trans. Mohamed A. El-Erian. Melbourne, Victoria: Serendib Pty Ltd, (originally published as *al-Wahda al-mawdū'iyya fī sūrat Yūsuf 'alayhi l-salām*, Cairo: Dār al-Kutub al-Hadītha, 1974).

Bakhtin, M. (1982) *The Dialogic Imagination: Four Essays*, ed. Michael Holquist, trans. Caryl Emerson and Michael Holquist, Austin: University of Texas Press.

Bal, M. (2008) *Loving Yusuf: Conceptual Travels from Present to Past*, Chicago, IL: University of Chicago Press.

Balsamo, G. (2004) *Joyce's Messianism: Dante, Negative Existence, and the Messianic Self*, Columbia, SC: University of South Carolina Press.

Barthes, R. (1986) 'The Reality Effect', in R. Barthes, *The Rustle of Language*, trans. R. Howard Oxford: Blackwell, 141–8.

Bashir, S. 'Anger', in *EQ*.

_____ (2003) *Messianic Hopes and Mystical Visions: The Nūrbakhshīya between Medieval and Modern Islam*, Columbia, SC: University of South Carolina Press.

Baudelaire, Ch. (1965) 'The Salon of 1845', in *Art in Paris 1845–1862: Salons and Other Exhibitions Reviewed by Charles Baudelaire*, ed. and trans. J. Mayne, Oxford: Phaidon Press, 1–32.

Baukham, R. J. (1978) 'The Rise of Apocalyptic', in *Themelios* 3.2: 10–23.

Baumgarten, A. I. (ed.), (2000) *Apocalyptic Time*, Boston, MA: Brill.

Bayat, M. (1982) *Mysticism and Dissent: Socioreligious Thought in Qajar Iran*, Syracuse: Syracuse University Press.

Becker, C. H. (1912) 'Islam', in *Archive für Religionswissenschaft* 15: 543–4.

Beeston, A. F. L. (1963) *Baidāwī's Commentary on Surah 12 of the Qur'ān*, Oxford: Clarendon Press.

Beissinger, M. et al. (eds), (1999) *Epic Traditions in the Contemporary World: The Poetics of Community*, Berkeley, CA: University of California Press.

Beja, M. (1984) 'Epiphany and the Epiphanies', in *A Companion to Joyce Studies*, ed. Z. Bowen and J. F. Carens, Westport, CT: Greenwood Press, 707–25.

Beltz, W. (1979) *Sehnsucht nach dem Paradies: Mythologie des Korans*, Berlin: Buchverlag Der Morgen.

Benin, S. D. (2000) 'Jews, Muslims, and Christians in Byzantine Italy', in *Judaism and Islam: Boundaries, Communication and Interaction: Essays in Honor of William M. Brinner*, ed. B. H. Hary et al., Leiden: Brill, 27–35.

Bernstein, M. S. (2006) *Stories of Joseph: Narrative Migrations between Judaism and Islam*, Detroit, MI: Wayne State University Press.

_____ (2000) 'The Story of our Master Joseph: The Spiritual or the Righteous?', in *Judaism and Islam: Boundaries, Communication and Interaction: Essays in Honor of William M. Brinner*, ed. B. H. Hary et al., Leiden: Brill, 157–67.

Bishop, J. (1986) *Joyce's Book of the Dark: Finnegans Wake*, Madison, WI: University of Wisconsin Press.

Bouguerra, M. L. (2005) 'Water: Symbolism and culture', in *Les Rapports de l'Institut Veolia Environment*, no. 5, available at: www.institut.veolia.org/en/cahiers/water-symbolism/.

Boullata, I. J. (ed.) (2000) *Literary Structures of Religious Meaning in the Qur'ān*, Richmond: Curzon.

Bowen, Z. R. and J. F. Carens (eds) (1984) *A Companion to Joyce Studies*, Westport, CT: Greenwood Press.

Böwering, G. 'Time', in *EQ*.

_____ 'God and His Attributes', in *EQ*.

_____ (1999) 'Ideas of time in Persian Sufism', in *The Heritage of Sufism: Classical Persian Sufism from its Origins to Rumi (700–1300)*, ed. L. Lewisohn, repr., Oxford: Oneworld, 99–233.

_____ (1997) 'The concept of time in Islam', in *Proceedings of the American Philosophical Society* 141.1: 55–66.

_____ (1994) 'Ibn 'Arabi's concept of time', in *Gott ist schön und Er liebt die Schönheit: Festschrift für Annemarie Schimmel zum 7. April 1992 dargebracht von Schulern, Freunden und Kollegen (God Is Beautiful and Loves Beauty: Festschrift for Annemarie Schimmel presented by students, friends and collegues [sic] on April 7, 1992)*, ed. J. C. Burgel and A. Giese, Bern: Peter Lang, 71–91.

_____ (1992) 'Ideas of time in Persian sufism', in *Iran* 30: 77–89.

_____ (1980) *The Mystical Vision of Existence in Classical Islam: The Quranic Hermeneutics of the Sūfī Sahl At-Tustarī (d. 283/896)*, Berlin: de Gruyter.

Bowra, C. M. (1952) *Heroic Poetry*, New York: St. Martin's Press.

Bravmann, M. M. (1972) *The Spiritual Background of Early Islam: Studies in Ancient Arab Concepts*, Leiden: E. J. Brill.

Bray, J. (2003) 'Lists and memory: Ibn Qutayba and Muhammad b. Habīb', in *Culture and Memory in Medieval Islam: Essays in Honour of Wilferd Madelung*, ed. Farhad Daftary and Josef W. Meri, London: I. B. Tauris; Institute of Ismaili Studies; Distributed in the USA and Canada by St. Martin's Press, 210–31.

Brinner, W. M. (trans.) (2002) *'Arā'is al-majālis fī qisas al-anbiyā', or: Lives of the Prophets as Recounted by Abū Ishāq Ahmad ibn Muhammad ibn Ibrāhīm al-Tha'labī*, Leiden: Brill.

Brockelmann, C. (1937–49) *Geschichte der arabischen Litteratur*, Leiden: E. J. Brill.

Brown, N. O. (1984) 'The Apocalypse of Islam', in *Social Text* 8: 155–71.

Bull, M. (2000) 'The End of Apocalypticism?' Review of *The Encyclopedia of Apocalypticism*, ed. J. J. Collins, B. McGinn, and S. J. Stein, in *Journal of Religion* 80.4: 658–62.

Burge, S. R. (forthcoming) 'Compilation criticism: Reading and interpreting hadith collections through the prism of fragmentation and compilation', in *Fragmentation and Compilation: The Making of Religious Texts in Islam: A Comparative Perspective*, ed. Asma Hilali.

_____ (2016) 'Myth, meaning and the order of words: Reading hadith collections with Northrop Frye and the development of compilation criticism', in *Islam and Christian–Muslim Relations*, 27.2: 213–28.

_____ (2011) 'Reading Between the Lines: The Compilation of *Hadīt* and the Authorial Voice', in *Arabica* 58.2: 168–97.

Bushrui, S. (1982) 'Joyce in the Arab World', in *James Joyce, an International Perspective: Centenary Essays in Honour of the Late Sir Desmonde Cochrane*, Irish Literary Studies Vol. 10, Gerrards Cross, Bucks.: C. Smythe and Totowa, NJ: Barnes & Noble, 232–7.

Bushrui, S. and B. Benstock (eds) (1982) *James Joyce, an International Perspective: Centenary Essays in Honour of the Late Sir Desmonde Cochrane*, Irish Literary Studies, Vol. 10 Gerrards Cross, Bucks: C. Smythe and Totowa, NJ: Barnes & Noble.

Cameron, A. 'Late Antique Apocalyptic: A Context for the Qur'an?', www.academia .edu/12304787/Late_Antique_Apocalyptic_a_Context_for_the_Qur_an, accessed 28 September 2015.

Campbell, J. (2004) *The Hero with a Thousand Faces*, Princeton, NJ: Princeton University Press (1st edn 1949).

Campbell, J. and H. M. Robinson (2005) *A Skeleton Key to Finnegans Wake: Unlocking James Joyce's Masterwork*, Novato, CA: New World Library.

Carlyle, T. (1900) *Heroes and Hero-Worship*, Chicago, IL: W. B. Conkey Company.

Casanova, P. (1911) *Mohammed et la fin du monde: étude critique sur l'Islam primitif*, Paris: Paul Geuthner.

Catana, L. (2011) 'The Coincidence of Opposites: Cusanian and Non-Cusanian Interpretations', *Bruniana & Campanelliana* 17.2: 381–400.

Cave, T. (1979) *The Cornucopian Text: Problems of Writing in the French Renaissance*, Oxford and New York: Clarendon Press and Oxford University Press.

Chittick, W. (1989) *The Sufi Path of Knowledge: Ibn al-Arabi's Metaphysics of Imagination*, Albany, NY: State University of New York Press.

Chodkiewiczs, M. (1992) *Un océan sans rivage: Ibn Arabî, le Livre et la Loi*, Paris: Seuil, trans. D. Streight (1993) as *An ocean without shore: Ibn Arabi, the Book, and the Law*, Albany, NY: State University of New York Press.

Clarke, L. (2005) 'The rise and decline of *Taqiyya* in Twelver Shi'ism', in *RII*, 46–63.

Classen, C. (1998) *The Color of Angels: Cosmology, Gender and the Aesthetic Imagination*, London: Routledge.

Classen, C. et al. (1994) *Aroma: The Cultural History of Smell*, London: Taylor & Francis.

Colby, F. S. and C. J. Gruber (eds) (2010) *The Prophet's Ascension: Cross-cultural Encounters with the Islamic Mi'raj Tales*, Bloomington, IN: Indiana University Press.

Cole, J. R. I. (1998) *Modernity and the Millennium: The Genesis of the Baha'i Faith in the Nineteenth-Century Middle East*, New York: Columbia University Press.

_____ (1997) 'Individualism and the Spiritual Path in Shaykh Ahmad Al-Ahsa'i', *Occasional Papers in Shaykhi, Babi and Baha'i Studies*, 1.4: available online at: http://www.h-org/~bahai/bhpapers/ahsaind.htm.

Collins, A. Y. (ed.) (1986) *Semeia 36: Early Christian Apocalypticism: Genre and Social Setting*, Decatur, GA: Scholars Press.

Collins, J. J. (2013) *The Dead Sea Scrolls: A Biography*, Princeton, NJ: Princeton University Press.

_____ (2007) Response to 'Islamicate Apocalypsis: Methodological Considerations', American Academy of Religion Panel, San Diego, November.

_____ (2005) 'Apocalypse: Jewish apocalypticism to the Rabbinic period', in *ER2*, i, 414–19.

_____ (ed.) (1999) *The Encyclopedia of Apocalypticism*, i, *The Origins of Apocalypticism in Judaism and Christianity*, New York: Continuum.

_____ (1997a) *Apocalypticism in the Dead Sea Scrolls*, New York: Routledge.

_____ (1997b) 'Was the Dead Sea sect an Apocalyptic Community?', in *Seers, Sibyls and Sages in Hellenistic-Roman Judaism*, ed. J. J. Collins, Leiden: Brill, 261–86.

_____ (1989) *The Apocalyptic Imagination: An Introduction to the Jewish Matrix of Christianity*, New York: Crossroads.

_____ (1987) 'Apocalypse: An overview', in *ER2*, i, 409–14.

_____ (ed.) (1979) *Semeia 14: Apocalypse: The Morphology of a Genre*, Decatur, GA: Scholars Press.

Collins, J. J. and R. A. Kugler (eds) (2000) *Religion in the Dead Sea Scrolls*, Grand Rapids, MI and Cambridge: Wm. B. Eerdmans Publishing.

Cook, D. (2002) *Studies in Muslim Apocalyptic*, Princeton, NJ: The Darwin Press Incorporated.

_____ (1997) 'Moral Apocalyptic in Islam', in *Studia Islamica* 86: 37–69.

Cook, W. R. (1984) 'The "Glory" Motif in the Johannine corpus', in *Journal of the Evangelical Theological Society* 27.3: 291–7.

Corbin, H. (2008) *Face de Dieu, face de l'homme – Herméneutique et soufisme*, Paris: Entrelacs.

_____ (trans.) (1996) *Les Orients des Lumières*, Lagrasse: Editions Verdier.

_____ (1993) *History of Islamic Philosophy*, trans. L. Sherrard, with the assistance of P. Sherrard, New York: Kegan Paul International (originally published as *Histoire de la Philosophie islamique*, Paris, 1964, 1986).

_____ (1983) *Cyclical Time and Ismaili Gnosis*, trans. Ralph Manheim and James W. Morris, London and Boston: Kegan Paul International in association with Islamic Publications.

_____ (1981) *Le Paradoxe du Monothéisme*, Paris: Éditions de l'Herne.

_____ (1980) *Avicenna and the Visionary Recital*, trans. Willard Trask, Irving, TX: Spring Publications.

_____ (1978) *Man of Light in Iranian Sufism*, trans. N. Pearson, Boulder, CO: Shambhala.

_____ (1971a) *En Islam iranien: Aspects spirituels et philosophiques*, 4 vols, Paris: Gallimard.

_____ (1971b) *L'Homme de Lumière dans le Soufisme iranien*, Saint-Vincent-sur-Jabron: Éditions Présence.

_____ (1970) *Annuaire de l'École Pratique des Hautes Études: Section des Sciences religieuses, 1969–70*, Paris: Imprimerie nationale.

_____ (1967) 'De l'Épopée héroïque à l'Épopée mystique', in *Eranos-Jahrbuch* 35, Zurich: Rhein-Verlag, 177–239.

Coudert, A. P. (1999) 'Newton and the Rosicrucian Enlightenment', in J. E. Force and R. H. Popkin (eds), *Newton and Religion: Context, Nature, and Influence*, Dordrecht and Boston, MA: Wolters Kluwer, 17–43.

Cragg, K. (2009) *The Iron in the Soul: Joseph and the Undoing of Violence*, London: Melisende.

Cross, F. M. (1998) *From Epic to Canon: History and Literature in Ancient Israel*, Baltimore, MD: Johns Hopkins University Press.

Cusa, Nicholas of (1999) *The Vision of God*, trans. E. G. Salter, intro. E. Underhill (repr. of London 1928 edn), Escondido, CA: Cosimo Classics.

Cuypers, M. (2015) *The Composition of the Qur'ān: Rhetorical Analysis*, London and New York: Bloomsbury Academic.

_____ (2014) *Une Apocalypse coranique: Lecture des trente-trois dernières Sourates du Coran*, Pendé: Éditions J. Gabalda et Cie.

_____ (2012) *La Composition du Coran: Nazm al-Qur'ān*, Pendé: Éditions J. Gabalda et Cie.

_____ (2009) *The Banquet: A Reading of the Fifth Sura of the Quran*, trans. Patricia Kelly, Miami, FL: Convivium.

_____ (2007) *Le Festin: une lecture de la sourate al-mâ'ida*, Paris: Lethielleux.

Dadbeh, A. et al. (2009/2012) 'Joseph', in *EIr*.

Dan, J. (2011) 'Messianic Movements in the Period of the Crusades', *WLL*, 285–98.

Davidson, O. M. (2008) 'Persian/Iranian Epic', in *ACAE*, 264–6.

de Premare, A.-L. (1989) *Joseph et Muhammad: Le chapitre 12 du Coran*, Aix-en-Provence: Publications de l'Université de Provence.

Denham, R. (2004) *Northrop Frye: Religious Visionary and Architect of the Spiritual World*, Charlottesville, VA: University of Virginia Press.

Dennett, D. C. (1992) 'The Self as a Center of Narrative Gravity', in *Self and Consciousness: Multiple Perspectives*, ed. F. Kessel, P. Cole and D. Johnson, Hillsdale, NJ: Erlbaum, 1992, 103–14.

DeWeese, D. A. (1994) *Islamization and Native Religion in the Golden Horde: Baba Tūkles and Conversion to Islam in Historical and Epic Tradition*, University Park, PA: Pennsylvania State University Press.

Dumas, F. (2011 access) 'Funny in Farsi', www.randomhouse.com/highschool/RHI_magazine/pdf3/Dumas.pdf.

Dundes, A. (2003) *Fables of the Ancients: Folklore in the Quran*, Lanham, MD: Rowman & Littlefield Publishers, Inc.

Ebied, R. Y. and M. J. L. Young (1975) *The Story of Joseph in Arabic Verse: The Leeds Arabic Manuscript 347*, Leiden: Brill.

Eco, U. (1994) 'Telling the Process', author's postscript in *The Name of the Rose*, trans. W. Weaver, San Diego: Harcourt.

_____ (1989) *The Open Work*, trans. Anna Cancogni, intro. David Robey, Cambridge, MA: Harvard University Press.

_____ (1989) *The Aesthetics of Chaosmos: The Middle Ages of James Joyce*, Cambridge, MA: Harvard University Press.

Eliade, M. (1971) *Myth of the Eternal Return*, trans. Willard R. Trask, Princeton, NJ: Princeton University Press.

_____ (1958) 'La Coincidentia oppositorum et le mystère de la totalité', *Eranos-Jahrbücher* 27: 195–236.

Elias, J. J. (ed.) (2010) *Key Themes for the Study of Islam*. Oxford: Oneworld Publications.

_____ (2001) 'The Sufi Robe (*khirqa*) as a vehicle of spiritual authority', in *Robes and Honor: The Medieval World of Investiture*, ed. Steward Gordon, New York: Palgrave, 275–89.

_____ (1995) *The Throne Carrier of God: The Life and Thought of 'Alā' ad-Dawla as-Simnānī*, Albany: State University of New York Press.

Eliot, T. S. (1938) *Selected Essays*, 2nd edn, London: Faber & Faber.

Ellmann, R. (1982) *James Joyce*, New York: Oxford University Press.

_____ (1954) 'The Backgrounds of Ulysses', *The Kenyon Review*, 16.3: 337–86.

Ernst, C. W. (2011) *How to Read the Qur'ān: A New Guide with Select Translations*, Chapel Hill, NC: University of North Carolina Press.

Fahd, T. 'Sakina', in *E12*.

Fairbairn, P. (1854) *Typology of Scripture: Viewed in Connection with the Entire Scheme of the Divine Dispensations*, 2 vols, in 1, Philadelphia, PA: Smith and English.

Fargnoli, N. A. and M. P. Gillespie (2006) *Critical Companion to James Joyce: A Literary Reference to His Life and Works*, New York: Facts On File.

Fatoohi, L. (2007) *The Prophet Joseph in the Qur'an, the Bible, and History: A New Detailed Commentary on the Quranic Chapter of Joseph*, Birmingham: Luna Plena Publishing.

Filiu, J.-P. (2011) *Apocalypse in Islam*, Berkeley, CA: University of California Press.

Firestone, R. 'Yusuf', in *EI2*.

_____ (1990) *Journeys in Holy Lands: The Evolution of the Abraham-Ishmael Legends in Islamic Exegesis*, Albany, NY: State University of New York Press.

Fleischer, C. H. (2000) 'Mahdi and Millenium: Messianic Dimensions in the Development of Ottoman Imperial Ideology', in *The Great Ottoman-Turkish Civilization*, iii, ed. K. Çiçek (et al.), Ankara: Yeni Türkiye, 42–54.

_____ (1992) 'The Lawgiver as Messiah: The Making of the Imperial Image in the Reign of Suleyman', in G. Veinstein (ed.), *Soliman le Magnifique et son temps: Actes du Colloque de Paris...mars 1990 (Suleyman the Magnificent and his time: Acts of the Parisian Conference...March 1990)*, Paris: La Documentation Française, 159–77.

Foley, J. M. (ed.), (2009) *A Companion to Ancient Epic*, Malden, MA: Wiley-Blackwell Publishing.

Force, J. E. and R. H. Popkin (eds) (1999) *Newton and Religion: Context, Nature, and Influence*, Dordrecht and Boston, MA: Wolter Kluwer.

Fox, J. J. (1909) 'Glory', in *The Catholic Encyclopedia*, ed. C. 'G. Herbermann et al., New York: R. Appleton, 6:585–6.

Franke, P. (2000) *Begegnung mit Khidr: Quellenstudien zum Imaginären im Traditionellen Islam*, Beirut, Stuttgart, In Kommission bei Franz Steiner Verlag Stuttgart.

Friedmann, Y. (1989) *Prophecy Continuous: Aspects of Ahmadi Religious Thought and its Medieval Background*, Berkeley, CA: University of California Press.

Frye, N. (2008) *Words with Power: Being a Second Study of the Bible and Literature*, Toronto: University of Toronto Press.

_____ (1991) *The Double Vision: Language and Meaning in Religion*, Toronto: University of Toronto Press.

_____ (1990) 'Cycle and Apocalypse in Finnegans Wake', in *Myth and Metaphor: Selected Essays, 1974–1988*, ed. R. Denham, Charlottesville, VA: University Press of Virginia.

_____ (1982) *The Great Code: The Bible and Literature*, New York and London: Harcourt Brace Jovanovich.

_____ (1964) *The Educated Imagination*, Bloomington, IN: Indiana University Press.

_____ (1961) in *The American Scholar* 30.4: 606.

_____ (1957) *Anatomy of Criticism: Four Essays*, Princeton, NJ: Princeton University Press.

_____ (1947) *Fearful Symmetry: A Study of William Blake*, Princeton, NJ: Princeton University Press.

Funkenstein, A. (1993) *Perceptions of Jewish History*, Berkeley and Los Angeles, CA: University of California Press.

Gallez, E. M. (2005) *Le Messie et son Prophète: Aux Origines de l'Islam*, 2 vols, Versailles: Éditions de Paris.

Garcia Martinez, F. (2007) 'Apocalypticism in the Dead Sea Scrolls', in *Qumranica Minora I*, ed. E. J. C. Tigchelaar, Boston, MA: Brill, 195–22.

Gasmi, L. (1986) 'Les Réseaux connotatifs dans le Texte coranique (le récit de Joseph: Sourate XII, Vols. 4–102)', *Arabica* 33: 1–48.

_____ (1977) 'Narrativité et Production de Sens dans le Texte coranique: Le Récit de Joseph', Paris: École des hautes études en sciences sociales (unpublished dissertation).

Geller, F. B. (2008) *Qur'ān in Vernacular: Folk Islam in the Balkans*, Max Planck Preprint 357, Berlin: Max-Planck-Institut für Wissenschaftsgeschichte.

Ghaemmaghami, O. (2012) 'A Youth of Medium Height: The Bab's Encounter with the Hidden Imam in *Tafsīr Sūrat al-Kawthar*', in *A Most Noble Pattern: Collected Essays on the Writings of the Báb, ʿAlí Muhammad Shírází (1819–1850)*, ed. T. Lawson and O. Ghaemmaghami, Oxford: George Ronald, 175–95.

Ghazālī, A. H. al- (1895) *Tafsīr sūrat Yūsuf*, Tehran: n.p.

Gillespie, M. P. (2003) *The Aesthetics of Chaos: Nonlinear Thinking and Contemporary Literary Criticism*, Gainesville, FL: University Press of Florida.

Glasheen, A. (1957) *A Census of Finnegans Wake: An Index of the Characters and Their Roles*, London: Faber & Faber.

Gluck, J. J. (1982) 'Is there Poetry in the Qur'ān?', in *Semitics* 8: 43–89.

Goldman, Sh. (1995) *The Wiles of Women, the Wiles of Men: Joseph and Potiphar's Wife in Ancient Near Eastern, Jewish, and Islamic Folklore*, Albany, NY: State University of New York Press.

Goldziher, I. (1971) *Muslim Studies,* ed. S. M. Stern, trans. C. R. Barber and S. M. Stern, Vol. 2, London: George Allen & Unwin Ltd.

_____ (1893) 'La Notion de la Sakina chez les Mohametans', in *Revue de l'Histoire des Religions* 28: 1–13 and 177–204.

Goppelt, L. (1982) *Typos: The Typological Interpretation of the Old Testament in the New*, trans. D. H. Madvig, Grand Rapids, MI: William B. Eerdmans Publishing Company.

Gordon, C. H. (1955) 'Homer and Bible: The Origin and Character of East Mediterranean Literature', in *Hebrew Union College Annual* 2: 43–108.

Greifenhagen, F. V. (2009) 'Garments in Surah Yusuf: A Prologomenon to the Material Culture of Garments in the Formative Islamic Period', in *JQS* 11: 72–92.

Grunebaum, C. E. von, 'Bayān', in *EI2*.

Gunkel, H. (2006) *Creation and Chaos in the Primeval Era and the Eschaton: A Religio-Historical Study of Genesis 1 and Revelation 12*, trans. K. William Whitney Jr., Grand Rapids, MI: Wm. B. Eerdmans Publishing.

Günther, S. (2011) '"Gepriesen sei der, der seinen Diener bei Nacht reisen ließ" (Koran 17:1): Paradiesvorstellungen und Himmelsreisen im Islam – Grundfesten des Glaubens und literarische Topoi', in *Jenseitsreisen: ERANOS 2009 und 2010*, ed. E. Hornung and A. Schweizer, Basel: Schwabe, 15–56.

_____ (2005) 'Introduction', in *Ideas, Images, and Methods of Portrayal: Insights into Classical Arabic Literature and Islam*, ed. S. Günther, Leiden: Brill, xiii–xxxiii.

_____ (2003) 'Literacy', in *EQ*.

_____ (2002) 'Muhammad, the Illiterate Prophet: An Islamic Creed in the Quran and Quranic Exegesis', *JQS* 4.1: 1–26.

_____ (1999) 'Hostile brothers in transformation: An archetypal conflict figuring in classical and modern Arabic literature', in *Myths, Historical Archetypes and Symbolic Figures in Arabic Literature: Towards a New Hermeneutic Approach. Proceedings of the International Symposium in Beirut, June 25th–June 30th, 1996*, ed. A. Neuwirth et al., Stuttgart, In Kommission bei Franz Steiner Verlag Stuttgart, 309–36.

Günther, S. and T. Lawson (eds) (2017) *The Roads to Paradise: Studies in Islamic Eschatology*, 2 vols, Leiden: Brill.

Hajjaji-Jarrah, S. M. (2005) 'Āyat al-Nūr: A metaphor for where we come from, what we are and where we are going', in *RII*, 169–81.

_____ (2000) 'The enchantment of reading: Sound meaning and expression in the *Sūrat al-ʿĀdiyāt*', in *Boullata*, 228–51.

Hallaq, W. 'Law and the Qur'ān', in *EQ*.

Hamori, A. (1974) *On the Art of Medieval Arabic Literature*, Princeton, NJ: Princeton University Press.

Hanson, P. D. (1979) *The Dawn of Apocalyptic: The Historical and Sociological Roots of Jewish Apocalyptic Eschatology*, Philadelphia, PA: Fortress Press.

Hardie, P. (1999) 'Metamorphosis, Metaphor, and Allegory in Latin Epic', in *ETCW*, 89–107.

Harries, K. (1975) 'The Infinite Sphere: Comments on the History of a Metaphor', *Journal of the History of Philosophy* 13.1: 5–15.

Hart, C. (1963) *A Concordance to Finnegans Wake*, Minneapolis, MN: University of Minnesota Press.

Hastings, J. (ed.) (1913) *Encyclopaedia of Religion and Ethics*, 13 vols, Edinburgh: T. & T. Clark.

Haubold, J. (2002) 'Greek Epic: A Near Eastern Genre?', in *Proceedings of the Cambridge Philological Society* 48: 1–19.

Hellholm, D. (ed.) (1989) *Apocalypticism in the Mediterranean World and the Near East*, Tübingen: J. C. B. Mohr (Paul Siebeck).

Heyden, D. (2005) 'Caves', in *ER2*, Vol. 3: 1468–73.

Hirsch Jr., E. D. (1967) *Validity in Interpretation*, New Haven, CT: Yale University Press.

Hirtenstein, S. (1999) *The Unlimited Mercifier: The Life and Thought of Ibn Arabi*, Oxford: ANQA Publishing and Ashland, OR: White Cloud Press.

Hodgson, M. G. S. (1974) *The Venture of Islam: Conscience and History in a World Civilization*, 3 vols, Chicago, IL: University of Chicago Press.

Hoffman, T. (2009a) 'Koranisk/kaotisk: Om Koranens semantik, retorik, ritualisering, reception og konstruktion i lyset af begrebet "kaos"', in *Chaos: Dansk-norsk tidsskrift for religionhistoriske studie*, Copenhagen: Forlaget Chaos, 75–94.

_____ (2009b) 'From the Chaotic to the Chaordic: Rethinking Chaos and Quran', unpublished paper presented at The Quran: Text, History & Culture, a conference convened by the Centre of Islamic Studies, School of Oriental and African Studies, University of London, 12–14 November (typescript kindly provided by the author).

Hopkins, J. (1985) *Nicholas of Cusa on Learned Ignorance: A Translation and Appraisal of De Docta Ignorantia*, Minneapolis, MN: Arthur J. Banning Press.

Horace, *Ars Poetica or Epistle to the Pisos*, trans. A. S. Kline, available at: http://www.poetryintranslation.com/PITBR/Latin/HoraceArsPoetica.htm#_Toc98156243.

Hoyland, R. (2012) 'Early Islam as a Late Antique religion', in *The Oxford Handbook of Late Antiquity*, ed. Scott Johnson, New York: Oxford University Press, 1053–77.

_____ (1997) *Seeing Islam as Others Saw It: A Survey and Evaluation of Christian, Jewish, and Zoroastrian Writings on Early Islam*, Princeton, NJ: Darwin Press.

Hutcheon, L. and M. (2004) *Opera and the Art of Dying*, Cambridge, MA and London: Harvard University Press.

Huwayzī, ʿA. ʿA. al- (2001/1422) *Kitāb tafsīr nūr al-thaqalayn*, 8 vols, ed. ʿAlī ʿĀshūr, Beirut: Muʾassasat al-Taʾrīkh al-ʿArabī.

Ibn al-ʿArabī, M. D. (1980) *The Bezels of Wisdom*, trans. R. W. J. Austin, New York: Paulist Press.

_____ (1966) *Fusūs al-hikam*, Beirut: Dār al-Kitāb al-ʿArabī.

Ibn Bābawayh, M. (1970) *Ikmāl al-dīn wa-itmām al-niʿma fī ithbāt al-rajʿa*, Najaf: al-Matbaʿah al-Haydarīyah.

Ibn Hanbal, A. (1969) *Musnad al-imām Ahmad Ibn Hanbal wa-bihāmishihi muntakhab Kanz al-ʿummāl fī sunan al-aqwāl wa-l-afʿāl*, 6 vols, Beirut: al-Maktab al-Islāmī lil-Tabāʿah wa-al-Nashr.

Ibn Hishām and Ibn Ishāq (2003/1464) *al-Sīra l-nabawiyya*, 4 in 2 vols, Beirut: Dār al-kutub al-ʿilmiyya.

_____ and _____ (1992) *The Life of Muhammad: A Translation of Ishāq's Sīrat Rasūl Allāh*, trans. A. Guillaume, New York: Oxford University Press.

Ibn Qutayba, ʿA. (1936/1355) *al-Qurtayn*, Cairo: Maktabat al-Khānjī.

Izutsu, T. (1966) *Ethico-religious Concepts in the Qurʾan*, Montreal: McGill University Press.

____ (1964) *God and Man in the Koran: Semantics of the Koranic Weltanschauung*, Tokyo: Keio Institute of Cultural and Linguistic Studies.

Jarrett, M. (1999) *Drifting on a Read: Jazz as a Model for Writing*, Albany, NY: State University of New York Press.

Jeffery, A. ʿAyaʾ, *EI2*.

Johns, A. H. (1999) 'She desired him and he desired her' (Quran 12:24): ʿAbd al-Raʾūf's Treatment of an Episode of the Joseph Story', in *Tarjumān al-mustafīd*, *Archipel* 57: 109–34.

____ (1993) 'The Quranic Presentation of the Joseph Story: Naturalistic or Formulaic Language?', in *Approaches to the Qurʾān*, ed. G. R. Hawting and Abdul-Kader Shareef, London: Routledge, 37–70.

____ (1981) 'Joseph in the Qurʾān: Dramatic Dialogue, Human Emotion, and Prophetic Wisdom', *Islamochristiana* 7: 29–55.

Joyce, J. (1959) *Critical Writings of James Joyce*, ed. E. Mason and R. Ellmann, New York: Viking Press.

Jung, C. G. (1977) *Mysterium Coniunctionis: An Inquiry into the Separation and Synthesis of Psychic Opposites in Alchemy*, Princeton, NJ: Princeton University Press (first published in German in 1956, Jung's last book-length work).

Kassis, H. E. (1983) *A Concordance of the Quran*, foreword by F. Rahman, Berkeley, CA: University of California Press.

Kawashima, Robert S. (2004) 'Verbal Medium and Narrative Art in Homer and the Bible', *Philosophy and Literature* 28.1: 103–17.

Keeler, A. 'Joseph ii: In Qurʾānic exegesis', in *EIr*.

____ (2006) *Sufi Hermeneutics: The Qurʾan Commentary of Rashīd Al-Dīn Maybudī*, Oxford: Oxford University Press, in association with the Institute of Ismaili Studies.

Kennedy, P. F. (2016) *Recognition in the Arabic Narrative Tradition: Discovery, Deliverance and Delusion*, Edinburgh: Edinburgh University Press.

Kermani, N. (2000) *Gott ist schön: Das ästhetische Erleben des Koran*, Munich: C. H. Beck, trans. T. Crawford (2015), *God is Beautiful: The Aesthetic Experience of the Quran*, Cambridge: Polity Press.

Khalafallah, M. 'Badīʿ', in *EI2*.

Kia, C. (2012) 'Joseph iii: In Persian Art', in *EIr*.

Kierkegaard, S. (2009) *Repetition and Philosophical Crumbs*, trans. M. G. Piety, New York: Oxford University Press.

Kinberg, L. 'Paradise', in *EQ*.

Kister, M. J. (1962) '"A Booth like the Booth of Moses...": A Study of an Early *Hadith*', in *BSOAS* 25: 150–5.

Koch, K. (1972) *The Rediscovery of Apocalyptic: A Polemical Work on a Neglected Area of Biblical Studies and Its Damaging Effects on Theology and Philosophy*, trans. Margaret Kohl, London: SCM (formerly, Student Christian Movement) Press.

Kohlberg, E. and M. A. Amir-Moezzi (2009) *Revelation and Falsification: The Kitāb al-qirāʾāt of Ahmad b. Muhammad al-Sayyārī*, Leiden: Brill.

Kooten, G. H. van and J. van Ruiten (eds) (2008) *The Prestige of the Pagan Prophet Balaam in Judaism, early Christianity and Islam*, Boston, MA: Brill.

Kreuzer, S. (2007) 'Ark of YHWH', in *Religion Past and Present,* i, ed. H. D. Betz et al., Leiden and Boston, MA: Brill, 381–2.

Kristeva, J. (1987) *Tales of Love*, New York: Columbia University Press.

Kugel, J. L. (2003) *The God of Old: Inside the Lost World of the Bible*, New York: Free Press.

_____ (1990) *In Potiphar's House: The Interpretive Life of Biblical Texts*, San Francisco, CA: HarperSanFrancisco.

Kulaynī, M. al- (1954/1374) *al-Uṣūl min al-Kāfī*, 2 vols, ed. ʿAlī Akbar al-Ghaffārī, Tehran: Dār al-Kutub al-Islāmīyah (Maṭbaʿat al-Haydarī).

Lamb, C. (1886) *The Adventures of Ulysses, Edited with Notes for School*, Boston, MA: Ginn & Company.

Lambden, S. (1986) 'An Episode in the Childhood of the Bab', in *In Iran, Studies in Babi and Baha'i History*, Vol. 3, ed. Peter Smith, Los Angeles, CA: Kalimat Press, 1–31.

Landolt, H. (2003) 'Walāyah', in *ER2*.

Lange, C. (2015) *Paradise and Hell in Islamic Tradition*, Cambridge: Cambridge University Press.

Lawrence, B. B. (2017) *The Koran in English: A Biography*, Princeton, NJ and Oxford: Princeton University Press.

_____ (2006) *The Quran: A Biography*, London: Atlantic.

Lawson, T. (2017) 'Paradise in the Quran and the music of apocalypse', in *Roads* 1: 93–135.

_____ (2015) 'Joycean modernism in a nineteenth-century Qur'an commentary? A comparison of the Bab's Qayyūm al-Asmā' with Joyce's Ulysses', in *Erin and Iran: Cultural Encounters between the Irish and the Iranians*, ed. H. E. Chehabi and Grace Neville, Washington, DC and Boston, MA: Ilex Foundation & Center for Hellenic Studies Trustees of Harvard University, 79–118.

_____ (2014) 'The Quran and Epic', in *JQS* 16.1: 58–92.

_____ (2012a) 'Typological Figuration and the Meaning of "spiritual": The Quranic story of Joseph', in *JAOS* 132.2: 221–44.

_____ (2012b) 'Apocalypse', in G. Böwering et al. (eds), *The Princeton Encyclopedia of Islamic Political Thought*, Princeton, NJ: Princeton University Press, 38–9.

_____ (2012c) 'The Bahá'i Tradition: The Return of Joseph and the Peaceable Imagination', in *Fighting Words: Religion, Violence, and the Interpretation of Sacred Texts*, ed. J. Renard, Berkeley, CA: University of California Press, 135–57.

_____ (2011) *Gnostic Apocalypse in Islam: Qur'an, Exegesis, Messianism and the Literary Origins of the Babi Religion*, London and New York: Routledge.

_____ (2010a) 'Le Coran et l'imaginaire apocalyptique', trans. G. Rivier, in *Religions et Histoire* 34: 48–53.

_____ (2010b) 'Coherent Chaos and Chaotic Cosmos: The Quran and the Symmetry of Truth', in *Weltkonstruktionen: Religiose Weltdeutung zwischen Chaos und Kosmos vom alten Orient bis zum Islam*, ed. P. Gemeinhardt and A. Szgoll, Tübingen: Mohr Siebeck, 177–93.

_____ (2008a) 'Duality, Opposition and Typology in the Qur'an: The Apocalyptic Substrate', in *JQS* 10.2: 23–49.

_____ (2008b) 'Divine Wrath and Mercy in Islam: Their Reflection in the Quran and Quranic Images of Water', in *Forschungen zum Alten Testament*, 2nd series, ed. Reinhard G. Kratz and Hermann Spieckermann, Tübingen: Mohr Siebeck, 248–67.

_____ (2005a) 'Orthodoxy and Heterodoxy in Twelver Shiʿism: Ahmad Al-Ahsa'ī on Fayd Kashaní (the *Risalat al-ʿIlmiyya*)', in *Religion and Society in Qajar Iran* ed. R. Gleave, London: RoutledgeCurzon, 127–54.

_____ (2005b) 'The Bab's Epistle on the Spiritual Journey towards God', in *The Baha'i Faith and the World Religions: Papers Presented at the Irfan Colloquia*, ed. M. Momen, Oxford: George Ronald, 231–47.

_____ (2004) 'Akhbārī Shī'ī Approaches to Tafsīr', in *The Koran: Critical Concepts in Islamic Studies 4*, ed. C. Turner, New York: RoutledgeCurzon, 163–97.

_____ (2003) 'Seeing Double: The Covenant and the Tablet of Ahmad', in *The Baha'i Faith and the World's Religions: Papers Presented at the Irfan Colloquia*, ed. M. Momen, Oxford: George Ronald, 39–87.

_____ (2002) 'The Hidden Words of Fayz Kashani', in *Actes du 4e Colloque de la Societas Iranologica Europaea, Paris, Septembre 1999*, Vol. 2, ed. M. Szuppe et al., 427–47.

_____ (2001) '*Coincidentia Oppositorum* in the Qayyúm al-Asmá': The Terms "Point" (*nuqta*), "Pole" (*qutb*), "Center" (*markaz*) and the Khutbat al-Tatanjiya', *Occasional Papers in Shaykhi, Babi and Baha'i Studies* 5, no. 1, available online at: /www.h - net. org/~bahai/bhpapers/vol5/tatanj/tatanj.htm.

_____ (1989) 'The Terms Remembrance (*dhikr*) and Gate (*bab*) in the Bab's Commentary on the Sura of Joseph', in *Studies in Honor of Hasan M. Balyúzí (Studies in the Babí and Baha'í Religions)*, Vol. 5, ed. M. Momen, Los Angeles, CA: Kalimat Press, 1–63.

_____ (1988) 'Interpretation as Revelation: The Quran Commentary of Sayyid 'Alí Muhammad Shírází, the Báb', in *Approaches to the History of the Interpretation of the Quran*, ed. Andrew Rippin, Oxford: Oxford University Press, 223–253.

Leemhuis, F. 'Apocalypse', in *EQ*.

Levitin, D. J. (2006) *This Is Your Brain on Music: The Science of a Human Obsession*, New York: Penguin Group.

Lumbard, J. E. B. (2015) 'Covenant and Covenants in the Qur'an', *JQS* 17.2: 1–23.

Macdonald, J. (1964) *The Theology of the Samaritans*, London: SCM Press.

_____ (1956a) 'Joseph in the Quran and Muslim commentary, pt. I: A comparative study', in *MW* 46: 113–31.

_____ (1956b) 'Joseph in the Quran and Muslim commentary, pt. II: A comparative study', in *MW* 46: 207–24.

MacEoin, D. (2009) *The Messiah of Shiraz: Studies in Early and Middle Babism*, Boston, MA: Brill.

_____ (1992) *The Sources for Early Bābī Doctrine and History: A Survey*, Leiden: E. J. Brill.

_____ (1990) 'Orthodoxy and Heterodoxy in Nineteenth-Century Shi'ism: The Cases of Shaykhism and Babism', *JAOS* 110.2: 323–9.

Madelung, W. (1978) 'Ḳā'im Āl Muhammad', in *EI2*.

Madigan, D. A. (2001) *The Qur'an's Self-image: Writing and Authority in Islam's Scripture*, Woodstock: Princeton University Press.

Mahdi, M. 'Farabi, Abu Nasr: Philosopher-King and Prophet-Legislator', in *EIr* 9: 228.

Majlisī, M. B. (1983/1403) *Bihār al-anwār*, 111 vols, Beirut: Mu'assasat al-Wafā'.

Mann, T. (2005) *Joseph and His Brothers*, 4 vols, English trans. J. E. Woods, New York: Everyman's Library.

Martin, R. (2009) 'Epic as Genre', in *ACAE*, 9–19.

Mayer, T. (2009) *Keys to the Arcana: Shahrastānī's Esoteric Commentary on the Quran*. Oxford: Oxford University Press, in association with the Institute of Ismaili Studies.

Mays, J. L. (1993) 'The Question of Context in Psalm Interpretation', in *The Shape and Shaping of the Psalter*, ed. J. Clinton McCann, Sheffield: JSOT Press, 14–20.

McDonald, L. M. and J. A. Sanders (eds) (2002) *The Canon Debate*, Peabody, MA: Hendrickson Publishers.

McGaha, M. (1997) *Coat of Many Cultures: The Story of Joseph in Spanish Literature 1200–1492*, Philadelphia, PA and Jerusalem: Jewish Publication Society.

McHugh, R. (1979) 'Mohammad in Notebook VI.B.31', *A Wake Newslitter: Studies in James Joyce's Finnegans Wake*, n.s., 16.4: 51–8.

_____ (1976) *The Sigla of Finnegans Wake*, London: Edward Arnold.

McIntyre, J. L. (1903) *Giordano Bruno*, London: Macmillan.

Meier, F. (1966) 'Some Aspects of Inspiration by Demons in Islam', in *The Dream and Human Societies*, ed. G. E. von Grunebaum and R. Caillois, Berkeley and Los Angeles, CA: University of California Press, 421–30.

Merkur, D. (2011) 'Cultivating Visions through Exegetical Meditations', in *WLL*, 62–91.

Mir, M. (2001–6) 'Names of the Qur'ān', in *EQ*.

_____ (2000) 'Irony in the Qur'ān: A Study of the Story of Joseph', in *Boullata*, 173–87.

_____ (1986) 'The Quranic story of Joseph: Plots, Themes, and Characters', in *MW* 76: 1–15.

Momen, M. (2011) 'Perfection and Refinement: Towards an Aesthetics of the Bab', in *Lights of 'Irfan* 12: 221–43.

_____ (1985) *An Introduction to Shi'i Islam: The History and Doctrines of Twelver Shi'ism*, New Haven, CT: Yale University Press.

_____ (1982) 'The Trial of Mullá 'Alí Bastámí: A Combined Sunní-Shí'í Fatwá against the Báb', *Iran* 20: 113–43.

Moreen, V. B. (1994) 'Moses in Muhammad's Light: Muslim Topoi and Anti-Muslim Polemics in Judaeo-Persian Panegyrics', in *Journal of Turkish Studies* 18 (*Annemarie Schimmel Festschrift*): 185–200.

Murata, S. (1992) *The Tao of Islam: A Sourcebook on Gender Relationships in Islamic Thought*, Albany, NY: State University of New York Press.

Nagy, G. (2008) 'The Epic Hero', in *ACAE*, 71–89.

Nawfal, A. (1976) *al-I'jāz al-'adad li'l-Qur'ān al-karīm*, Cairo: n.p.

Nguyen, M. (2012) 'Exegesis of the *hurúf al-muqatta'a*: Polyvalency in Sunni Traditions of Quranic Interpretation', *JQS* 14.2: 1–28.

Nelson, K. (1985) *The Art of Reciting the Qur'ān*, Austin, TX: University of Texas Press.

Neuwirth, A. (2017) 'Paradise as a Quranic Discourse: Late Antique Foundations and Early Quranic Developments', in *Roads* 1: 67–92.

_____ (2008) 'Two Views of History and Human Future: Quranic and Biblical Renderings of Divine Promises', in *JQS* 10: 1–20.

_____ (2000a) 'Negotiating Justice: A Pre-Canonical Reading of the Quranic Creation Accounts. Part II', in *JQS* 2.2: 1–18.

_____ (2000b) 'Referentiality and Textuality in Surat Al-Hijr: Some Observations on the Qur'ānic "canonical process" and the Emergence of a Community', in *Boullata*, 143–72.

_____ (1984) 'Symmetrie und Paarbildung in der Koranischen Eschatologie: Philologisch-Stilistisches zu Surat ar-Rahman', in *MUSJ* 50.1: 443–75.

_____ (1980) 'Zur Struktur der Yūsuf-Sure', in *Studien aus Arabistik und Semitistik: Anton Spitaler zum 70. Geburtstag von seinen Schülern überreicht*, ed. W. Diem and S. Wild, Wiesbaden: Harrassowitz, 123–52.

Neuwirth, A. et al. (eds) (2009) *The Quran in Context: Historical and Literary Investigations into the Quranic Milieu*, Leiden: Brill.

_____ (eds) (1999) *Myths, Historical Archetypes, and Symbolic Figures in Arabic Literature: Towards a New Hermeneutic Approach: Proceedings of the International Symposium in Beirut, June 25th–June 30th, 1996*, Beirut: In Kommission bei Franz Steiner Verlag Stuttgart.

Nicholson, R. A. (1921) *Studies in Islamic Mysticism*, Cambridge and New York: Cambridge University Press.

Niditch, S. (2009) 'Epic and History in the Hebrew Bible: Definitions, "ethnic genres", and the Challenges of Cultural Identity in the Biblical Book of Judges', in *Epic and History*, ed. D. Konstan, West Sussex and Malden, MA: Wiley-Blackwell, 86–102.

_____ (2008) 'The Challenge of Israelite Epic', in *ACAE*, 277–87.

Nuʿmān, Ibn Hayyūn al-Tamīmī al-Maghribī al- (2008) *Kitāb Asās al-taʾwīl*, Salamiyya, Syria: Dār al-Ghadīr.

Nwyia, P. (1970) *Exégèse coranique et langage mystique: nouvel essai sur le lexique technique des mystiques musulmans*, Beirut: Dar el-Machreq.

O'Regan, C. (2002) *Gnostic Apocalypse: Jacob Boehme's Haunted Narrative*, Albany, NY: State University of New York Press.

Ogden, C. K. and I. A. Richards (1949) *The Meaning of Meaning: A Study of the Influence of Language upon Thought and of the Science of Symbolism*, London: Routledge & Paul.

Padwick, C. (1961) *Muslim Devotions: A Study of Prayer-manuals in Common Use*, London: SPCK.

Paret, R. 'Ibrahim', in *EI2*.

Parkin, D. (2007) 'Wafting on the Wind: Smell and the Cycle of Spirit and Matter', *JRAIns* 13: 39–53.

Pellat, C. 'Hamasa: i. Arabic Literature', in *EI2*.

_____ 'Hilm', in *EI2*.

Qāḍī, Wadād -al (2006) *The Primordial Covenant and Human History in the Quran*, Beirut: American University of Beirut.

Quinn, Sh. A. (2000) *Historical Writing during the Reign of Shah Abbas: Ideology, Imitation, and Legitimacy in Safavid Chronicles*, Salt Lake City, UT: University of Utah Press.

Qutb, S. (1981) *Mashāhid al-qiyāma fī l-Qurʾān*, Cairo: Dār al-Maʿārif.

Rafati, V. (2012) 'Colours in the Writings of the Báb (trans. O. Ghaemmaghami)', in *A Most Noble Pattern: Collected Essays on the Writings of the Báb, ʿAlí Muhammad Shírází (1819–1850)*, ed. T. Lawson and O. Ghaemmaghami, Oxford: George Ronald, 33–51.

Rahman, F. (1982) *Islam & Modernity: Transformation of an Intellectual Tradition*, Publications of the Center for Middle Eastern Studies, no. 15. Chicago, IL: University of Chicago Press.

_____ (1980) *Major Themes of the Qurʾān*, Minneapolis, MN: Bibliotheca Islamica.

Rashtī, K. (1270 [1853 or 54]) *Sharh al-qasīda al-lāmiyya*, Tehran: Chāpkhānah-i Mirzā Muhammad Riżā Nūrī.

Ravasi, G. (1995) *The Crypt of the Cathedral of Anagni: A Miniature Underground Sistine*, Genoa: Edizioni d'Arte Marconi for Basilica Cattedrale Anagni.

Ravasio, E. (2014) *Il Padre di Bloom e il Figlio di Dedalus: La funzione del pensiero tomista, aristotelico e presocratico nell'Ulisse di Joyce*, Tricase: Youcanprint.

Reda, N. (2017) *The Al-Baqara Crescendo: Understanding the Qurʾān's Style, Narrative Structure, and Running Themes*, Montreal and Kingston: McGill-Queen's University Press.

Renard, J. (2008) *Friends of God: Islamic Images of Piety, Commitment, and Servanthood*, Berkeley, CA: University of California Press.

_____ (1996) *Seven Doors to Islam: Spirituality and the Religious Life of Muslims*, Berkeley and Los Angeles, CA: University of California Press.

_____ (1993) *Islam and the Heroic Image: Themes in Literature and the Visual Arts*, Columbia, SC: University of South Carolina Press.

Rendsburg, G. A. (1988) 'Literary Structures in the Quranic and Biblical Stories of Joseph', in *MW* 78: 118–20.

Revard, S. V. and Newman, J. K. (1993) 'Epic. I. History (Revard) and Epic, II. Theory (Newman)', in *The New Princeton Encyclopaedia of Poetry and Poetics*, Princeton, NJ: Princeton University Press, 361–75.

Reynolds, D. (2009) 'Epic and History in the Arabic Tradition', in *Epic and History*, ed. David Konstan, West Sussex and Malden, MA: Wiley-Blackwell, 392–410.

Ricks, S. D. (2000) 'The Garment of Adam in Jewish, Muslim, and Christian tradition', in *Judaism and Islam: Boundaries, Communication and Interaction: Essays in Honor of William M. Brinner*, ed. B. H. Hary et al., Leiden: Brill, 203–25.

Rippin, A. (ed.) (2001) *The Qur'ān: Style and Contents*, Aldershot and Brookfield, VT: Ashgate.

_____ (1983) 'The Qur'ān as Literature: Perils, Pitfalls and Prospects', *Bulletin (British Society for Middle Eastern Studies)*, 10.1: 38–47.

Rosenthal, F. 'History and the Qur'ān', in *EQ*.

Roth, C. (1965) *The Dead Sea Scrolls: A New Historical Approach*, New York: W. W. Norton & Co. Inc.

Rubin, U. (1997) 'Apocalypse and Authority in Islamic tradition: The emergence of the Twelve Leaders', in *Qantara* 18.1: 11–42.

Ryan, P. (1975) 'The Descending Scroll: A Study of the Notion of Revelation as Apocalypse in the Bible and in the Quran', in *Ghana Bulletin of Theology* 4: 24–39.

Saleh, S. (1971) *La Vie future selon le Coran*, Paris: J. Vrin.

Salier, W. H. (2004) *The Rhetorical Impact of the Sēmeia in the Gospel of John*, Tübingen: Mohr Siebeck.

Sanders, J. A. (1984) *Canon and Community: A Guide to Canonical Criticism*, Philadelphia: Fortress Press.

Schimmel, A. (1999) 'Yūsuf in Mawlānā Rūmī's poetry', in *The Heritage of Sufism*, Vol. 2: *The Legacy of Medieval Persian Sufism*, ed. L. Lewisohn, Oxford: Oneworld, 45–60.

_____ (1994) *Deciphering the Signs of God: A Phenomenological Approach to Islam.* Edinburgh: Edinburgh University Press.

Schmidtke, S. 'Pairs and pairing', in *EQ*.

Scholem, G. (1995) *Major Trends in Jewish Mysticism*, New York: Schocken Books.

Sells, M. (1999) *Approaching the Qur'ān: The Early Revelations*, Ashland, OR: White Cloud Press.

_____ (1991) 'Sound, Spirit, and Gender', in *sūrat al-qadr*, *JAOS* 111.2: 239–59.

Shoemaker, S. J. (2012a) *The Death of a Prophet: The End of Muhammad's Life and the Beginnings of Islam*, Philadelphia, PA: University of Pennsylvania Press.

_____ (2012b) 'Muhammad and the Qur'ān', in *The Oxford Handbook of Late Antiquity*, ed. Scott Johnson, Oxford and New York: Oxford University Press, 1078–108;

Smith, M. (1989) 'On the history of ΑΠΟΚΑΛΥΠΤΩ and ΑΠΟΚΑΛΥΨΙΣ', in *Apocalypticism in the Mediterranean World and the Near East*, ed. D. Hellholm, Tübingen: J. C. B. Mohr (Paul Siebeck), 9–20.

Snouck Hurgronje, C. (1916) *Mohammedanism: Lectures on its Origin, its Religious and Political Growth, and its Present State*, New York: G. P. Putnam's Sons.

Sperl, S. (2006) 'Epic and Exile: Comparative Reflections on the Biography of the Prophet Muhammad, Virgil's *Aeneid*, and Valmiki's *Ramayana*', in *Comparative Studies of South Asia, Africa and the Middle East* 26.1: 96–104.

Stern, M. S. (1985) 'Muhammad and Joseph: A Study of Koranic Narrative', in *Journal of Near Eastern Studies* 44: 193–204.

Stetkevych, J. (1996) *Muhammad and the Golden Bough: Reconstructing Arabian Myth*, Bloomington, IN: Indiana University Press.

_____ (1993) *The Zephyrs of Najd: The Poetics of Nostalgia in the Classical Arabic Nasīb*, Chicago, IL: University of Chicago Press.

Stetkevych, S. P. (2010) *The Mantle Odes: Arabic Praise Poems to the Prophet Muhammad*, Bloomington, IN: Indiana University Press.

Stewart, D. J. (2013) 'Divine Epithets and the *Dibacchius: Clausulae* and Quranic rhythm', in *JQS* 15.2: 22–64.

_____ (2011) 'The Mysterious Letters and Other Formal Features of the Qur'ān in Light of Greek and Babylonian Oracular Texts', in *New Perspectives on the Qur'ān: The Qur'ān in its Historical Context*, ed. G. S. Reynolds, London: Routledge, 321–46.

_____ (2010) 'Prophecy', in *Key Themes for the Study of Islam*, ed. J. J. Elias, Oxford: Oneworld, 281–303.

_____ (2009) 'Poetic license in the Qur'ān: Ibn al-Sā'igh al-Hanafī's *Ihkām al-rāy fī ahkām al-āy*', in *JQS* 11.1: 1–56.

_____ 'Smell', in *EQ*.

_____ (2000) 'Understanding the Koran in English: Notes on Translation, Form, and Prophetic Typology', in *Diversity in Language: Contrastive Studies in Arabic and English Theoretical and Applied Linguistics*, ed. Z. Ibrahim, S. T. Aydelott, et al., New York: American University in Cairo Press, 31–48.

_____ (1990) 'Saj' in the Qur'ān: Prosody and Structure', in *JAL* 21.2: 101–39.

Stock, B. (1996) *Augustine the Reader: Meditation, Self-knowledge, and the Ethics of Interpretation*, Cambridge, MA: Harvard University Press.

Stowasser, B. (2005) 'Time sticks', in *Alltagsleben und materielle Kultur in der arabischen Sprache und Literatur: Festschrift fur Heinz Grotzfeld zum 70. Geburtstag*, ed. Th. Bauer und U. Stehli-Werbeck, Wiesbaden: Harrassowitz, 201–10.

Strothmann, R. (1974) 'Taḳīya', in *The Shorter Encyclopaedia of Islam*, ed. H. A. R. Gibb and J. H. Kramers, Leiden: Brill.

Subtelny, M. E. (2007) 'Visionary Rose: Metaphorical Application of Horticultural Practice in Persian Culture', in *Botanical Progress, Horticultural Innovations and Cultural Changes*, ed. Michael Conan and W. John Kress, Washington, DC: Dumbarton Oaks Research Library and Collection. Distributed by Harvard University Press, 13–36.

Suchocki, M. (1982) 'The Symbolic Structure of Augustine's Confessions', *JAAR 50*, no. 3, 365–78.

Suhrawardī, 'U al- (1965) *'Awārif al-ma'ārif*, 2nd edn, Lahore: Shaikh Ghulam 'Ali.

Suyūtī, J. al- (1973) *al-Itqān fī 'ulūm al-Qur'ān* (2 vols in 1), Beirut: al-Maktaba al-Thaqāfiya.

Tayob, A. Muhammad, 'Role of the Prophet in Muslim thought and practice', in *The Oxford Encyclopaedia of the Modern Islamic World*, Oxford, accessed 21 February 2013, www.oxfordislamicstudies.com.myaccess.library.utoronto.ca/article/opr/t236MIW/e0550.

Thackston, W. M. Jr (trans.) (1978) *The Tales of the Prophets of al-Kisā'ī*, Boston, MA: Twayne Publishers.

Tihrānī, Āghā Buzurg al- (1978/1398) *al-Dharī'a ilā tasānif al-shī'a*, 25 vols. Tehran and Najaf: distributed through author.

Tindall, W. Y. (1959) *A Reader's Guide to James Joyce*, New York: Noonday Press.

_____ (1955) *The Literary Symbol*, New York: Columbia University Press.

Toelle, H. (1999) *Le Coran revisité: Le Feu, l'Eau, l'Air et la Terre*, Damascus: Institut français d'études arabes de Damas.

Toorawa, S. M. (2007) 'Referencing the Qur'an: A Proposal, with Illustrative Translations and Discussion' *JQS* 9.1: 134–48.

Tottoli, R. (2002) *Biblical Prophets in the Qur'ān and Muslim Literature*, trans. M. Robertson, London: Curzon.

Valentine, S. R. (2008) *Islam and the Ahmadiyya Jama'at: History, Belief, Practice*, London: Hurst & Co.

van Dijk, T. (1972) *Some Aspects of Text*, Grammars, The Hague: Mouton.

van Duzer, C. A. (1996) *Duality and Structure in the Iliad and Odyssey*, New York: Peter Lang.

Van Dyck Card, J. (1984) *An Anatomy of 'Penelope'*, Rutherford, NJ: Fairleigh Dickinson University Press and London: Associated University Presses.

_____ (1973) '"Contradicting": The Word for Joyce's "Penelope"', *James Joyce Quarterly* 11.1: 17–26.

van Ess, J. (1988) *The Youthful God: Anthropomorphism in Early Islam: The University Lecture in Religion at Arizona State University*, Tempe, AZ: Dept of Religious Studies.

VanderKam, J. C. (2000) 'Apocalyptic Tradition in the Dead Sea Scrolls and the Religion of Qumran', in *Religion in the Dead Sea Scrolls*, ed. J. J. Collins and R. A. Kugler, Grand Rapids, MI and Cambridge: Wm. B. Eerdmans Publishing, 113–34.

_____ (1998) *Calendars in the Dead Sea Scrolls: Measuring Time*, London and New York: Routledge.

Vermès, G. (2010) *The Real Jesus: Then and Now*, Minneapolis, MN: Fortress Press.

Vielhauer, P. (1964) 'Apocalyspes and related subjects', in *Edgar Henneke New Testament Apocrypha*, ii, ed. W. Schneemelcher, tr. R. Mcl.Wilson, Philadelphia, PA: Westminster Press, 581–683.

Voelker, J. C. (1976) '"Nature It Is": The Influence of Giordano Bruno on James Joyce's Molly Bloom', *James Joyce Quarterly* 14.1: 39–48.

Wacker, N. (1990) 'Epic and the Modern Long Poem: Virgil, Blake and Pound', in *Comparative Literature* 42.2: 126–43.

Walbridge, L. (ed.) (2001) *Most Learned of the Shia: The Institution of the Marja' Taqlid*, New York: Oxford University Press.

Waldman, M. R. (1986) 'New Approaches to "biblical" materials in the Qur'ān', in *Studies in Islamic and Judaic Traditions: Papers Presented at the Institute Islamic-Judaic Studies, Center for Judaic Studies, Univ. of Denver*, ed. W. M. Brinner and S. D. Ricks, Atlanta, GA: Scholars Press, 47–64.

_____ (1978) 'Review: Islamic Studies: A New Orientalism?', in *The Journal of Interdisciplinary History* 8.3: 545–62.

Waltke, B. K. (1981) 'A Canonical Process Approach to the Psalms', in *Tradition and Testament: Essays in Honor of Charles Lee Feinberg*, ed. John S. Feinberg and Paul D. Feinberg, Chicago, IL: Moody Press.

Wansbrough, J. (1978) *The Sectarian Milieu: Content and Composition of Islamic Salvation History*, New York: Oxford University Press.

_____ (1977) *Quranic Studies: Sources and Methods of Scriptural Interpretation*, Oxford: Oxford University Press.

Weinfield, M. (2007) 'Presence, Divine', in *Encyclopaedia Judaica*, xvi, ed. M. Berenbaum and F. Skolnik, Macmillan Reference USA in association with the Keter Publishing House, 481–4.

Weir, D. (1996) *James Joyce and the Art of Mediation*, Ann Arbor: University of Michigan Press.

Wheeler, B. (2002) *Moses in the Qur'ān and Islamic Exegesis*, London: RoutledgeCurzon.

Wilson, E. (1956) *Red, Black, Blond and Olive: Studies in Four Civilizations: Zuni, Haiti, Soviet Russia, Israel*, New York: Oxford University Press.

Winter, I. J. (1994) 'Radiance as an Aesthetic Value in the Art of Mesopotamia (with some Indian Parallels)', in *Art, the Integral Vision: A Volume of Essay in Felicitation of Kapila Vatsyayan*, ed. B. N. Saraswati and S. C. Malik et al., New Delhi: D. K. Printworld, 123–32.

Yared, A. (2001) 'Introducing Islam in Finnegans Wake: The Story of Mohammed in VI.B.45', *Genetic Joyce Studies* 1.

_____ (1998) '"In the Name of Annah": Islam and *Salam* in Joyce's *Finnegans Wake*', *James Joyce Quarterly*, 'ReOrienting Joyce', 35.2/3: 401–38.

Yücesoy, H. (2009) *Messianic Beliefs and Imperial Politics in Medieval Islam: The 'Abbāsid Caliphate in the Early Ninth Century*, Columbia, SC: University of South Carolina Press.

Zarandi, N. (1974) *The Dawn-Breakers: Nabíl's Narrative of the Early Days of the Baha'i Revelation*, trans. Shoghi Effendi, Wilmette, IL: Baha'i Publishing Trust.

Zwettler, M. (1990) 'Mantic manifesto: The Sura of the Poets and the Quranic foundations of Prophetic Authority', in *Poetry and Prophecy: The Beginnings of a Literary Tradition*, ed. J. L. Kugel, Ithaca, NY and London: Cornell University Press, 75–119.

Index

Abbasids xxiv, xxv, 56
Abd al-Muttalib 16
ablutions 115
action 13–14
Ad 171
Adam 7, 118–19
afterlife xix, xxiii, 28
Ahmadis xxv, 56
al-Ahsa'i, Shaykh Ahmad 68, 135–6
Alexandria xxiv
Allah, see God
angels 9–10, 170, 171
anger, see wrath
Antioch xxiv
apocalypse xii, xv, xvii–xxv
    and definition 78
    and genre 28–34, 52–6, 79, 130–1
    and Islam 34–5
    and literature 76–7
    and paradise 35–7, 49–52
    and the Quran 170–3
    and reunion 63
Apocalypse of St John, The 28–31
Aristotle 15
audience xiv
Avicenna 96

Bab, the 74, 132–4, 135–9, 141–6, 153,
    154–5
    and hidden imam 163, 164–5, 167
    and interconnectedness 147–8
    and scandal 167–8
    and suras 156–62
Babis xxv, 56, 66

Badr, Battle of 47
Baha'is xxv, 56, 138
Balkans, the 2
basmala (with the help of God) 6, 7,
    105, 157
bees 74
Bible, the xiv, xvi, 1, 7
    and apocalypse 28–31, 78
    and creation 119
    and paradise 36
    and structure 21
    and typological figuration 41, 58
Boshru'i, Hoseyn 137, 142
Brown, Norman O. 84
Bruno, Giordano 150–2, 166

Campbell, Joseph 15–16
canon 21–2
Casanova, Paul xxi, 34–5
Cathedral of Anagni 46
Cave, the 97–8
Central Asia 2
chaos 116–18, 119–20, 129–30
chiasmus 4, 20
Christians xx, xxv, 29–31
civilisation 19–20
coincidentia
    oppositorum 148–53, 164
Collins, John xviii–xix, xxvi, 76–7
Constantinople xxiv
Cook, David 77
Corbin, Henry xxvi, 7, 25, 59, 72
covenant, see Day of the Covenant
creation 10, 14, 118–19, 130

damnation xxiii
Day of Alast, *see* Day of the Covenant
Day of Judgment xx–xxi, 6–7
   and the Bab 142–3, 154
Day of the Covenant xiv–xv, xx–xxi, 7,
   28, 43–7
   and the Bab 142–3, 154
   and order 118–19
   and path 6–7
disconnected letters 146, 165
divine intervention 13
divine presence (*al-sakina*) 28, 44, 46,
   47–9
duality xxii, 5, 79, 80–9, 92–3

Eliot, T. S. 98, 106
epic xii–xvii, xxvi, 1–5
   and evolution 7–8
   and heroes 14–15
   and interconnectedness 147–8
   and Joseph 70
   and Joyce 153–4, 161–2, 163–4
   and lists 8–9
   and the Quran 169–70, 172–3
epithets 11–12

false gods 9
false witness 101
al-Farabi 114
fasad (rottenness) 122
al-Fatiha (The Opening) 5, 6–7, 8, 12,
   99–100
Fatimids xxiv
Finnegans Wake (Joyce) 134, 143, 161
Firdawsi 2
fitna (disorder) 120–1
floods 108–9
forty-two 157–8
Frye, Northrop xiv, xxvi, 91–2
   and typological figuration 42, 60–1
futur (fissures) 121

Gabriel xix
genre 78–9; *see also* epic
Ghazali, Abu Hamid xxv, 64–5
Gilgamesh xii, xv, 1, 5, 18
glory motif 28, 37–41, 48
God 94–5, 96, 99–105
   and creation 119
Goppelt, Leonhard 58
Gospels 30

Hadith 95–6
Hallaj xxv
hamdala (verse) 6
hell xxiii, 9
hereafter, *see* afterlife
heroes 14–20, 24, 25
hidden imam 135–6, 137, 148, 156–7,
   163, 164–5
Hijaz 23, 122
hijra (refuge) 17, 47, 129
Homer xiii, 1, 11, 19, 85; see also
   Odyssey, The
Hour, the xxi–xxii, xxiii–xxiv, 45
al-Hudaybiya 47
humanity xiv–xv, xix, 19–20, 169–70
Hurufis xxv, 56

Ibn Abbas 128–9
Ibn al-Arabi xxv, 64, 83, 88, 96–7
Ibn Taymiyya xxv
idolatry 101, 102–4
ignorance 116, 121–7, 129
inspiration 5–6
invocation 6
Iran xxv, 136, 138–9, 167
Islam 23–4, 55–6, 116–17
   and apocalypse 34–5
   and civilisation 126–7
   and culture 7–8
   and enlightenment 62, 86–7
   and Fall 128–9
   see also Shi'ism; Sunni Islam

Jacob 63, 66, 69–70, 73–4
jahl (ignorance) 116, 121–7, 129
Jerusalem xxiv
Jews xxv
jihad (holy war) 18
jinn 106
Joseph 57, 63–8, 128
   and the Bab 137, 142, 154, 156
   and shirt 68–75
Joyce, James 132–4, 139–41, 143–4,
   146, 147–56
   and the epic 161–2
   and religion 165–7
   and scandal 167–8

Kaysanis xxv
Kermani, Navid 106
Khadir (Khidr) 97–8

al-Khalwati, Shaykh Ya'qub b. Shaykh
     Mustafa 65
Kharijis xxv
Khomeini, Ayatollah xxv
Khurramis xxv
Kindi xxv

laws 10–11
Light verse 120
lists 8–11
literature xiv; see also Bab, the; Joyce,
     James; Odyssey, The

Mahdi of Sudan xxv
Majlisi, Muhammad Baqir 67–8
Mawdudi xxv
Mecca 19
Medina 19, 127
mercy 96–7, 98–9, 104–5, 106
     and water 112–14
messengers xxi, 8–9, 171
mi'raj (night journey) 17
monotheism xxii, 6
Moses 40, 97–8
Mount Hira 17
Muhammad xix, xxi, xxii, xxiv, 90–1
     and apocalypse 34–5
     and cloak 72
     and hero 15–18
     and typological figuration 42, 58–9,
          62, 63
murder 101
muse 5–6
mushafi order xvi, xvii
Muslim community xxiii, 95

al-Naqavi 65
narrative xiv–xv, xvi–xvii, xx–xxi, 4–5
     and apocalypse 54–5
     and duality 84–5
     see also typological figuration
nature 89, 106–7
New Testament, see Bible, the
Night of Power 59–60
Ni'matullahis xxv
Ninety-Nine Beautiful Names 95
Nuqtawis xxv

Odyssey, The (Homer) xii, 4
     and Joyce 133, 139–41, 149–50, 156,
          162

olive trees 19
opposition xxii, 79, 80–9, 92–3; see
     also coincidentia oppositorum
Ottomans xxiv, 56

parables 12
paradise xix, xxiii, 9, 28
     and apocalypse 35–7, 49–54, 55
path 6–7, 8
performance 22, 46
Persian Bayan (Bab) 142
poetics 98–9, 106
poetry 90
prophets xxi, 127
     and heroes 20
     and lists 8–9
     and typological figuration 61
     see also Joseph; Muhammad

al-Qaeda xxv
Qa'im 67–8
Qarmatians xxv
Qayyum al-asma' (Bab) 132–4, 137–9,
     141–6, 153, 154–5
     and the epic 162–4
     and scandal 167–8
     and suras 156–62
Qutb, Sayyid xxv

Rahman, Fazlur 96
al-Rahman, see God
Rashti, Seyyed Kazem 73, 135, 136, 137
rebellion 19
recitation 25–6
religions 9, 10; see also Christians;
     Islam
revelation xiv, xv, 27–8
     and apocalypse xviii–xix
     and dreams 128
     and natural world 106–7
rhyme 80
ring composition 4–5, 20, 54–5
road, see path
Rome xxiv

al-Sadiq, Ja'far 73
Sadra, Mulla 65
Safavids xxiv, 56
saints 25
sakina, see divine presence
Salih 91, 171

salvation xxiii
Sarbadarids xxv
scale 13–14
scent 68, 70, 71, 73–5
Sells, Michael 59–60
Semeia xxiii
Shaykhis xxv, 66, 136
Shi'ism 65–7, 71–2, 121
   and the Bab 135–7, 138–9, 163,
     164–5
Shirazi, Ali Muhammad, *see* Bab, the
shirk (violation of tawhid) 83, 90, 128,
   129
shirt (*qamis*) 57, 67, 68–75
Shoemaker, S. J. 35
signs 129–30, 152–3
similes 12–13
sira (biography) 16, 18
Sirhindi, Ahmad xxv
speeches 13
spiritual truth 62
storytelling 20
structure xvi–xvii
Suhrawardi xxv, 96
Sunni Islam 121
suras 8
Surat al-Baqara xv–xvi, 20
Surat al-Ma'ida 10–11
Surat al-Rahman 80–1
Surat al-Shu'ara 90, 93
Surat Yusuf 20
symmetry xxii, 79, 127–8

al-Tabari 118
tafawut (disharmony) 121

tafsir (scriptural commentary) 155, 156
taqiyya (hiddenness) 66, 67
tawhid (oneness) 81, 82, 83, 127–8
Thamud 171
time 45–7, 59–62, 143–4
trope of intensity xxvi
al-Tustari, Sahl 72
typological figuration 41–2, 45, 57–62,
   170
   and Joseph 71
   and Muhammad 90–1

Ulysses (Joyce) 132–3, 139–41, 143,
   146, 149–56
   and the epic 161–4
   and religion 165–7
   and scandal 167–8
Umayyads xxiv
umma (community) 17, 19, 129
Uthmanis xxv

vengeance 100–1
verses xix–xx

walaya (authority) xxv, 25, 147–8
wali (guardian) 25
warrant xxvi
water 99, 107–15, 117
World of Images 115
worship 19
wrath 97–104, 106, 114

Yusuf, *see* Joseph

Zwettler, Michael xxvi, 90